TONY EVANS' BOOK OF
ILLUSTRATIONS

TONY EVANS' BOOK OF
ILLUSTRATIONS

Stories, Quotes, and Anecdotes
from more than 30 years of preaching and public speaking

TONY EVANS

MOODY PUBLISHERS
CHICAGO

All Scripture quotations, unless otherwise indicated, are taken from the *Holy Bible, New International Version®*. NIV®. Copyright © 1973, 1978, 1984 by International Bible Society. Used by permission of Zondervan Publishing House. All rights reserved.

Compiling Editor: Chrystal Hurst
Editor: Christopher Reese
Cover Design: Paetzold Associates
Cover Image: Donald Fuller
Interior Design: Ragont Design

Library of Congress Cataloging-in-Publication Data

Evans, Anthony T.
 Tony Evans' book of illustrations : stories, quotes, and anecdotes
from more than 30 years of preaching and public speaking / Tony Evans.
    p. cm.
 Includes bibliographical references and indexes.
 ISBN 978-0-8024-8578-6
 1. Homiletical illustrations. I. Title. II. Title: Book of
illustrations.
 BV4225.3.E93 2009
 251'.08--dc22
                                    2008031093

This book is printed on acid free recycled paper containing 30% PCW
(Post Consumer Waste) and manufactured in the United States of
America by Thompson-Shore, Inc.

We hope you enjoy this book from Moody Publishers. Our goal is to provide high-quality, thought-provoking books and products that connect truth to your real needs and challenges. For more information on other books and products written and produced from a biblical perspective, go to www.moodypublishers.com or write to:

Moody Publishers
820 N. LaSalle Boulevard
Chicago, IL 60610

5 7 9 10 8 6 4

Printed in the United States of America

This book is dedicated to Ikki Soma,
one of my special sons in the ministry.

———❖———

Special thanks to my daughter Chrystal Hurst
for her labor in compiling and
editing the material for this work.

CONTENTS

INTRODUCTION

I AM REGULARLY asked where I get my illustrations. My answer is always the same: everything for me is an illustration, because I have learned to think illustratively. The wonders of God's creation make everything that exists, as well as all the events that occur, possible illustrations. The key is to learn to view everything through this lens.

Illustrations are important because relevancy is important. The Bible was not written as a systematic theology with all the truth on any given subject neatly packaged in one location. Rather, it is a biblical theology where forty authors over fifteen hundred years recorded for us God's interface and interaction with the history of mankind where real life unfolded. Scripture deals with real people in real life dealing with real issues and needing real answers. In fact, the New Testament exhorts us to look to the Old Testament for the purpose of illustrations and examples (1 Corinthians 10:11).

Therefore, for someone to speak on God's behalf and be irrelevant, esoteric, and ethereal is to commit the sin of boring people with the Word of God. Illustrations are one primary way of keeping the truths of God's Word relevant to the contemporary audience who needs to hear and understand His Word as it relates to them and their real-life realities. It was Jesus' ability and practice of bringing God's truth to life through the use of illustrations that made Him the master teacher and storyteller that He was.

Illustrations are also important for understanding and comprehension. Because so much of what the Bible addresses involves comprehending the workings of the spiritual realm and how it interfaces with the physical realm, and because many of the ancient ideas, vocabulary, and culture are foreign to us, there needs to be clarity of understanding of the meaning of terms, concepts, and perspectives that may be difficult for the hearer to grasp. The biblical communication must successfully bridge the gap between the biblical author and audience and the contemporary audience. Illustrations are one major way of constructing such a bridge.

Effective and clear illustrations enable both the speaker and hearer to more firmly grasp spiritual truths in ways that make those truths come alive both to the mind and to the heart.

There is, however, a danger in the use of illustrations, and that is allowing them to become an end unto themselves. Illustrations are designed to illustrate, not simply to entertain. Thus, they need to be tethered to some point or truth and not be allowed to dangle alone, disconnected, from anything meaningful and informative.

It is my prayer that God will use this volume to help enhance the effectiveness of the user to bring home the truth of God to those who desperately need to hear a word from Him. In addition, it is my hope that it will encourage and inspire you to look at life illustratively, so that your speaking, preaching, and teaching will be full of fresh, relevant illustrations that will enhance your audience's understanding of God's truth and enable them to see how really relevant and applicable God's Word is to their lives.

SERMON Illustrations

A

ABIDING

A DINNER plate left out overnight will be hard to clean in the morning. An alternative to scrubbing is soaking the dish in hot water and dishwashing liquid. Letting a dish abide in the solution will allow a hard cleaning job to become a lot easier. This is what abiding does for Christians. We are much easier to clean up when we've been hanging out in the right environment.

Religion says "Scrape off the dirt." It tells us to apply elbow grease to fix a problem. Relationship says "Soak." Just sit in the hot water for a while. Abiding will set you free.[1]

Eph. 2:8–9; 2 Cor. 11:3

SADLY, these days there are many young ladies who are being coerced indirectly into bad situations because they meet somebody over the Internet. Even thirteen-year-old girls can be lured to a location to meet somebody they don't know because they "fell in love" over the Internet. Their initial relationship with this stranger is only by reading. Both parties sit at the computer and read each other's words, but after awhile, the words take on life because behind the word is a real, living person. Those words for a young girl grow into emotions and then turn into actions as she figures out how to sneak out to meet him. Those words take on life because the girl spent time abiding in the presence of someone she couldn't now see.

You can't see the Living God. He's a spirit, but He's written to you and wants to have an eternal love affair with you. If you hang out there with His words, next thing you know you'll be packing your bags to meet Him. You'll have fallen in love with Him and have become transformed by abiding in His presence.[2]

[Transformation; God's Presence]
John 3:16; 15:3–5; Rom. 12:2

THE PLANET Mercury is hot. Pluto is cold. Why is Pluto cold and Mercury hot? Mercury is really close to the sun and Pluto is a long way off. The farther you get away, the colder things become, but the closer you get, the hotter things are. You may say that you are not a Pluto Christian or a Mercury Christian. Maybe you are an Earth Christian where things get hot and cold. You may be a seasonal Christian who has changes depending on whether it is wintertime, summertime, springtime, or fall.

God is looking for some Mercury Christians. He is looking for some folks who want to get close and stay hot all the time because they stay close to the S-o-n.[3]

[Discipleship]
James 1:8; Rev. 3:16

I WAS talking on my phone one day and it began going "beep, beep, beep." The beeping noise indicated that the battery was low. After a couple of minutes,

I heard a clicking noise. The battery had died because it had been off its charger too long. In other words, it was putting out with no refill and so it lost its power. It lost its "anointing." It lost its ability to function at the level it was designed to function at because it had stayed away from its source too long.

We can't keep running on spiritual empty and wonder why we're only limping along in the Christian life. We are regularly caught unexpectedly on empty because we don't stay close to our source of strength on a regular basis.[4]

Phil. 4:13

A LOT OF people talk about how hot it is in Texas. The heat doesn't really bother me, though, because everything is air-conditioned in Texas. Your car is air-conditioned. Your house is air-conditioned. Every building you go in is air-conditioned. So while you do sometimes have to be under the sun, and while you're in it, it's hot, most people here just don't hang out in the sun.

Actually, I'm a hot-weather person. The hotter it is, the nicer it is for me. Where some people like air conditioners blasting in their cars, I prefer to roll down the windows. I'd rather have hot air than cold air-conditioning. It's just my particular temperament, and I know something is wrong with me, but that's just the way it is. I don't mind hanging out in the sun.

That said, most people I know don't want to hang out in the sun. They just want to *pass through* the sun. What a lot of people want to do with the s-u-n they want to do with the S-o-n. They just want to pass through.

When you hang out in the sun, you're going to sweat. Why? Because you can't be under that much power and it not affect you. If you hang out under the S-o-n, you're also going to sweat. You're going to sweat His commandments. You're going to sweat pleasing Him. You're going to sweat His Word because you can't hang in His presence without Him rubbing off on you.

The way you know He's rubbing off on you is that you begin to walk as He walks. You begin to pick up some of His habits. You begin to pick up some of His direction. You begin to pick up some of His influence.[5]

[Discipleship]
Luke 6:40

I HAVE abided over the last twenty years with American Airlines. They have been my airline of choice, and as a result I have been awarded a level of intimacy. That level of intimacy is called Platinum. They have awarded my consistency with them. That Platinum card affords me various privileges that come simply because I have the card. I can ride first class if the first class seats haven't been purchased. I can get bumped up simply because I have this Platinum card and I've flown two million miles with American over the years. They've given me a card that says I'm a preferred customer. They send things to my house because they appreciate the fact that I have abided with them. They like the fact that they can pretty much count on me to fly American when I travel.

When I walk up to a booth, if people are ahead of me, and first class is full, they have a waiting list. If they tell me they have Gold members in front of me, I pull out my Platinum card. My status bumps me to the top of the list. I take precedence because I have a deeper, longer, and more regular relationship with American than the Gold members do.

However, once a man behind me asked the clerk if there were any first class seats. The clerk told him there were, but then added that the first person was a Platinum member and would be awarded the upgrade first. The man reached into his pocket and pulled out an Executive Platinum card. I felt like slapping him. To remain Platinum you have to fly fifty thousand miles a year. To be Executive Platinum you fly one hundred thousand miles a year. When I walked up to the counter, they let me know they liked me by putting me first. When he came up they let me know they *loved* him. His level of abiding was deeper.

Some Christians are satisfied with Gold status, others are happy with Platinum, and yet others are after Executive Platinum. What kind of Christian are you? We need to know that until we are ready to make the commitment of abiding, we will never get all the benefits that occur with ongoing intimacy.[6]

[Commitment; Intimacy, with God]

SUNFLOWERS are beautiful flowers that start off as tiny sprouts. The reason sunflowers are called sunflowers is because they follow the sun. The sun rises in the east, the sunflower will point east. The sun sets to the west, and the flowers will point west. These flowers throw off a lot of seeds. They are pro-

ductive because they are always looking for the sun. They always locate the s-u-n, and because they always are looking for the s-u-n, they're always growing.

When you and I look for the S-o-n, like the sunflower looks for the s-u-n, then we will find the effects of His rays softening our hearts so we can throw off new seed, new life. It is our response to the Word that determines our productivity. Abiding in our relationship with the S-o-n will result in the transformation and growth that many Christians are looking for.[7]

[Transformation; Spiritual Maturity, Growth]

Rom. 6:4

THERE ARE two ways to drink tea. Some people are dippers. They dip their tea bag up and down in the mug. A lot of Christians are like that. They dip in on Sunday morning then dip back out. They dip back in on Wednesday night then they dip back out. But there's another way to drink tea and that's to be an abider. It involves the act of just dropping the tea bag in the water and letting it stay there. Without touching the bag an amazing thing will happen. The color of the water begins to change as the influence of the bag in the hot water effects change in the cup. A person can just sit and watch the transformation take place because of the act of abiding.

When you are a dipper you've got to make things happen by your own effort. You've got to move the bag up and down, dip a spoon in and out of the cup, wrap the string around the spoon, jerk, and then pull. It can require a lot of human effort. But when you are abiding, the water changes all by itself.

Once I was meeting with a guy and we were both drinking tea. He was dipping and pulling away. I just let my tea bag sit. He told me that he couldn't let his tea bag sit in the bag like that because his tea would get too strong. That's exactly what happens when you abide. The depth of your abiding will determine the rate of your progress in the spiritual life. Jesus wants you to stay there and experience the full strength of His presence.[8]

[God's Presence]

ABUNDANT LIFE

A WHILE back I went to McDonald's and ordered a value meal. The cashier asked me if I wanted to supersize my order. He wanted to know if I wanted my order to be bigger. I told him no; I just wanted my regular-sized order. He asked me again to make sure I didn't want my order supersized. I told him no thank you, got my regular-sized order, and drove off.

If you're tired of regular or ordinary living, God is offering you supersize.[9]

ADDICTION

A POW IS a prisoner of war. He or she is a person who has been captured by the enemy and is held hostage in the context of a conflict. The situation is where the opposition or the enemy now controls the movements, the actions, or the reactions of the person who has been captured.

Many Christians are POWs, prisoners of spiritual warfare. The Enemy has captured them, and there appears to be no way of escape. They feel trapped by situations and circumstances that the world calls "addictions." Whether it's drugs, sex, pornography, alcohol, codependency, gambling, or food, they feel trapped, and there seems to be no way out.[10]

ADVERSITY

IN ORDER for God to bring out the best in His children, He brings about scenarios in our lives to build strength and character.

When building our physical bodies, development takes on the form of pumping weights, running on a treadmill, and participating in activities that require tennis shoes. Workouts involve some sweat, heavy breathing, and perspiration because something is being developed. God allows trials and adversity to put us in gymnasium situations. Just like the Father did with His Son Jesus, He creates a workout scenario that includes a difficulty that we must work through.

A lady came to work out at the gym. Everything about what she had on said she was going to go for a killer workout. She wore the typical attire, the headband around her head, wristbands around her wrists, and had a water bottle on her side. She stepped into a clear area and bent down to touch her toes in order to stretch. This woman looked very serious about working out. She grabbed some dumbbells, walked over to a bench, and sat down. Lifting the weights, she did a couple of bicep curls, put the weights down, and wiped herself off with a towel. In an exasperated voice she said, "Whoof! That's enough for today!" This lady looked the part but she had not truly come to the gym for a workout.

Many Christians come to church every Sunday looking like they are ready for a workout. We wear the right clothes, sing the right songs, and talk the right talk, but building real strength requires real effort and a little sweat.

God figures that we will not voluntarily go to a spiritual gym so He brings the gym to us. Adverse circumstances, cross-bearing situations, difficult scenarios, and problematic encounters all serve as opportunities for Christian growth.[11]

[Trials; Tests; Character, Importance of]

Prov. 3:11; Phil. 2:12; Heb. 12:6; James 1:2; 1 Peter 1:6–8

A CATERPILLAR is ugly, slow, slimy, and it takes all day to go two feet, but when it undergoes the process of metamorphosis and the caterpillar becomes a butterfly, something beautiful is born. Metamorphosis is the process of something at work on the inside trying to show up on the outside.

There's only one reason a butterfly can fly: its wings are strengthened by the work it does to break through the cocoon. If a bystander were to slit open a cocoon prior to the butterfly breaking itself loose from the cocoon, it wouldn't fly. Its wings are developed through the struggle. No struggle, no flight.

Every Christian is a butterfly waiting to happen. A saint may feel like a caterpillar or even think they look like a caterpillar, but the idea is to work out their salvation in the midst of adversity because God is at work within them to do His good pleasure.[12]

[Transformation; Trials; Tests; Spiritual Maturity, Growth]

Phil. 2:12–13

ALIENS

AMERICA has ambassadors. Ambassadors are in a foreign land that is not their own. They go away temporarily to a foreign land to spend time away from home. Ambassadors have to learn the language and learn the customs, but they're never to belong there. They are just to live there in order to carry out their mission.

In order to carry it out, they've got to live there. In order to carry it out, they've got to talk the language. To carry it out, they've got to function in the context of the people, but they are to never forget it's not where they belong. The Bible says your citizenship is in heaven.

What good is an ambassador who doesn't represent the homeland? The problem is that today we've got a generation of ambassadors who like the foreign country. In fact, they have fallen in love with the foreign country.[13]

[Ambassadors, for Christ]

Phil. 3:17–21; 1 Peter 2:11

WHEN HURRICANE Katrina hit New Orleans, thousands of people were displaced. Thousands of people had to leave their homes and move to other places. Some moved to other cities in Louisiana, others moved to Houston, other people moved to Dallas, not knowing when they could return home.

Months later, many people could still not return home and they were frustrated. Although they had places to sleep, food to eat, and clothes on their backs, they were not happy. Although they had opportunities for new lives, new jobs, and a new start, they were not excited. Although the victims of Katrina had the ability to send their kids to new schools, to see new places, and to do new things, they were not thrilled. No matter how great the new places were, many Americans displaced from New Orleans were frustrated. Why? Because they were not home. It didn't matter how wonderful Dallas or Houston could be, these cities were not New Orleans.

As Christians, we should never be satisfied with the things that this world holds. We should never be thrilled with the things this world has to offer. No matter how wonderful this world is, for the Christian, it will never be home. We are aliens in this world.[14]

[Ambassadors for Christ]
Heb. 11:12–14

AMBASSADORS, FOR CHRIST

I USED TO love the television show *Charlie's Angels*. First there was a TV show, and then there were the *Charlie's Angels* movies. These three young ladies would go in harm's way for Charlie. What's interesting is, they had never seen Charlie. Charlie was invisible to them, yet they were willing to do his bidding. They would get a call and receive information about what Charlie wanted them to do. They would go out to represent Charlie's interests, even though it meant difficult times for them. They were Charlie's Angels.

The word *angel* in the Bible means *messenger*. The original Greek word is *angelos*. It means to be a messenger for someone else. Now if invisible Charlie could get three ladies to go in harm's way for a man they had never seen, how much more should Jesus' angels, messengers for Jesus Christ, be willing to go in harm's way to represent somebody they've never seen? Even though we haven't seen Him, we should be ready to fulfill His mission and share His love with others.[15]

[Witnessing]
2 Cor. 5:20; 1 Peter 1:8–9

ANGER

A MAN said, "My wife and I promised that we would never go to bed angry. We haven't slept together in seven years."[16]

[Marriage]

B

BAPTISM

WHEN a lady gets married, she puts on a ring. That ring does not make her married. She could be married without a ring, just like you could be saved without being baptized. But what the ring does do is serve as a sign that she is married.

Many times when you see a guy talking to a girl, you will see his eyes go south as he is looking at the left hand to see whether or not she has already been spoken for and belongs to another.

I am certain that a wife who refused to wear her ring would insult any man. He would probably take that as a rejection of him. The ring is more than a piece of jewelry. The piece of jewelry represents an institution and a covenant. Like a ring is symbolic for marriage, baptism is a sign of our covenant with God.[17]

[Salvation; Marriage; Spiritual Identity, in Christ]

Acts 2:38; 8:13; Matt. 28:19

THE IDEA OF A baptized believer is that they have gone public in declaring that they are wedded to another—to Jesus Christ.

We would think it odd if a husband never wanted to go out in public with his wife. He might say, "I'll eat dinner with you as long as it's at home," or "I'll watch a movie with you as long as it's at home," or "I'll talk to you as long as it's at home." That kind of behavior would be an insult. Jesus Christ is insulted regularly by His children because in private they will identify with Him, but in public they don't want folks to know that they are associated with Him.[18]

[Witnessing; Spiritual Identity, in Christ]

Luke 9:26; Rom. 1:16; 2 Tim. 1:8

BIBLE

FOR MANY people, the Bible is like the Queen of England. She holds the top position, but has no real power.[19]

RECENTLY, I decided to do something I never do. I took out my car manual and read it. I'm a real simple guy. I get in a car, get behind the wheel, turn it on, and roll. That's it. But one day I was just fooling around, opened my glove compartment, and there was my car manual. Now this manual has been in this car for three years. As far as I'm concerned, this is unnecessary reading.

I see a steering wheel, I see brakes, I see an accelerator, a radio, heat, and air-conditioning. Good to go.

But on this particular day, I decided to flip through my manual. I was shocked at some of the stuff I read in there. There is so much stuff in this car that has never been used! I realized that I'd been doing things manually that the car was set up to do automatically. I realized that I'd not been taking advantage of all that the manufacturer had provided.

On one particularly rainy day, I was trying to look out of my rear window and couldn't see anything. After three years of having this car, I had no idea there was a windshield wiper back there. It wasn't that it was not provided, it's that I was ignorant of the provision. I didn't know what was provided and I certainly didn't know how to take advantage of it.

What the Bible, the grace manual, is designed to do is show you all the provisions that God has provided for every believer. The problem is I not only need to know that the manual is there, but I also need to know what it tells me I can do and how things work.[20]

[God's Will; Scripture, Importance of]

Josh. 1:8; Ps. 119; 2 Tim. 2:15

WHEN MY oldest son was small, I bought him a bicycle for Christmas. It came with a manual that explained how to put it together. I did not intend on using the manual. After all, I was finishing my doctorate degree. After studying for twelve years post high school, I considered myself to be a smart brother. The bicycle that I had bought for my son had all these nuts and bolts and various parts, but I had decided that I didn't need this manual. I'd had too much edu-ma-cation. I decided to depend on my own human intelligence.

Eight hours later and with just the handlebars on, my wife, Sister Evans, came to the door and said, "Why don't you read the manual?" Could it be, just maybe, that the bicycle maker knew more about bicycle fixing than I did? Could it be that the Life Maker knows more about life living than you do?[21]

[God's Will; Scripture,
Importance of]
Prov. 3:5–6; Mark 12:24;
2 Tim. 3:14–17

BIBLE, APPLICATION OF

MY WIFE at various times over the years wanted to take classes at Dallas Seminary. She didn't want to take the class in the traditional way. She want-ed to audit the class. You see, when you audit the class, you can go and sit and get the information but there are no out-side requirements. You don't have to study. You don't have to take any tests. You get the information but you don't have the burden of the class.

Many Christians come to church on Sunday mornings and audit the sermon. They go to class, have text-book in hand, sit in their regular seat, and listen to the professor. But all they want to do is audit the class. They don't want to be expected to do any homework. They don't want to pass any tests that God sends their way to check their understanding. These Christians will pay the money to take the class but they don't want to have to meet any requirements. They also don't expect to receive a de-

gree and diploma from the school.

As long as my wife audits her sem-inary class, she will have no credit on her transcript. There will be no grad-uation ceremony and nobody will ever hand her a degree. As long as you audit your Christian life, there will be no passing grades, there will be no di-vine recognition, and there will be no experience of your calling.[22]

[Church; Commitment]
1 Sam. 15:22; James 1:23–24;
1 Cor. 9:23–25

A COUPLE decided that they should do something together to strengthen their marriage. They decided to go duck hunting together. They'd heard of other people going duck hunting with dogs, so they figured they needed to buy a good hunting dog and buy the dog they did. They got all of their equipment and their dog and took off to go duck hunting for the day. They tried getting some ducks, but they came to the end of the day and hadn't gotten one. The husband looked at the wife and said, "Honey, we've got to be doing some-thing wrong here. We haven't caught a duck yet."

The wife said, "Well, maybe, if we throw the dog up a little higher, he can catch a duck this time."

That's what a lot of us are doing. We're trying to get a dog to do what a gun was meant to do. We're trying to accomplish things in our lives with tools that don't work or don't make sense. A dog is not the right weapon to get ducks. You need fire-power to bring a duck down.

A lot of us have "hound dogs" try-ing to fix our marriage. We're on the phone with "hound dog" girlfriends or guy friends. All they're doing is barking us up into more mess. We're doing everything but using firepower from heaven. It's not that we're not trying. The question is, *what* are we trying.

The Word of Christ must dwell in us richly. It has to be the basis of our decisions.[23]

[Marriage; Scripture]

Josh. 1:8; Col. 3:16; 1 Peter 2:1–3

BIBLE, AUTHORITY OF

A NAVY captain was sailing and came upon a big light. He thought it was a ship coming toward him. He was the highest-ranking officer in the U.S. Navy at this particular time. So he got on a big bullhorn and said to the ship behind the light, "Move ten degrees south or we're going to crash!"

It said, "I shall not move! You move ten degrees north so you don't crash!"

The captain was getting irritated. He said, "Don't you know who I am? I am a captain in the United States Navy. I say, 'You move ten degrees south so we do not crash!'"

The voice came back, "I shall not move! You move ten degrees north so that you don't crash!"

The captain got back on the speaker and said, "Did you hear me say that I am a captain in the United States Navy?"

The voice came back, "Yes, but I am the lighthouse!"

The Word of God must be the authority for the life of the disciple who is living with a kingdom perspective.[24]

BIBLE, CENTRALITY OF

IN THE game of football, there is no game without the ball. Players can put on the gear, wear the helmets, and walk in the cleats, but there is no game without the pigskin. Nothing really matters much in football if you don't have the ball.

When you think about it, that little piece of pigskin controls a lot. A touchdown is only a touchdown measured by where the ball is. A first down is only a first down measured by where the ball is. You're onside or offside in relationship to the ball. Whether it's a catch or an incomplete pass depends on control of the ball. Everything has to do with the ball. Three points or a lack of three points has to do with where the ball went. Isn't it amazing? You can have all the other stuff right, but if there is no football, you just wasted your Saturday afternoon.

In the Christian faith it is possible to have a bunch of stuff right. You can go to the right church, carry the right Bible, and use the right "Christian-ese." You can have all the accessories of Christianity and still not have the main thing. If you don't have the main thing, everything else is a waste of time. Just like we can't play football without a football, we can't be effective Christians without the gospel.[25]

[Gospel; Scripture]

Rom. 1:16–17; 1 Cor. 9:23

BIBLE, GUIDANCE OF

I HAD a speaking engagement once that required about a forty-five-minute drive. So I got my directions. It was a men's breakfast at a church, so I left my house with plenty of time to spare, put the directions beside me in the seat, glanced at them, and then got on the freeway headed to the breakfast. After driving for about forty minutes, I glanced at the directions to double-check my exit. I made sure it was the right one, then I exited and made a left. I began driving past the mall, past the light, past another light, and I wasn't seeing anything I thought I was supposed to see. I figured I hadn't gone far enough, so I kept driving.

Things were getting worse, not better. I figured that I ought to pull over and ask somebody. So I pulled over to a convenience store, thinking that I could trust the people who worked there to give me directions. A clerk told me that I hadn't gone far enough. Now, I thought that the church was supposed to be not too far off the freeway, but I figured I had missed something and assumed that the clerk knew what he was talking about. After all, he was from the area. He told me to just keep going and that I'd run right into it. I get in the car and I keep going.

I started seeing cows and realized that I was now in the country. Something about this didn't feel right. I wasn't arriving at where I thought I was supposed to be. So I figured I'd asked the wrong person. I needed to talk to somebody else, get somebody else's opinion. So I asked another guy.

Time was getting late. I was supposed to start speaking at 7:30 a.m. I'd given myself plenty of time, but now it was 7:15 and I didn't know where I was. I was in a bad situation. So, I did ask somebody else. They said they'd never heard of the church. It was now 7:20 and I was getting a little nervous

because I hate being late to anything. I started winding down my window at stoplights, asking random people to help me find my way. It was 7:25 p.m., then 7:30.

I had gone to five different people to tell me where I was supposed to be. Everybody meant well, but nobody could tell me where I needed to go. I decided to read the directions one more time. I picked it up and looked at it closely. Originally, I had only glanced at it. Then I let well-meaning people try to help me. Now, I decided to look closely at the directions. When I exited the freeway, I should have turned RIGHT!

First of all, I listened to myself and turned left. Then I listened to everybody else and really went farther out of the way. But the instructions said turn right. Because I did not pay attention to the instructions but listened to my own understanding and listened to everybody else's understanding, I went left when I should have gone right. So I had to backtrack, and when I backtracked and went two blocks to the right of the freeway, I found the church.

I had lost time; I had lost patience. I was sweating, frustrated, mad, and irritated because I had gone the wrong direction.

Some of us have gone left. "There is a way that seems right to a man" (Proverbs 14:12). Where I wound up was wrong. A lot of us have spent five, ten, fifteen, twenty, thirty years going left and you're running out of time; the hour is late. It's time to backtrack because where God wants to take you is really not that far away.[26]

[Repentance; God's Will]

Prov. 3:5–6; Ezek. 18:29–31; Acts 17:30–31

THERE was a show I used to watch a couple of years ago called *Early Edition*. The host of the show would get the next day's newspaper, read it, and then do a show about the upcoming news. He'd read a newspaper about the morrow and related it to his viewers today. Because he had tomorrow's newspaper today, he had information nobody else did.

Most of our coworkers don't have the information. Most of our neighbors don't have the information. But as Christians, we've got an Early Edition. God has given us the Early Edition. We can function today in light of what we know about God's plan for the future.[27]

[Providence]
1 Thess. 4:13–18; Titus 2:11–13

WHEN you are on the highway, you are expected to choose one lane to drive in, though there may be lanes to your left and right. You are expected to stay in your lane and not to swerve into the other lanes, because if you start to swerve to the left or to the right, you're an accident waiting to happen. There's a time and an appropriate way to change lanes.

God's Word gives you a lane to stay in. That lane is based on the written Word and then affirmed by the work of the Spirit in terms of specific application. Stay in that lane and do everything He tells you to do and He will make your way prosperous.[28]

[Bible, Centrality of; Bible, Sufficiency of; Blessing; Focus]
Josh. 1:7–9; Ps. 1; John 13:17; James 1:22–25

BIBLE, NEGLECT OF

THE PREACHER came to have dinner with one of the families in his congregation. The woman of the house was very pleased to have the minister in her home and wanted to impress him. She wanted the preacher to read something to the family after dinner. She asked one of her daughters, "Darling, please go and get the good book. Go and get the book we love. Go get the book we read every day."

The girl came back with the Sears catalog.[29]

Josh. 1:8; Acts 17:11

BIBLE, PROVISION OF

A MAN was in prison and was in need of some money. He wrote his mother and asked her to send five hundred dollars immediately. Soon after, he got a package in the mail. It was a Bible. On the top of the Bible, there was a letter that said, "Son, I love you. Pray and read your Bible."

The man was ticked off. He got on the phone and called his mother. "Mama, I appreciate the Bible, but what I need right now is five hundred dollars."

She told him over the phone, "Son, pray and read your Bible." He got more ticked off and hung up on his mother.

He then wrote a letter. "Mother, I know you believe in God, but that's the problem with you Christians. You are so heavenly minded that you don't know how to function in the real world. When I need five hundred dollars, I don't need a Bible. I need a check or five greenbacks! If I need money, don't send me a Bible and tell me to pray!"

He got a letter back that said, "Son, pray and read your Bible."

He was so irritated at his mother, that for the six months he was in jail that Bible stayed in the corner.

After a long while, he finally got out. His mother was there to meet him. He could hardly speak to her. "Mama, you let me down. I needed you as my mother and you let me down."

She said, "What do you mean, son?"

"I wrote you. I called you. I begged you for five hundred dollars and every time you gave me this same old line to pray and read my Bible."

"Well, son, did you pray and read your Bible?"

"Yeah, I prayed and read my Bible, and I'm still as broke now as I was when you told me the first time to pray and read my Bible."

"Son, do you have your Bible?"

He reached in his bag and he handed her the book.

"Son, let me ask you one more time. Did you pray and read your Bible?"

"Yes, Mama. I told you I prayed and read my Bible."

"Son, you neither prayed nor read your Bible."

She opened up the Bible and at every major divisional section within the text, there was a hundred-dollar bill taped inside of it. If the boy would have just read his Bible he would have understood that the thing he was looking for was in the text. Because he didn't take seriously the Word of God, what the Word of God had to offer he never received.[30]

BIBLE, SUFFICIENCY OF

THERE WAS a commercial not too long ago for Prego spaghetti sauce. A mother is cooking the spaghetti and the pot is full of what looks like a vibrant, red spaghetti sauce. The aroma appears to be filling the house. The son comes up and looks at his mother cooking the sauce and asks, "Mom, where are the mushrooms?"

She says, "It's in there."

"But what about the sausage?"

"Why, it's in there."

"What about the ripe tomatoes?"

"It's in there."

Prego's spaghetti sauce had kick and flavor, because of what was inside. Every time the boy looked for something to explain what he smelled, his mother would reply, "It's in there."

If you are looking for victory, it's in the Bible. If you're looking for transformation, it's already in there. If you're looking for power, it's in there. If you're looking for deliverance, it's in there. If you're looking for a brand-new you, it's already there. The divine nature has given you everything you need and you can learn about what's available to you by studying the Word of God.[31]

2 Tim. 2:15; 2 Peter 1:3

I AM SURE many of you have mothers like I do. My mother thought castor oil was the medicine for everything.

"Ma, I got a stomachache."

"Bring the castor oil."

"Ma, I got a headache."

"Bring the castor oil."

"Ma, I got a hanged toenail."

"Bring the castor oil."

My mother had a view that castor oil could fix anything. Now, let me explain something about castor oil. I didn't prefer castor oil. I didn't like the way castor oil tasted. It didn't matter. I grew up hearing my mother say, "Boy, put this castor oil in your mouth, because it's good for you." She believed that castor oil could fix anything and that it was sufficient for whatever ailed me.[32]

BIBLE, USE OF

A PREACHER was late for his appointment and pulled into a parking lot. He went around the parking lot ten times looking for an empty space. The only spot he could find was one where a sign said No Parking. He put a note on his window: "Late for my appointment." Then he wrote underneath, "Tried ten times. Forgive our trespasses."

He came back to his car an hour later. There was a note next to his note from the policeman. It read, "Been riding in this neighborhood for ten years. Will lose my job if I don't ticket you. Lead us not into temptation."[33]

[Temptation]

THE WORD, like medicine, is designed to address the comprehensive issues of life. A Bible that is falling apart usually belongs to somebody who isn't.[34]

[Spiritual Maturity]
Ps. 19; James 1:25

BLESSING

ALL OF us know people who are living unproductive lives. Our society is filled with people who offer no productivity to the well-being of themselves, their families, their jobs, or society in general. They are just hanging on.

A leech sucks blood from a host. It takes nutrients without leaving its host anything beneficial in return. Similar to leeches, unproductive people take, but do not give.

One of the ways God will bless you is by making your life productive. He will enable you to do more with your life than exist. He will enable you to make a life that is worth something.[35]

[Giving; Christian Living, Power]
Ps. 1; 1 Cor. 12:4–7; Eph. 2:10

HAVE YOU ever been to a real pizzeria? Especially a real, authentic Italian place? The dough is the best! That dough goes through some major abuse before it is ready to be served and eaten. It is slammed down on the counter. Bam! It's treated very rough. A rolling pin mashes it and flattens it out. It is twirled around on a single finger, then thrown spinning up in the air.

Now, most people aren't thinking about the process of making the dough. They just want the good stuff —the pepperoni, sausage, cheese, and sauce. But the good stuff doesn't happen unless the dough has been made ready to receive it.

See, many people want to see the goodness of God, the power of God, or the blessing of God and wonder why it's not happening the way they think it should. God is trying to tell them that "the dough isn't quite ready to receive it." Sometimes we are just not ready for the blessings of God to be fulfilled.[36]

[Sanctification; Maturity]
Luke 14:11; James 4:10; 1 Peter 5:6

CREDITCARD companies send mass mailings to people with amazing news of great grace. The recipients have not applied for a new card or a new level of credit, but the credit card company freely offers unsolicited spending power. These gracious companies write customers to tell them they are prequalified or preapproved. The only thing left for the customer to do is to accept the offer and spend! The limit has already been negotiated and all that's left to do is use it. By accepting Christ, we have accepted His terms and are prequalified for the spiritual benefits and resources available to us.[37]

> [Grace; Provision, God's]
> Rom. 5:17; Eph. 2:8

CITIES have food banks and blood banks. They're designed to help other people live. Although these banks are set up to collect, they are not designed simply to hoard and to store. The resources they gather help other people to live—either by the infusion of food or by the infusion of nutrients from blood.

God has saved and blessed Christians so that we can share the blessings God has given us with others.[38]

> [Giving]
> Gen. 12:3; Acts 2:44–45;
> 1 Cor. 16:1–4

THE STORY is told of Mr. Yates, who owned a farm in Texas. The Great Depression came and he was having trouble keeping up with the payments on his farm. The bank began to press Mr. Yates and gave him thirty days to pay his back payments or face foreclosure. With three weeks left to go, a man came to Mr. Yates's door. He worked for an oil company. He asked Mr. Yates to give the company a lease to drill on his farm for oil. Yates knew he was going to lose the farm anyway, so he decided that

it couldn't hurt. Well, that oil company did drill and hit a gusher—eighty-two thousand barrels of oil a day. Mr. Yates immediately became a multi, multi, many-times-over millionaire.

Now, there's a question on the floor. Exactly when did Mr. Yates become a millionaire? Did Mr. Yates become a millionaire when the oil company struck oil or did Mr. Yates become a millionaire when he bought the farm? Mr. Yates was a millionaire the moment he purchased the farm, but he lived in poverty because he didn't know what was underneath the ground.

When you came to faith in Jesus Christ as your personal sin bearer, the moment you came to faith, you were blessed "in the heavenly realms with every spiritual blessing" (Ephesians 1:3). Like Mr. Yates, many of us are living in the Great Depression. We are living spiritually poor, spiritually defeated, spiritually weak, and spiritually anemic lives even while sitting on top of all this wealth, because we don't know what's down there.[39]

> [Provision, God's]
> Col. 2:2

WILLIAM Randolph Hearst, the great publisher, read about a painting and became greatly interested in it. Desperately desiring to own this painting, he sent his people all over to try to locate this painting but they couldn't find it anywhere. A year later, out of the blue, one of his employees came to him and told him that the painting had at last been found. Hearst, excited about the discovery, asked where it had been all this time. His employee said, "It was in your basement. You've owned it all the time."

Mr. Hearst had never read the ledger that had record of everything he owned. He did not understand the wealth that he already possessed. Many believers operate their lives never fully understanding all of the blessing that is available to them in Christ.[40]

A MAN died who was extremely wealthy. His will was full of art pieces—very expensive art pieces. This man had a son who had died before him, a son whom he loved, and this son would have been his only heir. Soon after the death of the wealthy man a public auction was held that included the valuable art pieces. People came from all over the world because of those works of art. Over a thousand people gathered to participate in the auction. The auctioneer began the auction by offering up for sale a portrait, painted by the deceased son. It was a rather plain painting—not at all like the other expensive art pieces. The floor opened for bids, but there weren't any. After what seemed like a long silence, a little old man walked down the aisle. As he neared the front of the room, the auctioneer recognized him. He had been the servant of the wealthy man.

He meagerly and almost shamefully offered a couple of dollars from his pocket for the child-drawn portrait. The auctioneer hit his gavel and said, "Sold!" The many people in the room shifted with excitement, preparing for the main part of the selling to begin. But much to their surprise and chagrin, the auctioneer hit the gavel again and said, "Auction over." The room filled with loud chatter and confusion, wondering at the early close of the auction. The auctioneer went on to explain. In the will of the master, the instructions specifically said to offer for sale the painting drawn by his son first, and that whoever gets the painting of his son gets the whole art collection. The master had decided well in advance that whoever loved his son and accepted him could not only have his son's work, but all the other benefits that belonged to the father.[41]

[Salvation, Benefits of]
John 5:22–23; 2 Peter 1:17

WHEN I first started traveling and speaking in other places, my kids were small so I'd go by the gift store in the airport and I'd buy a gift to bring back to them. I would buy them a blessing. I'd buy a little toy or a trinket from the gift shop like some jacks for my girls or a little car for my boys. On my return I would give them the gift. They would always be excited. I would always get a hug and a kiss. There would be great gratitude and thanks because I had come back with a blessing and they were excited about the blessing. What made me feel good and excited me was the fact that they were excited about the blessor. I got a hug and I got a kiss as they expressed gratitude. But after a while, they began to look forward to my trips. They wanted me to leave again. In other words, my kids were so into the blessings that they had lost sight of the bless-er. As long as the bless-er brought back a blessing, they were fine. A lot of folk want to come to church and don't want to mess with the bless-er. They just want the bless-er to leave behind a blessing. God has said, "Return to me" (Malachi 3:7). He wants us to be focused on Him.[42]

[Thanksgiving, Motivation for;

Intimacy, with God;
First Love]
Deut. 8:10–11; Rev. 2:3–5

THE GREEK word for blessed, *makarios*, was the name of an island off of Greece—the Makarios Island. It was known as the blessed island because it was self-contained. The residents didn't need to leave the island in order to get their needs met. The island offered everything that they needed. The natural resources of the blessed island were so thick, so rich, so fruitful, and so productive that everything they needed to enjoy their lives was already built-in. The inhabitants of the island were self-sustained and self-contained without having to run to another island to get their needs met. The blessed island provided everything they needed.

All the stuff you get is outside of you. The new car, the new house, and the new money are all fine . . . but they are all extra. They are a bonus. In the biblical world of being blessed, you should be okay being on the island. Just being in the Kingdom with the King ought to put you in a blessed location. One of the ways you know that you aren't blessed yet in the biblical sense of the word is that you got to keep leaving the island to have fun. You need more than your relationship with God to have peace. You crave more than your communion with the Father to have joy. The blessed person finds their sufficiency with Him.[43]

[Kingdom of God; Contentment; Provision, God's]
Matt. 5:1–12; 1 Tim. 6:6

IF YOU were to go to Universal Studios, either in Florida or in California, they will take you on a tour in a tram through their movie lots. In these movie lots you'll see western towns and modern-day types of towns where films are made. The tour guides will explain to you as you drive through that what you are looking at is a facade. The external may look like it's a town or a city, but if you were to go on the other side, there's nothing there. There's no reality behind what you see. It looks good, but there's nothing else there. The lots are simply there to create an impression of a town or a city for the purposes of the film.

Unfortunately today, much of what goes on in the lives of Christians is not a reflection of true blessing but more like a facade. Beyond the external, their lives have nothing solid on the other side.[44]

[Weakness]

BLESSING, SOURCE OF

ONE OF the reasons that we don't recognize the goodness of God is that we confuse the means of delivery with the source. Many times we think that unless a blessing falls miraculously from heaven into our laps that it didn't come from God. We mix up medium and source.

When we listen to the radio, we can do so only because the radio is a method of delivery. There are no drums in the radio. No horns and no guitars reside inside the equipment. The radio is only a conduit—a point of contact. Even when your radio stops working, there's music in the air. All the radio does is receive a signal that comes from another source and deliver it to you. If you lose sight of that fact, you'll give the radio more credit than a radio ought to have. If you place too much weight on the medium, you'll forget the source.[45]

James 1:17

NORMALLY, when people eat a balanced evening meal, it includes vegetables. Those vegetables will have been purchased at a grocery store. Of course, a grocery store bought the vegetables from someone who farmed and harvested them. The farmer had those vegetables to sell because he planted seeds in the ground. The land in which the seed was planted was also supported by both rain and sunshine. Rain and sunshine are dependent on heaven.

Rain from heaven must come down upon the land in which the seed has been planted—so the fruit and vegetable can sprout, so the farmer can deliver it to the grocery store, so that we can pick it up when we go shopping, so that we can have a nice evening meal. If a person gets stuck appreciating the grocery store, then they've missed the source.

The grocery store is simply the mechanism of delivery. Now, if God stops the sunshine and rain, stops the replication of the seed, or does not allow the land to be fruitful, then there is no trip to the grocery store.[46]

[Provision, God's]
Matt. 5:44–45

THE CEREAL that we eat with milk comes from the grain, which came from the mill, which goes back to the provision of God in the wheat fields. The milk came from the cows that ate the grass that came from the ground that God provided. Everything you have is traced back to God.[47]

BLESSING, SURPRISE

A MAN took his girlfriend out for dinner and when they sat down, he laid an elaborate box on the table for her birthday. All the while they were eating dinner, she just kept thinking about this box, because it was a big box, and she wanted to know what was inside. She could hardly eat. The waiting to open the gift was killing her, but her boyfriend told her to open the gift after dinner. All she could think about was what was in the box.

Finally dinner was over. "Can I open the box now?"

"Yeah, you can open the box."

She opened the box and pulled out a pillow. "Oh, wow, I mean, this is a nice pillow . . . but it's a pillow."

She turned the pillow over, thinking that something was taped to the backside. There was nothing.

"Well, thank you." It was obvious she was disappointed that she got a pillow.

Her boyfriend got up, took the pillow from her, and laid the pillow on the floor. He got down on one knee, took her by the hand, and said, "Will you marry me?"

She forgot about the pillow. The one who gave her the pillow now became a lot more important.[48]

BODY OF CHRIST

SYMBIOTIC growth is the growth that occurs between two organisms where both benefit. Parasitic growth is growth that occurs in one organism because it's feeding off of another. Christians must ask themselves how they are functioning in the organism of the Body of Christ.

Am I a spiritual parasite? Sing to

me. Preach to me. Pray for me. Counsel me. Help me, but expect nothing from me. That is a parasite. A Christian interested in symbiotic growth says, "Yes, I have needs, but I'm willing to give too because everyone needs to benefit."[49]

[Commitment; Giving]

Eph. 4:1–16

YOUR HUMAN body is made up of systems. These include the nervous system, circulatory system, muscular system, lymphatic system, skeletal system, and immune system. These are systems that are interdependent upon one another and when one system goes down, the rest of the body is negatively impacted.[50]

1 Cor. 12:12–26

GOD DIDN'T put a hand on your wrist so your wrist could look good. He didn't put a foot on your ankle just so you could have something dangling. Every part of you was prescribed to accomplish a function. A nonfunctioning, noncontributing body part is something that you would have checked by a doctor, 'cause something is wrong.[51]

FOR TWO years, a little girl was an only child. She knew nothing about sharing because there was no competition. No competition for attention. No competition for love. All the dresses were hers. All the toys were hers. All the ingratiating elements were hers. It was all about her until the second child was born. When the second child, a girl, was born and brought home from the hospital, things had to be shared. Time had to be shared. Attention had to be shared. Love had to be shared.

One day, the father of the two girls walked into the nursery to find the eldest daughter standing and snarling over the new baby girl as she slept in the cradle. And then she did it. She took her hand and slapped the little baby. If a little girl can be that sinful at two years of age, imagine how sinful people are at twenty-two, thirty-two, or forty-two—especially when they've learned to become pros!

Needless to say, this little girl did not go without punishment because she exhibited a heart filled with evil! Because love had to be shared, she rebelled. But she needed to understand that rebelling against her sister also meant getting her in trouble with her father. When you are a rebellious member of the Body of Christ, your Daddy is upset.[52]

BODY OF DEATH

YEARS AGO cars were not as sophisticated as they are now. When the power steering fluid level was good, turning the wheel was a breeze with one finger. When your power steering fluid got low, you'd have to force the wheel to turn. You'd have to pull and tug. It wasn't natural. The pull of the wheel back to the center was so strong that without power steering, when you'd take your hands off the wheel, it would snap back to its neutral position.

Some of our lives are like this. We pull and tug trying to make ourselves better and different. After awhile we get tired and go right back to where our bodies are naturally programmed to be. That is what happens when you try to fix the "body of this death" (Romans 7:24) through human effort. It is naturally bent to sin.

So it is always going to go back there. Once you take your hands off of it for one minute, it is going to roll right back to its natural bent.[53]

[Flesh]

Rom. 7:13–18; Gal. 5:17

BOUNDARIES

PARENTS of teenagers know that the boundary lines between parent and child can get blurry real quick. The older the young person gets, the more apt they are to rebel against restrictions. Many a parent has had to remind their teenagers of who's who. The propensity of the young person is to mentally erase the parent-child distinction because they don't want to be told to clean up their room. They don't want restrictions; they want freedom without boundaries, which erases the line of demarcation.

God wants it to be clear that there is a major difference between man and God—a big-time difference. God is transcendent. God is infinite. Man is not. There is only one God. Man is not Him, so he needs restrictions.[54]

BROKENNESS

THE PICTURE of brokenness is of a wild stallion that wants its independence. It does not want to be ridden; it does not want to be told what to do. Now, it doesn't mind the cowboy feeding it or keeping the trough full of water. It doesn't mind having a place to go into out of the rain. It just doesn't want anyone to get on its back. But the process of breaking a stallion or breaking a wild horse involves the cowboy getting on its back and riding it. The stallion usually bucks and bucks and tries to throw the cowboy off.

"Get off my back!"

"Bless me with the food. Bless me with the water. Bless me with a covering. But don't get on my back!"

The cowboy gets on the back of the horse and rides it out. Sometime he's thrown off, but if the goal is the breaking, he rides that wild horse until it yields. How do you know when a horse has been broken? It doesn't lose its strength; it doesn't lose the muscles in its legs. It does not lose its God-given uniqueness and identity as a horse. It's just now a horse under somebody else's control.

Many of us want the blessings from God, but we don't want Him riding us and bringing us into submission to His will.[55]

[Blessing; Submission]

James 4:7

BROKENNESS, IMPORTANCE OF

TO ENJOY the fragrance of perfume or cologne, you must break the seal of the bottle in which it comes. To see a plant rise from the ground, the shell must be broken open by the substance inside. To enjoy roasted peanuts, there must be a breaking of its outer core. For a baby chick to experience life, it must break the egg that surrounds it. If you and I want to see God's face, we must be broken first.[56]

Matt. 21:44

BROKENNESS, PROCESS OF

THE REFINISHING of antique furniture is an awesome process. Strong chemicals strip away the old varnish. Then sandpaper machines sand it down, exposing all the crooks, nooks, and crannies that need repair. The sanding continues until the surface is even. Then it is varnished, over and over until it has a smooth, refinished surface. It is varnished until it gets back the glory of its originally intended look.

God will strip you down. He will sand and sand. He sands until He exposes every scratch, every nook, and every cranny. This is the part that hurts the worst. This is the part where most believers will cry out to the Lord in pain. This is the part when we must trust that His grace is sufficient. God follows the sanding process with the varnish. This is the point at which the life of Christ shines through in the life of the Christian. Your identity in Christ begins to reveal itself, and you'll find power you've never had because you've been broken.[57]

[Transformation; Character, Importance of; Trials; Tests]
Heb. 12:5–7; 1 Peter 1:6–7

A NUMBER of years ago, our kitchen was remodeled. The remodeler came in and showed us some great plans. He showed us pictures of what the new cabinets would look like, samples of our options for wallpaper, and color cards with choices for paint. It was a glorious sight to see what our new kitchen was going to look like on paper. In fact, there was so much excitement and anticipation about the new kitchen, we forgot about the process. To get that kitchen remodeled, stuff had to be torn down and torn up. Things got so bad in our house, that at one point, we had to move in with our daughter to get away from all of the flying dust. The remodeler had to tear up the floor, tear down the cabinets, move out the appliances, and sand down the walls. We had to get out

of there. We couldn't take it! But we wouldn't have been able to get a new kitchen if the old one wasn't torn up first.

Many people want God to give them a new life, a new job, or a new situation; but they don't want Him to touch anything. If I would have told my remodeler that I didn't want him to touch anything, he would have told me that I didn't want to remodel. If I wanted new paint, a new floor, or new cabinets, none of that would be possible if the old stuff wasn't messed up first. We have got to trust God and give Him permission to tear things up so that He can make all things new.[58]

[Transformation; Character, Importance of; Trials; Tests; Surrender, Benefits of]

WE HAVE recycling bins in our church. They take paper, bottles, and cans. They are designed to give them new life. These materials are taken to recycling centers where fire is used to break down the core components of the paper, or the glass, or the aluminum in order to reshape them into something brand-new. But the materials can't be reshaped until they are put under enough heat that they can be stripped of all the external and only the inner essence it left. Then the materials can be remade. God wants to recycle us. He'll keep us in the fire as long as it takes to strip us.[59]

[Transformation; Character, Importance of; Trials; Tests]
Ps. 66:10; Isa. 48:10

ALL OF you have bought concentrated juices that are packed in the can. That juice will go a long way. In order for it to go a long way, you have got to break the seal. A breaking must occur to get the juice.

Most of us have used cologne or perfume. In order to get that fragrance out of that bottle, you have to break open the top. No matter how much you try to pour it out, if you do not crack open the top, all of the fragrance will stay inside and will not benefit your body.

Guess what? When you come to Christ, the Scripture says that you were sealed with the Holy Spirit of promise. But if you want your soul to benefit from it, a cracking must occur.[60]

[Transformation; Character, Importance of; Trials; Tests]

Eph. 1:13–14

WHEN WE were kids, many of us had a piggy bank that had a little slot in the top for us to drop change into. There was only one way to get that money out of the piggy bank back then, when it wasn't sophisticated. You had to flip it over and shake it. If I wanted a lot of change, I had to do a lot of shaking. Why? Because there was something of value on the inside that I needed to come out on the outside. The only way to get it from the inside to the outside was to shake it loose. God's given us a great treasure in our earthen vessels, but there's so much callousness, hardness, independence, and self-sufficiency on the outside, that it keeps the beauty of Christ trapped on the inside. What God's got to do is to shake us up until He can get out of us what He knows is in there.[61]

[Transformation; Character, Importance of; Trials; Tests; Spiritual Maturity]

2 Cor. 4:7

C

CALLING

WHEN I have trips to go on, I have to go to the airport to catch a plane to my destination. My assistant gives me my plan. She makes sure that I know my destination and what gate I have to go to in order to board the right plane. When I go to the airport, that means that I'm intending to go somewhere. I don't just go to the airport to hang out. I go to the airport because I have a destination.

One time, in the days before cell phones, I was at the airport and heard over the intercom, "Dr. Tony Evans, will you please pick up the white courtesy phone." So I look around, wondering if that call was for me or not. Finally, it dawns on me that I'm the Tony Evans referenced in the announcement. So, I make my way to the white courtesy phone. My assistant was on the other line. She tracked me down because she had new information for me related to my travel plans. She needed to give me the directions necessary for me to know the new flight information.

Now, of course, there are thousands of people at this airport. There are people all over, but my assistant needed me, so she called my name. I heard my name and I got my message even in this busy place.

God has invited every Christian to the airport. He wants to take us somewhere, and He's got a flight plan for our destination. When we have decided that we are committed to the calling of God on our lives and when we are committed to answering

His call, God will interject, intervene, and change our plans if necessary to get us to the right destination. He knows how to find us wherever we are located and call us each by name to give us the information that we need to go in the direction of the plans He has for us.[62]

[God's Will]
Eph. 2:10; Phil. 2:13

BEING prepared for your calling is like going to a pizzeria. I'm talking about a real pizza place where they make the pies on the spot. It all starts with a ball of dough. They roll the dough, pressing and mashing it. Then they start pounding on it. After banging it around for a while, they start throwing it up in the air and twirling it. That dough goes through a whole lot so that you and I can have the pleasure of eating it.

But when you go to a pizzeria, you don't ask for dough. You want the good stuff. You want the sauce, the cheese, and maybe some meat or veggies on top. Everyone wants the good stuff, but you can't get the good stuff until the dough has been prepared.

In the same way, one has to be prepared for their calling. Sometimes, our preparation starts with some pressing and some mashing. Sometimes it means being thrown around or banged up for a little while. But this is only in preparation for the good stuff.[63]

[Sanctification; Trials; Tests; Spiritual Maturity]

CARNAL CHRISTIANS

THE GREEK word for *dull* has to do with slowness of perception due to moral laxness. It was the word used as an epithet for a mule. Now mules are not your greatest thinkers. Mules are not your most intelligent animals. They are kind of the dummies of the horse line. They are basically only good for carrying the loads of others on their backs. You don't really ride them. You don't really exercise with them. You just kind of use them as labor for work because they are dull. Christians can be mule-minded. Christians can regress to the point where they are of very little value to the things of God—not because God made them that way, but because they have become that way. They have become dull of hearing.[64]

[Flesh, Walking in]
Heb. 3; 5:11

CHAOS

YEARS ago, mental institutions were crude in working with people who were disturbed. In Europe, a particular sanitarium had a very antiquated way of determining whether an inmate was sane enough to be released back into society. They would put the patient into a janitor's closet. Then they'd put a stopper in the sink and turn on the water. The water would eventually overflow and the inmate would be given a mop and told to clean up the mess. For about five minutes or so, the person would be left in the closet alone, and then a doctor would come back to check on him. If he was mopping the floor with the water still running, the doctor would know that the patient was not ready to go anywhere because he did not make the connection and fix the root of the problem. That patient would not be declared sane.

Many people today are trying to mop up messes in their lives, families, or circumstances and they are mopping hard! The problem is that, even with all of that effort, there is still a mess because no connection has been made between the cause and effect of the situation. We must start with the cause or else we will forever be cleaning up. We'll forever be mopping but things will not get clean and dry.[65]

Matt. 23:25–27

A FATHER wanted to give his daughter something to do and there was a picture of the world on a sheet of paper. He tore it into smaller pieces and told her to see if she could put the pieces back together correctly, kind of like she would work a puzzle. The little girl agreed. Five minutes later, she showed her father the pieces put back together perfectly. He was stupefied. When he asked her how she had done the task so quickly, she said, "Oh, on the back was a picture of Jesus and I figured if I got Him right, the world would fall into place." Our worlds are in chaos because we aren't focused on getting Jesus right first.[66]

Eph. 2:11–13

CHARACTER, IMPORTANCE OF

A WALL Street broker had fallen in love with a young lady and began dating her. He was very wealthy and he had to be careful whom he related to. He didn't want to relate to somebody who would damage him or only come after him for his money. So he had one of his associates hire a private detective to find out everything there was to find out about this lady. He didn't want to make a mistake. He also didn't want the private eye to know whom he was doing the investigation for, lest the girl find out

later and think that her love didn't trust her.

The broker got his associate to hire a private eye to check up on this lady without telling the detective who it was that was making the assignment and paying the bill. After a number of weeks, the report came back on the young lady whom the broker was considering. The report said, "I have investigated this young lady and she has a squeaky clean life. Perfect in every detail, no flaws, no known mistakes. She is on the up and up in every possible way. However, there is one little possible blip on the screen of her life. She is often seen around town in the company of a young broker whose dubious business practices and principles are well known."

You see, the problem may just be you.[67]

Matt. 7:2–4

CHILDREN, TRAINING

MANY people spend more time training their dogs than they spend training their children.[68]

Prov. 22:6

CHOICE

IN ONE of the Indiana Jones movies, Indiana was looking for the Holy Grail. When he and his team finally arrived at the site where it was located, he had to go through a number of tests to get to the specific room where it rested. He weathered death. He had to spell the name of Jehovah correctly in Latin. He had to take a step of faith across a deep precipice. Finally, making it through the tests successfully, he came into a room with an assortment of cups. He was faced with the challenge of having to choose which one belonged to the carpenter from Nazareth. His enemies were pursuing him and they too wound up meeting him in the room with the assortment of cups.

There was a guardian knight there, and that guardian knight said that the person who chose the cup must choose carefully. In fact, his exact words were "Choose wisely" because there were consequences tied to the choice. Choosing the wrong cup led to death. Choosing the right cup led to life.

Moses says "Choose wisely" because within the covenant of God there are blessings and curses.[69]

[Blessing; Sin, Consequences of]
Deut. 28; Josh. 24:15

CHRIST, FREEDOM IN

IN JANUARY 1863 the Emancipation Proclamation was declared. This legal document said that all slaves were now free. But in Texas, someone kept it a secret. They didn't tell us that we were free. So for a couple of years after the Emancipation Proclamation, we were still in bondage.

We were acting like slaves because no one had told us we were free. In fact, we were so glad that someone finally told us, we made that date a holiday and African Americans celebrate Juneteenth every year. Thank God, someone told us! If no one had ever shared the good news, then we would have stayed in slavery much longer.

Jesus Christ, on Calvary two thousand years ago, signed your Emancipation Proclamation. He declared that you are free but Satan is

trying to keep it a secret from you. He's trying to keep you from coming into the realization that you don't have to stay tied down.

You don't have to say "Yes sir" to his control of your life any longer. You can now put down that plow and move "North." You can now take the freedom that has been offered to you and act on it. You can collect your forty acres and a mule and start plowing your own land now. You can start living through the freedom that you have because you have now been made free in Christ. That's who you are but you must live like it.[70]

[Race Relations]
John 8:36

CHRIST, SUFFICIENCY OF

RESPIRATORS are machines that do the breathing for you. If you are laid down on the hospital bed and there is a problem with your breathing, they put you on the respirator. If you insist on breathing on your own, the respirator does you no good. There's only one thing you can do with the respirator—cooperate. Now, you are involved because it's your lungs going up and down. It's your mouth and nose that are taking in and expelling the oxygen. The two of you are working together but the respirator is doing the work; you are just cooperating with it rather than resisting it.

Christ wants to express His life through you and be your respirator. He does not want you being your own respirator because then you don't need Him. He doesn't want to do it apart from you, so you must cooperate. You must yield yourself to the person of Christ. We have too many

Christians today hyperventilating in the spiritual life.[72]

[Surrender, Concept of; Grace]
2 Cor. 12:9

CHRIST, UNION WITH

ON THE day that you came to faith in Christ, you entered into a spiritual union with Him. What exactly is a spiritual union? Many people drink coffee with cream. When cream is added to coffee, a union occurs. The blackness of the coffee and the whiteness of the cream are now integrated and made one. The coffee becomes brown because of the union. The coffee is not considered black-and-white coffee; it's just a cup of coffee! When you drink it you now have to drink the black coffee with the white cream because they have become one. If someone were to try to separate the cream from the coffee, there would be chaos in the cup. Once the union of cream with coffee has occurred, no separation is possible.

The Bible says that when we came to Jesus Christ for salvation, we entered into an indissolvable union with Him so that what happened to Christ happened to us. Christ died. We died. Christ arose. We arose with Him. Christ ascended. We ascended with Him.[73]

[Salvation; New Life in Christ]
Rom. 5; Gal. 2:20

CHRISTIAN, DEFINITION OF

THERE IS an American embassy in England. Located in that building is all the power of the U.S. government on one square block. Everything needed from an American standpoint is inside that building, because when it speaks, it speaks on behalf of the government.

Suppose another world leader said to the president, "Let's have negotiations." The president can say, "I already have an ambassador in your country." What he would be implying is that to talk to an ambassador is the same as talking to him.

The Bible says that you are ambassadors of Jesus Christ. When people hear from us, they have just heard from God. He has given us delegated authority to speak on His behalf. How can we be ambassadors with our mouths closed? He has given us the privilege of being a spokesperson. Speak up, man! Speak up, lady![74]

[Ambassadors, for Christ; Spiritual Identity, in Christ; Witnessing]
2 Cor. 5:19–20; Eph. 6:19–20

HANGING around a hospital doesn't make you a patient. And hanging around a church doesn't make you a Christian.[75]

CHRISTIAN, SIGNIFICANCE OF

A STORY is told of the Pope when he was scheduled to speak to the United Nations delegates. His plane was to land in New York, from where he would be taken by limousine to the UN building. However, there was bad weather in New York and the plane couldn't land. The plane landed instead in Newark, New Jersey. They sent the limousine to pick up the Pope in Newark but they were running awfully late. The Pope got in the car. The driver was driving much too slow for the Pope. He said, "Driver, can't you go faster?"

The driver said, "I'm sorry, sir. I can't. I'm already in trouble. I've got outstanding tickets. If I drive fast and risk getting another ticket, I would jeopardize my license and then wouldn't be able to drive anybody and would lose my job."

The Pope thought for a second, then said, "Well, I've got to get there. I'll tell you what. Let me drive." So the driver got in the backseat and the Pope got behind the wheel. The Pope put his hand on the wheel, revved up the engine, and took off. He went winding down streets like he was driving a race car.

As he got close to the UN building, a policeman saw the speeding limousine doing all kinds of twists and twirls and turns. The police car's lights began to spiral as he went after the limo and pulled it over. One of the policemen got out, the other stayed in his car. The ticketing officer got out, got his ticket book, and went over to the window. He knocked on the window and signaled to roll the window down. He looked at who was driving the car, closed his book, and then went back to his own vehicle. The policeman who was still in the vehicle asked his partner, "Aren't you going to write him a ticket?"

"Nope!"

"You're not going to write him a ticket?"

"No, no, I'm not writing this guy a ticket. You don't understand the importance of this guy who's in this car."

"Well, he can't be more important than the mayor, can he?"

"Oh yes, he can!"

"Wait a minute. He can't be more important than the governor of New York, can he?"

"Yes, he can!"

"Well, he cannot be more important than the president of the United States, right?"

"Yes, he can!"

The officer was confused. "Now wait a minute! Who can be more important than the president of the United States?"

"I don't know who the guy is, but the Pope is driving him!"

You don't ever have to feel like you're a nobody if Jesus is in your life. You're never a nobody if He's behind the wheel of your car. You're never a nobody, no matter what anybody says about you, because if Jesus is behind the wheel, Satan can't ticket you. You are somebody because Jesus is in your life.[76]

[Spiritual Identity, in Christ; Blessing]
Rom. 8:28–39

CHRISTIAN, VALUE OF

A $100 bill can be crumpled, mashed, or spit on and it is still worth $100. Its value is not determined by what happens to it, but instead by the one who consigned it. The government says that this is worth $100. So it is worth $100 even if it is mistreated, stepped on, and spit on. It can even be ripped and taped back together and still be worth $100.

Many Christians feel that in their lives they have been stomped on, crushed, and bruised. However, their worth is not affected because their value has been consigned by another.[77]

Eph. 2:4–7

WHEN God saved you, He made you a diamond. If I rub a diamond in dirt, what I have is a dirty diamond. I have not lost the value of the diamond; I just let it get dirty. I shouldn't let the dirt on the diamond distract me from knowing the true worth of what I hold in my hand. However, in order to truly appreciate the beauty of the diamond, I would have to get the dirt off the diamond and then restore it back to its original luster.[78]

I SAW a lady who had some roses, and the roses were dead. They were drooping and lifeless. They were good for nothing else but to be thrown away. But she wasn't throwing them away. I saw her crumpling them in her hand. She explained that the roses were dead, but if she dried them and crushed them, she would then have potpourri. While the flowers were dead on the outside, they still had a lot of fragrance on the inside. Even in their apparent demise, they still could be turned into something sweet.[79]

[Death; Sacrifice; Victory]
Phil. 2:17–18

CHRISTIAN LIVING

SCRABBLE is a challenging game. It involves the bringing together of letters to form words. Although at first glance this may seem like an easy game to play because there are only twenty-six letters in the English alphabet, these letters come together to form enough words to fill the Encyclopedia Britannica, the Library of Congress, and the World Wide Web!

The game of Scrabble involves the ordering of items that originally have no implicit order. The words already exist, but the letters must be arranged a certain way to be made into words. The goal of this game is for players to set out letters so that they now make sense.

Christians are to live their lives in a way that their actions come together to form the picture of salvation. Salvation is a gift and for the Christian already exists. The goal of living the Christian life is to arrange one's lifestyle so that it now looks like the existence of a person saved by grace.[80]

[Life, Management of; Salvation; Discipleship]
Matt. 5:16; Rom. 12:2; Phil. 2:12

IF YOU go to a doctor, he diagnoses your ailment and prescribes a treatment. He gives you a prescription for medication. He gives you everything you need to feel better, but you've got to work it out. In other words, you've got to go to the pharmacist, you've got to get the prescription filled, and, most importantly, you've got to take the medicine in order for it to benefit you. See, God knows how to measure whether we value His salvation because if you do, you work it out. If you value it, you work it out. If you don't value it, then you don't work it out. You ignore it, you bypass it, or you marginalize it, but what you don't do is work it out.[81]

[Carnal Christians; Discipleship; Salvation]

CHRISTIAN LIVING, AUTHENTICITY

A FEMALE PRESENCE was requested for the monetary system and the Susan B. Anthony dollar was created. This dollar took the form of a large coin. Unfortunately, this coin did not reach the level of circulation of other coins more familiar. Why? Because it looked too much like a quarter. People had trouble distinguishing it and opted not to use it. A lot of Christians are like that. We are worth a dollar but the way we live our lives makes us look like we're worth a quarter.[82]

[Weakness; Witnessing; Flesh, Walking in]
Heb. 12:14–28

THE STORY is told of a gymnast who was out of work. He was reading the newspaper and he read that the gorilla in the local zoo had died. He went down to the zoo and said, "I hear your gorilla has died." He said, "I know you are probably planning to get another one, but I have an idea. Give me a gorilla suit; I am a gymnast so I can do all kinds of moves. I'll make the people think that I'm the gorilla. I'll have a job and you'll have a gorilla. If this arrangement works out, then you can keep me on."

Well, they didn't have anything to lose, so they gave him an authentic gorilla outfit. He practiced a bit making some gorilla sounds and then got in the cage. Everyone thought he was real. People kept showing up until the crowd had grown very large.

Next to his cage was a lion's cage. There was a rope hanging down in the gorilla's cage, so he said to himself, "I'll start swinging on the rope and dazzle the crowd with my moves. They'll really get riled up if they see me swinging over the lion's cage." He started swinging. The people did get excited as they watched him swing over the lion's cage and back. The zoo loved him and kept him on as the fake gorilla.

One day he swung over to the lion's cage and the rope broke. He fell down, and found himself looking straight into the mouth of the lion. Out of fear, he forgot his role of go-rilla and yelled out, "HELP!"

Immediately after his scream for help, he heard a female voice say, "Shut up, or you're going to get us both fired!"[83]

IF YOU'RE going month after month and year after year and there are no negative repercussions that ever come upon you because of your faith, then your faith has not been clearly demonstrated. You are a secret agent Christian or a Spiritual CIA member. You are a covert operative because there have been no repercussions for your faith.

To put it another way, if you were accused of being a Christian, would there be enough evidence to convict you or would you be found innocent of all charges?[84]

[Witnessing; Spiritual Identity, in Christ]
Luke 6:26; John 15:18–21;
2 Tim. 1:8; 3:12

THERE'S something I don't understand about Christmas. Why do we wrap gifts? I don't understand, and I certainly don't understand paying folks to wrap them. Trust me, the person you are giving a gift to is not interested in your wrapping. Now, they may placate you by noticing the wrapping and telling you how pretty the bow looks, but in the end they are going to tear it off.

Wrapping paper and all the accompanying accessories are a camouflage that disguises what people are really interested in. We get all hyped and geeked when we see people wrapped well. They drive a well-wrapped car; they live in a well-wrapped neighborhood. They work at a well-wrapped job, they wear well-wrapped clothes, and they have well-wrapped money. But God wants to know what the wrapping is covering. He's interested in knowing what is on the inside.[85]

[Spiritual Life, Manifestation of]
1 Peter 3:2–4

ONE YEAR at Christmastime, my wife wanted some wrapped boxes to use for decoration. She took eight empty boxes and had them wrapped to use as a decoration at our front door. Those boxes sat in the front of our house, impeccably wrapped, topped with bows, and empty. I didn't worry at all about a thief coming and stealing any of those wrapped boxes on the outside of our house. There wasn't anything in there!

A lot of folks are well wrapped but there's nothing going on in the inside. Unfortunately today, many people don't want to be truly blessed; they just want to be well wrapped. True, authentic Christian living starts on the inside and the evidence of that life works its way out.[86]

James 2:18

A BODYBUILDER was visiting an African tribe, and the tribal chief was just amazed at his physique. So the tribal chief asks the muscle builder, "What do you do with all of those muscles?"

The bodybuilder said, "Well, it's probably easier to show you than to explain." So he went into all these different presentations of his physique to show off the different muscles—the biceps, the triceps, the back, and the obliques. He just stood there, changing poses. After the presentation, the tribal chief said, "Now that's

impressive! But, I have a second question. What else do you do with all of those muscles?"

"Well," the bodybuilder said, "that's pretty much it. I work out to pose."

The African chief said, "What a waste. What a waste."

Many Christians work out only to pose. They don't work out to use the muscles they have developed. They carry their Bibles, stand during praise and worship, raise their hands in praise to the Lord, and absorb the Word of God from the sermon, only to leave the church and never use what they've learned.[87]

[Carnal Christians; Spiritual Maturity]
James 1:21–23

CHRISTIAN LIVING, BURDEN OF

A MAN one day was rushing to catch a plane. His plane was to leave at five but he left his watch home, so he was not quite sure what the time was. He came upon a gentleman lugging two heavy suitcases. The man who was rushing to catch his plane said, "Sir, excuse me, but I notice you have a watch. Could you tell me what time it is?"

The man, with great relief, dropped the suitcases and looked at his watch. He said, "Sure! It's 10:05 a.m. and it's fifty-three degrees outside. In Singapore it's seventy-four degrees right now and in Japan it's sixty-two. In Canada it is thirty-seven degrees outside and in the Congo it is one hundred and twenty degrees."

The guy stared at the suitcase man for a second and then said, "Your watch told you all that?"

"Oh yes," the man continued, "in fact, the Dow Jones is at 10,500 and the NASDAQ is 3,500. Anything else you want to know?"

"Wow! I can't believe that you got all that from your watch. Look, I have to run and catch my plane but I've got to have that watch. I will give you one thousand dollars for that watch!"

"Oh no. I'm sorry. I can't sell it to you. You see, I'm an inventor and I made this watch for my son. In fact, I'm on my way to give my son the watch now."

"Sir, I don't think you understand. I've got to have that watch. I'll give you twenty-five hundred dollars for that watch right now."

"I'm sorry, but this watch is only for my son."

"I'll give you five thousand dollars!"

"I'm sorry, sir."

"Look, I've got to catch my plane, but if you give me that watch right now, I'll give you ten thousand dollars. I'll give you the money right now."

The inventor reluctantly pondered the proposition. He figured that at $10,000, he could afford to invent another watch and pocket some extra change. "OK, why not!" He took the watch off and gave it to the man in a hurry.

The traveler wrote a check for ten thousand dollars and took the watch. He proudly held his new purchase and began heading toward his gate. Just as he started to run to make his flight on time, the inventor ran after him, struggling to carry his two suitcases, and yelling for the man to stop: "Excuse me, sir—just a minute! You for-

got your batteries!"

The hurried traveler looked shocked when it dawned on him that the batteries were in the suitcases. He did not realize that his purchase came with extra baggage.

Many Christians feel this way in their spiritual walks. When many of us met Jesus, we were fascinated by Him. We learned about the plan of salvation and figured that we had scored such a sweet deal. But after we got saved, we joined the church, met Christian friends, and then learned about the suitcases. All of a sudden, living the Christian life became heavy and burdensome. What we thought was going to be an easy thing now carried with it luggage that would seem to bury us.

The good news is that although many Christians feel that the Christian life is burdensome, it does not have to be this way.[88]

[Discipleship; Spiritual Life, Manifestation of; Power]
Matt. 11:29–30; 1 John 5:3

CHRISTIAN LIVING, COMMITMENT

AS THE offering tray passed, a little girl took the tray, put it on the floor, and stood up in the offering plate. The usher said, "Honey, why are you doing that?" And she said, "Because they taught me in Sunday school that my whole body was to be offered to the Savior." This little girl got the point that she was the one who belonged in the tray, and that God does not want donations.[89]

[Commitment; Sacrifice; Giving; Surrender, Concept of]
Rom. 12:1; 1 Cor. 6:20

THERE IS a story of a chicken and a pig who were walking down the street one day. They came to the grocery store and the grocer had a sign on the window that said "Bacon and Eggs Wanted." The grocer said, "Can you help me out? I need some bacon and eggs."

The chicken said, "Well, let's go help him out. He needs some bacon. Pig, you can give him the bacon, and I can give him the eggs."

The pig said, "You're crazy! All you have to give is a contribution. I have to give up the whole thing!"[90]

LIVING the Christian life is more than religion; it's a lifestyle. If you eat doughnuts all week long, drinking a Diet Coke is not going to help you. If you've operated apart from grace all week long, showing up at church on Sunday will not help you. Coming to church will make you feel better, but it doesn't solve your problem.[91]

[Life, Management of; Flesh, Walking in]

MCDONALD'S offers "combo meals." The company has made it easy for anyone to drive up and get a full meal by just saying a number. They have also trained their employees to take orders and always follow up with the question, "Do you want to supersize it?" The question basically implies that the customer is going to choose between taking a regular order or an oversized one.

In the same way, God continually offers His children the opportunity to "supersize" what He is offering to them. With just a little bit more of an investment of obedience and commitment on the part of the Christian, God will make so much more available.[92]

[Commitment; Sacrifice; Giving]
Matt. 17:19–21; James 4:8

SOME people participate in a scam. Due to a major event, such as a banquet or ceremony, they will go to a store and buy a dress, suit, or shoes to wear. They will adorn themselves with this outfit for the event, only to go back to the store the next day and return it! They never intend to buy these things to own them; they only want to use the goods for their own purposes and then give them back. Where the store intends to make legitimate sales to legitimate customers, the customers in this situation actually have an entirely different plan in mind. They are running a game on the establishment.

Many of us are attempting to run a game on God. We come to the store—the church—and say what we want and what we are committed to. We make declarations regarding what we want. We take for our own purposes what we want from the establishment, only to tell God later that we can't use it and don't want it anymore. We tell God that we want Him and that we are here for His purposes, and then at our convenience we live for our own fulfillment and purposes. That is running a game on God.

The difference is, with God, we can't run a game. He has the ability to search the heart.[93]

[Carnal Christians]
Jer. 17:10; Rev. 2:23

AN EVANGELIST was invited overseas to minister in a crusade. The first night of his visit, he was picked up by his host and was to be taken to the church in which he was to give his message. The car stalled. The driver's guage wasn't working and he had no idea he was without gas. The driver had in effect attempted to take his passengers somewhere with no tiger in his tank! Both the host and the traveling minister had to get out and push the car.

After awhile, they were able to get some gas and pour it into the tank. The motor began to rev up because the engine had been fed. Prayer wouldn't have solved that problem. The car even had two holy men in it, but it wouldn't budge without getting fed what it required in order to run.

Many of us want to give God everything except what God wants. We want to offer God a little of this and a little of that and wonder why our spiritual engines don't roar. God is requiring what we are not giving, and that is a committed life, using the time we have for spiritual development.[94]

[Commitment; Spiritual Maturity]
Ps. 90:12; Eph. 5:15–17

IN 1856, Henry Brown, a slave in Richmond, Virginia, decided he didn't want to be a slave anymore. Henry Brown found himself a box, a small wooden crate, and postmarked it to an abolitionist in Philadelphia, which was free territory. Henry Brown got inside the box, sealed the box from the inside, and mailed himself to Philadelphia.

Henry Brown was banking on the U.S. Postal Service to deliver him. He was in slavery and needed to be delivered. The abolitionist got the crate. When he opened the box, Henry Brown stood up, after being in that box for three weeks, and said, "How do you do, sir. My name is Henry Brown and I was a slave. I heard about you being an abolitionist, so I'm entrusting my future to you." That was a big risk. It was an oxygen risk, a risk of being discovered, and a risk of going hungry. But when Henry Brown stood up in Philadelphia, he was a free man. Henry Brown rejoiced because the risk was well worth the inconvenience. Living a committed Christian life involves taking a risk. It involves having faith that Jesus is going to come through for you. But living a committed Christian life is a risk that is well worth the inconvenience.[95]

[Risk; Trials; Commitment]
Phil. 3:7–11

GOD will always test you for the big things by looking at the little things. I knew at eighteen years old that God wanted me to preach. But, I started out on street corners and bus stops, not churches. I would go to bus stops and I would stand in front of the bus stop and there would be people waiting on buses and I'd go at it. There was no pay involved. There was no notoriety involved in that. In fact, I looked like a pure fool sometimes. But I was walking in what He wanted me to do. The church came later. A lot of us are waiting for this big blessing and God can't get us to move out of the seat we're in. If He can't get you to do little acts of good works, why should He entrust you with greater opportunities for good works?[96]

[Faithfulness; Calling]
Matt. 25:14–21

A MAN one day was writing the love of his life . . . her name was Betty. He wrote:

My dearest Betty,

I love you beyond words. Webster does not have in his dictionary the necessary vocabulary to explain the depth of my love for you. Thoughts of you dance across the portals of my mind. You are my all-consuming passion. So enraptured am I regarding my love for you that the Pacific Ocean would be like a pond if I had to swim it. I could do it as long as I knew you were awaiting me on the other shore. The heat of the Sahara Desert would never impede my progress to you, knowing that you would be the oasis that would refresh me when I arrive. There would be no inconvenience I wouldn't endure for you. Climbing Mount Everest would only seem like getting over an ant's hill if I knew you were at the precipice. All I'm simply saying to you, my darling . . . is that my love for you transcends time and space.

Signed, Sam.

P.S. I'll see you Saturday night if it doesn't rain.

Now I'm sure you would agree with me, Sam was only full of a bunch of noise. Sam could talk a good game but he didn't go very deep. While he could verbalize overcoming the elements to get to his love, a little bit of rain would keep him away. It's easy to verbalize being an overcomer. It's easy to say the words, "I am victorious. I've been made victorious in Christ." But it's a whole different thing to not let the rain slow you down. It's a whole different thing to take your position as an overcomer and turn it into your practice of overcoming.[97]

[Victory; Overcome]

A LITTLE girl came to her father and asked him for a nickel. The father reached in his pocket, but he didn't have any change. All he had was a twenty-dollar bill. He knew that was a lot of money, but he figured that his daughter had been a good girl. He decided to give her the twenty.

The little girl said, "Oh no, Daddy. You don't understand. I want a nickel."

"No, honey, you don't understand. This is a bunch of nickels. This is a twenty-dollar bill."

But the little girl didn't understand. She said, "Daddy, why won't you give me a nickel?"

He tried to explain. He tried to tell her how many nickels were in a dollar, and how many dollars were in a twenty-dollar bill. She wasn't getting it.

So she started crying and having a temper tantrum. "Daddy, you said you were going to give me a nickel. Why won't you give me a nickel?"

That's exactly what we do. We settle for a nickel when God offers us twenties.[98]

[Spiritual Life, Manifestions of; Blessing]
Eph. 3:16–19

MANY of us use sugar substitutes like Sweet'N Low. Sweet'N Low is used by people who want to taste some sweetness without having any caloric effect.

A lot of Christians want to be sweet, and low—sweet in their talk, but low in their walk.[99]

CHRISTIAN LIVING, IDENTITY IN CHRIST

THE STORY is told that one day the daughter of the Queen of England was sitting in a chair and slouching, sitting very awkwardly. They were out in public and the Queen's daughter had become an embarrassment because she was not behaving in concert with her identity. The Queen looked at her daughter and said, "Sit up, don't you know who you are?"[100]

MY WIFE and I got married in 1970. On that day a major change took place in her life. Her name changed. Although she had been Lois I. Cannings, her name became Lois Evans. She had a new identification.

We spent the first summer of our marriage in Harlem at 133rd and Lennox. I was involved in a ministry up there. We stayed, during that ministry time, in an apartment over a church. We'd just been there a day or so when someone called on the telephone and said, "May I speak to Mrs. Evans?"

My wife said, "Hold the line."

She went looking for Mrs. Evans until it dawned on her after she had left the phone that SHE was HER!

She came back to the phone, changed her voice, and said, "Hello, Mrs. Evans here."

She had forgotten who she was. She had forgotten her identity. When you forget who you are, you don't act like you should.[101]

1 Cor. 7:22–23; 2 Cor. 3:2–4

CHRISTIAN, don't you know who you are? Stop letting the world tell you who you are. You are a child of God. You are a saint. You are sanctified. You are secure. You are holy. You have royal blood flowing through your veins! That's who you are! A lot of us are not acting like we should act because we

don't remember who we are.[102]

1 Peter 2:9

WHEN your favorite sports team wins, you will say, "We won!"

WE who? You weren't on the field. You didn't get tackled. You didn't get hit. You didn't throw the ball. You didn't make an interception. You didn't block anyone. What do you mean WE won? WE won by identification. Because you identify with the team, when they win, you win.

We identify so much that we even call our buddies who live in another city and tell them, "We beat you!" We vicariously identify! We feel good when our team wins and we feel bad when our team loses. Why? Because we understand that we are related to the team by identity.

When Jesus died, you died. When Jesus arose, you arose. When Jesus comes back, you will rise to go with Him because that's who you are. We must identify with who we are in Christ. We have a new identity now.[103]

[Spiritual Identity, in Christ]
Rom. 8:9–17

DURING the Civil War, it was legal for a man who wanted to stay out of the army of the North to pay someone to fulfill his draft obligations. A man could actually buy someone to go to war for him. There was a man named Mr. Pratt who paid Mr. White to go fight a battle in the Civil War for him. Mr. White was killed. Mr. Pratt was redrafted. Mr. Pratt then took the agreement between himself and Mr. White to the draft board and told them that the second draft was invalid and ineffective because he "died" in Mr. White who had gone to war in his place.

When Satan comes up to you to redraft you into your old life, when Satan gives you a recall to your old way of thinking, your old way of talking, or your old way of acting, you've got to show him the agreement.

You can say, "Jesus Christ has already died in my place. You can't redraft me to that old life anymore. You can't take me back to that old way of thinking anymore. The payment has already been paid."[104]

[New Life in Christ; Satan]

ONE of the responsibilities of ministerial work is performing weddings, and in every wedding there is something I do all the time. I get to the place in the ceremony where I say, "Who gives this lady away to be married?" Generally, it's the father or some surrogate for the father who has positioned himself by the daughter and an exchange takes place. The father or surrogate then says, "I do."

Now I have bad news for the dad. Once he says, "I do," he can go sit down. I'm through with him. I will have no other conversation with him in the whole ceremony. Why? Because he's irrelevant now. Because in that ceremony, the man, the bridegroom, will then come and replace the father. The two of them will come up before me and I will go through the wedding vows. They will exchange the rings and then I will close the ceremony by saying, "I now pronounce you husband and wife." The audience will then stand and receive the new couple.

That young lady has been transformed. She has been transformed not because she's a different lady but because she has a new identity now.

When she came into the building, she was Jane Somebody. But once she has been presented by her father, she comes under a new authority and enters into a new relationship. The first man is now overruled by a younger, newer man, strictly for one reason and one reason alone: the young lady has transferred identities. The Bible says that you have transferred identities and when that old man called the flesh starts telling you what to do, you are supposed to tell it, "I have a new hubby now. I am married to a new lover now. I'm wearing a new ring now. I have a new name now."[105]

[New Life in Christ; Spiritual
Identity, in Christ; Natural Man;
Freedom]
Rom. 6:4; 2 Cor. 5:17

ON ONE of my shirts, I have my initials sewn onto the cuff. There will never be a question about whose shirt it is because my initials prove that it's my shirt. It's a shirt customized for me. Now I have some shirts that come off the rack and a lot of folks can possibly claim that they have one just like those, but not this one because this one is custom-made.

When something is custom-made it means it's fitted to your uniqueness. It has been crafted with you in mind. That means that it's not for everyone else to wear. We are all unique. We are all custom-made. There is no reason to try to be someone else or to live someone else's life. Why settle for off-the-rack living when there is an identity and life in Christ custom-made for each one of us?[106]

[Calling]

A MAN went to go visit a psychiatrist one day. When the doctor came in, he asked, "What can I do for you today? What seems to be the problem?"

"I have a problem. Every single time I go to the grocery store, when I pass by the dog food section, something in me tells me that I need to open a can of Alpo and eat it. Something inside tells me to pick up a can of Alpo, open it up, and start chowing away."

The doctor said, "Well, this is a little different from anything I've ever dealt with before. How long have you been dealing with this problem?"

The man said, "Ever since I was a puppy!"

This man was very confused about who he really was. If he were a dog by identity, then Alpo is what he would be looking for. Just as that gentleman was confused, many Christians are confused about their identity in Christ.[107]

I REMEMBER A few years ago we were driving down from Boston in the fall of the year. You know, the scene was beautiful. As leaves changed to brown, it was a wonderful fall sight along the Eastern coast. It was magnificent. People come from all over the country and even around the world to watch the changing of the colors.

But a lot of people don't understand the colors. They get the colors mixed up. They think the color is changing from green to brown. No, the real color of the leaves is brown, not green. The reason why brown leaves become green is that chlorophyll begins to reproduce on brown leaves during the spring and the summer, turn-

ing their natural brown color and camouflaging it so that what you see is green. But the green looks so impressive you think the green is the real deal, when actually the green is hiding the real deal. The real deal is brown. So in the fall, when the green chlorophyll begins to die, it unveils what's really there.

A lot of us have covered up the Spirit, so that we don't see our true colors or our true identity. We walk around projecting a fake identity. Many of us are fake Christians, trying to look like real Christians, when God wants to cut away the fake, so that the real deal shows up.[108]

[New Life in Christ; Spiritual Identity, in Christ]

Heb. 10:21–23

CHRISTIAN LIVING, NEW LIFE

WHEN you move into a new house that someone else lived in, it's your house, even though the owners are no longer there. The old people who were there may have been dirty, despicable, and filthy or unkempt and unclean. The house may have reflected who they were, but now you've purchased the home and you are a clean person. You are concerned about removing the dust, sweeping the floor, cleaning the dishes, and painting the walls. You move into that house and because you are there, the house takes on a whole different appearance. The grass is cut. The dishes are clean. The carpet is vacuumed. Why? Because a new person has moved into an old house.

Well, before you met Christ, the old person was living in that house called your body. But now that Jesus has moved in, it's the same body but you've got a new resident. This new resident is holy, clean, pure, and righteous. So even though He's living in that old house, He can make it look good. Even though He's living in that old house, He can paint it up. Even though He's living in that old house, He can clean it up. He can fix those carpets and hang those drapes and straighten out everything that's wrong in your life. Why? Not because your bodily house has changed but because somebody new has moved in. Christ has moved in. So stop keeping Him from painting and fixing up that old place so that you can live life as He meant it to be lived.[109]

[New Life in Christ; Transformation; Sanctification]
Rom. 6:21–22

CHRISTIAN LIVING, POWER

THERE'S nothing worse than a man who becomes a millionaire who doesn't understand the ramifications of his wealth, and who still lives like a pauper. And there's nothing worse than Christians, who have been made spiritual millionaires, living like spiritual paupers.

You would think when you look at the way some Christians live, that God has made absolutely no deposit of power in their account at all.[110]

Eph. 1:3, 6–8

SOMETIMES Christians look at other Christians and say, "Boy, I wish I could be as spiritual as they are." But don't you understand? You have the same identity that they do. So if they are progressing and you are regressing, it is because they are living in light of who they are and you are not.

In my house, I have a toaster, a can opener, a microwave, and a refrigerator. They are all different appliances, but they all work from the same power source. When I plug them in, the refrigerator refrigerates. When I plug the microwave in, the microwave does the microwaving. When I plug the toaster in, the toaster does the toastering, and when I plug the can opener in, the can opener does its can opening. Each appliance, though different, lives up to its manufactured specifications because each appliance is receiving the same power source.

Even though I am different from you and you are different from me, all of us have the equal potential of living up to God's manufacturer's specifications. You can be what God saved you to be and I can be what God saved me to be because the same electrical current is available to all God's kids. It's available to all who belong to Christ. So there are no special kids in the kingdom. God has the design for you but you must know who you are in Him.[111]

[Christian Living, Identity in Christ; Calling; Spiritual Gifts, Use of]
1 Cor. 12

I WAS talking on my cordless phone the other day and it started to make this clicking noise. It continued for a little while and then I heard one final click and then my phone went dead. I had no power. Do you know why there was no power? The receiver had been off the charger too long. It had been hanging out in the room, far away from the base, and so the power was all gone. So do you know what I did? I walked my receiver over to the base because the base had the power. After the receiver had a chance to hang out with the base for a little while, I walked over and picked up the receiver to find that it had power once more. Why? Because I brought it to where the power was. When I connected my receiver to the power, all of a sudden I could hear again.

Some of us have lives that are clicking and nothing is happening because we have not connected ourselves with the base.[112]

[Intimacy, with God]

Phil. 3:8–11

THE DATE was August 14, 2003. Mrs. Evans and I were in New York on our way back to Dallas. We went to LaGuardia Airport to catch our flight. I went to curbside check-in to check in our bags. The line was not moving. I waited twenty minutes, and still there was no movement in the line. I got out of the line to find out what was going on. The baggage handler said the airport had no power.

It was then that we found out that we were caught in the blackout of 2003 where the whole East Coast went dark due to a power grid failure. No planes were coming in, no planes were going out. We couldn't check in. The conveyor belts to deliver the baggage weren't working because there was no power. So we waited. We waited three hours along with thousands of other people at the airport who were also stuck in this miserable situation. It was a steamy, hot August day, with no solution in sight. Finally, as darkness was coming over the city of New York and the airport, we were told the airport was shutting down. Without power or light, or anything else, the airport was shutting down. So thousands of people like ourselves were stuck. We'd already checked out of our hotel room and had no place to go.

I got on my telephone and called my sister to ask her to help me find a hotel room. Everybody at the airport was looking for a room and I needed all the help I could get. She called me back soon after and said she'd found one room at the Crown Plaza LaGuardia. She said it was the last one and that they would hold it for me for ten minutes. We ran out into the dark of night, hailed a cab, and got to the Crown Plaza LaGuardia just in the nick of time.

Due to the power outage, candles were now lighting the hotel. We registered by hand because the computers weren't working. There was no TV, no air-conditioning, and no hot food because nothing was working. We pulled back the shades and opened the window to get some air in our room.

That's when we saw it. Immediately across the street from us was a Marriott Hotel. It was all lit up. I mean this place was popping. We heard music playing through our open window. The other hotel was so close we could see people moving around and eating outside. It was clear to me that we were in the wrong place. I had one simple question: How could there be that much light in this much darkness? It was about 9:00 at night, but I had to get my inquisitive question answered, so I walked back down the steps and crossed over to the Marriott.

I walked into an air-conditioned

Marriott Hotel. All the TVs were on and were tuned in to the newscast reporting on how dark New York City was. Folks were lined up at the restaurant to get hot food. There was all this light and joy and music and laughter and excitement in a dark situation. I went over to the assistant manager and I said, "Mister, I don't understand. It's dark everywhere. The airport is right over there and it's dark. My hotel is right over yonder and it's dark too. Everything is dark, and yet you are lit up like a Christmas tree. How can this be?"

He said, "It's really fairly simple. When we built this hotel, we built it with a gas generator. We've got power on the inside that is not determined by circumstances on the outside. Even though there's nothing happening out there, there's plenty happening in here."

When you accepted Jesus Christ, He came into the inside. So what's happening on the outside shouldn't determine whether or not you've got a lighthouse on the inside. What's happening out there shouldn't determine your joy. God has given us a generator of life and liberty in our souls through our relationship with Jesus Christ. We don't have to live our lives determined by life's circumstances.[113]

[Trials]

Phil. 4:4; 2 Cor. 12:9–10

I LIKE those truck commercials where they show the towing ability of a truck. They always show the truck pulling something, like a boat, up a hill. Do you know the thing that is being pulled is doing nothing but going for a ride? You never see a boat hitched onto a truck struggling to climb a hill. The power for the tow is located under the hood of the truck. The power is built into the vehicle. All the boat has to do is be hooked onto the truck.

The power for your Christian life is not in you. The power for your Christian life is Christ under the hood; it's Christ in you, the hope of glory.[114]

[Power. Accessing]

Col. 1:27

WHEN I was a boy in Baltimore, the way we "swam" on Saturday was to run through the water from the fire hydrant. The fire marshal would come around and open the fire hydrant enough for it to spray water for us. The fire hydrant would shoot out water; we'd put on short pants and have the time of our lives.

As a young boy, I didn't understand how all that water could come out of that little pipe for days. Water just kept gushing out of there. When I asked my dad about it, he explained that the pipe in the hydrant had no water. The water all came from underneath the ground. The pipe from the hydrant connected with another pipe that led to a reservoir and the reservoir had plenty of water. My Dad explained to me that as long as there was an underground connection, there would be plenty of water coming out of the pipe.

If there's nothing coming out of the pipe, you don't need a "pipe fixing," you need an underground connection. You need something underneath that connects you with the power source so that water can flow from your life.[115]

[Power, Accessing]

John 4:14

WE ALL know what it's like to have our car battery go dead. A powerless battery cannot take you anywhere. So you put up the hood of your car and pull out some jumper cables. You get another car whose battery is alive, and get the hood of that car close to yours. Then you take the cables and connect that battery's positive with your positive and the negative with a metal part on your engine. And then there is a transfer of power and a transfer of life. The living battery sends its life and its power through the cables to your dead battery. Then you can turn on your ignition and know that there has been a transfer of power via the cable. All of a sudden your dead car comes alive. All of a sudden your dead motor turns over. All of a sudden your dead car can now move. Why? Because it has power on its own? No. Because it borrowed power from another. Because it took power from a living battery.[116]

[Weakness; Power, Accessing]

CHRISTIAN LIVING, PURPOSE

VICTOR Frankenstein is known for bringing a lifeless creature to life. If you don't know about Victor Frankenstein, you know about his creation because the monster became synonymous with his creator's last name. The word *Frankenstein* conjures up thoughts of the monster, not his creator.

After going through a tragedy, Mr. Frankenstein desired to do something good. He decided to take lifeless items and make them come alive. He went to slaughterhouses, graveyards, and even coroner's offices to steal what he needed for his creation. He then put all of his materials together and brought his creature to life. This lifeless, dead entity did come alive. His goal was to take this monster and give it life. Well, he did it. He created it, and these days we know it by his last name—Frankenstein. What he didn't know is that he had created a beast.

The tragedy of Frankenstein is that after he was created, after he was given life, after he was nothing and then made into something, he turned on Victor and made his maker a victim of his own creation. Frankenstein became a monster because he took the life that was given him and used it for his own purpose.

You and I have been given life by our Creator. Yet many of our lives are nothing short of monstrous because we have taken the life that He has given us and used it for something other than the Creator had in mind.[117]

[Rebellion; Natural Man; Life, Emptiness of]
1 Cor. 6:19–20

MOST people have warranties on the major products they own in their homes. A warranty simply guarantees that the manufacturer will stand behind their product. It's a guarantee that if there's a defect, a fault, or a failure, that the manufacturer will stand behind the product. But all warranties have limitations. The warranty is not designed to cover abuse by the owner.

You can't take your toaster, throw it up against the wall, jump on it, or run it over, and then claim the product warranty. Warranties are offered under the assumption that the product will be used for its intended purpose.

God's got a warranty on your life as long as you're using it for His purposes and existing for His glory.[118]

A BOXCAR on a train has no power to move down the tracks on its own. It isn't going anywhere unless it's hooked up. The life of a Christian is like a boxcar on a train. It should be hooked up to the engine of God's purpose. If the boxcar of your life is not hooked up to the engine—the purpose for which God has you here—you are not going anywhere. You are stuck.[119]

A *MIX MASTER* is where a series of highways intersect. Normally, you can find a mix master near the downtown area of a city. At the point where the highways connect, you will find their purpose.

In a Christian's life there are also highways that lead to the center of their lives and their purpose. The highways of experience, opportunities, passions, and abilities are all designed to lead us to the intersection of our purposes in God and our calling for our lives here on earth. Where these four things intersect—experience, opportunities, passions, and abilities—our purposes begin.[120]

[Calling]

SAND is cheap. In fact, at the beach, it's free! Once it is bagged in order to put it on a playground, it costs to have access to it. Its value goes up. When sand is taken and bagged, what once was free on the beach now costs twenty-five dollars for a twenty-five-pound bag. Once this same sand is glued to a piece of paper to make sandpaper, its value has gone up again. Now it's five dollars for a sheet. The value has increased with a change in its purpose.

Now, sand is silicon dioxide. When sand is taken, heated, and processed, it becomes an intricate part of a computer chip that is now worth five hundred dollars. So what was once free on the beach now has value because it is in a bag, because it is glued on a piece of paper, or because it is in a computer chip that you can hardly afford. The sand is the same, but it has now found increased value in a greater purpose.[121]

IF A person walks around with one hundred dollars in their pocket but never uses it for what it was intended for, that one hundred dollars is just a piece of paper. It's valuable paper, but meaningless until utilized for its purchasing power.

Christians have value consigned by God. But until we live out our lives for the purposes intended, we walk around in a meaningless existence— valuable, but not useful. A Christian life not used for its purposes is a life not spent well.[122]

1 Thess. 2:10–12

MANY people today say they are trying to find themselves. These people are running around, trying to find themselves. This search is meaningless. If you don't know who you are, how do you know what to look for? And how do you know when you have found it, since you don't know what you are looking for?[123]

TOASTERS don't find themselves. Refrigerators don't find themselves. Appliances don't find themselves because their purpose has been assigned by another. A toaster doesn't have to find its reason for being; it's just got to do what the manufacturer had in mind.

Christians don't have to look for themselves. God has already consigned to us a divine reason for being. Our purpose is to fulfill it. If we are not fulfilling His purposes, days, weeks, and months go by as we watch more television, hook up with more friends, and try to get better jobs—and our lives still feel empty because we are disconnected from the purposes of God.[124]

> [Chaos; Life, Emptiness of]
>
> Eph. 2:11–13

YOU cannot discover your purpose until God is your reference point. Until and unless God becomes your reference point, you cannot discover your purpose in life.[125]

THE GREATEST example of purposelessness in the world is a dog. If you really want to see purposeless living, just watch a dog. If you really want to understand going through the motions, or just passing time, pay close attention to a dog.

First of all, a dog barks. Their bark can disturb and a dog will bark at just about anything. And you can't figure out what a dog is saying because all it's really doing is just making noise, desperately desiring to be noticed. One of the indications of purposeless living is a life that creates a lot of noise but doesn't really make a clear statement about anything.

Another thing a dog does is run in circles. It's not particularly going anywhere, but it's moving constantly. The ultimate purposelessness of a dog is when it's chasing its own tail, going around and around in a circle, and when it is finished moving, it's in the same place it started. Many of us are looking for purpose in activities. We've got our cell phones, PDAs, televisions, computers, and e-mail, stuff to distract us and keep us busy, but at the end of the day we're no further ahead with a sense of purpose than when we started.

Dogs function on the level of the external. They love to be petted and rubbed. They enjoy that good, momentary feeling. It's just a good feeling for the moment on a nice external coat. There are a whole bunch of folks today who get up and daily "put on the dog," hoping that someone will notice, and in some way make them feel valuable and significant.

Finally, dogs are consumers. Dogs don't only eat when they are hungry, they eat because food is there. Dogs live for the fun of life, not for its meaning.

At the end of the day, living life in this way results in hollowness in your soul. God's design and desire is to release you from that, but only on His terms.[126]

> [Chaos; Life, Emptiness of;
>
> Natural Man]
>
> Titus 3:3–5

WE'VE all watched the space shuttle lift off from planet Earth to go into outer space into the heavens. It sits there on the launchpad ready to move into a whole different realm. But that space shuttle is going absolutely nowhere until fire has been ignited, a blazing fire that takes it from the gravitational pull of Earth and delivers it to the glory of the heavens. No fire, no liftoff. No igniting, no destiny. The countdown begins. By the time they hit zero and the boosters are ignited, the ship is ready to take off into outer space.

Many of us have been earthbound

too long. No matter how much we desire to lift off to accomplish our mission, we don't seem to be able to get off the ground. What's keeping us from getting off the ground and getting to the mission? The countdown is taking place. We're getting older by the day. What keeps getting in the way?[127]

[Calling]
Ps. 90:12; Eph. 5:15–16

A PLAY-ACTION pass is where the quarterback receives the ball from the center. He turns and he fakes a handoff to the running back. The goal of the fake is to get the defense to trap the running back. The quarterback then tucks the ball and goes in the other direction to throw to a receiver. If he's done his job well, the defense has been distracted for a moment, thinking that someone else has the ball so that the quarterback can throw it to a wide-open receiver.

Satan has run a play-action pass on us. He has faked us out with the wrong purpose and we keep chasing it so that he can distract us from the real play. Like a pickpocket who loves a crowd, Satan has been robbing you of your purpose, getting you distracted from God's plan.[128]

[Satan, Strategy of]
John 10:9–10; 1 Peter 5:8–9

ONE of the ways that you know a bowler is serious about bowling is that they have custom-made balls. These are constructed to the appropriate weight and grip so that they fit the particular bowler's uniqueness. To have your bowling ball custom-made is to increase the possibility of effective delivery so that you can hit the mark. God

has constructed every member of His body in a customized way. God has uniquely crafted every one of us to hit the mark of His purpose and calling on our lives. We are not an assembly line of people with the same automated parts. We have been uniquely crafted for His purpose. You are, in fact, custom-made.[129]

[Body of Christ; Spiritual Gifts, Use of; Calling]
1 Cor. 12; Eph. 4:11–13

WHEN I grew up, I had tennis shoes. Tennis shoes were also called sneakers back then, and you used one pair for everything. You played basketball in them and ran in them. Whatever you did, you did with your sneakers.

But then Nike came along. Nowadays, people have to have designer tennis shoes and you have to have a different kind of tennis shoe for every sport. You can't just run and walk in the same shoe; you have to have a separate and different kind of shoe for each activity. How can there be a difference between a running shoe and a walking shoe?

The reason is that each shoe is specialized and crafted to fulfill the purpose for which it is being worn. Well, God is wearing you. He has crafted every single believer to wear based on where He wants to go or where He wants you to take Him and carry out His purposes.[130]

[Calling]

COMPANIES sometimes have staff audits. A staff audit is designed to analyze who is where, and whether they are producing at the level that they ought to be producing for the position that they occupy. The point is to make sure that the right people are in the right place, doing the right things in the right way. One of the questions on the floor during an audit is "Does each staff member's job and productivity contribute to the goals of the company?"

This is the same question God wants answered. How does the life of every Christian contribute to His kingdom?[131]

[Kingdom of God; Servanthood]

YOGI BERRA, the great catcher for the New York Yankees, used to talk a lot of noise. I can appreciate that. When I played baseball I was a catcher. One of the jobs of the catcher is to distract the batter. Part of my job involved saying mean things, irritating things, and offending things to the player up to bat. I'd talk about their mother, make fun of their batting abilities, or tell them that they hit like a girl. The point was to mess with their minds in order to take the focus off of the ball.

One time, Yogi Berra was behind the plate, and Hank Aaron came up to bat. Yogi said on this one occasion, "All right, Hank is getting ready to bat." Hank wouldn't say anything to him. Yogi continued, "Hank, you've got the writing on the bat in the wrong place. The words should be facing you." Yogi wanted to get Hank to look at the bat to make sure it was in the right place. Yogi kept going, "You better check it." Hank didn't budge. He didn't say a word. The next pitch Hank hit over the center field fence. Hank rounded the bases, stepped on home plate, and began walking toward the dugout. He stopped, turned back, looked at Yogi

Berra, and said, "I didn't come here to read."

It's vital to know why you are here. Don't let folk distract you from your calling.[132]

[Focus]

ONE OF the famous shows on television was *Seinfeld*. I watched about five minutes of it once, but it didn't look worthy of my time. But obviously, the show was popular because Seinfeld, the star, made a hundred million dollars from it. I've since discovered the key to the show's success. There is no plot. The episodes don't really go anywhere. So it's an aimless show that aimless people love.

Some folks are living their own *Seinfeld* show, because they wake up every day with no plot. They are not going anywhere. They are just existing day to day. There is no mission and no call of God on their lives.[133]

[Chaos; Life, Emptiness of; Natural Man]

APPLIANCES don't serve themselves. Toasters don't eat their own toast. Refrigerators don't cool the food that they are going to eat. Stoves don't eat the food that they cook. A microwave doesn't digest the food that it radiates. Can openers don't eat what is in the can they open. Appliances are there to serve somebody else. We benefit from their calling. God has assigned you a divine purpose and your fulfillment of that purpose should result in a benefit to others.[134]

[Servanthood]
Matt. 20:25–27; 1 Cor. 12; Eph. 4:11–13

THERE was a little boy who played on a football team who was something of a goof-off. He never really played hard, was always lazy, didn't practice diligently, and so he never got to play.

On the last game of his senior year, the running backs in front of him all got hurt, so they had to put him in. His teammates and coaches couldn't believe their eyes; he was playing like a wild man. They couldn't believe this was the same kid. After the game, they came over to him to ask him why he played so well after all those years of goofing off.

"Oh," he said, "it's simple. My father was blind. He died yesterday, so this is the first day he's ever gotten to see me play."

See, when you know Daddy is watching, it makes you want to perform at a higher level. It makes you perform for a greater reason. God has called you for His kingdom, which is what you do even beyond the church. Everything you do, you should do as if He's watching. You should do it for His glory.[135]

[Kingdom of God; God's Glory]
1 Cor. 10:31

ONE of the reasons so many of us are unfulfilled is that we are driving in the wrong lane. We operate in lanes of life that were never designed for us. We operate in purposes that were never designed for us. All exits are good exits, but not all exits are your exits. We don't get off at exits for no good reason when we are driving. We decide to get off at exits because they take us to our intended destination. We take exits that will lead us to where we are supposed to go.

Many people miss their purpose because they take any old exit where they see lights. We should only take exits that take us toward our destiny, our purpose, or our calling.[136]

[Calling; Focus]
2 Tim. 4:5

THE THING I loved most about the Lone Ranger was his horse, Silver. I loved to see Silver go up in the air at the end of the program. He was the perfectly trained companion for the Lone Ranger. Did you know Silver wasn't always like that? If you didn't see the first episode of the Lone Ranger, you can't appreciate Silver. In fact, if you didn't see the first episode of the Lone Ranger, you can't appreciate the Lone Ranger. He started off as a ranger among a whole group of rangers. One day his band of rangers got ambushed and he was the lone survivor of the ambush. This is how he came to be known as the "lone" ranger. The Lone Ranger was left for dead, but he alone recovered.

When he began to get his strength back, he heard in a canyon below him the sound of a horse, the horse that would come to be known as Silver. He saw the horse and figured that it could provide him a way of escape out of his situation. The only problem was the horse was a wild stallion. The whole first episode was about Silver being brought under the control of the Lone Ranger. Silver would throw him off; the Lone Ranger would get back on, only to be thrown off again. The bottom line is that the Lone Ranger rode Silver until Silver got the message that he was no longer in charge. When the Lone Ranger took over the reins of Silver's life, the horse could now do things that he would have never been able to do on his own—all because he was controlled by another.

God wants to ride you and me so we can do stuff that we could never do on our own. When the story of your life is written about how God rode you, what will He have accomplished? What will have happened in your life because you moved when God said "Giddy-up" and stopped when He said "Whoa"? What will God accomplish in your life because you yielded to His purposes?[137]

CHRISTIAN LIVING, SPIRITUAL GROWTH

GOD is not satisfied that you've taken one step, no more than you are satisfied that your children take their first step. All they did was get started. They still have to go to school. They still have to go through the teenage years. They still have to grow up and get married and have a family. The first step is great, but don't stop with excitement over the first step. All that's occurred is the introduction to spiritual life. There is an ongoing process of developing in the body of Christ.[138]

[New Life in Christ; Sanctification]
1 Thess. 4:1

MANY a parent has told their son or daughter how much potential they possess. They attempt to communicate to their child that they have so much more inside than what is visible right now. When a baby is born, that is only the beginning. Years of growth and development must occur before that infant grows into an adult.

In the same way, God has given every believer the promise of spiritual maturity. What is presently visible is not the end result of spiritual growth.[139]

HIS NAME was Thomas Anderson. He was just an ordinary computer programmer and occasional computer hacker. He was an ordinary man. But one day he got exposed to another realm. While working on his computer, he discovered that there was a reality beyond that which he was accustomed to. It was called the Matrix. He got transported into this other realm where he met another man named Morpheus. He discovered things were not as they appeared.

He discovered that in this realm, it was the computers who called the shots. He had settled for an ordinary life to sit down all day punching numbers into a computer until he discovered there was something bigger going on. He was then invited to participate in something much bigger than he was aware of. When he decided that he would participate, it became clear that he was the one—the chosen one whose job it was to save humanity from the takeover of the computers in the realm of the Matrix.

All of a sudden, his ordinary life became an extraordinary life. He received a new name; he would be called Neo. In the new realm, He could do things he couldn't do previously. In the new realm, he possessed abilities he didn't have before. In the new realm, he had a new love. His relationship with Trinity became his dominating relationship as they worked in partnership to keep the computers from overthrowing humanity. He discovered that life had something much bigger to offer him than his previous existence of sitting at a computer, punching away.

When Jesus Christ saved you, He invited you to partner in a new realm with Trinity—the Father and the Son and the Holy Spirit—in order to keep the agents of evil from dominating and taking over humanity. You have been called to something bigger. If you don't experience that new realm, if you are satisfied being a Thomas when you were made to be a Neo, you will not experience all that you were designed to experience.

Now Neo had to make a choice about where he wanted to live. He had to choose between two pills. One pill would take him into the new realm. The other pill would send him back to his ordinary life. He took the pill that would make his life no longer the same, ordinary existence. After choosing the pill of the new realm, he no longer got up every day to the same old life; he now got up and entered the Matrix.

The question is, which pill will you choose? Will you be satisfied with ordinary living or will you choose an existence that takes you into a new realm?[140]

Rom. 12:1–2; Eph. 6:11–13

CHRISTLIKENESS

MANY OF us are spending so much time being like the Joneses that we don't have enough time to be like Christ.[141]

WHILE IN seminary preparing for ministry, I was enrolled in a class that one day brought me great discouragement. Our class was asked to do a pa-

per. Now I always loved to do challenging things in class and I was committed to making an A on this paper; I was determined to spare no research effort, no dedication, nor any steadfastness to make an A on this paper. It was a particularly difficult class and it was rare that anyone ever made an A with this professor. I was sure that I would be the exception to the rule. My Type A personality kicked in and I was committed to ace this class, which meant acing this research paper. I was committed to it.

When I got my paper back, there was an F on it. Not only did I not make an A, I did not make a B, C, or a D either. There was an F in bold red across the top. You can imagine how crushed I was because I did my work, I clocked all-nighters, I researched, I studied the original languages, and I dug in. Even though the paper was only to be ten or twelve pages, I had eighteen to twenty pages. I had footnotes. I had gone the distance. How dare he give me an F!

I noticed a handwritten note on the bottom of the paper below the big, red F. It said, "Great scholarship, great detail, and magnificent effort, but you answered the wrong question." All that work mistakenly addressed the wrong thing. It wasn't that I was not sincere; it wasn't that I was not working hard; it was simply that I had addressed the wrong thing. I had been so focused on myself and what I wanted to achieve, that I missed the professor and what he wanted from me. In my desire to score high, I missed out on what could have been a wonderful assignment because I did not understand what the professor wanted from me.[142]

Heb. 12:1-2

MANY OF US are working hard at the Christian life. Many are doing overtime efforts; many are coming to church, reading the Bible, saying their prayers, and trying to do better, but they are failing. All their efforts are not working. They've made promises, committed, and then recommitted. These Christians are sincere. They are honest. They are doing their best. The problem is that many Christians are often so focused on themselves that they are missing out on what God is really looking for. God's goal for us is simple. He wants to conform us to the image of His Son.[143]

[Transformation; Sanctification]
Rom. 8:28-30

MANY people who have visited my home have marveled at a picture that we have on a little table by the door. There is a frame with two slots for pictures. On the right side of the frame is a picture of me when I was eighteen years old. On the left side of the frame is a picture of Tony Jr. when he was eighteen years old. What is amazing about this picture is that we look like twins. Even though I am many years older and even though we are father and son, in these pictures we look just alike. Why? Because of a DNA connection. My essence was transferred to him and in the process of his development, he wound up looking like me.

We should look like Christ. A connection has been made because of His sacrifice on Calvary, and His essence has been transferred to us. People should marvel at the resemblance.[144]

[Discipleship; Spiritual Identity, in Christ]
1 John 2:5-6

IF YOU take a poker and put it in a fireplace with the fire raging, the poker is just in the fire. But if you leave it in the fire, the fire gets in the poker. If the poker is left in the fire for any length of time, the environment of the fire will rub off on the poker so that it will become red-hot. It won't be red-hot because it said, "Let me be hot today," because it is in a hot mood, or because it stresses and strains to make itself red-hot. It becomes red-hot because of where it hangs out. Not only does the poker get hot because the fire is hot, but if it is taken out of the fire and gets near something, it will burn that something— not because of the power of the poker but because of the relationship of the poker to the fire. Because the poker was in the fire and the fire got in the poker, everything else is going to be set aflame.

If Christians are touching stuff and nothing's burning, nothing's changing, and there is no victory, it is because they do not understand that red-hot power does not come through effort but through relationship.

God's goal is Christlikeness, that is, being conformed to the character of Christ. Christlikeness simply means emulating who Christ is, not because you're stressing and straining, but because Christ is in you.[145]

[Grace; Victory]
Phil. 2:13; Rom. 8:13

LET'S SAY I want to play for the NBA. That's a great dream but I have a few problems. Problem number one is that I'm only six feet tall. Problem number two is that I can't fly. Problem number three is that I'm over fifty years old. As much as I might want to play for the NBA, I can't.

Now let's say that Michael Jordan writes a book and he calls it "Just Like Mike." The goal of the book is for Mike to share with his readers the secrets of his shooting ability, dribbling ability, passing ability, and jumping ability. So, even though I'm too old, too slow, too fat, and too short, playing for the NBA is my passion and I go and buy the book. I sit down and I read the book. I study the book. I digest the book. I have daily devotions with the book. Every day I'm in the book because I want to know how to be like Mike. But after all of this effort, when I go back outside to my basketball hoop, I still can't dunk. I still can't jump that high, and I have grown no taller. Everything is the same.

I get frustrated. I'm sincere. I'm reading the book. However, I can't get a connection between what I am reading and my experience on the court.

So I go to the church to request that the church pay to hire Michael Jordan to help me. It's clear that merely reading the book about how to play like Mike is not going to work. I need something else, and what better thing to do than to have Mike come and teach me. So Michael Jordan is now hired and he is now my tutor. He is going to take the book and personally guide me through it.

I'd still be frustrated because even though I would have read the book and even though I'd have the superstar as my coach, I'd still have my limitations. I'd still be the same size and the same age. Even with my sincerity in reading and listening to the expert, I'd still have a problem.

My problem is capacity. My problem is that I don't have the capacity to pull off what Mike is telling me and what Mike has written. Even though I'm reading it, even though I'm talking to Mike an hour a day, nothing has changed in my game. Oh sure, every now and then I'd make a few more shots and every now and then I'd pick up a few more moves, but when it comes to my goal of making it to the NBA, I'd be no closer after a year in the book and after a year of talking to Mike than I was before I got started. Why? Because I have limitations.

You've got a capacity problem. I've got a capacity problem. The problem is that your body is dead. Sin has killed it. Your human capacity to rise above your limitations cannot be corrected because it's dead. Sin has killed you. It has killed any capacity to be conformed to the divine standard. It doesn't matter how many New Year's resolutions, promises, rededications, or determinations you make. Oh yes, you may have a better day here and a better week there, but you are just looking better in the grave; sin has killed you.

There are many Christians today who are frustrated. They don't see a change in their life even though they are doing all of the right things. The only solution is for Christ to do for them what they can't because of their capacity problem. Just like being like Mike is not possible, so is being like Christ. Christlikeness is the Spirit of God inspiring the ability to emulate the person of Christ in and through your life.[146]

[Body of Death; Holy Spirit, Power of; Victory]

Rom. 8:11

CHRISTMAS, PURPOSE OF

A MOTHER was having a gathering to celebrate the birth of her newborn son. She invited a bunch of friends over to celebrate his arrival. She welcomed her guests, and they all had a great time celebrating, eating, and drinking.

After a while, one of the ladies said, "Well, bring the baby out. Let us see it."

The mother went to get the baby from his crib—he was nowhere to be found. She started to panic and feel fearful. Suddenly, she remembered that the baby was still at her parents' house, where she had left him that morning. She and the guests had been having so much fun they had forgotten what the party was about in the first place. During the Christmas season, many people get busy with celebration and forget that the birth of Jesus Christ is the reason for the season.[147]

CHURCH

FOR A three-hour football game, a sports lover will be on time. He will only miss the opening kickoff if it's unavoidable. He will sit in his favorite pew. He won't get up to eat. He will sit in front of the game for three hours and not complain that the game is going on too long. This sports lover will not budge because he has a high regard for whoever his favorite team is. If by chance the game goes into overtime, he will not even bother to look at his watch. He will be engaged be-cause the team on the screen is worthy of his respect.

Many times football games get more respect, time, and intensity than a visit to God's house on Sunday morning.[148]

Ps. 26:8; 27:4

MANY Christians today take the posture that they don't have to go to church to be Christians. While that is technically true, you do have to go to church to be a good Christian.

I asked my daughter one time, "Are you going to cook breakfast?" She said, "I'm not hungry." I probed again, "Are you going to cook breakfast?" She said yet again, "I'm not hungry." I tried one more time, "Are you the only person who lives here?" My daughter shrugged her shoulders and said, "I'm not hungry." I couldn't take anymore. "Well, I am hungry and I want breakfast!"

In order to be the kind of Christian that God wants you to be, you need the dynamic fellowship, dynamic motivation, and dynamic inspiration of the people of God. And not only do you need it, you should be willing to come, to serve, and to give to someone else. It's not just about you.[149]

[Fellowship; Servanthood; Spiritual Gifts, Use of]

Heb. 10:25; Eph. 4:15–16

CHURCH is like a hospital. It's where people who are sick, broken, bruised, beaten, and battered with life because of sin and unrighteousness come for help. It's okay if you are here and don't have all your life together. If you had all your life together, you wouldn't need to be here. However, hospitals do not tolerate sick people hanging around who don't want to get better. No doctor is going to keep fooling with a patient who won't take his medicine or won't accept a needle but wants to occupy a room.

What would you think if someone said, "Look, I know I'm sick. I've decided to stay sick because I just like this hospital. I'm going to put my name on the door to this room and live here for a while"?

You would condemn such a person for a misuse of the hospital because a hospital only exists to give life. That is what the church does. Just as people are born and go to a hospital to get equipped to live, you are born again to come into the church.[150]

Matt. 9:11–13

CHURCH, ATTENDANCE

MANY people have a feature called PIP, picture-in-picture, on their televisions. It means that you can look at your show and at any time bring up a little screen in the corner that has another channel going. You can watch a movie on the main screen and a football game on the little PIP screen. But the PIP is not the main show. The main show is what covers most of the screen. The PIP is simply another show to glance at while you're watching the main show on the television.

For many of us who attend church, the service is like a PIP. People go to church and receive a PIP experience. They receive spiritual information, hear spiritual truth, and sing spiritual songs, but it's not the main show. Instead, when they leave church is when the main show begins. They go back to work, family, and life—back to day-to-day struggles. Sunday morning is only PIP, something people glance at while they enjoy the main show.[151]

[Focus; World, Conformity to]
1 John 2:15–16

A MAN walked into a donut shop and, with a smile, asked for five donuts and a Diet Coke. Now, that Diet Coke was not going to cancel out the negative effects of five nonnutritional, sugar-soaked, fat-filled, donuts.

Some Christians think that "diet church" on Sunday morning will cancel out sinful living Monday through Saturday. It just doesn't work that way.[152]

CHURCH, MEMBERSHIP

TODAY, millions upon millions of spectators will watch the Super Bowl. People reorient their lives for three hours of athletic entertainment that will absolutely consume the nation and many parts of the world. The onlookers will be fans of one team or another, rejoicing when their team progresses and being heartbroken when their team falters. For approximately three hours of great intensity, spectators will watch twenty-two men on a field go to battle. The spectators, you and I, will cheer or boo, critique or analyze as the game is played. When the game is over, and the winner has been determined and everything is brought to finality, the fans will go back to business as usual with shirts that have not gotten dirty, pants that have not gotten ruffled, and bodies with no bruises or bumps. There is a big difference between being in the stands and being on the field.

Jesus Christ has a lot of fans. Folks

who want to show up to see what's going on. Folks who want to critique, analyze, or cheer. Folks who, when the dust settles, haven't broken a sweat.

They don't exert much energy. In fact, they picnic while the game is played. Jesus' spectators are quick to analyze how the folks on the field are doing. They analyze privately by getting on the phone and talking to friends, not understanding that there is a marked difference between sitting in the stands of the living room and being on the field.

It's easy for a person to ask why a play is not made when they are not the ones running the ball. It's easy for a person to blame a player for not executing when they are not on the field staring opposition in the face. The view from the field is a lot different from the view in the stands.

We must ask ourselves whether we are simply Jesus fans, or functioning members on the Jesus team. There is a marked difference between the two.[153]

MANY Christians today are spiritual orphans—children of God with no family relationship. Others are like foster children, bouncing from house to house, never finding a home; it just doesn't take five years to find a church.

We all know that babies grow best in families. When there are children in the world who have been orphaned or who are not a part of suitable families, we want to get them into good families. We don't want those children out there on their own. Why? Because we understand that children grow best connected.

If you are a disconnected saint, you are living out of the will of God. Being connected does not just simply mean church attendance either. Attendance only is simply attachment. Church membership is attachment accompanied by fellowship and service that gives you a chance to rub shoulders with people.[154]

[Fellowship]
Heb. 10:25; Acts 2:42

MANY people shirk church membership, using the excuse that they just don't like people. But just let things get bad enough in their lives. When they get sick they like people—such as doctors. When they are jobless, they like people—employers. The truth is, they only like people when those people are doing something for them.

Christians who receive and never give at their local churches are leeches. Leeches want all the benefit without doing any of the work.[155]

[Giving; Servanthood]

MOST of us are familiar with the old American Express slogan, "Membership has its privileges." When you become a member of various groups, usually associated with that membership are benefits. Even to be a part of the church, there are certain things that members have access to that visitors do not.

I remember receiving a packet from American Airlines some time ago—a Platinum booklet because I'm a Platinum flyer. It's a booklet that I've never read. I got it in the mail but put it aside because I had no knowledge of the privileges of membership that I possessed. There was a card in the book I never saw.

The other day, someone brought

to my attention something on the card that's been there all the time. This bit of information would have made life much more convenient, but because I'd never read what was available to me, there were benefits that did not accrue to me. Many of us who are part of God's family have little idea of all the benefits of membership.[156]

CHURCH, ROLE OF

A PASTOR'S wife often sits on the front row. While the pastor delivers his sermon, unbeknownst to the congregation, there is a lot of activity going on between him and his wife. Occasionally she rubs her ear as though she is scratching it. Now, if the congregation would look at her, they would think that she is massaging her ear because maybe the earring is irritating her ear or her ear itches. In reality, she is signaling her husband that he is talking too loud and that he should tone it down.

When she raises her hand to give what appears to be an "Amen!" she's saying to slow down because he is talking too fast. When she closes her eyes and nods her head, she is not saying she agrees. She is telling him that he is not panning the audience well—his eye contact is bad, he's looking too much to one side, and so on. When the pastor's wife rubs her shoulder, she is not having a shoulder ache, she is telling her husband that his tie is crooked, that he is embarrassing her by the way he looks, and to fix it!

Many of the good sermons that pastors preach are attributed to the fact that the pastor's wife is sitting there completing them for him. That's what the church does. It takes the message of Christ and it helps it to be laid out there so that the public gets it in the most refined form possible. The church takes the truth of Christ, and the truth of God, and the agenda of Christ and it lays it out there so that the world can see it operative in society.[157]

[Ministry, Importance of]
1 Tim. 3:15

IF YOU want to go somewhere in your car, you need gas to get there. If there is no gasoline in your tank, you're not going anywhere in your car because gas is the indispensable element needed for you to move from one location to another. Gasoline stations are places set up to give you what you need, but in order to fill up you have to get to where the gas is located. Many Christians ride on empty because they don't go to the place that will fill their tank.[158]

A YOUNG couple got married and was on their way home from the honeymoon. A tractor-trailer pulled out in front of them suddenly and the young groom swerved to avoid it. The car went into a tailspin and crashed. The groom was okay, but his new bride was bleeding profusely. He knew if he didn't get his new wife to a doctor, she was going to die. He got out of the car and saw a sign just a little ways away: "The Office of Dr. Rufus Jones—Internal Medicine." He picked up his beloved and struggled up the hill toward the doctor's home.

He began knocking on the door. An old man came to the door and the groom said, "Dr. Jones?"

The man said, "Well, yes?"

He said, "My wife is bleeding.

She's dying. Please save her!"

Much to this young man's surprise, Dr. Jones said, "I'm sorry, son, I can't help you. You see, son, I stopped practicing medicine many years ago. I don't have any equipment here. I don't have medical supplies. I stopped practicing medicine a long time ago."

Distraught with frustration and grief, the young man said, "Dr. Jones, if you can no longer help hurting people, then please take down the sign."

We've got a world out there bleeding to death. We tell people to come to the church where we offer Dr. Jesus, the medicine of the Holy Spirit, and the healing power of the Word of God. We tell people to come to the hospital. But if we're not going to be the hospital, then we need to take down the sign. There's no need in having a sign that says "Oak Cliff Bible Fellowship, Church of the Living God," if when people show up, they don't get surgery. Let's either be the real hospital or take down the sign. Let's not have everybody thinking that we're a hospital and practicing physicians and when they show up they die at our doorstep because we stopped being a church a long time ago. Let's be the church—the authentic representation of that which Christ gave His life for.[159]

IN EVERY community there are grocery stores. The job of a grocery store is very simple. It is supposed to provide life-giving food for those who live nearby because without food people can't live. Food is an absolute necessity for the well-being of a community because its inhabitants must eat to live. What good

are grocery stores whose shelves are empty or whose food is stale?

When you go shopping, you want to know that what you need is there and that it's fresh. You don't go to a grocery store to get year-old bread and year-old meat. You want it to be fresh, and you want to know that there's enough there so that regardless of how many other people shop, there's food for you. It's the job of a grocery store and those who work in it and own it to make sure that there is enough to service all the people looking for food. What a grocery store is to the physical well-being of a community, the church is supposed to be for its spiritual well-being.

What good is a church where the shelves are empty and the food is stale? What good is a ministry where, when people come for meat, there is none? Or when they come for bread, it's molded? Or when they come for vegetables, they are no longer firm? How could the church still call itself a spiritual grocery store?[160]

CIRCUMSTANCES, UNDERSTANDING

A LITTLE bird was flying south for the winter, but the air was so cold that it couldn't get to the warm climate before it began to freeze. It collapsed under the weight of the cold into a large field. A cow came by and dropped some manure on the freezing bird. At first, of course, the bird was upset, until the bird felt how warm the manure was. So the bird began to thaw out under the manure that the cow had left behind. In fact, the bird just got downright excited and started to sing at the joy of being thawed out by the manure. A cat was passing by and heard this sound of singing. He followed the sound to the manure. He started digging through the manure to get to the song, and discovered it was a bird. Then the cat ate the bird that was thawing out in the pile of manure.

Now there are a number of lessons in this story. The first lesson is, not everybody who drops manure on you is your enemy. Second lesson is, not everybody who digs you out of your manure is your friend. And finally, when you're in manure, keep your mouth shut.[161]

COMFORT

ON JANUARY 10, 2003, a young man named Terry Drier was in the water twenty hours after his boat had capsized. He gave a valiant effort at survival, although he later confessed he felt certain that he was going to die. After that long while, a helicopter located him, and sent word to a ship on its way to the Persian Gulf. The name of the ship was the USS *Comforter*. This vessel was on its way to do battle and paused to deliver one man. They went out of their way to save one man and there was a doctor on board who nursed him back to health.

Many people today are treading water, and they don't know how much longer they can hang in there. People are tired and feel like all is lost. All we must do is look up and see that our Deliverer is hovering nearby. He knows exactly where deliverance can be found. The God of all comfort will make sure that the comfort we need comes our way.[162]

[God's Deliverance]
Ps. 18:1–3; 40:16–17

WHEN A woman is in labor, she's hurting. In this situation, no one ever really knows exactly how long the pain is going to last. The husband is there, holding her hand, wiping her forehead, and patting her back. That's all he can do. He's limited. Holding her hand doesn't change the pain. He's just there to comfort her.

God is birthing something in the life of every believer, and He wants believers to comfort one another, while we go through the birthing process.[163]

[Encouragement]
Rom. 15:1–3; Gal. 6:2

COMMITMENT

IN MY HOUSE, we have a den that we use as a family room. We also have a living room that is rarely used. It just occurred to me that we don't do a lot of living in the living room. That room is not really named properly. It's more of the visit room than the living room. Now, the living room is in the house, but it really isn't the life of the house. It's not where we live. Most folks live in their den, or family room. Some folks live in the kitchen. Rarely do we live in those specially decorated places in our homes reserved for guests.

For many of us, God is in the house, but he's been relegated to the room in our house reserved for special occasions. He is only allowed in the living room. He's not allowed in the center—the den or family room. He's not allowed into the places where we live our lives. He's not allowed in the center of our lives; He's only allowed in designated areas.

Many Christians say that He is the centerpiece of their lives when He is really not at all.[164]

Matt. 6:33

COMMUNION

COMMUNION is a spiritual cleanser to flush the spiritual junk out of your system.[165]

MY MOTHER would tell me when we ate dinner, "Son, don't play at the table." When you partake of the Lord's Supper, be sure not to play at the table.[166]

1 Cor. 11:26–28

EVEN Jesus took Communion before he headed for the cross.[167]

BEFORE an NBA game, the team and the staff always eat a pregame meal. They have a spread laid out and the team sits down, eats, and fellowships. This is the meal they eat together just before they go into battle and face the enemy. The pregame meal provides the nutritional value they need in order to wage war on the field against folks who are trying to stop them.

When you come to the Communion table on Sunday, and you eat the bread and drink the cup, it is to give you the power you need to fight your spiritual enemy. Communion is designed to help you enter the world differently because you enter it with the power from on high.[168]

[Church]

CONFRONTATION

IT WASN'T too long ago that I was going down a one-way street, and I noticed somebody coming the other way. Obviously there was a problem. That car was going the wrong way. As I kept driving, I heard sounds all around me. After awhile it became clear that all these chorus of voices were trying to get my attention, trying to confront me with the reality that I was wrong. You see, I thought stuff was wrong with everybody else, when the problem was with me.

I suspected that there were two reasons for their concern. One is the damage that I could do to myself. The other is the damage I could do to others. They could have simply ignored it, and said, "That's his business." Or, they could do what they did, which is try to get my attention, because they understood that when you're going the wrong way, somebody needs to confront you, so that you can reverse your direction.[169]

Luke 17:3; 1 Thess. 5:14

CONSCIENCE

WE HAVE a built-in metal detector. When I go to the airport, I've got my keys in my pocket. I walk through security and beeps go off everywhere! The security guard will call me back and make me walk through again. When the machine beeps again, the guard will ask me to empty my pockets.

So I'll reach in my pockets and pull out my keys, take off my watch, and put them on the side because the alarm has gone off, indicating that I've tried to walk onto a plane with metal in my pocket.

You have in your person, like a metal detector, a sin detector, called the Holy Spirit. Now, we know He's a detector because He's holy. So whenever you introduce sin in your life, you are going to hear a beep! There's going to be an alarm, and that's what your conscience is. That's where the Spirit of God pricks your conscience.

It's like trying to fit a square peg in a round hole. If you keep twisting that peg and trying to force it, you will sooner or later cut down the square lines so that the square will become round like the hole, and it will eventually go in. That's what many of us do with our consciences. The Holy Spirit pricks us but we turn against it.[170]

[Holy Spirit, Role of]
1 Tim. 1:5, 19

MANY people have alarm systems in their homes. When they walk in the door they get a thirty or maybe forty-five second warning to disarm the alarm before it goes off.

God has given every believer an alarm system in your heart. We've gotten so used to not turning the alarm on that we don't hear it, or we've gotten so used to tuning it out that we might as well not hear it.[171]

CONTENTMENT

BETTER a smaller home with happiness than a bigger house with misery. At least that's the way it should be. Many people today pursue stuff that is bigger and better, then pop pills for the misery it brings.[172]

CONTENTMENT is being just as happy driving that Mercedes as you would be if you had to drive that jalopy from college. In both cases you'd have a ride. Contentment is taking as much pleasure in that big three-hundred-thousand-dollar house as you would a two-bedroom apartment. In both cases you'd have a roof over your head. Contentment is appreciating that T-bone steak as much as you would a hot dog. In both cases you are not starving. Contentment is being just as satisfied with the designer outfit as you would

with an outfit from the thrift store. In both cases you have clothes on your back and you are not naked. Contentment is realizing that God has met your needs.[173]

[Provision, God's]
Phil. 4:11–13

ADVERTISERS are well aware of our propensity toward covetousness, and spend an inordinate amount of time attempting to make us dissatisfied. They know if we become discontent enough, the frustration of our covetousness will make us spend and spend. Due to our chronic covetousness, many of us have adopted the motto, "I shop, therefore I am."[174]

[Covetousness]
1 Tim. 6:6–7

CORRECTION

IF YOU walk a dog on a leash and come to a post, and the dog goes to one side of the post and you go to the other side of the post, you will both be stuck. Although both of you are going in the same direction, you will not be able to move forward. So you will have to back up and pull the dog in the opposite direction in order to get him going the right way.

That's how it is with life. God will pull us back sometimes to move us forward. He'll jerk us back. He's not trying to be mean. He just is the One who knows how to get us going forward in the right direction.[175]

COVETOUSNESS

THE COVETOUS person, particularly the one who's become a materialist, will soon discover that money can give you a bed, but not sleep. It can give you books, but not brains; a house, but not a home; food, but not an appetite; and amusements, but not friends.[176]

[Contentment]
1 Tim. 6:8–10

MANY children struggle with discontentment during the Christmas holiday. If two siblings receive five gifts each, they will be excited about their own gifts for a little while. After some time has passed, one or both of the children will begin to covet something that their sister or brother has. Children will tend to meander away from being thankful for what was provided them and work their way over to what was given to another. They will begin the process of confiscation, being dissatisfied with what they themselves have been given.[177]

[Contentment]
Ex. 20:17

CRITICIZING, DANGER OF

WHEN my kids were small, I took them to the Ft. Worth Stock Show. This is a place where once a year various livestock are put on display. Now, I'm no Farmer Brown, but looking at the animals was fun for the kids, so I took them.

But, it smells out there. It stinks really bad. There are all these animals and they could only be kept so clean. It wasn't long after we got there that I was ready to go. My kids begged me to stay a little bit longer, but after awhile, I couldn't take the smell anymore. I had to get out of there!

I gathered everyone up and we made our way to the car. It was still stinky. We got in the car and made sure the windows were all up so we could escape the smell. It was still stinky! We got halfway home. It was still stinky. Finally, we pulled up at our house. The stink that was at the Ft. Worth Stock Show was in the house. How could it be stinking in Dallas when the problem was in Ft. Worth? Well, I had somehow gotten the problem on my shoes. It's easy to analyze everybody else, but you may actually be smelling yourself.[178]

[Judging]
Matt. 7:1–2

CROSS

THERE was a little boy one day who was lost; he couldn't find his way home and he began to cry because he was so lost. A stranger saw the little boy crying and came up to him and tried to comfort him. He said, "What's wrong, son?" The little boy said through a flood of tears, "I can't . . . I can't find my way home. I'm lost." Wanting to help, the man asked, "Is there anything near your house that you remember?" The boy thought for a moment and said, "There's only one thing that I can remember. There is a building near my home with a cross on it." The man knew exactly which cross the boy was talking about.

He took the boy by the hand and walked him to the church, the building with the cross. When the boy got to the church, he knew exactly how to find his home. When he found the cross, he found home.[179]

IN 1954, there was a landmark Supreme Court decision. It was Brown v. the Topeka Board of Education, which ended segregation in public education. Did it stop racism in schools? Absolutely not, but since then, when a lawyer stands up in a courtroom, he can reference the Brown v. Topeka, Kansas, Board of Education case to legitimize my rights today. It was a landmark decision.

In 1865, the Thirteenth Amendment abolished slavery. It was a landmark decision. In 1870, the Fifteenth Amendment gave the right to vote and it was a landmark decision. In 1964, there was the Civil Rights Act, another landmark decision that gave equal opportunity to all. Now, does that mean that all of the evils that those decisions were designed to address went away? Absolutely not, but what it does mean is that there is something in the past to use in an appeal when mess shows up in the present.

When mess shows up and somebody wants to deny a child the right to attend a certain school, a lawyer can reach back to the legal decision made in 1964 that frees people of color to go to any public school they are qualified to attend.

If somebody wants to say I can't go into this restaurant or drink from this water fountain, I can go back and pull from the Civil Rights Act that gives me the right to go anywhere I want as an American citizen.

Two thousand years ago there was another landmark decision. Jesus Christ hung on the cross between heaven and earth with all of hell watching, and He paid the price for your sin and my sin. That was a landmark decision.

When Satan comes up and tries to convince you that your needs will not be met, you can appeal to a landmark decision—"The Lord is my shepherd, I shall not be in want" (Psalm 23:1). That's a landmark decision. When Satan shows up and he says that he plans to ruin your life, you can appeal to a landmark decision. Two thousand years ago there was a landmark decision that establishes that you are more than a conqueror through Him who loved you and gave Himself for you. That landmark decision from two thousand years ago can be used today! [180]

[Salvation; Freedom; Satan; Race Relations]
Col. 2:14–15; Rom. 8:37

D

DAILY BREAD

BECAUSE of all of the laws regarding food safety, you can't take food allotted to be served on any given day and distribute what is unused. A friend of mine owns a restaurant and at the end of business each day, they pack up their unused food and take it immediately to a shelter, staying within the confines of the legal time period given by the laws, and share with others. They'd rather share the food with the homeless than discard it in a trash can.

"Give us this day our daily bread" does not just imply a selfish kind of request. It also involves being concerned about the needs of others. This verse says, "Give us." It raises the question of our personal need and the needs of others.[181]

[Giving; Provision, God's]
Matt. 6:11; Eph. 4:28

GEORGE Mueller of England was one of the great men of faith. He had an orphanage and ran the orphanage day by day, depending on God.

Once, they ran out of food. He set the table, and brought the kids around, although there was no food there. The kids glanced at each other perplexed and then one spoke up, reminding Mr. Mueller that there was no food on the table. Mr. Mueller answered that he realized that, but that they should give thanks anyway.

He prayed and thanked the Lord for His promise to give them their daily bread and to meet their need. He prayed and reminded the Lord that he was busy doing His business and that the children were hungry. At the conclusion of his prayer, there was a knock on the door. The baker up the street stood there and said that he felt led to bring his leftovers to the orphanage, as they had not sold all they had baked for the day.

It is only when you have experiences like that you know that your God is real. It's only when you have experiences like that you know He can be trusted. He wants us to have a daily dependency on Him in spite of the fact that we might have plenty of choices.[182]

[Provision, God's; Prayer]
Phil. 4:19

DARKNESS, WALKING IN

HAVE YOU ever gotten up in the middle of the night to go to the restroom or to the kitchen, failed to turn on the light, and miscalculated where the end of the bed was? That's a major miscalculation, especially if you don't have anything on your feet. Have you ever hit your pinky toe? It makes you want to lose your religion! Most of us have nightstands by our bed with a light. We use that in the middle of the night because we want exposure so that we can see where we're going. A lot of us have lived our lives making one bad decision after another because we've been walking in darkness, and we still want to know why our spiritual toes are always hurting.[183]

John 8:12

DEATH

DEATH is the door to eternity. A girl was cutting through the cemetery and her friends asked her why she would do such a thing. She told them it was the shortest way to get to her home. The cemetery is the quick way to go home.[184]

A FATHER WAS dying. He had his family come around. He only had a few minutes left to live. He had four children. He said, "Good night John, good night Butch, goodnight Betty, good-bye Ralph." Ralph said, "Wait a minute. You said good night to my siblings, but you said good-bye to me!" The father told his son, "Because the other three children have accepted Jesus, I will see them again in glory, but because you have not, I will never see you again."[185]

[Salvation; Heaven, Entrance into; Hell]

I LOVE MONOPOLY. I'm a consummate entrepreneur. I like taking something, crafting and building it to then see how I can expand it more. When I play this game I get very "Trumpheptic" in the way I try to take over. My main goal and aim is to purchase Park Place and Boardwalk because they are the most valuable properties on the board. If I get those two pieces of property, then I've begun building Mr. Evans's neighborhood. I will put up some green houses and start charging rent. And if you can't pay, then you must leave the game. I'm a barracuda when I am playing Monopoly.

There is also a depressing time when I am playing Monopoly. That is when the game is over. It is then that I'm reminded it was all a game. When the game is over, the green houses, the red hotels, and all that paper money must go back into the box. Then we close the box and I come back to the real world.

One day, they are going to close the box. When they do, it will not matter what you left behind because it's going to someone else. When they close the box, what will matter is what you forwarded ahead. What time, talents, and treasures you had that had eternity attached to them.[186]

[Eternity; Money; Reward]
Eccl. 5:15; 1 Tim. 6:7

AN OLD man asked a young boy, "What are you going to do with your life?"

The young boy replied, "I'm going to college and get a business degree."

The old man said, "Well, what then?"

"Oh! Then I'm going up to New York and I'm going to work on Wall Street, become a broker, and then become a millionaire."

"Oh! OK! And what then?"

The boy continued, "Then I'm going to buy myself a fine house. I may try to retire early so that I can enjoy the good life."

"What then?"

"Well then, after that, I'm just going to party, relax, and enjoy my grandkids."

"Alrighty. What then?"

"I guess after all of that, I'm gonna die."

The old man smiled wryly and looked the young boy in the eyes. "What then?"

For all of us in life, no matter how we live our lives and no matter what we fill them with, we will all die and we need to have a plan in place for that time too.[187]

[Eternity; Money]
Rom. 14:9–12

EPHESIANS 2:1 says, "And you were dead in your trespasses and sins." When some people hear that, their first response is that they weren't that dead.

Let me pose a question. Let's say I took you to a mortuary and we went downstairs where they embalmed the bodies, and there were two tables there with two dead people on them, one on each table. They were just being undressed and being prepared for the draining of their blood and their embalming for the funeral and burial. One had just died three hours before. The other had been there three months. In fact, the body had begun to decay. It had begun to stink. Rigor mortis had set in. The body was decaying.

I have one simple question. Which is the "deader" of the two bodies? One can look good and be dead, and the other can look like a freak show and be dead, and yet one is not deader than the other. The definition of death is the absence of life. The definition of death is not how ugly you look in the absence of life.

Men without God are dead. Some look good and are dead. Some look okay and are dead. Others are just ugly and are dead. But regardless of your state of decomposition, we were all dead before coming to Christ.[188]

[Natural Man; Sin; New Life in Christ]

Eph. 2:1–5

DEATH, FEAR OF

DONALD Grey Barnhouse, whose first wife died, was driving his kids from the funeral. One of the kids said, "Daddy, I don't understand, where did Mommy go? I don't understand what it means that she died." Barnhouse was trying to figure out how to explain death to his kids when, just then, a truck passed by and cast a shadow over the car.

He looked back at the kids and said, "Kids, would you have rather been hit by the truck or hit by the shadow?" Well, of course, they would have rather been hit by the shadow because the shadow doesn't hurt. It just darkens things for a moment. Then in his own wisdom, Barnhouse said these words, "Kids, when you die without Christ, you are hit by the truck. When you die with Christ, you are only hit by the shadow. The shadow is all you get."[189]

[Comfort]

Ps. 23:4; 1 Cor. 15:54–55

DEATH, INEVITABILITY OF

I'VE GOT bad news for you. Unless Jesus comes back, you are going to die. Your death will not be delayed because the Bible says you die by appointment. You are going to die.

Death today can look fairly nice.

The folks down at the funeral home know how to get us looking fairly good when we are dead. The funeral parlors have professional makeup artists who dress you up and make you look good. I've seen some people look better dead than they ever looked alive. But they're still dead.

Dead people used to be put into crude wooden boxes and carried around in horse-drawn carriages. You don't die like that today. Nowadays when you die, you die in style. We're talking bronze caskets lined with linen. If you die before you've had a chance to put your head on a satin pillow, no worries. Now's your chance. Always wanted to ride in a limousine? You've got it—a fleet, in fact. You will stop traffic that day. People will pull over just because you are riding by. But you're still dead.

Back in the day, the coffin would be lowered into the ground by ropes tied around the top and the bottom of the casket. Today, there are no ropes; a nickel-plated machine eases you down. They don't want to wake you up so you get put six feet under in the most comfortable way possible. But you're still dead.

Whether it's a coffin or a casket, a limousine, or a horse-drawn carriage, a nickel-plated machine or a rope, you are still dead. A fancy death doesn't change that reality.

What death should do is promote the idea of not wasting time in life. The older you get, there should be certain things you don't have time for because you realize that you are losing time every day. You can't waste it.[190]

[Time, Perspective on; Life, Management of]

Ps. 90:12; Heb. 9:27

ONE DAY a man came face-to-face with death. He was standing on the corner and death walked by. Death looked a little bit surprised, but he kept on going. Terrified, the man went and asked an old wise man what he should do. "I just saw death a second ago. He looked shocked to see me. What should I do?"

The old man said, "If I were you, I'd run to the next city in a hurry."

So the man got up and ran as fast as he could to the next city. As soon as he crossed the city line. he ran into death. Confused, he said, "I just ran into you yesterday and left the city to get away from you!"

Death said, "Yeah, I was surprised to see you yesterday too, especially since I'm scheduled to meet you today right here."

There's just nowhere to run. Nowhere to hide. Death has the ability to find you wherever you are.[191]

DEATH, UNEXPECTED

A MAN who came to the Pearly Gates ran into Saint Peter. Saint Peter asked, "Tell me what good things you did in your lifetime."

The man said, "Well, I can tell you about one thing I did. There was this biker who was stealing this old woman's purse. I saw him stealing it and I grabbed him, and threw him to the ground in order to help the woman whose purse was being stolen."

Saint Peter was impressed. "Wow! When did that happen?"

The man sheepishly said, "About two or three minutes ago."[192]

DEBT, BURDEN OF

MOST divorces are related to money. Many of us could be like Snow White and the Seven Dwarfs: "I owe, I owe, so off to work I go."[193]

[Money]

Prov. 22:7

DECEPTION

IT'S LIKE the man who hit another man's parked car. The offender got out of his car and began to write a note. The note said, "Everybody looking at me right now thinks I'm leaving my name, address, and phone number. I am not. Good luck."[194]

A LITTLE boy was lost one day and people were feeling sorry for him. They had begun to give him money because they were sad that he couldn't find his mother, until someone touched him and said, "I think I see your mother over there." He said, "Shhh, I see her too, but I don't need to find her right now."[195]

A MAN WHO went fishing had a very bad day. He caught nothing. On his way home he stopped by the grocery store, and told the person behind the meat counter, "Throw me ten of your largest fish so I can go back and tell my wife I caught them."[196]

POTATO chips these days are about one-fourth chips and three-fourths air. The potato chip companies can say it's a bag, call it a bag, and advertise it as a bag. But if you pay for a bag, you will get much less than what you bargained for.

We have too many potato chip Christians today. There are too many Christians who are half saved and half worldly. You open them up and they are full of air.[197]

[Carnal Christians; Worldliness, Concept of]
1 John 2:15–16; James 4:4

DUCK hunters use decoys. Today, these decoys have gotten pretty fancy. The decoys quack like ducks, move like ducks, look like ducks, and act like ducks. In fact, the ducks think that they are ducks and the real ducks end up being dead ducks because they can't tell what's real.

For the Christian, there are many roving decoys out there and their job is to extricate us from the intimate experience of our faith. We must look beyond what a person says or how they perform to determine their authenticity. We must evaluate and test the spirits. We must be on guard for decoys moving all around us, acting like the real thing, in order to deceive.[198]

[Focus; Wisdom]
1 John 4:1; 2 Peter 2:1

A LADY who lived in an apartment complex got up to answer a knock at her door. A man was there with a sad face. He said, "I'm sorry to disturb you, but we are collecting money for a destitute family in this apartment complex. They need help paying their rent so that they will have a place to live. The husband is out of work. The kids are hungry. The utilities are in danger of being cut off. They are going to be kicked out of their apartment any day if they don't have the rent by this afternoon."

Immediately the lady desired to help this family with such a great need. She asked the man to wait while she went to get some money.

"Here's some money to help with this family and their need. By the way, it's so nice of you to take your time seeking help for the family. Who are you, again?"

"Uh, I'm the landlord."

You can appear to have good motives, but not wholeheartedly serve God's interests.[199]

A MAN went to visit his friend who was a pig farmer. As he walked across the land toward the house, he noticed one unusual pig. The pig had a little limp when he walked. When he got a little closer, he noticed the pig had a prosthesis on. Well now, he had never seen anything like this in his life. Seeing a pig with an artificial leg was a first! He walked over to the farmer, who was rocking on the porch.

"Now that pig out there with the prosthesis, I have never, ever seen an artificial limb on an animal in general, and especially on a pig."

"Well," said the farmer, "let me tell you about that pig. One day, my little granddaughter was walking out in front of the tractor. The tractor was going to mow her down, but the pig jumped in and knocked her out of the way. On another occasion, my grandson was drowning, and the pig jumped into the water and saved him. I just didn't have the heart to eat the pig all at once."

Things are not always as they appear. Things are not always as clearly definable as they initially look.[200]

DECEPTION, COST OF

A GUY went to the doctor one day. He wanted to get a checkup, and the doctor did the traditional things. Then he brought in a little cat. The cat sniffed the guy, rubbed up against the guy, jumped on the guy's lap, and then the cat left. The man got a bill for two hundred dollars. The guy called the doctor's office immediately and said, "Two hundred dollars! What's this for?

The doctor replied, "Fifty dollars is for my checking you, and the other 150 is for the cat-scan."[201]

DECEPTION, SATAN'S

DECEPTION is like the solicitations that so many of us receive from credit card companies. A person from a bank will call your home and say, "I am happy to let you know that you qualify for our new Visa card. We are privileged to tell you that we have raised your limit to twenty-five thousand dollars and it would be our honor to send you your card today. You will be one of our preferred customers."

That conversation might leave a person feeling pretty good.

"Oh, I'm worth twenty-five thousand dollars!"

"Wow, I'm a preferred customer!"

"I'm somebody!"

Here's what they *won't* bother to tell you. They won't tell you that if you will simply use the limit, if you will simply spend twenty-five thousand dollars, if you will take advantage of everything they are offering, they will own you for the rest of your life. They don't tell you that they will tack 18 percent on everything you purchase.

There are people today who are owned by Satan. He may have told you to just take one pill, or just take one smoke, or just take one sniff. What he didn't say was that after that,

he'd own you.

That's what Satan does. He captures us with a thought, then owns us with a thought.[202]

[Satan; Debt, Burden of; Temptation]
1 Peter 5:8–9; James 1:14–16

DECISIONS

A YOUNG new bank president made an appointment to meet with his soon-to-retire predecessor to seek advice as he took on his new responsibilities. He had one basic question to ask. He wanted to know how the older gentleman had become so successful. His predecessor looked at him and said two words: "Good decisions." The young man, wanting more detail, pressed further and asked how one could come to make good decisions. The predecessor said, "Experience." The young banker continued his line of questioning by asking how one could come to gain experience. The predecessor said, "Bad decisions."[203]

DEDICATION, INCOMPLETE

WE HAVE dedications. We dedicate children. We dedicate houses. People ask us to come and dedicate their house. People ask us to come and dedicate their businesses. If you want me or one of the staff to dedicate something of yours, the dedication will be meaningless without an equal commitment to obedience. All you did was have a religious exercise in "ecclesiastical pomposity" when you have dedication that does not include obedience.[204]

[Commitment]
Isa. 29:13

DEMONS

IF YOU leave water stagnant for an extended period of time in the summer, you will attract mosquitoes. Mosquitoes are going to hang out where there is stagnant water because that's home for them. That's a nice environment for them. They are at rest in stagnant places.

If you leave trash out for an extended period of time, you're going to attract a rat and his cousins. You will have attracted them because you have created an environment in which they can be at home. If you leave food out at home too long, you are going to attract roaches. They will perceive as an invitation that you're leaving stuff out. They are going to make a connection between the environment that you have set and an invitation for them to share it.

Whenever there is uncleanness left alone in a life, it is an invitation for demons to make themselves a home.[205]

[Sin, Consequences of]
Eph. 4:27

IT'S ONE thing to see a roach, one roach. If you see a roach, that's a problem; but when you see a legion, that's a disaster. With one roach, Raid will do the trick. With an invasion of roaches, we will need the Orkin Man. An invasion means that you have a nesting of sorts hidden away somewhere.

Raid can't help you because all Raid can do is affect what you see, and maybe just behind the baseboard. But Raid can't go deep into the nooks and crevices of the wall. You will need a pro if you have an infestation of roaches.

If a problem jumps up in your life, you can just deal with it and then move on. That's not demons. Demons don't just visit. They come looking for homes. They are interested in setting up shop. They want to be in control.[206]

[Problems]
Matt. 12:43–45

DEPRESSION, OVERCOMING

PEOPLE have some unique ways of trying to overcome their depression. There was a lady whose husband died. She found herself, of course, extremely lonely. She told herself that she needed to do something to overcome her depression. She took a trip to the pet store to look for something to comfort her in her loneliness.

The proprietor introduced her to a parakeet that talked. The widow thought the idea of a talking parakeet was wonderful, so she took the parakeet home. She started talking to the bird, but the parakeet wouldn't talk back. The woman talked and talked. This went on for a week and, naturally, she was a little confused as to what was going on.

The widow made her way back to the pet store. "The parakeet is not talking."

The proprietor said, "Oh, you forgot to get the mirror. The parakeet needs to see itself in the mirror, then it will be encouraged to talk."

So she bought a mirror, took it back, and placed it in the cage. She made sure that the parakeet could see itself. For another week, she talked to the parakeet. The parakeet still would not talk.

The lady went back, yet again, to the pet store. "That parakeet is still not talking."

"Oh," he said, "you didn't get the swing. The parakeet's got to be on the swing and swinging and looking at itself in order for it to talk."

So she bought the swing, put the parakeet on the swing, and started talking to the parakeet.

Another week went by and she made her way back to the pet store.

"This dumb parakeet is not working. It's not doing what I hoped it would do."

"Oh, I am sorry. There's one more thing you forgot to get—the ladder. The parakeet has got to have the ladder to walk up and down on. That movement will allow it to talk."

Begrudgingly, she bought the ladder. Another week went by. That parakeet didn't say a word. However, at the end of the week, it fell over dead.

The widow was really mad now. She marched back to the store and sought out the store owner. She said, "That parakeet you sold me died. I bought the mirror, bought the swing, bought the ladder, and that bird didn't say a mumbling word. It just fell over and died."

The store owner said, "I cannot believe that it died. Did it say anything before it died?"

"Yeah, while it was falling over dead, it looked up with one eye open and said, 'Don't they serve any food at that pet store?'"

For four weeks, that bird hadn't eaten. The woman kept buying all the wrong stuff. That's what a lot of us look for—all the wrong stuff. The things we hope will solve our problems die on us. They don't produce what we expect.[207]

[Worldliness, Concept of]

DISCIPLESHIP

PEOPLE want salvation but don't want to put in the time to be strong disciples of Jesus Christ. What many Christians want to do is to audit the Christian life. An audit is where a person goes to class to get information, but is not required to do any of the work. They don't have to take a test or do any homework. They are only attending for informational purposes. They want the data without the responsibility. That's an audit. That's what some folks do every Sunday. They audit Jesus.[208]

[Carnal Christians]
1 Cor. 9:23–25; Heb. 12:1

MANY people after our services on Sunday line up to get a CD of the message. When I speak on Sunday mornings, the messages are taped and made immediately available for purchase when the service is over. People each week line up to get the CD. What they get is a copy of the master. There is a master CD that holds the original recording; then there are the copies that are made available to people who want to listen to the sermon again or share it with someone else. All that people can purchase are the replicas. The replicas of the master sound like the master, look like the master, and feel like the master, but they are not the master. However, they are so much like the master, it's as good as having the master itself.

Jesus is the Master, but what He wants to do is copy Himself onto His followers, so that when people see you or me, they are getting a recording of the Master, as we are committed to following our Master who has all authority. This is the essence of discipleship.[209]

Matt. 10:24–25; Eph. 5:1–2

THE GREEK word for disciple, *mathetes*, was a very meaningful word in the Greek world. Plato developed a form of thinking or a philosophy of life that separated the physical and spiritual realm. This disconnection between the physical and spiritual still affects our thinking today, as is apparent when we reference the secular versus the sacred. That form of thinking that Plato developed is called Platonic thought.

Plato had a follower named Aristotle. Aristotle was a follower of Plato. He was a student and he studied the Platonic philosophy. Aristotle, Plato's student, developed schools called academies, where he would train the next generation in Plato's thinking. So Aristotle, Plato's student, bought into the worldview of Plato, and began developing schools to train other students in this thinking of Plato. Part of this organized approach by Aristotle is known as Aristotelian logic. Aristotle systematized and organized the thinking of Plato and made it transferable. Out of these schools there were birthed men and women who now went into the marketplace with this Platonic worldview. They became doctors and lawyers and teachers, but they had this worldview.

In the meantime, Rome overtook Greece. The big military machine of Rome defeated Greece and Greece was now a defeated nation and now being occupied by Roman power. But there was a problem in Rome. The folks who had been trained in Greece with the thinking of Plato and the system of Aristotle were infiltrating Roman culture. We call it the Hellenization of the Romans. Rome was being "Greekenized," even though it was the prominent military power. The Greek influence permeated the Roman culture because of the power of discipleship.

This is the point of discipleship. When Jesus discussed discipleship, it was in the cultural context of Greek culture influencing the Roman Empire through the power of discipleship. Jesus Christ takes the concept of discipleship and intimates, "I'm looking for a generation of followers who are so saturated in My thinking, My worldview, and My orientation that when integrated into the culture in which they are situated, the culture will have to live with the influence of Jesus Christ, who permeates the culture."

So a schoolteacher really is a disciple of Jesus Christ disguised as a teacher. A lawyer is really a disciple of Jesus Christ disguised as a lawyer. A businessman is really a follower of Jesus Christ disguised as a businessman. The idea is to have people who use what they do as a disguise for who they are to impact the world for Christ.[210]

[World; Impact, Impacting the; Discipleship, Impact of]
Matt. 5:13–14; Luke 13:18–21

DISCIPLESHIP, FREEDOM OF

WHAT IF you were in jail and the bail was twenty-five thousand dollars? What if I came and deposited the bail for you, they did all the paperwork, and documented that you were now free? You would have legally been declared free. The problem is that you would still be in jail. Although the payment had been paid and the paperwork had been done, there would still be a gap of time between the bail being posted, the paperwork being done, and actually getting you out. The information on paper doesn't unlock the cell. Paperwork doesn't unlock the cell door. You've got to have a key.

Jesus has posted bail because He put the price for our sins on His tab. Jesus paid it all. The paperwork has been signed. You are accepted in heaven. If you still feel like you are in your cell, then you have yet to have your door unlocked. How does this happen? Believing in Him gets you free on record. Walking with Him and growing in Him gets you free in actuality. When you continue learning and applying His Word, the Son picks up the keys and makes you actually free.[211]

[Sanctification; Spiritual Maturity, Growth; Transformation]

John 8:36; Gal. 5:1

DISCIPLESHIP, IMPACT OF

PERHAPS you don't know what fifth columnists are. It goes all the way back to when the Spanish army would invade a nation and they would march the soldiers in four columns. The soldiers would march in four columns and do a frontal assault on whatever nation or city they were going to attack. The nation being attacked felt pretty secure, because they could see the four columns coming. But what they didn't know about were the fifth columnists.

The fifth columnists had moved into the city a year beforehand as covert operatives. They had become doctors and lawyers, politicians and businesspeople, and they infiltrated the land that would be attacked a year later. In other words, they were saboteurs.

What they did was to set things up for the army invasions. When the four columns marched, the fifth columnists would have already caused havoc on the inside. The four columns could do what they needed to do, because there were subversives internally.

God expects every Christian who is functioning in a secular, non-Christian society, business, or school to be a fifth columnist. He expects you to be part of His army that works behind enemy lines. He wants you to represent the interests of heaven in the locality of earth where He has placed you. Fifth columnists don't become part of the culture, they just function at the level they need to in order to bring about the bigger plan of the nation that they are a part of.[212]

[World, Impacting the]

Matt. 5:13–14; 1 Cor. 9:19–23

9/11 HAS changed our world. It's not only changed America, even though we were the ones directly affected. The reverberation is worldwide. A whole new system was set up because of 9/11 called Homeland Security. You have to wait in long lines now at the airport because of 9/11. You got different color codes indicating the seriousness of a potential threat, all because of 9/11.

Folks halfway around the world infiltrated our culture because of their belief system. They had a belief system that created an action and they infiltrated the culture. Even though we don't buy their belief system, we are affected by it. Their actions were wrong and the belief system that inspired the actions is illegitimate and evil, but it was effective. Their belief system acted. It didn't just talk. It made its presence here. Those men on 9/11 were disciples of their system. They didn't just *believe* it. They risked everything to advance it.

To be a disciple is to be a visible, verbal follower of Jesus Christ. It is to be clearly a representative of Him. There should be no question that you're a Christian in your world.[213]

[World, Impacting the; Witnessing]

2 Tim. 1:7–9

IN THE movies, there are previews of coming attractions. This is where the hot clips of the upcoming movies are shown. The cuts of the movies are always of the most exciting scenes: the fight scenes, the love scenes, or the chase scenes. The moviemakers show you the best clips because they want you to tune in to the whole show. Now, the movie itself may actually be terrible, but you'll never know it by the clips!

One day there is a big show coming to town. God is the Producer, the Holy Spirit is the Director, and Jesus is the Superstar. It will be a worldwide production. In the meantime, God has left you and me here as previews of the coming attractions. As disciples of Christ, we're supposed to be the hot clips of the upcoming show, so that when people see our clips, they conclude the show must be hot. From watching our previews, people should raise the question, "Where can I buy a ticket to the show?" It is then that we can tell them, "You don't have to buy a ticket; the price has already been paid."[214]

[World, Impacting the; Spiritual Identity, in Christ; Witnessing]

1 Peter 2:11–12

DISCIPLINE, LOVE IN

ONCE I got suspended from school in the eighth grade for fighting. Some boy messed with my fried chicken. They served fried chicken for lunch, and this boy took a piece of chicken out of my plate.

They had to call my father from his job. Now, my father worked by the hour, which meant he had to punch out to come see why his son, the preacher's kid, had gotten kicked out of school. He went to the school and came to the principal's office, where I sat, waiting. I'll never forget my father's face as he listened to the story of how I came to get in trouble. I'll also never forget my father's response. He told the principal, "Sir, you will never, ever, ever have to worry about my son ever being suspended from school ever again."

As we walked out he said, "Do you know how much this visit cost me? I am going to take the payment out on you." Even though I was disciplined, he still fed me. Even though I was disciplined, he still clothed me. Even though I was disciplined, there was still a roof over my head. Even though I did something to irritate him, he was my daddy, and he was tenaciously committed to me.[215]

[God's Discipline]

Heb. 12:5–11

DISCRIMINATION

I WAS amazed at some of the testimonies I heard as I participated in the funeral of Tom Landry, the former coach of the Dallas Cowboys, especially one testimony by one of the black players. This player said that he would have come even if he had not been asked to speak. He went on to explain how, during the sixties when society was still very racially divided, he always knew that when he came to the Cowboys' football camp, this coach would treat him fairly. One African-American player after another came up and said that they knew Landry to be a fair man at a time when the culture was unrighteous. What did this man have to show for it? Twenty years of winning and going to heaven with a good name. He didn't let what was happening in society mess with his team. Too many of us let folks on the outside affect how we feel in our hearts and therefore we break up our winning season for the kingdom of God.[216]

[Race Relations; Kingdom of God]

Acts 17:26; Rom. 12:2; Gal. 3:28

ONE of the least-thanked groups in our society is the people who empty the garbage. It's not what you would call a high-class job. However, in New York a couple of years ago, the garbagemen went on strike. All of a sudden, these typically underrated people became the most significant people in the city because the whole place was stinking.

If you let a couple of weeks go by and your garbage doesn't get picked up, all of a sudden, the nobodies become somebodies. God has said that He makes the nobodies of this world the somebodies, and He measures our significance by how we treat them. It is important to make time in your schedule for people rejected by society.[217]

[Servanthood]

Matt. 25:31–46; James 1:27

MANY people discriminate in the area of education. Now, let me explain something to the "edu-ma-cated." Whether you have a PhD or a GED, you have come into the kingdom through the same door. God did not look at your resume before He brought you into the kingdom. He didn't see whether you had a BS, MBA, or PhD. He wanted to give everybody in here a BA—born again.

Praise God if you got to go to school on a government grant. Praise God if your parents could pay for it. Praise God if you had to work like a dog to get it, and praise God for the person who had the tenacity to go back after dropping out. But our education or lack of it doesn't make us any better or worse in God's sight.[218]

Acts 10:34; Gal. 2:6

DIVINE NATURE

IF A PERSON has accepted the Lord Jesus Christ as their Savior, then God has deposited within them a divine nature. Divine nature is the nature of God deposited inside of the believer in seed form. Inside of the seed lies spiritual potential. It's all in the seed.

When a seed of corn is planted, in that seed is all the potential of a stalk with a bunch of ears. Watermelon seed is planted because inside is the promise of something so much bigger. An acorn has all the makings for a huge oak tree. Planted seeds grow, with the help of a little water and sunshine, into so much more than originally visible. However, they must go through a process of growth in order to fully mature into their possibilities.[219]

[Spiritual Maturity, Growth; Transformation; Sanctification]

Phil. 2:13; 2 Peter 1:3–10

YOU'RE like an old car that has had a new motor placed inside. When you look at the vehicle, it looks like the same old car. But there is a new life source within it, a new motor. When you have a new motor you don't need to be concerned about changing spark plugs or connecting wires. All you have to do is understand you have a whole new motor.

Many of us are trying to live our Christian lives by changing spark plugs on Monday, checking connections on Tuesday, changing wires on Wednesday, working on the gas line on Friday, and replacing the belt on Saturday. But all of the work was taken care of when you got the new motor.[220]

2 Cor. 4:10; 5:17

DIVORCE

A WOMAN, when asked why she was seeking a divorce from her husband, said, "When I got married I was looking for the ideal, instead it became an ordeal, so now I want a new deal."[221]

[Marriage]

WHEN SYLVESTER Stallone was making one of his Rocky movies, right after one of his fighting scenes, he said, "You know, boxing is a great sport as long as you can yell, 'Cut!'" Many of us feel that way about marriage—it's a lot of fun as long as you can yell "Cut!" and can get out of it when it's beating you up too badly.[222]

[Marriage]

DOUBLE-MINDEDNESS

WE ALL have AM and FM on our radios. Those are two different frequencies. There is no such thing as "AM-FMish." Each frequency is separate and distinct. When riding in the car, you can only listen to one or the other. You can't have both at the same time, even though both are there. We come to church for the "Heavenly Broadcast Network." We leave church for the "Flesh Broadcast Network." Flipping frequencies like this is double-mindedness.[223]

[Worldliness, Concept of]

MOST of us are double-minded and attempt to think two ways at the same time. We come to church for the wisdom from above. We go back out of church and get the wisdom from below and we try to mix them.

If a woman is making stew for her family, she'll probably put in some meat, potatoes, and some seasoning. However, if she decides to add just a tad of arsenic—just a little bit to "spice it up," that cook will have just killed her family. Attempting to integrate two contradictory realities doesn't work.[224]

James 1:6–8

YOU CANNOT mix unleaded and diesel fuel and still think you're going somewhere. The moment you introduce diesel and unleaded into the same "unleaded-only" engine, you have canceled the unleaded by the fact of diesel. Just because it looks like gas doesn't mean it is going to help you. What we do as Christians is we come to church to get unleaded, then on Monday go to the world and get diesel and wonder why we're only chugging along.[225]

[Worldliness, Concept of]
1 John 2:15–16

THE FIRST time I rode a horse, I figured I'd watched enough cowboy pictures to know how to do it. So I jumped up on the horse and said, "Giddyup."

The horse would take two steps forward, then back up three steps. I assumed I had a crazy horse. In fact, I told the attendant that I needed another horse. He let me know that my horse was fine, but that he needed another rider.

I didn't understand the problem with my riding. I was making all of the sounds that I'd always heard on TV and kicking him like I'd seen on TV. The attendant told me that all those sounds and kicking were fine but wouldn't work at the same time that I was pulling back on the reins. The horse was thoroughly confused. He didn't know whether I wanted him to go forward or step backward. Many of us are going two steps forward and three steps back and we wonder why we're not making progress.[226]

AN APPLE A day keeps the doctor away. But I don't like apples. They tell me apples are very nutritious. I just don't like them—except when I go to the Texas State Fair. At the fair, I get candied apples. They take the apple and they dip it in liquid sugar. Then, me and apples, we are all right. The problem is that the way the apples have been prepared, the nutritional value has been destroyed. By mixing the apples with the sugar, things are now kind of messed up. The apples will hurt me now, not help me. When you mix human wisdom with divine wisdom, you cancel divine wisdom. All you have is human wisdom. That's what the Bible calls being double-minded—being secular and sacred at the same time.[227]

[Wisdom]
Col. 2:8; James 1:6–8

E

EMOTIONS

WHEN my smoke detector went off one day, my first reaction, of course, was fear and shock because I assumed there was a fire. This makes sense because that's what the alarm is there for—to notify me when there is a fire in my house. The problem is there was no fire. There was only a bad connection in the wiring. My alarm made a loud noise signaling a fire when there was no fire. It would not have been wise of me to just dial 911 because I heard the noise, without determining the truth.

Determining the truth saved me time. I could have started emptying the house, pulling stuff out of the house, and breaking doors down because, after all, the detector made the fire noise. But upon examination, I had to compare the noise with reality. There was no fire.

When we experience various emotions, we must examine them. We must ask questions. We need to ascertain what the facts are that our feelings are responding to. The smoke alarm was real, as are our feelings. But it's up to us to make sure that they are correct indicators that we should act on.[228]

[Wisdom]
James 1:19–20

IN COURTHOUSES, you see policemen on post to keep the peace. The fact that a judge may have made you upset by ruling against you does not change the fact that you have to behave respectfully in the courtroom and stay in your seat. Your feelings of frustration do not justify an emotional response or causing chaos in the courtroom. You have got to control yourself in the courtroom. Why? Because if you don't, the policemen have the backing of the law to make you behave. Your feelings have to adjust to the reality of where you are.

In the same way, we must measure our feelings and emotions against the reality of God's Word. His Word sets the tone for how we live, not our feelings.[229]

[Scripture, Importance of; Faith]
2 Cor. 5:7

ONE DAY while flying his plane, a pilot noticed a small cloud up ahead. He decided to just fly through it. Once he got in the midst of the cloud, he realized that it wasn't as small as he had thought. He decided to pull up and out of it but after pulling up for a long period of time, he decided to try to point the nose of the plane down to get out of this cloud.

Still not able to come out of the cloud, the pilot began to get a little disoriented. With all of his maneuvering, he began to wonder if he was right side up or upside down. Sweat began pouring down his face, because he didn't know his position in the cloud. He started to feel upside down. He checked his instruments and they said the plane was still right side up. He felt like the plane had tipped over but the instruments said the opposite.

The pilot made a decision to believe the instruments even though his emotions were leading him differently. It took all of his energy to believe that those instruments were telling him the truth.

Finally, he came out of the cloud,

not far from the ground, because the cloud was low. When he came out, he was right side up. Had he believed what he felt, he would have been a dead man; but he acted on what the instruments said, even though he felt differently.

While many times our emotions and feelings will lead us into defeat, the Word of God is an instrument that gives solid guidance and direction we can count on.[230]

[Scripture, Importance of; Wisdom]
Ps. 119:105–6

IF YOU'VE ever had a police car pull up behind you with its lights flaring, you know what happens to your feelings. You probably begin to feel nervous. Your heart probably starts pounding—ba-boom, ba-boom, ba-boom, ba-boom. Even if you get a bit of relief when the car pulls out to the side of you in pursuit of somebody else, it can take a moment before your emotions get in line with the facts.

We can't depend on our emotions. We have to stick to the facts. When it comes to Christian living, we must learn to rely on the truth of the Word of God for our direction. Relying on our emotions can lead us astray.[231]

[Scripture, Importance of; Wisdom]
John 7:24

ENCOURAGEMENT

A FATHER and his son were walking on the beach and the boy happened to notice all the starfish lying there. There were hundreds and thousands of them that had been washed up onshore. Of course, they were dying, not being in the water. So they began throwing them back into the water.

Soon the boy realized that there were just too many. The boy then said, "Daddy, there are so many starfish up on the beach. It doesn't matter that we are throwing back a few here and a few there. It doesn't matter, because there's too many of them."

His father said, "It matters to the ones we pick up."[232]

IN THE 1996 Olympics, Keri Strug, the Olympic gymnast, had the weight of the Olympic gold medal for her team on her shoulders. All she had to do was have a successful vault, and the United States would get the gold. There was one problem. When she did her first vault, she sprained her ankle, and she could barely walk. She fell; she did not get the score she needed for the U.S. team to win. As she sat there on the mat with tears falling down her face, she cried for two reasons. One, she was in pain. And two, there was no way she could make the score to win the victory in this situation.

But she had another jump. She had another vault. She got up. She felt like giving up, but her coach stood on the sidelines and said, "You can do it, Keri. You can do it, Keri. I believe in you. You can do it."

As she limped to get ready to try to do a vault, she could barely move. She told an interviewer, after the vault, that all she could do to keep going was keep her eyes on the coach. He kept her from focusing on her ankle. This girl was really hurting. She was crying. But she had an encourager who believed in her. She found strength from his encouragement that she didn't have. Even with the limp, she took off running, and did her flip on the vault. She had to nail the landing in order to win. She had to try to do this with an ankle that was injured. With her coach's encouragement holding her up, she conquered her impossibility. She earned a high enough score for the U.S. team to win the gold—all because of her coach's encouragement. Encouragement changes your performance.[233]

[Perseverance]
1 Thess. 5:11; Heb. 3:13

IN IOWA there was a storm that had flooded out a major city. People were gathering their goods to save what they could. One of the policemen saw a sight that touched his heart. He saw a little boy carrying another little boy on his shoulders, all while still trying to carry goods and luggage and everything else. The policeman went over to help the boy and said, "My, you're trying to do too much. You've got all these bags and then you've got that boy on your shoulders. It's too much weight for you. It's too heavy."

The little boy looked at the policeman and said, "He ain't heavy, he's my brother."

When you know somebody is your brother, it makes it easier to bear the weight and carry them to safety.[234]

[Family of God; Fellowship]
Gal. 6:1–2

GEESE fly together in a "V" formation. Why? Because it actually gives them 71 percent more efficiency in their journey. When one goose is in trouble, two leave and join the one goose until it can get back up in the air again. They're committed to each other.[235]

ENCOURAGEMENT is like peanut butter on bread. If you spread it around, it just helps things stick together better.[236]

ENCOURAGEMENT, CHURCH AS

WHEN my youngest son played for Baylor, they didn't have one of the great winning programs in college football. But it was always amazing to me. I'd be sitting in the stands and watching those cheerleaders. Looking at them, you'd think we were winning. They'd be down there, on the sidelines, jumping around and yelling, "Yeah, yeah, yeah!" The score could be forty-five to nothing and the cheerleaders would still be out there supporting the team as if the team were contending for the national championship.

The church should be a place of heat that stirs people up. People need to be encouraged in their Christian walk. Sometimes, you may be the one who needs the encouragement, but when you are not the person, you should be the cheerleader who encourages others on.[237]

[Family of God; Fellowship]
Gal. 6:1–2

ENCOURAGEMENT, NEED FOR

ONE OF the immensely popular shows of our recent past has been the show *Cheers*. The show was centered around folks hanging out at a bar. Now, people just don't go to bars to drink. They can drink at home. People go to bars to drink in an environment of encouragement. In fact, they have a name for it; it's called a happy hour. Happy hour is designed not only to give you drinks at maybe a little cheaper rate but also to bring people together and to create an environment. The establishments figure that if people are not receiving happiness from their jobs or in their homes, it works to provide an environment where people get what they are missing out on.[238]

[Fellowship]
1 Thess. 5:11

MANY churches are in need of what every football team has: cheerleaders. The job of a cheerleader is to tell everybody "we're going to make it." No matter how bad things look on the scoreboard, there is still hope. Cheerleaders cheer all the way to the end of the game and will act like the team is winning by a big score even when there may be no way that a victory is possible. Their job is to be a cheerleader.

When folks come into today's sanctuary with broken lives, they need to run into some cheerleaders, folks who are willing to cheer them on and tell them that they are going to make it.[239]

[Encouragement; Praise]
Eph. 4:29; 1 Thess. 5:11

ETERNAL PERSPECTIVE

REGGIE Jackson was a baseball player known as "Mr. October." He got his nickname because he was known to shine when his team played in the postseason playoffs. Reggie would come up to bat, and the ball was going over somebody's fence. Reggie Jackson said once in an interview that he lived for the postseason because that is when he would shine. But Reggie Jackson, in order to get to the postseason, had to get through the regular season. His secret to shining in the regular season was to keep his eye on October. God is looking for some Mr. and Mrs. Octobers—people with their eyes on eternity who faithfully play the regular season because they're looking forward to post-season glory.[240]

[Eternity; Heavenly Mind-set; Kingdom of God]
John 14:2; Phil. 3:12–14

MYOPIA is the technical term for what is commonly known as near-sightedness. People who are near-sighted only see what's near or close to them. Their range of vision is limited. They need glasses to see things farther away due to their myopia. This same medical terminology has been used in the broader context of life to describe people who are shortsighted and who don't see the big picture in life. These folks tend to live for the moment, making choices that benefit them in the "right now." They live their lives existing only for this life.[241]

[Greed; Worldliness, Concept of]
Matt. 6:19–21; Luke 12:16–21

A TOMBSTONE contains a date of birth, date of death, and a dash. Above these things is the name of the deceased and below, usually, will be some kind of statement. The main part of the tombstone is the dash. It is all about the dash because the dash is talking about what happened while that person was here on earth.

When we meet God, He is going to want to discuss the dash. He is going to want to know what we did do that served His eternal purposes.[242]

[Life, Management of; Stewardship]
Matt. 25:14–30

ONE DAY a man was talking to an an-gel. The angel said, "What can I do for you?" The man said, "Show me the *Wall Street Journal* one year from today. This way, I will know where to invest and will become a multimillionaire." The angel snapped his fingers and out came a *Wall Street Journal* marked one year in advance of the date when they were talking. The man flipped the pages of the newspaper, studying the listings and observing which stocks would be high and which ones would be low. But in the midst of his joy, a frown came upon his face and tears began to roll down his eyes because when he looked over on the next page, he saw his face. His picture was in the paper under the obituary column.

You see, this life can only offer you so much. Unless you live now in light of eternity, you are going to waste time focusing on the things of this earth. Enjoy your life, but as a Christian focused on the things that matter to God.[243]

[Life, Management of; Money, Use of; Stewardship]
Matt. 25:14–30; Luke 12:16–21

ONE OF the greatest connections you could ever make is the connection between time and eternity. Expectations always affect behavior. You can always know what you expect by what you do.

If you expect to be a doctor, it will affect your educational plans. If you expect to be a pro athlete, it will affect your workout regimen. If you found out you were terminally ill, it would affect what you consider important. Expectations affect decisions.

Many Christians are living in perpetual defeat because their expectations are locked into time and they have lost sight of eternity.[244]

[Eternity; Time, Perspective on]

Ps. 39:5

THE REFLECTION from the sun is supposed to let us see the brilliance of the moon, which has no light of its own. The moon is dark 24/7. The sun reflects off of the moon so that the beautiful moon is actually the result of the work of the sun.

Now on some days we can see a full moon, on other days we can see a half moon. On yet another day, only a quarter of the moon is visible, and then at times we can't see the moon at all. How come we don't always get the full moon? Because whenever there is less than a full moon, it means the Earth is in the way. The Earth has gotten between a portion of the moon and the sun. The moon's reflection is interrupted as Earth moves in its orbit. Earth simply keeps getting in the way.

Many of us are not able to move forward in our lives, because Earth keeps getting in the way. We are so focused on time, and so foggy about eternity, that the benefits of eternity are not able to penetrate the realities of time and we are stuck with what we see.[245]

[Worldliness, Distraction of]

Rom. 12:2; 1 Cor. 13:12; Heb. 12:1

A MAN died and went to heaven. Saint Peter met him at the gate. The man wanted to know what the value system was in heaven. He said, "Peter, how much is a minute worth up here?" Peter said, "Well, in heaven, a minute is worth a million years." The man excitedly said, "Whoa! Well, then, how much is a nickel worth up here?" Peter said, "Well, up here, a nickel is worth a million dollars." He said, "WHOA! Well, Peter, can I have a nickel?" Peter said, "Yeah, in a minute."

It's all about your value system. It's all about what you're looking at.[246]

[Money, Love of; Perspective]

Ps. 90:12; Matt. 16:26

FLORENCE Chadwick was a world-class swimmer. She had already been successful in swimming the English Channel. Now she wanted to take on the twenty-six-mile trek from Catalina Island, California, to the California mainland, as no woman had ever done that before. So Florence went into the Pacific with a number of boats surrounding her as she made the trip. She swam. Hour after hour, she swam. It was a very foggy night when she tried to do this. As darkness set in, she could barely see her hand in front of her face as she stroked. After swimming fifteen hours and fifty-five minutes, she waved to the boats and said, "I can go no farther. I quit."

They hoisted her out of the water, and they asked her, "Why can't you keep going?" She said, "Because I can't see. The fog is just too thick." After getting on the boat, she discovered that she was only one-half mile from the coast of California. All that hard work, and she was ever so close but she didn't quite make it.

Florence Chadwick decided to try again two months later. She got in the water. It looked bright and sunny, but after about twelve hours, fog set in once more. This time the fog was even worse than before. Again, she couldn't see, but this time she kept swimming. She kept going. This time she not only swam from Catalina Island to the coast, but she swam there and beat the world record by two and a half hours.

When she arrived at the California coastline, she was interviewed and asked, "Last time you tried this, you quit. How did you make it this time?" She said, "This time it was easy because I kept a mental picture of the California coastline in my mind. And as long as I didn't lose sight of where I was going, I could handle the trip getting there."[247]

[Focus; Perspective, Power of; Trials, Patience in]
John 14:2–3; Gal. 5:7

HER NAME was Dorothy. He was the Wizard of Oz. Dorothy had a nice, comfortable life in a place called Kansas. But through a tornado, her life got turned upside down and inside out and she found herself in a magical place—a place unlike she'd ever seen before. But there was a problem; she didn't know how to get back home.

Somebody told her about a Wizard in the city of Oz and told her if she could only get to him, he'd get her home. So she began a tour down a yellow brick road. She picked up three friends along the way because everybody was hurting. She passed on the word, "There's this guy in Oz and I hear that he can fix it all. He can get me home, he can get you a brain, he can get you a heart, and he can get you courage. I hear that there's no need the Wizard can't meet, so I think we need to stop hanging out and we need to follow the yellow brick road."

So they skipped down the road, singing, "We're off to see the Wizard,

the wonderful Wizard of Oz," because he had the answer to their problems and their needs. And even though there were a lot of things trying to get in their way—there were monkeys, the wicked old witch, and all these problems—they were determined to get to him because he had the answers to all of the different dilemmas that they faced.

They finally get to the place called Oz. They finally get behind the curtain and they discover something very interesting. Dorothy's told to click her heels three times because the Wizard told her, "Dorothy, you're already home. You're looking to go where you already are. If you simply click your heels, you'll discover you've been there all the time."

Did you know you're already home? The Bible says that when you got saved, He raised you and seated you next to Jesus Christ in heavenly places. The Bible says when God saved you, He had already taken care of your eternal destiny. You are already home.[248]

[Heavenly Mind-set; Kingdom of God; Victory]
Luke 17:20–21

WHEN I travel, I stay in a hotel, but I never unpack my suitcase. I operate out of my suitcase. I never open up the drawers and put my clothes away. Why? Because I'm not coming to live there. I'm visiting the hotel for a day or two. I don't unpack all my stuff because that room is not my home. Now, I enjoy the hotel room but I just don't get too comfortable.

Whenever I travel out of the country, I don't learn the language of the country. I don't bother to spend mounds of time mastering the language of the culture because I'm not staying there. I may be there for a day or two, or maybe even a week if the country is far enough, but I don't invest much time and energy in language study because I know I'm not going to stay. I am only there for a temporary period of time to do my business. Then I'm going to catch a plane and leave. I am always conscious of my home. I'm always conscious of Dallas, Texas, because that is where my home is.

The problem with believers is that we make this world home. We unpack our bags and we become absorbed in the culture around us, forgetting that this world is not our home.[249]

[Heavenly Mind-set; Worldliness, Distraction of]
John 14:2; 1 John 2:15–17

STICK your finger in a glass of water, pull it out, and see what kind of dent you leave behind. The spot where you placed your finger will quickly fill in. While you may make an impression for a moment, as soon as you are off the scene, that place is going to fill right in.

This is what our lives are like. We are here on this earth for a moment. The impression we make in time is only but for a moment and then time will quickly fill in as we pass on into eternity.[250]

[Life, Brevity of; Time, Perspective on]
Ps. 39:5; James 4:14

SO MANY people today are living empty lives. There was a man who once said he was dying to finish high

school so he could go to college. Then he was dying to finish college so he could start his career. Then he was dying to get married and start a family. Then he was dying for the kids to turn eighteen so they could leave. Then he was dying to retire. And then . . . he was just dying. He never really got around to living because he never connected his temporal state with his eternal state. He never connected time with eternity.[251]

[Eternity; Life, Emptiness of; Time, Perspective on]
Ps. 90:12; John 9:4

ETERNAL SECURITY, ASSURANCE OF

IN ONE of the Superman movies, Superman saves a man from a burning building. He rescues him from the top floor and is carrying him to safety by flying through the skies. The man looks at Superman and then looks down to the ground. "I'm scared, Superman. Look how far down that is."

Superman gives him a great answer. "Now if I delivered you from the burning fire, what makes you think I am going to drop you when I'm carrying you to safety?"

If God has delivered you from a burning hell, what makes you think He will drop you before He safely puts you down?[252]

[Eternal Security, Assurance of; God, Power of; Salvation, Assurance of]
Ps. 23:1–6; John 14:1–4

ETERNITY

WHEN a mother is pregnant with a child for nine months, the time that the baby is growing and developing in the mother's womb is not an end unto itself. It is preparation for something bigger.

Those nine months are the preparation period for the entire lifetime.

Why is a mother concerned about diet and medical checkups? She understands that what she does in the short period of time she incubates new life can affect to a large degree a much greater amount of time in the future. Nobody goes through nine months looking for an unhealthy baby and God doesn't put you here for a lifetime looking for an unhealthy saint.

God created you for eternity and He has given you a slice of time—your "nine months." In this slice of time, His purpose is to prepare you for a reality called eternity.[253]

[Eternal Perspective; Life, Management of; Stewardship]
Eccl. 3:11; Matt. 6:19–20

ETERNITY is never-ending. This concept can be hard to grasp. Think of it this way: If we were to empty the Pacific Ocean, the largest body of water in the world, we'd be left with a hole that's beyond imagination. If we were then to fill that hole with sand and make a pile as high as Mount Everest, we'd be talking about a lot of sand because Mount Everest is the tallest mountain peak in the world. Since the ocean is fairly deep and Mount Everest is fairly high, we'd have a fairly sizable sandpile!

Now, if we had a bird that would take one grain of sand from that sandpile every 100 billion years, how long would it take the bird to finish the sandpile? I don't know that in human language we have such a number. It is probably beyond numerical count.

Whatever that number is, when the bird finishes the last grain of sand, you will have been in eternity your first second.[254]

[Eternal Perspective; Time, Perspective on]
Ps. 90:4; Eccl. 3:11; 2 Peter 3:8

EVANGELISM

DURING election time there are fierce battles waged to win the votes of Americans. Both Democrats and Republicans blitz the media, attempting to get people to vote for their respective party. Spinmeisters and pundits alike do everything they can to let voters know where they stand. Signs, posters, and bumper stickers serve to plaster candidate names in plain view of as many eyes as possible. Whether in the barbershop or in the foyer of the church, the discussion is thick about the pros and cons of each person. There is commitment to a party, to a man, and to a philosophy that is visible by the intent of efforts to persuade people to one side or the other.

As important as the American political process is, it pales in comparison to the spiritual conflict in which we are engaged. Here there are two opposing positions—two opposing kingdoms. Christians are called to be unashamed of our representative, our spokesperson, Jesus Christ. Your vote should be clear and there ought not be any ambiguity over who has it. If you name the name of Jesus Christ, somebody else, other than yourself, ought to know it.

God has called each one of His children to be public spokespersons for the King of Kings and Lord of Lords and for His kingdom, with the goal of winning folks over. We should be definitive in our purpose of calling people out of the kingdom of darkness into the kingdom of light. This process is called *evangelism* or *missions*. Has your voice been heard?[255]

[Evangelism, Responsibility of; Sharing the Gospel]
Acts 1:8; 1 Peter 3:15

WHEN a man is interested in a woman, he always runs the risk that she may reject him or turn him down. When a man strikes up a conversation with a young lady he takes a liking to, he is ultimately after a positive response. He may not get one, but that is his intent.

Evangelism is going after a response from a sinner. It's more than a casual conversation; it's seeking to get a response.[256]

[Repentance; Sharing the Gospel]
Col. 4:6; James 5:20

WHEN I travel, sometimes I have to ask an attendant at the airport to point me in the direction of the gate that will get me to my proper destination. Like the attendant, Christians should be able to point the lost in the direction of the gate that will lead them to the Savior.[257]

[Evangelism, Call of; Gospel; Sharing the Gospel; Witnessing]
1 Cor. 11:1; 1 Peter 3:15

WHEN you drop a letter in the mailbox, it is then delivered to the post office. The mail is then sorted by postal workers who group the mail by zip code so that your letter can reach its proper destination. In the same way, Christians have the job of making sure that others reach their divine destination.

It is hard to help somebody else reach their divine destination if you're lost too.[258]

[Evangelism, Call of; Gospel; Sharing the Gospel; Witnessing, Importance of]
1 Cor. 11:1; 1 Peter 3:15

EVANGELISM, CALL OF

WE ALL grew up in school having to say the Pledge of Allegiance. Day after day, we would begin our school day, saying, "I pledge allegiance to the flag of the United States of America, and to the Republic for which it stands, one Nation, under God, indivisible, with liberty and justice for all." Our schoolteachers would lead us or they would come across the PA system and the whole school would be reciting it together as a daily reminder of where our national commitment lies. We were being reminded at every turn about the awesome privilege it is to enjoy the freedoms of America and to commit ourselves to loyalty to the country.

Before sporting events, "The Star-Spangled Banner" becomes a musical reminder of a commitment to a country and a flag and a constitutional republic that is the essence of this democracy. This is not just done as a routine; it's done as a reminder of what the privileges are. As flawed as some of the aspects of our nation may be, this song and this pledge are a reminder of our commitment to be an American.

In a similar way, Jesus Christ asked His followers to make a pledge of allegiance—a statement of commitment to be both identified and associated with Him, if, in fact, we claim Him as our Savior. He has asked us to make it known that we are Christians, followers of Jesus Christ.

He invites us to come out of the closet and to go public. He invites us to stop being secret-agent Christians and CIA followers. He invites us to be clear and articulate representatives of Him.[259]

[Evangelism, Responsibility of; Witnessing]
Rom. 1:16; 2 Tim. 2:15

EVANGELISM, NEED FOR

THE REASON why we don't do more evangelism is that we've lost our concern for the lost. Most people are not concerned that they are lost. They're like the little boy at Disneyland who was enjoying Mickey Mouse and Donald Duck. He was enjoying the Ferris wheel and the roller coasters. He was having a marvelous time and in the midst of the crowd got separated from his parents. When he got separated from his parents, he didn't know that he was lost because he was having so much fun on the rides.

Satan has so constructed this world order to give you enough distractions so that you don't know you've gotten lost in your spiritual Disneyland. We've got a world full of people who don't know that the fun in this world and all this world is offering them—the movies, the parties, the clubs, the social relationships, the money, and the job—is all a satanic camouflage to keep them from realizing that they have been separated from God. Mankind spends so much time having fun that they don't know that they are lost.

However, the parents of this particular child were looking for him. They knew he was lost at Disneyland. They went to an officer and told security that they couldn't find their child. The security man led the parents to the lost child, who didn't even know he was lost.

God wants to find lost people. We are the security guards to bring lost people into contact with the God who wants to regain fellowship with them. That's our task in evangelism. We are the ones God has chosen to deliver this message.[260]

[Evangelism, Responsibility of; Satan, Strategy of; Witnessing, Importance of]
Luke 19:10; 2 Cor. 4:4

EVANGELISM, RESPONSIBILITY OF

THE PRESS secretary of the White House has one job—to speak on behalf of the head of state, represented in the White House by the president. What he thinks is irrelevant. Whether he agrees with the president is irrelevant. His job is to speak on behalf of the president. Period. Then, he should be ready and willing to take questions. "Be prepared to give an answer to everyone who asks you to give the reason for the hope that you have" (1 Peter 3:15).[261]

[Sharing the Gospel; Witnessing]
Col. 4:6; 1 Peter 3:15

WHAT kind of fireman would I be if I didn't warn you about fire? What kind of policeman would I be if I didn't warn you about criminals? What kind of doctor would I be if I didn't tell you about disease? What kind of pastor would I be if I didn't warn people about hell?

I would rather love folks into heaven, but if I have to scare them there, that will work too.

What would you say about a

fireman who saw your house burning down and who simply said, "It'll burn itself out in a little while"?

What would you say about a policeman who saw juveniles vandalizing your property and simply said, "Well, you know, boys will be boys"?

What would you say about a doctor who, when telling you that you had cancer, simply said, "Take two aspirin and rest"?

You would probably say they are not taking their jobs seriously. And I would not be taking my job seriously if I did not tell people about the place called hell.[262]

[Hell; Judgment Day; Witnessing, Motivation for]
Matt. 28:18–20; 1 Cor. 9:16

SUPPOSE you are a doctor and there was a disease that everybody had. Even though their symptoms were different, everybody who caught the disease died and everybody had it. Let's also say that you, as a skilled physician, came up with the cure.

What would you say about a doctor who knew everybody else was dying without a solution, and wouldn't share the solution he had?

This is the situation for many Christians. The Bible says that the whole world is dead in trespasses and in sin. If we have met Jesus, we've found the cure. How dare we keep it to ourselves! How dare we be on our way to heaven and not care that people are drowning and on their way to a Christless eternity! How can we not make sharing the gospel a priority![263]

[Evangelism; Witnessing, Motivation for]
John 14:6

EVILDOERS

ABOUT four or five years ago in Texas, a pilot left the motor running on a plane and somehow this plane engaged itself. It was without a pilot and took off. It was flying on its own. It stayed in the air for over ninety minutes. Then, the inevitable happened: it ran out of gas, crashed, and was totally destroyed.

For a while, you can fly on your own. For a while, you can take off and be somebody. For a while, you can act like God does not exist. For a while, you can play a little religion, but not be serious about subordinating yourself. And for a while, you can fly.

I know there are atheists, and they look like they're flying. I know, sometimes you look at evil people and you say, How come they can be so evil and can fly so high? I know sometimes you are jealous when you look at folk who have no respect for deity and seem to be flying high. Keep watching, because sooner or later, they will run out of gas, crash, and be destroyed. When you fly your life without God in the pilot's seat of your life, that's what happens. That's why the Bible says don't be envious of the evildoers. Just because they are making money and getting ahead by doing wrong, don't get jealous of them. One can only fly high on their own for a while, but there will come a point where they will run out of gas and will discover in an abrupt way there is a God who is Lord over the universe.[264]

[God's Ways, Unpredictability of; Independence, Consequences of]
Ps. 73:1–28; Jer. 12:1

EVOLUTION

THE BELIEF that nobody plus nothing equals everything.[265]

> Gen. 1:1; Isa. 64:8

IT IS natural for us to assume that if we see a watch, it has a watchmaker. Evolution would have us believe that we could take the contents of a watch, throw them up in the air, and expect them to fall down precisely in the correct order and positioning and automatically start ticking![266]

> [Workmanship]
>
> Job 38:4; Ps. 8:1–9

IF YOU walked into a quiet forest and stumbled upon a ball, the natural assumption would be that someone put it there. You would assume that someone had been there before.

If you stumbled upon a very large ball, like a ball the size of a house, you'd assume that someone really big had to put the ball there.

Suppose that ball is the size of planet Earth. Then someone *really* big would have had to put it there![267]

> [God, Power of; Workmanship]
>
> Rom. 1:20

IF THERE is a design, there is a designer. If there is a painting, there has to be an artist.[268]

> Col. 1:16

F

FAILURE

IN BASKETBALL one of the most important skills for players to have is the ability to rebound. Rebounds occur because a shot somewhere has been missed. There is no need for a rebound unless something has been missed. If a shot was missed, that means a shot was attempted, but somehow something went wrong in the attempt that caused the shot to be missed and therefore we have the need for a rebound.

One reason a shot can be missed is that a player was off in their perspective. They were looking at the goal, but what they saw and what they did didn't match. They were unable to sink the basket. They may have shot too short, too long, too hard, or too soft. There was not a correlation from the eye to the action.

Another reason that shots are missed in basketball games is because the opposing team is in a player's face. It's the job of the opposing team to wave their hands in the shooter's face and obstruct their view. They are supposed to provide a distraction.

Sometimes shots are missed because a player is fouled. A foul means that a player has been illegitimately handled, producing an inability for them to make the shot.

Any coach will want their player to go for a rebound on their missed shot. The player shouldn't walk off the court, quit the game, or throw in the towel because they have missed a shot. A good player will go back up for the ball and retrieve it to shoot again.

In the Bible, there are lots of people who missed shots. Many of God's servants missed their target and had to deal with the consequences of missing their shot. In fact, a study of the Word of God will turn up many people whom God used who were on the rebound.[269]

> [Brokenness, Importance of; Second

Chances; Sin, Victory over]
1 Cor. 15:9; Heb. 11:1–38

FAITH

WE CAN picture faith as a connection between the work of the Holy Spirit and the power at work in our new nature. Faith is a wire that conducts a current called grace that flows from the Spirit so that the new nature receives power.[270]

[Faith, Characteristics of; Grace; Holy Spirit, Power of]
Matt. 17:20; 1 Peter 1:3–5

MOST people don't come to church, stand in front of a pew, and wonder if that pew can hold them up. Most people don't study the pew, evaluate the pew, or wonder about the pew's strength. They just sit down. They exercise faith. The faith is not based on a feeling about the pew, but rather on the confident trust that the pew will hold them up.

The reverse is also true. If a person says they believe that the pew can hold them but they never sit down, they are not exercising faith because they did not act on what they said they believed. Faith is acting like God is telling the truth.[271]

[Faith, Acting in]
James 1:22

MOST things that are powered by batteries have an on and off switch. If the batteries are included when an item is purchased, then it is ready to be used immediately. However, it still must be activated by the switch. As Christians, our switch is faith. When we turn on our faith, we are able to access the power included in us.[272]

[Christian Living, Power; Faith, Characteristics of]
Luke 17:6; 2 Cor. 5:7

FAITH is not equal to feelings. To allow your feelings to guide your faith is like a truck driver being controlled by the cargo in his truck rather than by the wheel that he is steering. It is the wheel that controls the cargo, not the cargo that controls the wheel.[273]

[Faith, versus Feelings; Holy Spirit, Guidance]
Titus 1:15

ONE time I was battling a cold and couldn't shake it. I called my doctor, told him my symptoms, and he told me I didn't need to come in. He was going to call in a prescription for me. He told me what medicine he was prescribing and how he wanted me to take it.

Now, a number of things went into motion. First of all, I had to believe that I was talking to the person I thought I was talking to, because I couldn't see him. It was just a conversation over the phone. So I had to listen to his voice. I listened to his voice and he told me how to fix my problem. Now, I could've lain in bed and meditated. I could have believed him, but stayed in my bed thinking about how good it was that I had a doctor who understood my problem and provided me with a solution. I could have lain there thinking how great it was that I had a solution, but all that lying around and thinking about the good words that the good doctor shared with me wouldn't make me better. It may have given me warm fuzzies because he talked to me, but I'd still be sick as a dog.

Guess what I had to do. I had to get up, get in my car, drive to Walgreens, and say to the pharmacist, "Do you have a prescription with my name on it?" There's a lot of medicine in there, but I needed something with my name on it. I needed something that wasn't generic but personal to me. The doctor told me it was there, and because I believed his word I acted on it and went to Walgreens.

Taking this illustration further, I could have just received the medicine and looked at it. I could have gazed at it and made sure that it looked medicinally acceptable to me. But, I'd still be sick as a dog. The doctor's instructions were not for me just to drive to Walgreens and get emotionally fixated on the look of the medicine. He told me to take it. By following his instructions to the T, my faith was matching up with my works and I began to feel much better.

A lot of us are spiritually sick and every week we come to hear what the Doctor's got to say. Some of us stop there and just think about how good it was to talk to Him. Some of us leave church feeling good about how great the prescription sounds, but still sick as a spiritual dog because we don't take it and ingest it by acting on it. Therefore, we're not transformed.[274]

[Faith, Acting in]
James 1:22; 2:26

CEMENT, in order to become concrete, must be mixed with sand and water. If bags of cement in a store are never stirred in with water, that cement will never become concrete. Water and sand must be married if you want to get something that is cementable. In order for God to make your life concrete, you are going to have to learn to mix it. You've got to take faith, mix it with works, and watch God lay some concrete in your life.[275]

[Faith, Acting in]
Gal. 5:6; Eph. 2:10; 2:26

FAITH, ACTING IN

A BLIND girl, one day, was caught in a fire on the tenth floor of a building. She could make her way to a window, but she couldn't see anything. She felt the heat and smelled the smoke of the fire. Then she heard a fireman yell, "Jump, jump!"

She said, "I'm scared to jump. I can't see."

The fireman said, "If you don't jump, you're going to die. Take the risk, and jump."

It's bad enough to jump from ten stories high, but to jump when you can't see where you're jumping— that's terror. In the midst of the chaos and confusion, she heard another voice, "Darling, jump, I've got you." She smiled and said, "Okay, Daddy, I'll jump."

Jesus Christ is inviting us to jump. He knows we're nervous, but just jump. He knows you're scared, but just jump. Remember, we're talking about your Daddy. We're talking about Somebody you know. You've seen what He can do.[276]

[Jesus, Relationship with; Risk]
Matt. 14:22–33

A MAN slid over the side of a cliff and was able to grab a branch at the last second. He hung dangling over the precipice, hundreds of feet from the ground below. He screamed out with a loud voice,

"Help me! Somebody help me!"

A voice came out of the sky, "Do you believe that I can help you?"

The man responded, "Yes, I believe. Please help me!"

The voice came out of the sky again, "Do you believe that I have the power to help you?"

"Yes, I believe! I believe! Please help me!"

"Do you believe I love you enough to help you?"

"Yes, I know you love me. Please, oh please, HELP ME!"

"Because you believe, I will help you. Now let go."

After a brief silence, the man said, "Is there anybody else up there?"[277]

[Double-mindedness; Risk]

Matt. 19:16–22; Luke 6:46; James 1:6

FAITH, CHARACTERISTICS OF

FAITH has to have substance. If after a child has lost a tooth, their parent goes to bed, saying, "I am trusting the tooth fairy to put a dollar under my son's pillow," that's just wasted conversation. There's no such thing as a tooth fairy. There's no substance. In order for faith to do something, it must be based on something. Christians are told to have faith in the Word of God.[278]

[Bible, Authority of; Word of God]

Ps. 119:105; 2 Tim. 3:16

IN A farming community, it hadn't rained in a long time, and things were getting desperate. The ministers decided they were going to call a prayer meeting. They said, "Look, we want the whole town to come to the prayer meeting and bring their religious sym-

bols." So the whole town showed up for the prayer meeting and people brought crosses, they brought their Bibles, the Catholics brought their rosaries, and they all cried out to God. They finished the prayer meeting. No rain was in sight. They all went home.

The next day though, in the town square where they had had the meeting, there was a little boy. "Oh, God, we need rain. God, show Your power, and give us rain." The day before, with all the preachers and all the religious symbols, calling on God, no rain. The little boy shows up the next day by himself in the town square, and as he was praying, the sky got darker. As he was praying, rumbling occurred. As he was praying, the shower hit, and it was pouring down rain.

What was it about this little boy? He said the same things that all the people said the day before. The day before they had all the preachers, they had all the ministers; they even brought their religious symbols. But the day the young boy came, when the clouds got dark, he lifted up the symbol that he brought: an umbrella. He expected it to rain.

When you anticipate rain, you take an umbrella. When a man tells you it's going to rain, when a meteorologist says it's going to storm today, most people will get their umbrellas because they believe his word. Meteorologists are wrong half the time and we still take them at their word. Why is it, when it comes to God, who is never wrong, we hesitate to believe and act on His Word?[279]

[Faith, Acting in; Trust in God]

Mark 10:15; James 2:26

FAITH, DISTORTION OF

WHEN you place a spoon in a glass of water that's only two-thirds full, it appears that the spoon is bent or broken. This is called refraction. We know that the spoon is neither bent nor broken, it simply looks that way because of the light. As the light passes through the water, a distortion is created.

The world in which we are now living has created a refraction. It has created a distorted view of life, so that people are looking at life and living life in a way that the secular culture has defined it, actually creating a refracted view of reality. In fact, if you look at the world order closely, it will make you think your faith is broken. But it is not that your faith is broken, it is the distorted view of this world order being applied to your faith.[280]

[Faith; Worldliness, Distraction of]
1 Cor. 13:12; Col. 3:2

FAITH, SIZE OF

A BUSINESSMAN had to travel to a small town for a meeting and invited his wife to come with him. She was excited about the trip until she learned her husband was going to be flown to the small town in a twin-engine Cessna plane.

"Honey, I've decided not to go."
"What! Why not?"
"I am not going on a little-bitty, twin-engine Cessna."

Her husband smiled and knowingly said, "Honey, your faith is too small."

She quipped, "No, the plane is too small."

The businessman really wanted his wife to go with him, so he canceled the Cessna and booked travel on a major airline. His wife went with him because, as she put it, "her faith grew because the size of the plane grew."

The object of her faith determined how much faith she decided to have.[281]

[Trust in God]
Ps, 31:6; Prov. 3:5

THERE was a man one day whose wife was very ill. It was in the frontier days and he had to get to a place that had medicine to save his wife's life. The only problem was that it was wintertime and in order to get to the person with the medicine, he had to cross a lake. The lake had been iced over. His wife's life depended upon it, so he had to get up and cross this cold lake that had now been covered with ice. He was terrified. He was concerned that the ice would break. Scared to death but spurned on by love for his wife, he got down on his hands and knees and inched along, ever so carefully.

All of a sudden, he felt a rumbling on the ice. He was even more terrified. Maybe the ice was cracking. The rumbling got louder. It became thunderous. The man was living in terror. But as the noise got closer, he looked up behind him and saw a man driving a team of horses across the ice. The horses pulled a carriage that was loaded with a bunch of boxes and it just went thundering across the ice. All of a sudden, the man stood up, started walking, and then running. All of a sudden, this man that was full of fear became a man full of confidence. He learned something about the ice. He learned that if it could hold a team of horses thundering across it, it could certainly hold him.

If you want to have more confidence in God, then hang around somebody who's riding with God with a team of horses so that you'll know He can carry you with whatever you're facing. Find somebody who's been where you are and has experienced God's deliverance. Their story of faith will encourage you.[282]

[Encouragement]

1 Cor. 11:1

FAITH, VERSUS FEELINGS

WE CAN'T rely on how we feel. Our feelings, thoughts, and emotions go up and down.

If you go to a scary movie, you can know that the monster is not real and still feel afraid. You can still be scared because the moviemakers manipulate your mind so that you begin to feel a reality that is not truly there.

You may know it's not real, but you feel like it's real, so therefore you get scared. Feelings have no intellect. All they can do is react. Having faith is not based on how one feels.[283]

[Emotions; Faith, Characteristics of]

FAITHFULNESS

SUPPOSE a person went to their boss and said, "Boss, I know I've been doing a sloppy job, but the reason I've been doing a sloppy job is because you haven't given me a promotion. If you would promote me, I wouldn't do a sloppy job. So I tell you what you do, Mr. Boss—you give me that promotion and then you'll see how I can really work!"

Not only would that person not receive a promotion, they will be go-

ing job hunting. Why? Because that's not how it works. Christians many times want to give God slop and ask God for blessings. It doesn't work. God wants faithful people—people He can count on.[284]

[Christian Living, Commitment; Perseverance]

Gal. 6:9; Heb. 12:1

IN 1980, a young lady entered the Boston Marathon. She started the race looking great. And as the runners approached the finish line, she was leading the pack by a country mile, breaking all kinds of records. The crowd applauded as she crossed the finish line and was crowned champion.

It was suspicious, however, that a woman who had never won a marathon before could win the Boston Marathon—especially by a country mile. Lo and behold, when they examined the situation, the girl started the race but then left the run and got on the subway, rode the subway for sixteen miles, got off the subway, got back onto the route, and crossed the finish line first! When her cheating was discovered, she was, of course, disqualified from the race.

Some of us have started living the Christian life but have jumped on the subway and we want to cross the finish line with God saying, "Well done, My good and faithful servant." But when He opens the books and checks the record, He's going to know that you left the field. He's going to see that you didn't keep on until the end, that you didn't remain an alien and a stranger, and He's going to say, "You lose the medal, because you didn't faithfully follow the rules."[285]

[Carnal Christians; Judgment Day;
Perseverance]
1 Cor. 9:24; Gal. 5:7

THERE are some wives who get an anniversary present every year. Their husband comes home from work, takes his wife out to dinner, gives her a great gift, and makes a to-do about that special day. But that's it. The wife doesn't hear from him for the rest of the year.

The husband doesn't regularly do any dinners, no dating, or romances, but she can count on it—on the next anniversary, he's going to be there with a great present and a nice dinner and he's going to wine and dine her, yet practically say, "Okay, love you! I will see you again next year."

Any woman I know would gladly trade in an annual anniversary day for a consistent 364 days a year that were faithful and consistent and full of communication, even if it only included McDonald's. She's looking for something ongoing rather than just one big thing a year.

Some of us get happy because we do one big thing for God a year.

We say, "Boy, on November 26, I did a biggie for God. I know heaven was applauding because I did a whopper for God!"

We've got those two or three things a year we do for God. At the judgment seat, God is not going to want to know only about November 26. He's going to want to know about what you did every day over the course of your life.

He's going to ask you, "Did you live a life of faithfulness to Me?"

God is not concerned about the occasional biggies you do. He's con-cerned about the consistent obedience that you give. He wants to know whether or not we can be faithful. The definition of faithfulness is consistently giving God your best in what He calls you to do.[286]

[Christian Living; Judgment Day;
Life, Management of]
1 Cor. 9:24; Eph. 2:8–10

FALSE RELIGION

THE ESSENCE of false religion is a Christian being involved in religious activity while being void of spiritual intimacy. It is exemplified by a person having a ritual of religion without a relationship with God.[287]

[Carnal Christians; Intimacy,
with God]
Matt. 23:27–28; 2 Tim. 3:1–5

RELIGION VOID of a relationship will leave you spiritually hungry. Like drinking saltwater, the more you drink, the thirstier you get.[288]

[Intimacy, Importance of; Jesus,
Relationship with]
John 4:13–14

RELIGION devoid of a relationship is like a pacifier that a baby works hard to suck on, but from which no real nutrition flows.[289]

ON ONE occasion, I walked into a hotel lobby and saw a bowl of fruit set out for guests. I decided to grab an apple. I bit into it only to discover that it wasn't real. It was wax. It was quite embarrassing to bite into a wax apple thinking that it was real and then not know quite what to do with it! Do you put it back with teeth marks on it? Do you steal it and take it with you?

I had mistaken something artificial for something that was real. It's possible to have artificial church that looks real. It's possible to be an artificial Christian but look real.[290]

[Christian Living, Authenticity]
2 Tim. 3:1–5; 2 Peter 2:1

FAMILY

PLATO, the great philosopher, was right when he said, "The saga of a nation is the saga of its families written large."[291]

Prov. 22:6

FAMILY, OF GOD

YOU'VE been called into something staggering. If Bill Gates were to adopt a child, that would be staggering. If the president of the United States were to adopt a child, the implications of that are staggering.

Because we've been adopted into the family of God, the implications are beyond comprehension.[292]

[Salvation, Benefits of]
Rom. 8:17; Gal. 4:7

FASTING, POWER OF

IF YOU'VE ever watched the high jumpers in the Olympics, you will realize that there are two kinds. The regular high jumpers jump about seven feet. They run and throw their backs over the bar. But there is another kind of high jumper. They are called pole-vaulters. They jump about eighteen feet. They back up. They look down the runway. But they have that pole in their hand. They start running down the track, stick the pole in a hole in the ground, put all of their weight on that pole, and use the pole to lift them to a level that they could not lift themselves on their own.

Some of us have mountains. There is a crossbar and we have tried to high-jump it in the flesh. We have seen that mountain and we have backed up. We have said, "Mountain, you are not going to keep me down any longer." We grit our teeth with the power of positive thinking, New Year's resolutions, and resolves not to repeat our mistakes. We take off and we jump two feet when there is an eighteen-foot bar.

Some of us have been jumping that same two feet for fifty years and the bar is still up there. In fact, it keeps going higher every year. Maybe what you need is a pole vault. You need something that you can lean on when you get to your problem so that you can go higher than you could ever lift yourself. Maybe you need a pole that will help you jump over the mountain. The pole vault for the bars in your life are fasting and prayer.[293]

[Overcoming, Power of; Power, Accessing; Prayer, Deliverance through]
Est. 4:16; Luke 5:35

FATHER GOD

MY KIDS can always get through to me. In the busiest of times, they can still get through to me because I'm their father. I've told my assistant that whenever my family calls, put them through. I may not be able to talk to them long each time; I may even have to call them back. But I want them to know that even thousands of church members don't get in the way of me being their father.

Here is some good news. Just because God is God of the universe, that doesn't get in the way of Him being our Father. Even though He's got millions and millions of kids that He must govern, He's still Daddy. As our Father, God makes Himself available to us.[294]

> [Intimacy, with God; Prayer, Access in]
> Rom. 8:15

FATHERS

SATELLITES are often used to show us where the enemy is located. They provide pictures and perspectives so that we are kept from ambushes and traps. They provide information critical for being victorious in war. Fathers are supposed to be like satellites, providing a perspective for their kids in order to keep them from being ambushed in illegitimate relationships.[295]

> [Parenting]
> Deut. 6:6–9; Eph. 6:4

FEAR

MOST of us have experienced our children's dependence on us to face their fears when they have nightmares or when it's thundering and lightning during a storm. They'll wake up, scream, and jump out of their bed. They will walk through the valley of their bedroom, down the valley of the hall, to the valley of your room. They jump in your bed, because what they need is somebody to be with them.

Your hugging them doesn't stop the rain, the thunder, or the lightning, but it changes how they face it. They'll fall asleep in your arms. The fear that they have alone, they no longer have, because Mama or Daddy holds them. You help them face their fears in the midst of their struggles. This is exactly what the heavenly Father does for us when we face our own fears and insecurities.[296]

> [God's Presence]
> Ps. 23:4; Isa. 66:13

FELLOWSHIP

ALONG the California coastline, there are some of the largest living organisms in the world—redwood trees. The redwoods are three hundred feet high. Some of them are forty feet around. Some of them have been there for 250 years. They are a magnificent sight. The trees are so massive because they only grow in groves and their roots intertwine underneath the ground. No intertwining, no growth. No connectedness, no growth.[297]

> [Body of Christ; Christian Living, Spiritual Growth; Church]
> Acts 2:42–47; 1 Cor. 1:10

A FAKE I.D. is normally used to give the impression that a young person is older than they really are. Many Christians come to church with a fake I.D., giving the impression that all is well when all is not. We show an I.D. of harmony when our lives are really in discord. We show an I.D. of having it all together when we don't even know where all the parts have gone. However, God saved us for authentic relationships and fellowship with one another.[298]

> [Carnal Christians; Christian Living, Authenticity]
> Matt. 23:28

SUNDAY morning worship for many could be equated with attending a masquerade party where we put on a spiritual mask to hide the turmoil in our souls. We show up to the party but no one really gets to know who we are.[299]

> [Christian Living, Authenticity]
> Rom. 3:23

KOINONIA, biblical fellowship, concerns itself not with cookies and punch in a fellowship hall, or social gatherings where you "high-five it." Authentic biblical fellowship means the mutual sharing of the life of Christ between His family members.[300]

[Church]

Acts 2:42–47; Heb. 10:24–25

ANTHILLS are made when a bunch of insignificant creatures get together. If you ever mistakenly step on an anthill without shoes, their fellowship will make an impact on you. One ant bite might sting a little. Most folks can handle that. But if a person messes with the whole family in an anthill, those ants will gather around your foot and serve notice that you are unwelcome in their house.

One ant can't create that kind of impact by itself. Gathered together, their combined effect is much greater. Not only do they ward off intruders together, they will also work together to rebuild in a day and a half what was destroyed.[301]

[Body of Christ; Intimacy, Power of]

Eccl. 4:12

ONE of the ways used these days to cut down on traffic is the creation and use of HOV lanes—lanes for high occupancy vehicles, which are vehicles with more than one person in them. The idea is to discourage so many cars with only one passenger. This means that if you are not alone in your car, you can travel down an HOV lane and you will get there faster because you are not slowed down by a lot of individual people driving individual vehicles to the same location. This is like driving down the highway in koinonia—fellowshipping on your way to work.

On the highway to heaven, God wants you to travel down a high occupancy vehicle lane and He wants to be the other person in the car. On the highway to heaven, He wants there to be an intimate, meaningful connectedness or fellowship between you and Him as you are on your way to glory. He wants you to enjoy the trip. He doesn't want you to despise the journey.[302]

[Intimacy, with God; Jesus, Relationship with]

Lev. 26:12; 2 Cor. 6:16

FELLOWSHIP, MAINTAINING PROPER

A LITTLE boy tripped and fell outside and one of his hands fell in the mud. His mother said to him, "Go wash your hands."

He went in the bathroom and came out a few minutes later. He now had two dirty hands. His mother said, "I thought I told you to wash your hands!"

He said, "I did. I took my clean hand and wiped my dirty hand."

The dirt rubs off. If you want to be clean, hang out with clean folks.[303]

[Relationships; Sin, Stain of]

1 Cor. 15:33; 2 Cor. 7:1

FELLOWSHIP, PROOF OF

I RAN into a lady whom I knew but hadn't seen in an extended period of time. I asked her, "How far along are you?" referring to an apparent pregnancy.

She said, "I'm not pregnant."

That was one of my more embarrassing moments. Sometimes things look like they are happening, when really, there is not much going on.

You can go to church and look the part. You can look spiritually pregnant when there's really nothing on the inside going on. A Christian is not known by how well they act the part. They aren't known by how well they shout or how much they know or how often they are seen carrying a Bible under their arms. A Christian is not known by how much they say "hallelujah" or "amen" or "praise the Lord." A Christian is not known by how much "Christian-ese" they know or how big their smile is. We know Christians because they have faith in Jesus Christ and because they love others.[304]

[Christian, Definition of; Love]
John 13:35; 1 John 4:7

EVERYONE has had either a cold or the flu. Everyone is familiar with the feeling of a cold coming on. Stuffiness begins to coagulate within your system. You begin to feel a little weak, or perhaps even feverish. A runny nose ensues, followed by stopped-up nostrils, and it becomes clear that you are entering into a time of sickness. In fact, this phenomenon even has its own season designated. It's called "flu season."

Certain types of weather can bring it on or, sometimes, a weakened immune system. One thing is pretty clear, however: when you have a cold, you know it. Folks who get close to you know it. You can see the look of a cold or flu victim on their face. You can see the drowsiness of the eyes. You can hear the coughing or the sneezing or the perpetual use of the handkerchief designed to address some of the more unpleasant aspects of having a cold or the flu.

It's pretty impossible to have a cold or the flu and not have symptoms. If you've got a cold or the flu, it's going to show up somewhere, somehow. It's pretty impossible too to have fellowship with God and it not show up. Just like the cold or flu, it has its symptoms. It is fairly easy to recognize.[305]

[Christian Living, New Life; Sanctification]
Matt. 12:33

FIRST LOVE

I'M A Tabasco man. Anytime I eat virtually anything, I put Tabasco on it. When I go places, I enjoy discovering new kinds of hot sauce. I love fire in my food. The absence of fire for me means a bland dish. It's just there.

Jesus loves fire. He wants a little hot sauce on the relationship that we cultivate with Him. He doesn't want the basic Christian meal offering of duty and service. He wants my passionate, pleasurable pursuit of Him.[306]

[Jesus, Relationship with; Passion]
Matt. 22:37–40; Mark 12:30

ONCE I was flying from Atlanta back to Dallas and had to catch flight number 74. There is a famous soul food place in Atlanta called Pascal's, and this place is famous for its fried chicken. Pascal's has many booths in the Atlanta airport. So as I was at the airport waiting on my flight, the smell from Pascal's was calling my name. I went over and ordered two thighs and a biscuit. Just as I sat down to eat my chicken, I heard the last call for my flight, flight number 74 to Dallas.

I was on the horns of a dilemma.

Piping-hot chicken was calling my name. Flight number 74 was calling my name. Both of them were screaming in my ears. I had to decide if I would risk missing my flight to eat my chicken, or if I would leave my too-hot-to-eat chicken and catch my flight. I decided to take my chicken on the flight.

God is not saying to give up the "chicken" of religion. He's saying don't miss the flight of first love. Don't let what you do for God get in the way of your relationship with God. Don't mix, or miss, the connection.[307]

[Jesus, Relationship with; Priorities]
Rev. 2:4

FLESH

THE FLESH is like a defensive line set up in football to stop the offensive movement of the team with the ball. When you accepted Christ, God handed you the football and told you to score touchdowns. The flesh is a defensive line trying to stop your progress, to kill your drive, to stop you from scoring, and to keep you stuck in the same place on the field all game long. The flesh operates to keep you out of the red zone so you can't even score a field goal. The job of the flesh is to block your spiritual progress.[308]

[Flesh, Nature of; Spiritual Maturity, Growth]
Gal. 5:1; Col. 3:7–8; Heb. 10:26–30

FLESH, CONTROLLING THE

A LONG time ago, a movie came out called *The Blob*. This cosmic Jell-O had come down from space, fell into a little crater, and cracked open. An old man came and had a little stick in his hand and was playing with it, and it ran up on his arm and began to consume him. The more he tried to shake it off, the more it consumed him. Some folk found him and rushed him into a hospital room. The doctors couldn't figure out what was wrong and the professionals tried to fix it. When they left the room for a few moments and came back in, the man had been totally consumed by the Blob. In fact, when the doctor touched it, the Blob consumed the doctor too. The Blob then rolled outside of the hospital and consumed everything and everybody in its path.

By the time the movie comes to an end, the Blob is the size of a mountain. Throughout the movie, people had tried everything they could to get rid of the Blob. They'd shot at it. They'd tried to cut it. In fact, it absorbed some of the folk trying to kill it. But at the end of the movie, they discovered one little thing. The Blob could not handle cold. It could deal with anything else, but it couldn't handle cold. Someone noticed that when they sprayed something cold on it, the Blob would back up. They put some more cold stuff on it, and it backed up some more. Whenever they stopped putting the cold on it, it would come forward again, but when they sprayed something cold on it, it would back up.

They figured they couldn't get rid of it completely, but they could render it incapable of doing more damage. So what they ended up doing was freezing it, putting it in a crate, attaching the crate to an airplane, and flying it to Alaska. They could not destroy it, but they could change its environment so that it was rendered inactive. Not only did they remove the Blob, but they also transferred it to a new environment where it was so cold that the Blob could not express itself again.

When Jesus saved you, He moved you from the projects to the penthouse. He put you in a brand-new environment and the Blob of your flesh can't handle this new environment.[309]

[New Life in Christ; Salvation, Benefits of; Sanctification; Sin, Victory over]
Acts 3:19; 2 Cor. 5:17

FLESH, NATURE OF

IT'S BEEN awhile now, but a popular television show aired years ago called *Diff'rent Strokes*. It was a rather funny show. It was about two little boys named Arnold and Willis. The boys' mother had been the maid for a man named Mr. Drummond, but she died. Not wanting those boys to be left to meander and wander in the projects, he adopted them and brought them to live in his penthouse.

The whole show revolved around these two boys from the projects trying to learn how to live in the penthouse. Much comedy surrounded them bringing old ways into a new environment. There was great entertainment in seeing Mr. Drummond try to educate these young men in the finer things of their new environment. The question of the show was whether or not you could take boys out of the projects, put them in the penthouse, and expect them to leave the projects behind. The whole show was about how difficult it is for people to get rid of old patterns once they have been established.

When God found you and me, we were in the spiritual projects. He has now seated us in heavenly places. We are in the penthouse, but many of us have drug along with us a lot of the old patterns from the old neighborhood. Those patterns are called *the flesh* in the Bible. The flesh is not merely the body, but it is the body with its old patterns.[310]

[Flesh; New Life in Christ; Sin Nature, Residue of; Worldliness, Distraction of]
Rom. 5:12; 8:12–17; Heb. 12:1

FLESH, WALKING IN

BEFORE a balloon is filled with air or helium, it has no life. However, once helium fills a balloon it has the potential to fly high. Most of the time when we go to buy balloons at a carnival or a circus, we look for the ones that are filled with helium and ready for purchase. Those balloons are not flying around because the vendor, to keep them available for sale, ties them down. They will be tied to something intended to keep them on the ground.

Many Christians are aware of the power of the Spirit they have inside but are tied down. They can't fly high because they are tied down. Walking in the flesh keeps them from experiencing their potential to fly high.[311]

[Holy Spirit, Power of; Sin Nature, Residue of; Worldliness, Distraction of]
Mark 4:18–19; Heb. 11:1; James 1:14

YOU GO to any cemetery and among the dead you will discover the living—people who work there who take care of the grounds. These are living people operating among the dead. They are facilitating death even though they are very much alive. Unfortunately, today, many Christians who are alive are living in spiritual cemeteries. They are living among the dead. Of all the things the Bible promises, very few of them are very real to these people because they are finding it difficult to get out of the graveyard of their circumstances.[312]

[Sin Nature, Residue of; Worldliness, Distraction of]
Prov. 5:22; Rom. 6:11–14

FOCUS

SWEET Georgia Brown is a soul food restaurant in the Dallas area that serves good food. It would be a mistake if you were on a diet to spend a lot of time thinking about Sweet Georgia Brown because you'd be thinking about the source of your problem.

Most of us focus on the sins we are trying to overcome. We focus on what's wrong, but focusing on what's wrong is only going to refuel us in the wrong direction. The Devil wants us to focus on ourselves and our problems instead of focusing on Christ.[313]

[Satan, Strategy of; Temptation]
Heb. 12:2

MANY people have been on an airplane when turbulence occurs and the plane may have seemed out of control for a bit. If that's ever happened to you, you probably got a little nervous. Your seat belt may have already been buckled but you tightened it. You may have grabbed on to the armrest a little tighter. You may have felt a bit unsettled because you were suspended in air with nowhere to go. You may have started reading the same line over and over again in your book because you were destabilized by the turbulence.

But then you probably also know what it is to have the captain come over the loudspeaker and say, "We've run into some choppy air, so we're going to adjust our altitude and hopefully find some smoother air."

Now, your problem will not have disappeared. The turbulence is still there, but you will probably take a deep breath, relax, read, and feel much more at ease because you have moved from a focus on the turbulence to a focus on the pilot.[314]

[Fear; God's Presence]
Ps. 23:4; Isa. 66:13

ONE of the ways people train dogs is through the use of temptation. The trainer will take a piece of red meat and throw it in front of the dog. The first time that dog sees the red meat, he'll probably go after it because that's his nature. The second time, the trainer will throw out a piece of meat but then restrain the dog, telling the dog to "stay," and making the dog redirect his attention to the trainer before rewarding him with the meat. The trainer will continue to tempt the dog with meat while retraining him and making him give his attention to the trainer while repeating, "STAY!"

Eventually, the dog will learn that if he focuses on the trainer or the master, and gives him his attention, the trainer will reward him. The dog will learn to handle the presence of the meat because the meat is no longer the focus.

The Devil knows that we're not focused on the Master, so he continues to put temptations in front of us to keep us distracted. If we would only learn to focus on the Master, we would then be able to handle the temptations that are so often put before us.[315]

[Satan, Strategy of; Temptation, Nature of; Worldliness, Distraction of]
Rom. 6:12; 7:21–25; 1 Cor. 10:13

MOST of us are looking to our own human resources to be victorious, successful, and righteous, and we're really looking hard. Newsflash: We are looking at the wrong thing.

No one goes out to the doughnut shop just to look at the doughnuts. You go to the doughnut store to EAT donuts! One thing is guaranteed though—if you do go to the doughnut shop to look at donuts, you will end up eating them. Why? Because the more you stare at it, the more you are going to want it.

Satan's goal is to get us focused on our sin, but focusing on our sin can't help us. We have to focus on something else, someone else, who can help us overcome that sin.[316]

[Satan, Strategy of; Sin, Dealing with; Temptation]
Rom. 7:21–25; Heb. 12:2

A MAN wanted to learn to play golf and took a trip to the driving range to practice his desired hobby. That little white ball was really doing a number on the newbie and making him quite embarrassed. Six times in a row the first-timer swung and missed the ball. He thought to himself, "Now, this game provides a lot of exercise, but I don't have any idea what that white ball is here for."

A lot of us are involved in endless activity, not hitting a thing, because we are not living with focus. We are busy and getting a lot of exercise moving through life, but our lives are not coming into contact with the goals God has for us.[317]

[Christian Living, Purpose; Life, Management of]
Ps. 127:2; Matt. 13:22

FOCUS, ON THE RACE

AT THE Good Will Games in Edmonton, Canada, the Jamaican team was participating in the four-by-one hundred meter relay. The third leg for the Jamaican team had a friend who was competing in another event nearby. While the sprinter was waiting for the baton, he looked up for a moment to try to catch his friend doing his event. In the next moment, the guy running the second leg of the race came up to him with the baton and ran into him. Needless to say, the race was over for Jamaica because of the lack of focus of one of the team members. He wasn't focusing on his race. He was looking at somebody else's. Stop looking at everybody else's race, and run your own race.[318]

[Gossip; Worldliness, Distraction of]
1 Cor. 9:24; Gal. 5:7

IN THE Olympics, one of the games involves a bunch of guys who row boats. They row their boats with their backs to the finish line. They can't see the finish line. But at the front of the boat is the cockswain, a guy with a horn. He sits at the front of the boat, shouting instructions. "Pull, Pull! Row, Row!"

The guys in the boat keep their eyes fixed on the cockswain while they row. While they can't see where they are going, he can. So, they fix their eyes on him. The cockswain gives them a cadence and keeps them on track.

If you don't know where you're

headed, put your eyes on Jesus because He knows where your finish line is. He knows how to get you in the start of the race and take you to the finish line.[319]

[Focus]

Heb. 3:1; 12:2

FORGIVENESS

TWO CARS were involved in an accident. One of the drivers had insurance; the other didn't. The driver without insurance also did not have a job, and his license was expired. The insured driver had a choice after he left the scene of the accident. He could live for the rest of his life sour about his messed-up bumper, or he could use his insurance to get his car fixed. He chose to get his car fixed rather than be held hostage by someone else's lack of insurance.

When we sin, we must lay it before God and admit our sin. If someone has sinned against us, we must relieve them of the sin so that we can move on.[320]

[Sin, Confession of]

Matt. 5:23–24; Col. 3:13; 1 John 1:9

ONE of the things I loved to do when I was in elementary school was to write on the blackboard. Whenever the teacher wanted a volunteer to write on the blackboard, I would regularly raise my hand. One of the beautiful things about the blackboard was if you made a mistake with the chalk, there was always the eraser to rid yourself of the error. Forgiveness works the same way. It is the cancellation of something. It is the deletion of an error. It is the ability to erase a mistake and start over again.[321]

[Forgiveness, of Sin; Second Chances]

Ps. 103:12; Prov. 28:13; 1 John 1:9

WE'VE all seen, even if just in a picture, a bell in a bell tower. These hang up high and have a rope attached to them. To ring the bell, the rope must be pulled down a few times. There is a constant pulling and constant ringing of the bell. Now, after the pulling is over and the person pulling the rope lets go, the bell will keep swinging. The bell does not stop swinging just because the rope is not being pulled anymore. It will swing for a while before it slows down and eventually stops.

Forgiveness is the act of letting the bell rope go. It means that you choose to no longer hold the rope. A lack of forgiveness is when you constantly pull the rope. Each ring of the bell reminds us of each wrong inflicted on us by another. Our constant pulling of the rope keeps the wrongdoings on our minds. Now, if we choose to let go by a decision of the will, our emotions will still hear the bell for a little while. But, if you let the rope go and leave it alone, after awhile, the bell will slow down until it stops.

Don't let the fact of the feelings of the pain get in the way of your forgiveness. You are responsible for not constantly ringing the bell. If you don't pick up the rope, the sound will die down. Sometimes forgiveness is hard because we've been ringing the bell for so long that we don't know how life is without the bell. Sometimes we leave the bell alone for a while but then we pick up the rope and we start all over again.[322]

[Freedom]

Luke 17:3–4; Eph. 4:32; Col. 3:13

THERE'S hardly a person in this world who doesn't have a scar on their soul. God's only solution for a hurt heart is forgiveness.

A gentleman owed his pastor eight thousand dollars. The pastor had offered to help the man out of a jam. Over time, it became obvious that the man was not going to pay the pastor back. Every time the pastor saw the man, he also saw his lost eight thousand dollars.

What made it worse was the fact that the man had not yet bothered to offer an explanation as to why he hadn't paid up. After many weeks, the man came to his pastor and offered his sincere apologies. He was not going to be able to pay his debt. The pastor made a decision in that instant. He chose to forgive the man. He released him from the debt he owed and promised never to raise the subject of the debt again.

In releasing his debtor, the pastor also released himself from the frustration, anger, and hurt of being owed a debt. He didn't have to look at the man from the pulpit and think of the debt, because it had been forgiven.[323]

[Debt, Burden of; Restoration]
Luke 17:4; Col. 3:13; Eph. 4:32

FORGIVENESS, FROM GOD

I LOVE that Motel 6 commercial. It says, "We're gonna leave the light on for you." God's light of forgiveness is always on, welcoming those sinners home who want to repent and ask His forgiveness.[324]

[God's Goodness]
Luke 15:11–32; 1 John 1:9

IN 1929, a man named George Wilson robbed a mail carrier and killed him. He was sentenced to die but received a presidential pardon. To the shock of the Oval Office, he rejected the pardon. The president of the United States had set him free. George Wilson said no. The case went to the Supreme Court and the issue was simply this: If the president of the United States gives you a pardon, aren't you pardoned? Can you reject a pardon given by a sovereign? Chief Justice Marshall rendered the decision. It simply read: "A pardon rejected is no pardon at all. Unless the recipient of the pardon accepts the pardon, then the pardon cannot be applied." A pardon has two sides—the offeror and the offeree. Unless the offeree accepts the offer from the offeror, then the pardon cannot be mandated. On the cross, the eternal God, having been satisfied by the death of His Son, has offered every man and every woman and every boy and every girl a pardon. We just have to accept the pardon offered.[325]

[Salvation, Rejection of;
Sin, Victory Over]
Ps. 1:23–33; 1 Tim. 1:18–20

FORGIVENESS, OF SIN

THE WONDERFUL thing about electronic calculators is that if wrong buttons are pressed and the calculation is thrown off, all is not lost. The problem does not have to be unraveled or figured out. By pressing "clear," the calculation can be restarted.

Some people are in situations that they can't unravel. Their lives are so twisted and turned that they can't figure things out. They are too confused. The great thing about God is that He is ready and waiting to press "clear." He's ready to abundantly pardon.[326]

[Forgiveness, from God; God's
Goodness; Second Chances]
Eph. 1:7; 1 John 1:9

A DIRTY diamond is still a diamond; it just needs to be cleaned.[327]

[Sin, Contamination by]
John 13:8; Rev. 7:15

EVERY week, people have the habit of taking clothes to the cleaners that have been soiled. The job of the cleaners is to freshen them up and get them smelling good again. Jesus has a pick up cleaning service. He picks up dirty people—people who have allowed their lives to sink into the mud for one reason or another—and cleanses them.[328]

[Forgiveness, from God;
Sin, Contamination by]
John 13:8; Rev. 7:15

THE BIGGEST bulldozer in the world is the D575A. It's 16 feet long, 25 feet wide, and 41 feet high. It weighs 225,000 pounds. It's a huge machine to bulldoze dirt. A couple of years ago it came to a county where there was an overload of garbage, and the bulldozer was brought in to dig a big hole that would collect the garbage and remove it from the lives of the citizens.

On the cross, God dug a hole so big He could collect the sins of the whole world—past, present, and future. On the cross, He gathered all the sin and took out His eternal wrath on Jesus Christ for you and for me. "God made him who had no sin to be sin for us" (2 Corinthians 5:21).[329]

[Cross; Forgiveness, from God;
Sin, Victory over]
Ps. 103:12; John 1:29; 2 Cor. 5:21

FREEDOM

THE WONDERFUL thing about living in America is that we have options. In many countries around the world, actions are limited. The government controls everything, and the ability to choose is lost. The wonder of the American experience and experiment is the opportunity, at least on paper and in principle, for a person to freely pursue life, liberty, and what makes them happy.

But there are also restrictions in a democracy. There are limitations. We do not enjoy freedom without boundaries. We can't just drive through a red light. We can't just shoot through a stop sign. Why are there limits? Because, very simply, in order to enjoy freedom, there must be sufficient restrictions so that freedom is maximized.[330]

[Boundaries; Law, Purpose of]
Ps. 119:145; James 1:25; 1 Peter 2:16

A TENNIS player isn't free to play tennis if there is no baseline. A baseball player isn't free to play baseball if there is no foul line. A football player is not free to play football if there are no sidelines. There are some "nots" in athletic games in order for the game to be maximized. The reason that God allows boundaries is to create the opportunity to take full advantage of freedom.[331]

[Boundaries; Law, Purpose of]
Ps. 119:145; James 1:25

YOU CANNOT be free without restrictions. A fish is not free to roam the jungle. It wasn't made for that. A lion is not free to live in the ocean, because it wasn't made for that. Freedom is having the benefits accrue to you that you were created to receive. Freedom doesn't mean there are no boundaries. Freedom means that within the right boundaries you can maximize your potential.[332]

[Boundaries; Law, Purpose of]
Ps. 119:145; James 1:25

IN NEW York Harbor, there is a lady who stands tall. She holds a torch in her hand, giving light. Inscribed on the pedestal upon which this lady stands are these famous words:

Give me your tired, your poor,
Your huddled masses
yearning to breathe free,
The wretched refuse of
your teeming shore.
Send these, the homeless,
tempest-tossed, to me:
I lift my lamp beside
the golden door.

We know this lovely lady as Lady Liberty, and she stands there in New York Harbor with a crown on her head that has seven spikes. The spikes speak of seven seas and seven continents. In other words, no matter where you are in the world, you can come to America. You can come with all your mess. You can come with all your problems. You can come with all your burdens. You can come with all your needs. You can come because Lady Liberty is holding a torch to show you the way.

At the bottom of Lady Liberty's feet is a chain that has been broken. She is inviting the broken and bruised people who have been held hostage in one situation or another. No matter where they are in the world, they are welcome to come to America to find freedom.

God is holding the same promise of freedom to those who are looking to escape bondage. He welcomes all to come and to bring their problems, burdens, and needs. He is faithful to show us the way.[333]

[Forgiveness, from God; Gospel, Good News of; Sin, Victory over]
John 8:36; Rom. 8:20–21

FREEDOM, FIGHTING FOR

ONE OF the great contradictions of the Revolutionary War was that men fought long and hard to be free. They risked their lives that they might be removed from the tyranny of England and enjoy the wonders of freedom in what would be the United States of America. The irony, however, is that the very men who fought for freedom endorsed slavery and owned slaves. Freemen owning slaves—there's a contradiction there somewhere. So cataclysmic was the reality of slavery that it became one of the primary reasons for a civil war.

You see, when you find freedom you ought to offer it to other folks too. When you've discovered that you've been made free, then slavery ought not to be part of your vocabulary. What was true of the Revolutionary War is also true for us.

Freedom is worth fighting for; freedom is worth risking your life for. There's nothing like being free. When you find it for yourself, don't hold other folks in slavery.[334]

[Double-Mindedness]
Luke 4:18; 1 Peter 2:16

FREEDOM, ROAD TO

SOME people live their lives like hamsters. A hamster looks outside the glass of his cage and sees freedom. He decides to run for it. He gets on the wheel. He runs on the wheel, trying to get to his freedom. He soon realizes that he's not getting anywhere. So, he runs faster. An hour later, he's still in the same spot.

Many of us have been trying to break a habit for years, and ten years later we are still in the same spot. We've made New Year's resolutions to quit bad habits or to have better marriages or to work on bettering our finances. A year later, we are in the same position.

Why does this happen? We are using the wrong method. When we are trapped, we cannot change things ourselves. The only way for a hamster to find freedom is for the owner of the hamster to reach inside the cage and lift it out of there. Somebody bigger than the hamster has to take over.

Trying to get out of a caged situation using only our own human effort is not good enough.[335]

[Salvation, Need for; Self-Sufficiency, Danger of; Stronghold]
John 14:6; Rom. 3:23; Eph. 2:8–9

A MAN who lived in a foreign country became a citizen of the United States of America. In the country where he was raised and grew up, there was a curfew overseen by the military. Beyond a certain time, the streets had to be cleared and everyone had to be in their homes. When he immigrated to the United States, he began immediately sightseeing to see part of the country that he was now becoming a part of. However, when he saw darkness set in and looked at his watch, he saw that he was about to pass his curfew time.

Seeing a man getting in his car, he said, "Sir, would you please rush me to my hotel so that I won't overstay my curfew and get in trouble?"

The gentleman in the car couldn't figure out what in the world the man was talking about until it dawned on him that he was a foreigner and that he was a little mixed up about his new life in America. He explained to and assured the man that in the U.S. the law that he had been used to no longer applied. He explained that he was no longer under the jurisdiction of the country he came from. He was in a new country now and that meant he was free to stay up and stay out. The restrictions of the old homeland no longer applied. This man was in the United States. but had not yet learned to cast off the bondage of the old country.

A lot of us are in Christ, but we've not yet learned how to cast off the old bondage of being in Adam. So we sing about freedom, talk about freedom, and yet we feel the pressure of the curfew and the bondage and oppression of the old law system under which we operated. Far too many Christians today are in chains because they've just spent so much time in the old country. In getting used to this thing about being free in Christ, they have not adapted yet.[336]

[Forgiveness; Law of Sin and Death; Sin Nature, Residue of]
Rom. 8:1–17; 2 Cor. 5:17

FRIENDSHIP, NATURE OF

REAL friends are those people who, when you make a fool of yourself, don't think that you have done a permanent job.[337]

[Second Chances]

A FRIEND is someone who is there when the good times aren't.[338]

[Adversity; Commitment; Trials]
Prov. 18:24; 27:10

A FRIEND is someone who always gets in your way when you are on your way down.[339]

[Confrontation]
Matt. 18:15–17; James 5:19–20

A FRIEND is someone who comes in when the world walks out.[340]

Prov. 18:24

G

GAMBLING

A STORY is told of a cowboy who was desirous of getting health insurance. The health insurance agent wanted to see what kind of condition the cowboy was in before he would insure him.

"Sir, have you had any accidents?"

He said, "Well, I really haven't had any accidents. Now, once I was bitten by a rattlesnake, and I did have a horse that kicked me in the ribs . . . laid me up for a few weeks. But I haven't had any accidents."

Somewhat confused, of course, the insurance agent said, "Excuse me, now you just said you didn't have any accidents, but you were bitten by a rattlesnake and kicked by a horse. Well, what do you call that?"

The cowboy said, "Naw, those weren't no accidents. They did those things on purpose!"

Insurance companies are going to be concerned about their risk. That's why they want to know about pre-conditions. They want to limit their exposure to risk. They are in the business of gambling and they want to gamble right.

To gamble is to take a risk.[341]

[Greed; Risk]
Heb. 13:5

IT'S LIKE the guy who told the preacher, "Preacher, I'm going to gamble, but if I win, I'll give it to the church." Now this man had been really sick. So sick that he thought he was dying. He was gambling because he was hoping in his last days to win money to enjoy the remainder of his life. Well, he did win. He won big. But he also got better.

The preacher said, "What happened to the money you said you'd give to the church?"

The man said, "Now, you know how sick I was. I was too sick to comprehend what I was saying!"[342]

[Greed; Money, Love of]
Luke 16:13; Acts 5:1–11

GIVING

A LITTLE boy was given the assignment of planting a seed. His project was to then take it home with him so he could watch his plant develop and grow. He placed it carefully in the windowsill in the kitchen. The next morning the boy ran into the kitchen with great excitement only to stop suddenly at the windowsill with a curious frown on his face. Very upset, he questioned his mother about the state of his plant and the fact that nothing appeared to be happening. His mother carefully explained to him that seeds didn't grow up to plants overnight.

It's the same way with the principle of sowing and reaping. Reaping

doesn't occur immediately after sowing. Reaping, many times, doesn't
even occur a month after sowing.
Reaping occurs when the season is
right.[343]

[Sowing and Reaping]
Gal. 6:9

A COUNTRY preacher once delivered a sermon on giving. He said, "Now
church, you know we've got to go
somewhere and so we need the church
to walk." And the deacons lined up on
the front row and they said, "Rev, let the
church walk. Let the church walk."
The preacher said, "We've got to start
moving." And the deacons said, "Let it
walk." The preacher saw that he had the
deacons with him, so he said, "And then
after we've walked for a little while,
church, we've got to run." The deacons
said, "Yeah, let the church run!" He went
on preaching, getting the congregation
and deacons more excited as he continued. He said, "Then, after we've run
for a little while, it's time for the church
to fly! We've got to fly!" The deacons
said, "Yes, Reverend, we've got to fly!
We've got to fly!" Then the preacher
said, "Well, now, you know it's going to
take money for the church to fly." The
deacons said, "Let it crawl, Rev! Let it
crawl!"[344]

[Giving, Priority of; Money, Use of]
Matt. 6:24; 1 Tim. 6:10

THERE is the story about the guy who
was giving and he gave one thousand
dollars per week in the offering when he
was first saved. Later on in his Christian
walk, he went back to his pastor and
said, "Pastor, when I was first saved, I
was so excited about Jesus Christ—so
excited about the Word; I was being so
blessed. I was growing so much. There

were so many changes taking place in
my family when I was first saved and I
wanted to thank God with all I had because of the amount of money He allowed me to make. I gave one thousand
dollars every week to the offering because I was just so thankful for His
goodness. However, the more I grew,
the less I gave. Now I'm not appreciating His grace anymore and I only give
fifty dollars a week even though I make
more money." He said, "Pastor, pray for
me."

The pastor said, "Heavenly Father,
right now my brother is in trouble because You know when he was first
saved, he loved You enough to give one
thousand dollars. But now he's going
downhill and he only gives You fifty
dollars. My prayer right now is that You
take him back to when he was making
only a few dollars."[345]

[Giving, Priority of; Greed, Influence
of; Money, Love of]
Mal. 3:8–12; 2 Cor. 9:7

A FAMILY sat down to the dinner
table and started talking about the
church service. The son started off by
saying, "The sermon was boring today,
Dad." The sister chimed in, "Boy, you sure
are right; the pastor stumbled over the
Scripture." The mother jumped in and
said, "Yeah, and the choir, Lord have
mercy! They were pitiful! They weren't
in tune at all." The father finally threw in
his comments. He said, "Well, you know
you guys really ought to hush. What do
you expect for a quarter?"[346]

[Materialism, Perspective of;
Money, Use of]
Mal. 3:8–12; 1 Tim. 5:18

ONE day the elder board of a church

was faced with a situation that was a little uncomfortable. A man named Jim in the church who had a serious heart condition had just inherited one million dollars and they wanted to tell him, but they were afraid that the shock would kill him.

They asked the pastor if he could figure out a way to tell Jim that he had inherited such a large sum of money. The pastor agreed. He approached the man after church one day and casually said, "Jim, if you had one million dollars, what would you do with it?" Jim looked up and said, "Pastor, if God gave me one million dollars, the first thing I would do before I did anything is give half of it to the church." The pastor had a heart attack and died.[347]

[Giving, Types of; Money, Use of]
Luke 6:11; 2 Cor. 9:7

STEALING from God is like robbing the local police station—not a good idea.[348]

[Greed, Emptiness of; Sin, Consequences of]
Mal. 3:8–12; Luke 6:11; Acts 5:1–11

ONE day a man was lost in a desert without water, but he saw an old shack. He was dying of thirst. He knew he didn't have much longer so he painfully made his way to the shack. Inside the shack was a little jar of crystal clear water set on the floor next to a pump. Flooded with relief, he walked over to the jar to quench his overbearing thirst. As he reached down to pick up the jar of water, he noticed a sign. The sign said, "Use this water to prime the pump out back. When you are satisfied, refill it and leave it for the next person who will pass this way."

He found himself on the horns of a dilemma because he was so very thirsty. What if he followed the directions on the sign and there was no water in the well? He had to make a decision to either serve himself now, or invest and take the chance that deep down there was so much more.

Giving is a method of priming the pump of God's blessing in the life of a believer. You have a choice. You can take the little that God has given you now and consume it for yourself. Or you can use it to prime something that's got so much more. It all boils down to whether you believe there's something underneath the ground.[349]

[Blessing, Source of; Giving, Motivation for]
Mal. 3:10–12; Matt. 10:8; Luke 6:38; 2 Cor. 9:7

AS CHRISTMAS was approaching quickly, a young man started thinking about what he could give his father, who lived far away. He wanted to get him something special—something that would manifest how much he valued him. He looked around and found something he thought would be unique, special, and unusual. It was an exotic parakeet. It was so unique that it could speak five different languages and it could sing "The Yellow Rose of Texas" standing on one leg. It was a most unusual bird.

He thought to himself that his father would surely think a bird like this was extra special. In addition, it cost ten thousand dollars. This guy thought for sure that this most unique bird would show his father how much he loved him. He purchased the bird and had it shipped to his father. He couldn't wait to hear his dad's response to this most phenomenal gift.

He called his father on Christmas Day. He said, "Dad, did you get my gift?" His father said, "I certainly did, son." The man said, "Well, Dad, how did you like it?" His dad replied, "Oh, it was delicious!"

His dad obviously missed the point. He didn't understand the nature of the gift and because he didn't understand the nature of the gift, he treated it in a way other than how it was to be utilized.

Unfortunately, many Christians miss the point of the gift of giving.[350]

[Grace, Appreciation of]

Matt. 6:2; Luke 6:11; Acts 5:1–11

THE DOLLAR said to the dime, "You are a skinny, valueless little runt." The dime said to the dollar, "But I go to church more often than you do."[351]

[Giving; Money, Use of]

Mark 12:41–44; 2 Cor. 9:7

GIVING, METHOD OF

A STORY is told of a circus strong man who had particularly powerful hands. One of the things he would do is take an orange before the crowd and squeeze it with his bare hand until every drop of juice came out. Then he would dare the audience to find another drop because of how strong he was. He'd have other big strong men come up and try to squeeze more out, but to no avail. No one could get more juice.

On one occasion, a skinny man came up and said he'd like to try. They laughed, but gave him the orange. He took one hand, and with all the strength he could muster up, he squeezed it. To the shock of the

strong man and the crowd, there was a drop of orange juice that dripped out. They couldn't believe it. When asked how in the world he was able to squeeze out another drop of orange juice and where his power came from, the man replied, "Oh, it's easy. I'm the treasurer for the church down the street. I know how to squeeze stuff out of folks."[352]

[Giving]

2 Cor. 9:7

GIVING, MOTIVATION FOR

I REMEMBER when I was teaching my oldest son, Anthony, about giving. At the time, he was getting one dollar a week for an allowance. I explained to him that he now had to give ten cents to God before he spent the other ninety. I also explained that ten cents was the minimum and that he could give more based on his gratefulness. My son understood that he had to tithe before he could buy candy. Anthony was not a happy camper.

First, he explained to me that one dollar wasn't enough to buy anything. He started quoting the prices of all his favorite candies. Second, he couldn't believe that he had to cut into his too-little allowance to share with God.

So, I had to teach him. I said, "Now, Son, where did you get the dollar?"

"Well, Daddy, you gave it to me."

"Where did Daddy get the money to give you the dollar?"

"Well, you got the money from your salary at the church."

"Well, how did I get money from the salary at the church in order to give you the dollar?"

"Because the people go to work and then they give and then you get a salary from which you gave me a dollar."

"So, where did the people get the money out of which I got a salary to give you a dollar?"

"Well, the people have jobs and when the people got paid at their jobs, they gave a portion of their income from which you got a salary to give me a dollar."

"Tell me some of the kinds of jobs that the people do who got the salary who gave the money that provided me the salary to give you a dollar."

My son started naming a bunch of different kinds of jobs. For each job he mentioned, I explained to him all of the natural resources it took, under the good hand of God the Father, to make those jobs possible—that also made my salary and his dollar possible.

After that conversation, he put fifteen cents into the offering. When you understand that everything starts with God, it motivates you to give to Him first.[353]

[Blessing, Source of; Giving, Motivation for]
Lev. 27:30

GIVING, PRIORITY OF

A PREACHER out in the country was testing out one of his rich members. John was a farmer and the preacher asked him, "John, if you had 100 pigs, would you give 25 to God?"

"Yes, Pastor, I would."

"John, if you had 20 pigs,would you give 5 to God?"

"Absolutely, Pastor."

"John, if you had two pigs, would

you give one to God?"

"Preacher, cut that out! You know I only have two pigs!"

As long as we're being hypothetical, we'll be generous, but once God asks us what we're going to do with what we have in our hands, we have a problem.[354]

[Giving; Sacrifice]
Luke 16:10

GIVING, TYPES OF

THERE are three kinds of givers: the flint, the sponge, and the honeycomb. To get anything out of the flint, you have got to hammer it. Then you only get chips and sparks. To get water out of the sponge, you have got to squeeze it. The more you squeeze, the more you get. But the honeycomb simply overflows with sweetness.

When a person understands what God has done for them, you don't have to prime them to give and you don't need ten collections. They understand that He is a great God. In fact, at offering time, we ought to jump to our feet and applaud that we are *here* to give, have something to give, and have been blessed to have strength enough to work that we might be able to give. We ought to just applaud the privilege of giving.[355]

[Giving; Money]
Deut. 15:7; Luke 6:38; 2 Cor. 9:7

GOD, AUTHORITY OF

THE QUEEN of England is a prestigious figure. She looms larger than life. She even has her own palace. There's only one problem. She has no power. She looks good. She looks like one of the most powerful women in the world, but she can't vote and she can't veto. Her position in her country is one of courtesy. What England does to the queen, we do to the King. We give Him verbal recognition. We encase Him in beautiful palaces called churches. We've got people coming to pay homage to Him, but when it comes to decision making, veto power, and voting, we don't need Him. We acknowledge His position without giving Him the credit for power that accompanies it.[356]

[God, Power of; Jesus, Authority of; Surrender, Concept of]
Josh. 4:24; Job 12:13; 1 Cor. 4:20

GOD, EQUALITY WITH

YOU'VE heard a teenager say it or maybe you've even said it yourself. You may be staying up fairly late until you are ready to go to bed, and your child wants to know how come he or she can't stay up because you're doing it. They have lost the distinction between parent and child. Hopefully you'll tell them that there is a difference and that you are doing it because you are the adult! Our children simply can't do everything we do because we are the parents and they are the children. There is a distinction. They cannot ever be fully like us. We will always be the parents and they will always be the children.[356]

When Satan comes on the scene and says we can be like God, it's just not true. It's just not possible.[357]

[God's Holiness; Pride, Problem of; Satan, Lies of; Satan, Strategy of]
Gen. 3:1–6; Prov. 16:18

REMEMBER the Nike commercial? "I wanna be like Mike." They sold a lot of tennis shoes with folk wanting to be like Mike. They sold a lot of #23 jerseys because folk wanted to be like Mike.

The problem is that it takes a lot more than tennis shoes to be like Mike! You got to be able to fly to be like Mike, because Mike is in a class by himself. He is unique among professional basketball players, so desiring to be like Mike and wearing the paraphernalia that gives the impression you're like Mike does not make you like Mike, because he is too unique.

When Satan offered the possibility of being like God to Adam and Eve, he was offering an impossibility. He told them that the reason why God set up a boundary is that He didn't want them to be like Him. However, the truth is that boundary or no boundary, they could never be like Him. We can never be like Him. He is in a class by Himself.[358]

[Deception, Satan's; God's Holiness; Satan, Lies of; Satan, Strategy of]
Gen. 3:1–6

MUHAMMAD Ali, true story, got on a plane one day and he was sitting in first class and a flight attendant came to him and asked him to buckle his seat belt as they were nearing takeoff. The flight attendant came back; Muhammad Ali had not buckled his seat belt. She said, "I'm sorry, Mr. Ali, but you are going to have to buckle your seat belt." She came back again, right before the plane was getting ready to taxi down the runway; Ali had not buckled his seat belt. She said, "Mr. Ali, we can't move until you buckle your seat belt." Mr. Ali replied, "I don't need to buckle my seat belt."

"What do you mean you don't need to buckle your seat belt? Everybody has to buckle their seat belt."

"Well Superman don't need no seat belt."

The flight attendant now was ticked off. She looked squarely at him and said, "Superman don't need no airplane, either."

A man has got to know his limitations. Autonomous man, man who believes he can live without God, make it without God, do science apart from God, or create apart from God will be rudely awakened.[359]

> [Boundaries; Pride; Pride, Problem of; Self-Sufficiency, Danger of]
> Prov. 16:18; 29:23; Matt. 23:12

GOD, FEAR OF

THE REVERENCE and fear of God is the starting place for wisdom. If a driver is going 80 mph and notices a police car parked up ahead on the side of the road, they will slow down. In fact, a whole series of things goes into motion. First the driver's heart starts beating a little more heavily. His brain tells his leg to get off of the accelerator and ease down on the brake, being careful not to slam on it. His eyes look down at the speedometer to ensure the speed is shifting to lower and then they move to the rearview mirror to see if he has been caught or not.

The policeman's presence has produced a healthy respect for the law. When an officer is present, drivers adjust to the law because of respect for the officer's authority. A driver may not like his authority, may not want his authority, or might even be rebellious against his authority—but he still respects it.

What would most people think about a person who speeds up to 90 mph when they see a policeman? They would call him a fool. Why? Because that driver is showing no reverence for the law.

Many Christians live their lives according to their own set of laws because they do not respect God or acknowledge His rule over every area of their lives. Just as a driver should fear the authority of a police officer whether they see him or not, a Christian shows true fear of God by how they acknowledge His authority. Truly fearing God means that God is the reference point wherever the Christian goes or whatever they are involved in.[360]

> [God, Authority of; Jesus, Authority of; Self-Sufficiency, Sin of]
> Deut. 6:13; Ps. 111:10; Isa. 8:13

THE FEAR of God is two-sided. One side has to do with awe or reverence. The other has to do with being dreaded. This is similar to the dual role parents have with their children. Not only do they wish for their children to respect them, but they also want their children to know that their improper behavior could invoke discipline.[361]

> Isa. 8:13; 1 Peter 1:17–18

THE OLD belief, centuries ago, was that the sun revolved around the earth. As we now know, this belief was wrong. The earth revolves around the sun. Many of us have got it wrong in our spiritual lives. God doesn't revolve around us. We revolve around Him. We know that we fear God when we have made Him the centerpiece of our lives.[362]

> [Jesus Christ, Centrality of; Self-Sufficiency, Sin of]
> Ps. 118:22; Matt. 21:42

WHAT IF the president told you he was coming to your house? What if he chose your house above all the other homes in the community to come and visit? What if he told you that he wanted to come and have dinner with you? Everything would change. Your cleaning habits would change. Your schedule would change. What you do with your kids would change. Everything would change, because somebody great was coming your way. We will change for a man what we won't change for God.[363]

[God's Glory]

Ex. 3:5; Acts 7:33

ELECTRICITY is good. We're warm because of electricity. We cook because of electricity. We freeze food because of electricity. Lights come on because of electricity. Electricity is a good thing. However, I would not advise you to take a screwdriver and stick it in an outlet!

You don't want to do that because the same electricity that can help you can also fry you. The same electricity that can illumine you can make your hair pop out. In other words, electricity, while being helpful, must be handled properly or else the help it is designed to give winds up hurting. The hurt won't be intentional. It will happen because you are not handling it right.

God wants to show you your destiny. He wants to guide and govern your life, but He's got to be handled right. That's why He says, Fear Me.[364]

[God, Power of; Power, Accessing]

Ex. 19:12; Heb. 12:18–21

GOD, IMAGE OF

PICTURE frames are sold with a valueless picture displayed. The point of it is just to take up space. It means noth-

ing. A person will purchase the frame, take it home, and put in a picture of somebody who means something—a relative, a friend, a special memory. The picture that is placed inside the new frame has value. Why? Because it is an image of real life.

Now, all of a sudden that picture frame has greater value because the image it holds represents something or someone cared for. When there's life in the womb, God has placed His image in the frame. Now the frame has greater value because it bears the mark of God.[365]

[Humanity; Life, Perspective on]

Gen. 1:26–27; Ps. 139:13; Isa. 44:24

GOD declared Himself so unique that He says we are not even to make a replica of Him. He doesn't even want us to take His picture. He doesn't want us to paint any likeness of Him because even if we try our best to come up with an idea of what He looks like, we're going to mess Him up.

It is like going to one of these mall photograph booths with those cheap dollar photographs, taking a picture, and then having to apologize for taking it because rather than complimenting you, it made you look worse. God says, "Don't even make or come up with an idea of what I look like cause anything you come up with is going to make Me look bad."[366]

[Idolatry; Idols]

Ex. 20:4–6

A BOY one day was talking to his pastor and he was doodling on a piece of paper. The preacher said to him, "Son, are you drawing a picture?" He said, "Yes." "What are you drawing a picture of?" The boy replied, "I'm drawing a picture of God." The preacher said, "But we don't know what God looks like." The little boy said as he continued drawing his picture, "Well, you will when I'm finished."[367]

[God's Holiness; Idols]
Ex. 20:4–6

GOD, KNOWING

SPORTS buffs know a lot about celebrities and athletes whom they've not even met. They can cite statistics on touchdowns, home runs, and points scored. Gossips know a bunch about the latest scoop on people they don't talk to—who divorced who and who's hanging out with who. Pop culture junkies read the tabloids even though the people they are so interested in would pass them on the street without a nod.

A Christian can come to church for years and only know about God. True knowledge of God requires a two-way conversation. Many Christians say they want to know God but don't put the effort in to do so.[368]

[Christian Living, Spiritual Growth; Jesus, Relationship with]
John 17:3; Heb. 5:12–14

GOD, POWER OF

THE DAUGHTER of the elementary school principal got in trouble one day. She was doing something that she shouldn't have and one of the teachers corrected her. The girl ignored the teacher's reprimand and continued to do exactly that which got her into trouble. The teacher then leaned down and got eye to eye with the girl to threaten her with a punishment if the young lady didn't change her behavior.

The little girl looked up at the teacher and said confidently, pulling rank, "Do you know who my father is?"

Do you know who your Daddy is? He is God almighty and King of the universe. When you've got that kind of Daddy, you can pull rank. You can pull rank over the Devil. You can pull rank over people. You can pull rank over problems. You can pull rank over difficult situations.[369]

[Father God; God, Authority of; Trials, Confidence in]
Rom. 8:15; 1 John 3:1

VOLTAIRE, the French philosopher, was a pagan who cursed God. He believed that there is no God. He believed that thinking about God was an exercise for people of lower intellectual ability. Voltaire ridiculed the thought of God. But then as it goes for all men, it came time for him to die. He lay there on his deathbed desperately in need of God. He screamed and hollered. In fact, Voltaire's nurse is recorded as saying that she never wanted to see another man die like Voltaire did because this man died in agony, foaming at the mouth with hell looming before his eyes. Here was a man who cursed God and God's Word.

Now, if you go over to his house today, it's a Bible factory where they make Bibles that are sent around the world. God can take folk who cuss Him out and use the place they used to cuss Him out to write His Word and distribute it to other people. He is a God who can take evil and make it turn out for the good. God could take men who condemned Jesus to death and then use their condemnation for our salvation. They can allow sinful men to pin Him to the cross so that you and I might be redeemed. So don't get upset because evil men are doing evil things. Just tell your King to use His power to take their evil for your good. That's the kind of God you have.

God's power is unlimited. God's power is potent.[370]

THERE is a true story of a Reverend Taylor who pastored a church over in Jamaica. One Sunday he was preaching and a man kept coming and interrupting the services. Reverend Taylor would stop preaching and wait for the man to settle down; then he'd start preaching again. The man would interrupt the service again. Reverend Taylor would stop. This happened a few times and finally he just asked the man not to interrupt him anymore. The next time the man interrupted the service, Reverend Taylor prayed aloud, "Lord, I am seeking to communicate Your Word to these people. This man refuses to respect that. Would You demonstrate to him before this people today, that he is not to play with the Living God?"

Reverend Taylor picked up where he left off in his sermon. The guy interrupted yet again. Within five minutes, he dropped dead of a heart attack in the middle of the aisle right in the middle of the service in front of the congregation. It's a fearful thing to fall into the hands of the Living God.[371]

[Sin, Consequences of]
Isa. 8:13; Acts 5:1–11

THERE was a lady who lived out in the boondocks. She did not have electricity, but she wanted it. She called the electric company and they made arrangements so that a line could be gotten out to her so that she could have the benefits of electricity.

After delivering electricity to her home for almost six months, someone at the company noticed that only one unit of electricity was used. A serviceman was sent out to check and make sure there was no problem. He rang her doorbell, and when she answered, he asked, "Hello, Miss. Are you using your electricity?"

She said, "Why, yes, I am!"

"May I ask what you are using it for?"

"Well, when it gets dark I turn it on long enough for me to light my kerosene lamp."

This woman didn't understand the power she had. She had all this power that could keep things well lit all night long, but she was settling for a kerosene existence.

Many Christians are settling for taking this great power that God has given them only to light their own human efforts. They are not maximizing the power of His presence.[372]

[Fasting, Power of; Power,
Accessing; Praise, Power of]
Acts 1:8; Eph. 3:20

A LITTLE boy one day was trying to pick up a rock. He said "Dad, it's too heavy."

He said, "Son, you can do it."

The boy strained and tried, but he said, "Dad, it's too heavy."

The father insisted, "Son, you can do it."

He tried again. "Dad, it's too heavy."

He said, "Son, you're not using all your strength."

"Dad, I am. I am. It's too heavy."

"Son, you're not using all your strength."

"Dad, why are you continually saying I'm not using all my strength? It's too heavy."

"I know you're not using all your strength, because you haven't asked me to help yet."

There is more strength available to you than what you have. Be strong in the strength of His might.[373]

[Father God; Power, Accessing]
Eph. 6:10; Col. 1:29

GOD, PRIORITIZING

ONCE I had to go to Wal-Mart to get some stuff. I wanted to be the first one there when they opened because I hate anything with "mart" in its name. If it's a "mart," I don't want to be there. I got up early to hit Wal-Mart and when I got there, to my dismay, the parking lot was full. I've never been so irritated in my life. I got up thinking that day that I was getting a head start!

I walked inside the store and there were lines of people. I retrieved what I came there for and got in line, still a little baffled as to why the store was so congested. I shortly discovered that on this particular day, at this particular Wal-Mart, there was a storewide sale. The place was full because everybody had showed up to get their goods at reduced prices.

It dawned on me as I stood in line, that is the problem with most people today. Everyone wants to show up with God when He's on sale. As long as He comes at reduced prices and low expectations, we'll shop there. We'll come to church when nothing is expected, but the moment He comes at full price, the parking lot gets empty.[374]

[Christian Living, Burden of;
Priorities; Sacrifice]
Matt. 8:18–22; 16:24; Luke 9:57–62

I-635 is the freeway that loops around Dallas. You can circle the city on 635. It sits on the margin of the city. It's far enough to keep you from being bogged down with downtown traffic, yet close enough to give you access to the city.

Most people have God on the loop—close enough to look respectable, far enough not to be bothered with. They don't understand that the true God wants to be in city hall because that is where the legislation is made. He wants to be in the middle of the things that matter—not just on the outskirts.[375]

[Jesus Christ, Centrality of;
Priorities]
Matt. 8:18–22; 16:24; Luke 9:57–62

GOD, WAYS OF

HAVE YOU ever talked to one of these brilliant PhD-kind-of-people and you don't know what they're talking about? You know it's deep, even though you don't understand any of it because they're just communicating on a whole different plane, on a whole different level.

At the heart of many of our dilemmas is our inability to know God's ways. God says that as high as the heavens are above the earth, so are My ways higher than your ways and My thoughts than your thoughts. They're not only bigger, they're higher. His thoughts are at another level.[376]

[Circumstances, Understanding;
God's Ways, Unpredictability of]
Ps. 92:5; Isa. 55:8–9

I REMEMBER telling God as a teenager, "God, I'm going to do anything You want, but I will not pastor." He said, "Um-hmm."

He's full of surprises and His ways are not your ways. His thoughts are not your thoughts.[377]

[God's Ways, Unpredictability of]
Isa. 55:8–9; 1 Cor. 2:16

ONE difference between God and us is that we have different viewpoints. Take a parade. We watch a parade progressively. We watch one band come after another. We watch the parade go by one band at a time. God sees the whole parade. He doesn't have to wait for each band to turn the corner. From the starting place to the finish, He sees the whole parade. He sees the whole package. That's why "without faith it's impossible to please God." You've got to believe He sees what you can't. You've got to believe that He sees what is not visible to you because you can't see around the corner.[378]

[Faith; Time, Perspective on; Trust in God]
Ps. 33:13; Heb. 4:13

GOD'S DELIVERANCE

A LIFEGUARD was on duty when he noticed a gentleman was in trouble. He dove into the water and swam out to the struggling man, stopping about three feet from him. From this short distance, the lifeguard realized that the victim was a large fellow. Not wanting to be taken under, the lifeguard considered his dilemma. Not only was his ward sizable, he was also trying to save himself. He was afraid. He was swinging. He was panicking. He was in trouble. In an effort to save himself, the man was swing-

ing wildly against the water and was draining his energy quickly.

The lifeguard continued to tread water at a short distance, not because he didn't care but because he was waiting on the man to stop trying to save himself. He knew that he would be unable to save the drowning man as long as he was using his own methods, insisting on his own strength, and relying on his own ability. His cry for help contradicted his efforts to save himself. His approach was hindering the lifeguard's planned approach.

Finally the man's energy left and he had no more fight. When he stopped beating the water, stopped leaning on his own understanding, and stopped using his own methods, the lifeguard took over. The lifeguard worked his way around to the man's back, reached over his shoulder, cupped the chin under his hand, and put an elbow in the middle of his shoulder blade. This allowed the man's body to come closer to the surface of the water and rest on the hip of the lifeguard as he sidestroked in to the edge of the pool.

Even though the man was large, the rescue was possible because he was resting in the strength of his savior.

Once the man was calm, he thanked the lifeguard. He gave the lifeguard complete credit because he realized his own resources couldn't have gotten him out of the mess he had found himself in.[379]

[Salvation, Need for; Surrender, Benefits of]
Ps. 33:16; Rom. 3:23; Eph. 2:8–9

THERE'S a magnificent hotel in the Bahamas. It's named after the lost city of Atlantis. It is a monstrosity of a hotel and is viewed as one of the greatest hotels in the world. There is a water park in the middle of the hotel. In the middle of the water park is a water slide disguised as a huge Egyptian pyramid. This pyramid water slide goes straight down at lightning speed. Lines are always long for this slide. Not only is it a thriller, but as you go down you slide through an aquarium that holds some of the most dangerous fish in the world. The aquarium is contained by thick glass that acts as a barrier between the hotel guests and that which would eat them alive. That slide is a scary drop through a tank of scary fish, but there is a protective covering to keep the fish away from the visitors.

Sometimes life is a scary slide. Sometimes there seems to be trouble all around. But God protects those who fear Him and delivers them out of their trouble. Sometimes He keeps us from the trouble altogether; sometimes He lets us slide right on through. Either way, we come out on the other side.[380]

[Adversity; Life, Perspective on; Trials, Endurance during]
Ps. 34:4; James 1:2–4

THERE are a ton of Court TV shows on today. Most of those are true stories with real people. But normally, there is only one way you can get on the program. You have to agree in advance that all decisions by the judge are final. In other words, there can be no appeal. Whatever the judge renders is final in his court. God has a court, a judgment on earth, through the church, and all decisions are final as long as they are in keeping with the Word of God.[381]

[Judgment; Surrender, Concept of]
2 Cor. 5:10; Rev. 20:11–15

GOD'S DISCIPLINE

WHEN I travel for a long period of time, I normally don't do a good job of sticking with my exercise program. So when we return and I have to face the pain of getting back into my workout routine, I'm usually a little discouraged about that because I know what's going to happen. I'm going to be hurting. My wife is going to have to help me put on my shirt the morning after. She's going to have to help tie my tie. I'm going to be hurting because I took a break from lifting weights. But if I want to get on the right track again, there's no way I can bypass that pain. There's no way I can bypass that inconvenience. In order for me to get where I want to go because I took a break, I've got to pay the price.

We want to lay off of Christ and not pay the pain of getting back on track. It's always going to be painful when you veer away from Christ and He has to get your attention to pull you back in. But God's discipline is always to restore you.[382]

[Discipline, Love in; Sin, Consequences of; Trials, Value of]
Ps. 94:12; Prov. 3:11–12; Heb. 12:11

THE STORY is told about a little boy who was out in a pond. He had his little toy boat floating on the pond and the boat began to drift way out. He couldn't get it. A man came by and saw the boat way out in the pond and he did something very interesting. He picked up stones and threw them on the other side of the boat. He threw them beyond where the boat was. The boy didn't understand what the man was trying to do. The stones were causing quite a disturbance in the water. Something very interesting began to happen. As the man threw the stones out in the pond, they created ripples of water that moved backward toward where he and the boy were standing. Those ripples slowly pushed the boat back to shore.

That's how God's discipline is. When we wander away from Him in the "Sea of Sin" or the "Pond of Unrighteousness," He throws the disturbing actions of His loving discipline in order to create a disturbance to push us back onshore. God wants to push us back to where we should never have wandered from in the first place.[383]

[Discipline, Love in]
Prov. 3:11–12; Heb. 12:11

GOD'S FAITHFULNESS

THE SUN is a light twenty-four hours a day, seven days a week. All year long, all decade long, all century long, the sun just keeps on shining. The problem, however, is that the earth gets dark. How can there be all that light and the earth still gets dark? It's because the earth turns. The earth gets dark because the earth is spinning on its axis. Therefore the side that faces the sun gets light and the side that is facing away does not.

If there is darkness in your life, it's not because God, the Father of Lights, is turning; it's because you are turning. He is the Father of Lights and in Him there is no shadow. There is no darkness in Him. Because God is faithful, He's consistent. Just like the sun, He is always shining and in His light, there is no shifting or moving

shadow. We just have to make sure we are turned toward Him.[384]

[God's Presence; Light; Rebellion]
Isa. 57:15; James 1:17

GOD'S GLORY

GOD wants to be shown off among His people. He wants to be revealed among His people. He doesn't want apologies. I mean, any man who would apologize that his wife is by his side, is a fool. Any woman who would apologize that her husband is by her side is a fool. And any Christian who apologizes for belonging to the Lord Jesus Christ is a fool![385]

[Jesus, Relationship with; Worship]
Rom. 1:16; Eph. 1:6

ALL around us are invisible electronic waves. The air is thick with them. It's because of those invisible waves that you can speak to someone on a cell phone, or listen to a radio in your car, or watch the football game on TV. You cannot see these waves. They are invisible to the naked eye, but when you sit down in front of your television and turn it on, the television set will give you a visual of the invisible. That which you cannot see will be made visible through the vehicle of a TV set. You will be able to see in living color the invisible become alive.

God is invisible. The Bible says no man has seen God at any time. He's a spirit. The air is thick with His presence. He is everywhere. The problem is the human eye can't see Him so He must then make Himself visible. The process by which the invisible reality of God comes across in living color is called glory. When we say that God is glorious, we are saying that God has made Himself visible in such a way He can now be seen.[386]

WATER is wet because that's the way water is. Wetness is intrinsic to the nature of water. You can't talk about sky without talking about blue because blue is intrinsic to the nature of sky. You can't talk about sun without talking about hot because hot is intrinsic to the nature of sun. It is irrelevant whether you like the idea of the sun being hot, water being wet, or the sky being blue. The qualities are just intrinsically there.

God is glorious intrinsically. When you recognize it, He's glorious. When you don't recognize it, He's glorious. When you like it, He's glorious. When you don't like it, He's glorious because that's just who He is. God's glory is beyond human comprehension. It is beyond what you can conceive of.[387]

MANY STORES have mannequins. Another word for a mannequin is a dummy. The job of the dummy is to magnify the fashion of the store. They put clothing on the dummy and the dummy is supposed to act as an attraction to lure the customer into the store. They are to look at the clothes on the dummy and be drawn into the store. The clothes on the dummy didn't come from the dummy. The clothes on the dummy came from the owner of the store and the owner of the store put clothes on the dummy so that folks out-side would be attracted to come inside based on how the dummy looks. Need I say more?

On our best day, we are nothing but dummies. What God wants to do is dress us up. He's given you a new nature. He's given you a new life. He wants to dress you up and He's saying, "Listen, dummy, I want you to attract people to Me not only when times are going good but when times are going bad. Your job is to make Me look good." God is after making sure that He looks good. If you can make this switch, a small switch because it only involves one thing, and yet a whopping switch because it involves everything, God will be glorified in your life.[388]

WHEN entertainers develop a name for themselves, they go into designer clothing with their name. Sometimes it's clothes or sometimes it's cologne or perfume. They put their name on their product so you're not only buying a product, you're buying a name. When ladies go into the section of a department store that houses the "couture collection," they are not just looking at merchandise priced high because of the material. A part of the high price is because of the name.

I walked into a store with Sister Evans once that had a large couture collection on one of its floors. All of these items were designer items and carried the designer's name. I saw a dress for eight thousand dollars. I decided to feel the material. Now, it was nice, but I don't care how good that material was, it ain't worth eight thousand dollars. I made sure we didn't stay on that floor long. That dress was not worth eight thousand dollars. It was pretty. It was cute, but not that cute. The price, however, didn't just reflect the intrinsic value of the material. The price tag included the designer's name. Once the designer's name is attached to some nice material, the price of the material automatically increases in value.

Once you put God's name on something, it increases in value. Once you say, "God, I'm doing this in Your name," your service increases in value.

Another thing about these couture shops is that they always make your visit there a nice one. The way the store is laid out just makes it a nice place to be. It's always clean, spacious, and well laid-out in there and they even provide lounge chairs for husbands like me to sit. Why, I went to one store and they asked me if I wanted something to drink! They offered me a choice of coffee, coke, or tea with cookies. This was no bargain basement! This place offered the best because the names represented in the store were great. The presence of the name increases the value of the service. If you're giving God sloppy service, it means you don't understand His name.[389]

[Father God; God's Name]
Eccl. 7:1; Phil. 2:10–11

GOD'S GOODNESS

THE BIBLE says that God has stored up goodness for those who fear Him. God has plenty of goodness in storage.

Many people today have so much stuff that they can't hold all of it in their homes. In an effort to control the overflow, they've rented storage spaces.

God's got goodness in storage that belongs to those who revere Him. He has stuff that He wants to share, is ready to share, and desires to share with His beloved.[390]

[Blessing, Source of; Grace, Provision of]
Ps. 31:19; Phil. 4:19

MANKIND has been breathing oxygen ever since the first man was created. Since that time billions of folks have lived and died. There are six and a half billion people on Earth now. This number is also about the total number of all mankind who has ever lived on planet earth up until the present. So, literally in the history of mankind, about thirteen billion people have lived. No one yet seems to be worried about running out of oxygen for everyone to breathe. There are concerns about the quality but not the amount.

God has more than enough. Fish have been swimming in the water since creation and there is still more than enough. Animals have been eating foliage in forests and jungles. A little while after they eat, it just pops back up. God has built in His goodness to naturally replicate itself.[391]

[Blessing, Source of; Nature; Provision, God's]
Ex. 16:1–31; Phil. 4:19

GOD is good. The problem is that many of His children are ungrateful—quick to complain about what they don't have but slow to give thanks for what they do.

A little boy went grocery store shopping with his mother. They were in the checkout line and the grocer asked the mother if he could offer her son some candy. The mother agreed. As the grocer held out the jar, encouraging the boy to reach in, the little boy shook his head. The man stretched the jar out a little further and told the boy he could take as much as he would like. The boy continued to say no. With a confused look on his face, the grocer gave one last effort. The boy finally said, "I want you to give it to me." The grocer happily took some candy out of the container and handed it to the boy who quickly offered his thanks.

When he and his mother were in the car and on their way, she curiously asked, "Why wouldn't you take the candy? Why did you tell him to give the candy to you?" Her son replied, "Because, Momma, his hands were bigger than mine!" Smart boy. He understood that the hands of the source were bigger.

If God's children would simply let Him be God, they would soon discover that His hands are bigger than their own.[392]

[Blessing, Source of; Provision, God's]

Matt. 7:11; Phil. 4:19

GOD'S HOLINESS

GOD and sin are irreconcilable. The two don't get along. It's sort of like you and the garbage in your house. I hope you don't get along with it too long. At least twice a week, you take it outside because you and your garbage were not made to live together. Garbage after awhile should be designated for delivery outside of your home so it can be picked up and disposed of. Now, more garbage will show back up again in a day or two, but hopefully you will take it back out again because you and garbage are irreconcilable. We would have a problem with people who find themselves reconcilable to garbage.

Well, God and sin are irreconcilable. The two can't meet because of the holiness of God. He can't be comfortable where unrighteousness is allowed to express itself freely.[393]

[Divine Nature; Jesus, Perfection of; Sin; Sin, Stain of]

2 Sam. 6:6–7; 1 Peter 1:16

MY WIFE is the wife of Mr. Clean. She's Mrs. Clean, all right. She's a cleaning fanatic. Some people get high on drugs. She gets high on detergent. Our kids will tell you, she doesn't want to ever see any dishes ever left in the sink. It's a rare day if anything is left in our sink.

Sometimes I will walk into our home, being the busy man that I am, and happen to lay something in a place that it ought not be in. Or sometimes, because I'm tired and busy, my tendency is to step over something that may be lying in a place it ought not be. My wife will say, "Excuse me, um, dear, didn't you see that?"

Now the answer to that question is sometimes yes and sometimes no. Sometimes I see it, but I just don't care, okay. Sometimes I didn't see it because my mind is somewhere else. Either way, what my wife has a penchant for doing because of her cleaning perfectionism is to expose me to the light. She speaks the word to bring my attention to the fact that there is something wrong that I have let go unaddressed and that I have walked in "darkness." She lets me know that I've missed the boat, whether intentionally or unintentionally.

That means I have two options now. I can either change my actions and walk in the light that has been given to me, or I can continue to walk the way I'm walking. The Bible calls this "walking in darkness" because if I keep walking in the same direction when the light has exposed my wrongdoing, then I am no longer walking in the light. I am now walking in darkness because I can see what the light has shown me and have chosen not to respond to it.[394]

[Confrontation; Darkness, Walking in; Light]
James 5:19–20; 1 John 1:7

GOD'S NAME

WHEN people hear the name Bill Gates, they think of money because his name is associated with wealth. When people hear the name Serena Williams, they think of tennis because she plays this game with excellence. If the name Tiger Woods is mentioned, a person will think of golf because he is a pro in the sport. No one would think to name their child Hitler, as this name is associated with evil. Names have significance. No one would think to name their child Benedict Arnold because there is a negative meaning attached. Well, if names matter, then you can imagine how God must feel about His name![395]

[Ten Commandments]
Ex. 20:7; Deut. 5:11

A FORM of forgery is the unauthorized use of someone else's name. It is signing a document unapproved. It is caused by a name being written on a piece of paper when the actual person behind the name has not been consulted. A person convicted of forgery can be thrown in jail due to unauthorized use of another person's name.

Businesses trademark their names. They legally establish ownership of their names so that they are in full control of their usage. Their trademarked name belongs to them. Any other person or business desiring to use the trademark must first be licensed to do so. God's name has been licensed to Christians to use because He's the Lord our God. However, His license comes with a restriction. His name can't be used in vain.[396]

[Father God; Ten Commandments]
Ex. 20:7; Deut. 5:11; John 20:31

A MINISTER received a letter from the governor welcoming him to open a city council meeting in a word of prayer. This letter also requested that the minister pray generically and not mention Jesus so as not to offend people of other religious persuasions. The minister accepted the call. The day of the event, he took his place at the podium and began to pray, "Father, I want to thank You for this opportunity to pray before the city council. I would like to thank You first of all for creating them, because if they were not here, then they could not take on this responsibility. According to Your Word, everything created was created by Christ Jesus. Thank You, Lord, for creating government. Government is an institution of God according to the apostle Paul who met Jesus Christ on the Damascus Road. And Lord, if there are any city council people here today who do not understand that Jesus was born of a virgin, lived a perfect life, died a substitutionary death, and bodily arose from the dead, would You explain that to them! I ask that You bless their proceedings today in the name of Jesus. Amen."

The governor approached the minister after his prayer and expressed his disappointment in how the minister had imposed his religion on other people. The minister gently replied, "I don't do neutral prayers. I don't do Muslim prayers. I don't do Buddhist prayers. I do Christian prayers because I'm a Christian . . . and that means to follow Jesus Christ!"[397]

[Jesus, Authority of; Prayer, Jesus' Name; Spiritual Identity, in Christ]
John 20:31; Acts 4:18; Phil. 2:9–11

GEORGE ZIMMER of the Men's Warehouse appears on the company commercials to advertise the company's level of customer service. Mr. Zimmer explains the company's quality product and services then ends each commercial by saying "I guarantee it" and showing his signature. In doing this, Mr. Zimmer is saying he owns the company, takes responsibility for its product, and guarantees the product and the service. Well, God owns His company and He stands behind His name. He signs off on what He produces in your life, and the service that He gives will be of the highest quality.[398]

Phil. 2:9–11

GOD'S PERSPECTIVE

MANY a person checks the traffic reports before they head out onto the roads to go to work. By listening to the traffic report, they can figure out which freeways are clogged up and determine how much time needs to be allotted to getting to their destination or which route is best to take.

Any traffic report worth its salt is given from a helicopter. Somebody up in the sky looks down at the whole situation and can give direction to drivers so they know how they ought to proceed. Now, a person can say, "I am not listening to the traffic report. I am going to take my chances." The only problem is that when they are in traffic, they can't see what's going on. All they will know is that there is a long line and they will be stuck in it.

Now which is better? Does it make more sense to try and make the traffic decision on one's own and possibly get stuck or does it make better sense to follow the instructions from the helicopter? Of course, following the helicopter makes more sense because the person flying above in the chopper sees the big picture.[399]

[Holy Spirit, Guidance; Perspective, Importance of; Perspective, Power of]
Ps. 33:13; Heb. 4:13

GOD'S PRESENCE

A GROUPIE is somebody who likes to hang in the presence of a celebrity. God created the world to be made up of six billion people who are groupies and want to hang out in His presence.[400]

[Abiding; God, Knowing; Jesus, Relationship with; Worship]
Ex. 33:15; Ps. 84:10

A TRUE story is told of Mendelssohn, the great composer and musician. He went to a cathedral in Europe. They had just bought a new organ. The guy whose charge it was to take care of the organ didn't recognize the talented musician.

Mendelssohn said, "Sir, may I please play this organ?"

The caretaker of the organ said, "Oh no! This is our brand-new organ. We can't just allow anyone to play it."

Mendelssohn asked again, "Please ,sir, let me play the organ."

"I'm sorry. You don't understand. This is a million-dollar organ. We can't let you play this organ."

The composer tried yet again. "Please, please let me play."

To get rid of the visitor, the man said, "Okay. Here, you can play for just a minute."

Mendelssohn sat down and started playing. Music like the man had never heard started coming through the pipes of this organ. He had never heard such harmonious sounds in his life. He said, "Mister, who are you?"

Mendelssohn introduced himself.

The man just stared at him with his mouth open, now recognizing who stood in front of him. He felt embarrassed to think that he had been foolish enough to forbid Mendelssohn to play the organ. He just didn't realize who was in his cathedral. We ought to be embarrassed that we don't recognize the power of the presence of God and give Him the right to have His way.[401]

[God's Will; Pride, Problem of; Rebellion]
Prov. 3:5–6; John 1:10–11

GOD'S STANDARD

IF WE were to have a jumping contest and aim for the ceiling of the church sanctuary, no one would win. You may jump higher than I can, but I can guarantee you that everyone in the room is going to fall short of the ceiling. If the ceiling is the standard, the fact that you jumped higher than me is irrelevant. You still would have failed to meet the goal.[402]

[Jesus, Perfection of; Sin, Contamination by]
Rom. 3:23; 6:23

IF SOMEONE is sixty minutes late for a plane and another person is sixty seconds late for a plane, which one is better off? They both miss the flight. Some folks are missing heaven by a lot, while others are missing it by a little, but everyone's missing it because, unless you're as good as God, you are unacceptable to God. God's very nature will not allow Him to lower His standard of perfection.[403]

[Jesus, Perfection of; Heaven, Entrance into; Sin, Contamination by]
Rom. 3:23; James 2:10–11

MY SON came to me one day and asked me to accompany him to the gym. He told me that he wanted to show me something. He was about eleven years old and barely five feet tall. He wanted to show me that he could dunk! I had to see this!

I took him over to the gym and he bounced the ball, approached the goal, and cupped the ball under his hand in preparation. My eleven-year-old son, not even barely five feet tall, went up and dunked the basketball. It was an amazing sight . . . until I realized how he did it.

Before we went over to the gym, he called and asked the maintenance man to lower the goal. The standard had been lowered. I had the guy to raise the standard back to its correct height. I explained to my son that the goal should not be lowered so that he could meet it, but that he should continue to work hard to rise to the standard.

Sometimes, we lower the standard and then get all excited because we meet it and think we've done something. God is after us meeting His standard. He wants us to rise from wherever we are and rise to His level of excellence.[404]

[Children, Training; Christian Living, Spiritual Growth; Truth, Importance of]
Lev. 11:45; 1 Peter 1:15–16

IF YOU'VE ever traveled to England, you know the English are fairly prim and proper. A lot of the men wear three-piece suits, and they often carry in the little pouch inside their vests one of those round, stopwatch kind of things on a chain. If you ever happen to see a Londoner take out their timepiece to check the time, you will probably also see them look up and then look back at their watch. Sometimes they will make an adjustment to their watch. What they are doing is looking at Big Ben and adjusting their watch to Big Ben's time.

In London, Big Ben is the standard for the time of day. Englishmen reach into their pockets, pull out their watches, and adjust it to Big Ben. If your time is different from Ben's time, Ben doesn't change. You must

change, because there is a fixed standard that is nonnegotiable.

God wants us to adjust our ministry, our program, and our thinking to His ministry, program, and thinking for us. Sometimes we look at one another and measure our spirituality or effectiveness by others, but if are not measuring ourselves against the standard the Lord has set for us, then we are not looking at the right standard.[405]

[Divine Nature; Jesus Christ, Centrality of; Spiritual Identity, Basis of]
Lev. 19:2; Heb. 12:2; 1 Peter 1:15–16

WHENEVER I'm scheduled to go to the dentist, I spend extra time brushing my teeth. I try to do a good job so I will make a good impression. So I do extra scrubbing, extra flossing, and extra work to make myself look good to the dentist. The only problem is that when I arrive, the dentist is not satisfied with my good works. He's not satisfied with how much I brushed or how much I flossed. He looks deeper. He takes X-rays of my mouth and then uses sharp tools to dig in between my teeth, coming up with stuff I never even knew was there.

When I go to the dentist he reveals things that I thought I had taken care of on my own. That's because he's operating on a different standard. You can brush your teeth all your life long but if you don't get the stuff that's down deep, there will still be problems.

The Bible declares that on our best day we've still got stuff under the gums. On our best day we do not satisfy the demands of a holy God. We cannot meet the demands of perfection without being perfect.[406]

[Illumination]

1 Sam. 16:7

GOD'S VOICE

A NATIVE American was walking down the street with a businessman one day. The Native American stopped.

"Listen!" he said.

"For what?" the business replied.

"Don't you hear it?"

"Hear what?"

"Crickets."

"Crickets? I do not hear any crickets."

The Native American continued to try to help the businessman hear what he heard: "Oh, they're loud. Just listen! Don't you hear them?"

Getting a little disgruntled, the businessman said, "I don't hear any crickets."

The Native American looked around, and right over on the side, there was a cricket. He went and picked it up.

The businessman looked shocked. "I can't believe that. We are here downtown with all these people. You and I are talking and you can hear a cricket. I don't know how you did that."

The Native American reached into his pocket and took out some change. He threw it on the ground. Twenty people stopped walking. Then he said, "You always hear what you are tuned in to. You are tuned into money; you are going to hear a penny when it's dropped. I am tuned in to nature, I hear a cricket."

A lot of Christians will miss the still small voice of God because they are not tuned in.[407]

[Worldliness, Distraction of;

Worship, Benefit of]

1 Kings 19:9–18; Ps. 46:10

GOD'S WAYS, UNPREDICTABILITY OF

A MAN one day was walking through the woods with a friend. His mouth was dry, so he kept licking his lips. The problem was that the more he licked his lips, the more they got chapped. The more his lips got chapped, the more he licked his lips. He had no Chapstick.

He asked his friend, "What can I do? My lips are so dry and it's only getting worse."

"Oh," he said, "there's a simple solution to chapped lips out here. Go over yonder, get some horse manure, and rub it on your lips. Two things will happen. Number one, the horse manure will deal with cracking of the lips. Number two, you won't be licking your lips anymore." Some of God's solutions come in the strangest ways.[408]

[Problems]

Isa. 55:8

GOD'S WILL

WHENEVER you run from God, you must pick up the tab. Whenever you run from God, you've got to pay for the trip of deserting His presence. When you're in God's will even if you don't like God's will, God will pick up the tab.

If your company sends you on a trip, then they're responsible for paying your way. Now, when you go on your own trip or vacation, your company doesn't pay for that. It's your trip so you must pay.[409]

[Materialism, Deception of; Self-Sufficiency, Danger of]

Deut. 29:18–19; Judg. 17:6; Isa. 53:6

EAGLES are known for soaring. They glide in the air. The amazing thing about eagles is that they don't work that hard to hang in the air like they do. Eagles depend on wind gust and updraft.

When an eagle catches the wind, he can soar for a long time, just pausing ever now and then to flap his wings a bit. An eagle doesn't fly, furiously beating the air with his wings. If it did, many of them would probably poop out because their wings are too heavy to do that for any length of time. They rest on the power of the wind.

Many people are tired of furiously fighting their way through life, trying to do the best they can. God would have us to catch the wind. He wants us to link into His will so that we don't have to struggle unnecessarily where He's provided a way. His commandments are not burdensome.[410]

[Christian Living, Power;
Power, Accessing]
Matt. 11:29–30

IF YOU are driving and headed for the highway, you will eventually have to drive on a service road, up onto the on-ramp, and then onto the highway. You will have to merge into the traffic. In order to merge, you will have to slow down and look behind you to pay attention to the rest of the cars on the highway. They will be rolling and you will be the one to have to merge. You are merging with the cars traveling on the highway; they are not merging with you.

You merge onto the highway because it is the most direct route to lead you to where you want to go. Many of us want to get on the on-ramp and have the highway traffic stop to let us on, but that's not the way it works.

God is going somewhere and He's the main highway. He wants us to merge with Him and His program. He's not trying to stop His program to merge with us. That would be backward. This is not how it works. We ought to be willing to submit to the will of God.[411]

[Submission; Surrender, Concept of;
Trust in God]
2 Chron. 30:8; John 3:30; 17:4

A DRUNK driver is told not to drive. If he or she drinks, they are not to drive because they could hurt themselves or somebody else. People who have had a drink should hand over the keys to somebody who's sober and let this other person take control of the steering wheel so that each passenger in the car can get from where they are to where they are supposed to go.

Many of us are driving the steering wheel of our own life and shouldn't be. We are crossing the line, swerving, and going out into the ditch because we are out of control. God stands available to take the keys of our life and to drive us home. He can take us from here to eternity safely and on time, but He's got to have control of the wheel. He must be in charge.[412]

[Self-Sufficiency, Danger of;
Submission; Surrender, Concept of]
Rom. 8:7; James 4:1–7

IF I'M headed to downtown Dallas by way of the highway, then downtown is my intended goal and the highway is my route. But if I begin making my way to downtown and the highway is backed up due to construction or an accident, the backup interferes with me reaching my goal. That's no problem. I can exit the freeway and take an alternate route downtown. It may take me a little out of the way or take a bit longer but I can still use the alternate route to get me to my goal. The accident may have interfered with my preferred route but it does not interfere with my goal. Even if I get blocked on my alternate route, I still have yet another route that I can take to get to my same destination.

God's comprehensive will means that when He's going downtown and when He has determined His ultimate goal, He will always reach that goal. If human beings or the Devil himself create a block in God's plan, God is never limited to one highway. He is never limited to one route. Now, you know why that's good news about the will of God? That means folk can't stop the will of God for you.[413]

[God, Power of]
Isa. 55:11; Jer. 29:11

GOOD

MOST kitchens have blenders. These blenders are designed to take independent foods and integrate them, coagulate them, unite them, interface them, and create something new, bigger, and better than any one item could be on its own. A blender takes these items and crushes and forces them together so that what started out as separate, unrelated things now become amalgamated into something wonderful.

What a cook does in the kitchen when using a blender to mix ingredients is what God does with the universe. He is the consummate blender. He has an absolutely amazing ability to take unrelated things and come up with something bigger, better, and

more beautiful than what He started with.[414]

[God, Power of; Nature]
Isa. 64:8; Rom. 8:28

GOSPEL

THE GOSPEL is simply one beggar telling another beggar where to find food.[415]

[Bible]
Rom. 15:4

GOSPEL, GOOD NEWS OF

A YOUNG lady one day was speeding through a small Georgia town. She was traveling 70 mph in a 55 mph speed zone. The police pulled her over and wrote her a ticket that would cost her $100. She didn't have the money to pay it and ended up having to go to court over the ticket.

In the courtroom, the judge said, "You were found guilty of going 70 miles an hour in a 55 mile speed zone. You have to pay $100."

The young lady said, "I'm guilty, but I can't pay it. I don't have $100."

"Well, if you don't pay the ticket, we'll have to lock you up for the weekend."

"I can't pay the ticket, but I don't want to go to jail. Can you please just have mercy on me?"

The judge matter-of-factly replied, "I can't change the law. The law says that you've got to pay $100, or you have to spend the weekend in jail. Those are the rules, and I can't change the rules."

Starting to tear up she spoke in a small voice. "Isn't there something you can do? I can't pay it, but I don't want to get locked up. Have mercy on me."

The judge looked down on her, pushed his chair back from the bench, zipped down his robe, and took it off. He went over to the side, picked up his jacket, and put it on. He walked down and stood beside the girl, reached in his wallet, and brought out a hundred- dollar bill. He put the $100 bill on the bench, took off his jacket, then went over and picked up his robe. He zipped his robe and got back behind his bench.

"Young lady, you've been found guilty of going 70 miles an hour in a 55-mile-per-hour speed zone. The law is the law. I can't change it; the law says you must pay $100, or spend the weekend in jail. Ah! But I see somebody else has already paid the price."

God saw us speeding down the highway of sin. He zipped down the independent use of His deity and put on the jacket of humanity. He came down, died on the cross, and paid the price that you and I could not pay. He picked up the tab, rose from the dead, zipped up his glorified body, and ascended up to heaven. The good news of the gospel is that a bill we could not pay has already been paid. It has been paid by God Himself, in the person of Jesus Christ. Isn't that good news?[416]

[Cross; Gospel; Justification; Mercy]
Isa. 44:22; Eph. 2:8–9; Gal. 3:13

GOSSIP

FOUR preachers were out together and wanted to have a confession time. They were talking about their various failures. One preacher said, "Well, you know, I sometimes watch movies I shouldn't be watching." Another preacher said, "Well, you know, I go to the casino and gam-ble occasionally." The other guy said, "You know, when I'm by myself I smoke cigars and cigarettes." The fourth preacher said, "Well, my sin is gossip and I can't wait to get out of here."[417]

[Sin, Confession of]
Prov. 11:13; James 5:16

A YOUNG boy one day went to a monk and said, "I have slandered my neighbor. What can I do?"

The monk said, "Take a feather and put it on every step in the neighborhood."

And so the boy put out a couple of hundred feathers. He went back to the monk and said, "OK. Now what?"

"Now go pick them up." But when the boy went to pick them up, most of them had been blown away by the wind, to which the monk said, "Once you gossip, it's nearly impossible to stop it."[418]

[Sin, Effects of; Sin, in the Believer]
Prov. 11:13; 16:28; 1 Peter 3:10

GRACE

A FOCUS on grace can change one's perspective. For a little bit of joy in your life, wake up in the morning, and rather than complaining about what you don't have, start with the grace of God, start with what He's already done that you don't deserve in the first place. As the song says,

Count your blessings
Name them one by one
Count your blessings
See what God has done
Count your blessings
Name them one by one
And it will surprise you
What the Lord has done.[419]

[Blessing; Grace, Appreciation of]
Titus 3:3–7

A FATHER took his boys to the fair. He went to the ticket booth and bought a roll of tickets and dispensed it to his sons. Then one of his sons saw a school friend and brought him over to introduce him to his father. The school friend went over to the father, introduced himself, and then asked for a ticket! The father held back the tickets and said, "I'm sorry, I can't give you a ticket. I need to hang on to them to give rides to my sons today." But his son said, "That's OK, Dad, I don't mind sharing. You can give it to him." When the father heard the son give his okay, the father dispensed the ticket for the fair to the young man in the name of his son. When you come to God the Father, He looks at the Son for His OK. Why? Because the gift of the "ticket' is dependent on the Son. This is what we call grace.[420]

[Christ, Union with; Father God]
John 1:17; Rom. 3:23–24

GRACE is a force. It is like a tailwind that pushes us toward the will of God.[421]

[God's Will]

SOME purchases come with extras that have to be purchased. A new car is a sizable investment in and of itself, but there is always a long list of additional purchases that can be added on to enhance the new car and increase its price. There is the base price and then there's the price that includes all the extras. This is the case unless the car is considered "top of the line."

Many toys purchased for children during the Christmas season indicate on the box that batteries are not included and must be purchased separately. The toy is now accessible but doesn't include power. What good is a toy that needs a battery?

Grace is different. Grace comes with everything included. God says that everything He's ever going to do for you He's already done. Grace is also all-inclusive.[422]

[Grace, Sufficiency of; Justification; Power, Accessing]
Eph. 1:3; 2 Peter 1:3

A CONDUIT is a tubelike object that typically conveys water or some other fluid. There is a conduit for grace. It is the gospel of Jesus Christ. Jesus Christ is the conduit for grace.[423]

[Blessing, Source of; Jesus]
John 1:17; Titus 3:4–7

THE FACT that you live a better life, do better things, and are a nicer person may make you a better neighbor, but it doesn't make you fit for heaven. That can only happen by grace.

Suppose three men decided they wanted to swim to Hawaii. Well, one may swim farther than the others, but all three would end up dead because Hawaii's too far.

God is too high; He's too holy for us even on our best days, weeks, or years to make ourselves acceptable to Him. Our salvation is based on God's grace.[424]

[Salvation, Means of; Self-Sufficiency, Danger of]
Rom. 4:1–8; Eph. 2:8–9

GRACE, APPRECIATION OF

WHEN a person truly understands that oxygen is a gift, they will not smoke. If a person comprehends that good health is a gift, they are not going to abuse drugs. When a Christian understands that grace is a gift of God, they will make the choice to say no to wrong and yes to right. If a Christian loses sight of grace, then they become irresponsible with the life given to them by God.[425]

[Life, Management of; Self-
Sufficiency, Danger of]
Rom. 6:1; 2 Cor. 5:7

PEOPLE who love old westerns remember the old movie with Gary Cooper called *The Hanging Tree*. Gary Cooper is a doctor and he saves people's lives. In one scene, a young man gets shot; he's dying. Gary Cooper goes in and he pulls out the bullet and is able to save the man's life. The man, grateful for having been rescued, asks what he can do for the doctor. Gary Cooper says, "Well, you know, I've always needed an assistant, so why don't you assist me. I'll teach you what to do." When the young man asked how long the doctor wanted his help, Gary Cooper replies, "For the rest of your life because that's how long you would have been dead if I hadn't saved you."

God has said to you and me this is what He wants. For the rest of your life on earth, since He saved you, He wants you to yield yourself to His purposes, to His pleasure, and to His goals.[426]

[Salvation, Cost of; Salvation,
Gratefulness for]
Eph. 2:10

GRACE, LAW AND

HAVE you ever seen a person with a big dog on a leash and the dog is dragging the person or the person is pulling the dog? That is the way a lot of us are living our Christian lives; we're living it on a law leash. Stop that! Don't do that! Come here! Read your Bible! Pray! Go to church! There is nothing wrong with those things. It's just that a leash is jerking us around.

But have you ever seen a dog walked by its master without a leash and without ever leaving its master? The person walks and the dog walks. The person stops and the dog stops. He doesn't need a leash because he's got a good relationship with the dog.

You can always tell the difference between a grace dog and a law dog when you walk into a house. A law dog has its tail tucked underneath. Its master intimidates it. It's afraid of its master. It is a miserable dog. But a grace dog's tail is wagging when its master comes home because there's a relationship there.[427]

[Grace; Jesus, Relationship with;
Law, Effect of]
Rom. 7:7–25; Col. 2:20–23

GRACE, NEED FOR

THE NEED for grace is the problem of sin and the problem of sin cannot be solved by the efforts of man. Nothing you do can cancel out the problem of sin. Crushing five million oranges still won't give you an apple.[428]

[Heaven, Entrance into; Sin; Sin,
Dealing with]
Rom. 3:23–24; Eph. 2:8–9

GRACE, POWER OF

THE POLICEMAN has a law book. The policeman shows up because a law has been broken. But the book does not take you to jail. The book does not condemn or go after the person who's hurt you. All the codebook does is give you the guidelines by which the laws can be manifested.

When somebody is breaking in your house unauthorized, you don't need a codebook. You need a person who represents the codebook. That is, you need the codebook brought to life in an individual. You need a person to bring alive what's been written in the law book against trespassing on private property. You can't say to the criminal, Here is the law. You're trying to break in my house, let me read to you what the law says: "Thou shall not trespass on private property." While you are right with the law, there is no power in simply reading it. You will have to pick up and dial 911 because you want the law enforced by somebody who's got the power to pull off what the book talks about.

The grace of God has appeared. It teaches us from the book what's godly and what's not, but you're looking to the officer to enforce the book in the context of your environment. When you get the combination of the written Word connected with the Living Word, you get to experience the engine called grace.[429]

[Bible; God, Power of; Holy Spirit, Power of; Power, Accessing]
John 1:14

GRACE, PROVISION OF

ONE TIME, my wife and I were walking through the airport. We were changing flights and had to walk from one terminal to another. I got on the moving sidewalk, but she decided to just walk down the hallway without assistance. So, I am walking down the moving sidewalk with ease, because I am walking in the Spirit. In other words, I was mov-

ing, but I was resting my weight on the moving sidewalk, which was carrying me along. She was walking in the flesh, her own human effort, and her own ability. With less effort, I covered more distance in a lot less time. She was huffing and puffing; I was chilling. She was walking in the flesh, I was walking in the Spirit, and so my progress was much greater than her progress. Hers was purely human effort; mine was resting on the movement of something else underneath me. That made me able to enjoy my progress whereas she had to endure hers. After a bit, I turned around and waved just to rub it in how far I was ahead of her.

Once I got down to the end of the walkway, I was feeling pretty good and started wondering exactly how far back Sister Evans was. So I looked back and oddly enough didn't see her at all. She was not anywhere to be found.

All of a sudden I heard her call my name. I had to turn to look at her because her voice was coming from ahead of me. I was so confused because her position was impossible based on how she and I had traveled through the hallway. I had been walking in the Spirit, making great progress. She had been walking in the flesh and had been delayed. How was this possible? Well, it dawned on my wife that walking in the flesh wasn't going to work. It dawned on her that her human effort wasn't going to get her where she wanted to go. So she saw one of those carts driving by, waved it down, sat down, and passed me up.

She hitched a ride on a cart of grace.[430]

[Flesh, Walking in; Holy Spirit,

Power of]

Rom. 9:16; Gal. 3:3; Eph. 2:8–9

GRACE, SUFFICIENCY OF

SOME of us have service policies in our home that we haven't looked at for years. We have no clue as to what our benefits are. I was thumbing through the service contract for my car. I'd never looked at it, and one day I was sitting in my car waiting and decided to flip through it.

I discovered some benefits that I never knew I had simply because I had the vehicle. I had been paying for AAA but my service contract told me that because I own the car, the manufacturer would take care of any problems I had. I had been paying to get my tires rotated. The ser-vice contract told me that for the type of tires I have on the car, no rotation is needed. So I'd been fooling with stuff that's already been taken care of. I didn't understand the benefits that accrued to me by virtue of my having this vehicle.

We must realize that the relationship we have with the Lord Jesus Christ has benefits. The covenant brought about by salvation has provisions that we should be aware of.[431]

[Blessing; Grace, Provision of; Jesus, Relationship with; Salvation, Provision of]

2 Peter 1:3

THE STORY is told of a man who went on a voyage. He had been longing for so long to go on this voyage. It was a cruise and it cost him all he had. He packed himself peanut butter and jelly sandwiches because he knew he wouldn't be able to afford to buy any-thing on the cruise. It was a weeklong cruise and he planned to eat his peanut butter and jelly sandwiches the whole time for the length of the trip. As he finally embarked upon his long-awaited vacation, he was excited about the upcoming fun although it included the same meal day in and day out. At first, he was fine with his chosen fare, but after awhile, he began to notice all the food available to the other travelers. People were gorging themselves on beef, ham, turkey, chicken, and vegetables. He saw people having room service. He thought to himself, "Lord have mercy. I am here with peanut butter and jelly and these people are eating all of this!"

One day he saw one of the guys coming by with a big plate of food and the man asked how much would it cost just to get a little meal. This guy with the plate stared at the man. The man continued to explain that he only had enough money for his ticket, didn't bring enough for the meals, but now thought he would like to try something small. With disbelief, the guy told the man that the meals were included in the price of the ticket.

There are a lot of Christians today eating peanut butter and jelly sandwiches, wondering why they can't enjoy a megameal. They look around at other Christians who seem to be victorious, seem to be "on top," or seem to be eating spiritual steak and potatoes, and wonder why they are limited to peanut butter, jelly, and bread. What that man on the cruise ship didn't understand is what far too many Christians don't understand, and that is the principle of grace.

When Jesus went through the heavens and was seated on the right-hand side of the Father, all the meals were included in that ticket. All the help is in that ticket. All the enablement is in that ticket. All the strength is in that ticket. Leave the peanut butter and jelly sandwiches alone and avail yourself of the provisions of God that are in the ticket. Keep in mind, however, that they are only dispensed at the throne of grace.[432]

[Blessing; Christian Living, New
Life; Grace, Provision of; Salvation,
Provision of; Spiritual Food]
Luke 11:11–13; Phil. 4:19; 2 Peter 1:3

GRATEFULNESS

A MAN needed his pants ironed. His wife, as she ironed the pants for him, burned the pants. These pants were brand-new pants that he was looking forward to wearing. Her husband started to get mad but stopped to think before reacting and said, "Lord, thank You that my leg wasn't in those pants." There is always a reason to give thanks. ("Be anxious for nothing, but in prayer and supplication with thanksgiving.")[433]

[Perspective; Thanksgiving,
Importance of]
1 Chron. 16:8; Ps. 7:17; Phil. 4:6

A MAN got on the bus one day, found a seat, and sat down. On the next stop, a lady got on and had to stand up because there were no seats. The man who had boarded the bus earlier stood up to give her his seat as he was taught to do as a boy. When the lady sat down, she fainted because she was so astonished that someone would offer his seat to her.

When she came to, she thanked the man. Then he fainted out of shock that somebody would be that grateful.[434]

[Thanksgiving, Motivation for]
Ps. 105:1; Luke 17:11–17; Heb. 12:28

MATTHEW Henry, the famous Bible scholar wrote in his diary, "Let me be thankful first, because I was never robbed before; second, because although they took my purse, they did not take my life; third, let me be thankful that although they took my all, it was not much; and fourth, because it was I who was robbed and not I who robbed."[435]

[Gratitude; Thanksgiving,
Motivation for; Perspective]
Ps. 103:2; 1 Thess. 5:1–18

I HATE squash. One of the worst things I could do at the dinner table is exclaim my distaste for squash. That was only a signal to take the squash bowl and forcibly serve me, putting the squash on my plate. Mom always put more on my plate than I would have put had I humbled myself to eat it in the first place. Then my mother would just sit and watch me eat, ensuring that I ate it all up.

Complaining would only make things worse. It would only make my mother go "overseas" on me and start talking about kids in India who would love to be having squash right now. If I insisted on not eating the squash, I would quickly hear, "Well, you ain't hungry then."[436]

[Children, Training; Ungratefulness]
Num. 11:1; 1 Cor. 10:10; Phil. 2:14

I DON'T eat fish. My father was a longshoreman and as a longshoreman he loaded and unloaded boats. Sometimes there would be periods where ships weren't coming in regularly or maybe the longshoremen would go on strike so we would go without income for segments of time. My father had to feed his family so he would go out on a boat and catch herring.

Herrings have hundreds of small bones inside. My dad would catch herring by the net and he would bring them home. So we would have herring for breakfast, lunch, and dinner! Boiled egg and herring, herring sandwich for lunch, or herring and rice for dinner. Although I gradually developed a hatred for anything in the fish family, my daddy would always say that this was all we had and he would give thanks because we were eating *something*.[437]

[Daily Bread; Provision, God's]
Num. 11:4–6; 1 Kings 17:7–16

THERE is the story of a little boy who wanted his mother to pay him for all the services he was rendering in the home. He left her a note that read:

For washing the dishes, you owe me a dollar. For cleaning my room, you owe me a dollar. For hanging up my clothes, you owe me a dollar. For mowing the lawn, you owe me a dollar. Mama, you owe me, pay up.

He printed a bill for her, totaling four dollars and gave it to her.

The mother came and put four dollars on the kitchen table with a note of her own. The note simply said:

For carrying you nine months and being sick as a dog, no charge. For staying up all night with you, night after night when you were sick, no charge. For working overtime so that I could get you those special tennis shoes, no charge. For entertaining your friends when you wanted to bring 'em over without notice, no charge. Signed, your mother who loves you. Total, zero.

After reading the note, that young man realized that he had lost sight of the goodness of mother. He had turned a love relationship into a business deal. He had said to his mother what a lot of God's children say to Him: "Pay up. What's in it for me?"[438]

[Father God; God's Goodness; Ungratefulness]
1 Sam. 10:17–19; Ps. 118:12

I USED to have a dog. I was feeding it one day. I was reaching down to move the dog's plate to get it in the right position and the dog growled at me. This didn't sit well with me at all!

My thoughts went something like this: *What! I've been feeding you for years. I've been buying you food when I didn't know how I was going to eat; I've cleaned up messes that you've made in this house. Don't bite the hand that feeds you.*

Let's just say that he used to be my dog. He couldn't snap at me and me still be his provider. He wasn't going to get ticked off at me and have me as his provider. He was not going to get an attitude with me and keep me as his provider.

The only reason this dog was eating was because he was in my house. I bought the bowl and put the food in it. When he needed water, he couldn't reach the sink! I filled the bowl with water and put it down for him to drink. When he needed to go outside to use the restroom late at night, I got up and opened the door. That dog should never have barked at me!

In the same way, God doesn't want any attitudes from us. Every time we see Him approach, He expects us to give thanks and have attitudes of gratitude.[439]

[Provision, God's; Thanksgiving, Motivation for; Ungratefulness]
Heb. 12:28

GREATNESS

WHILE I was going through seminary, I worked at Trailways Bus Station loading buses. I worked on the dead man's shift from eleven at night until seven in the morning. When I came to work there, I realized that the guys had a scam going. A guy would punch out for lunch and then have his buddies punch him back in when in reality he was asleep on the job.

Each guy would get his turn and the other guys would cover for each other and await their turn to get three hours or so of sleep while on the job. Put simply, what they were doing was stealing. It was theft. They had agreed to work for eight hours but were stealing a few hours every night from the company.

After I'd been around a few days, one of the guys came to me and asked me which part of the night shift I wanted to take for a long break. He explained the system to me, how long I could take, and who I was to punch in. When I told him that I couldn't do it because I was a Christian, what I thought would be a great witnessing opportunity didn't go over too well. The guys all decided to teach me a lesson.

When buses would show up during the night needing to be unloaded and then loaded again, the other guys wouldn't show up and help. I found myself loading and unloading buses by myself. That situation was hard. It was very painful both emotionally, knowing people were against me, as well as physically, because it was a lot of work. And to top it all off, I'd have to still, after all of that work, go to class. It was rough.

About six months into this, I got called to the office—the Trailways office. The supervisor said, "Unbeknownst to the night crew, we have had various night supervisors come down and observe the activities. We are aware of the scam. We have also noticed that you haven't participated and have not been supported when the buses came in. We would like to offer you the opportunity to become the supervisor for the night shift and we will double your salary!"

My enemies became my footstool.

God is watching. Some of the greatness comes in time. Most of it comes in eternity. If you want to be great, take advantage of every opportunity to serve for the benefit of others, to the glory of God.[440]

[Conscience; Deception, Cost of; Faithfulness; Reward]
Ps. 73:1–28; Matt. 10:28; Gal. 6:9

GREED

SOME thieves one day broke into a store but didn't steal anything. They just exchanged the tags. They took a $6,000 tag off of a diamond ring and put it on an imitation diamond. They took the imitation diamond tag of $99.95 and put it on the $6,000 ring. They took an imitation print painting and reversed its tag with that of an expensive original. People came in and bought stuff up. They spent a lot of money on the worthless and a little bit of money on the expensive.

We live in a culture today that has switched the tags. We put a lot of money on the flashy and put thirty-nine cents on character. We put a lot of money on expensive cars and high positions of career, but we put ten cents on integrity, truthfulness, dignity, and character. We have switched the tags. Don't let anybody switch your tags.[441]

[Materialism, Deception of; Money, Love of]

Ps. 90:12; Matt. 6:19–21; 16:26

GREED, EMPTINESS OF

MONEY cannot bring satisfaction. It is like the man who said, "Last month my aunt died and left me $25,000. Last week, my brother died and left me $38,000. I am so depressed."

His good friend said, "Why are you depressed?"

He said, "Because this week, nobody died."[442]

[Materialism, Deception of; Money; Perspective, Need for]

Eccl. 5:10; 1 Tim. 6:9–10

MANY of us were like the dog in the fable carrying a juicy steak across a bridge. As he walked and crossed the bridge, he looked over and saw the reflection of his face with the steak in his mouth. He thought it was another dog with a bigger steak. So he went after the bigger steak and got neither.[443]

[Greed; Materialism, Deception of; Money, Love of]

Eccl. 5:10; Luke 12:15; 1 Tim. 6:10

GREED, INFLUENCE OF

ONE DAY a man called the church. He got the secretary and said, "I would like to speak to the head hog at the trough."

The secretary said, "What did you say?"

The man gladly repeated himself, "I would like to speak with the head hog at the trough!"

"If you mean the pastor, it would be more appropriate if you would say, 'I want to speak to the pastor.'"

The man, a bit taken aback, said, "Well, I had $25,000 that I wanted to give to the church."

The secretary quickly replied, "Hold the line. I think the big pig is coming in right now."

Money changes people.[444]

[Money]

H

HARD HEART

MANY people smoke day after day, month after month, year after year and all of a sudden their ability to breathe is impacted and the lungs become hard. A lung is supposed to be soft and pliable but when a person smokes like that, their lungs become hard and the air can't penetrate them.

You can read the Bible until you are blue in the face, but if it is being read by a hard heart, the Spirit won't penetrate it.[445]

[Bible, Use of; Spiritual Maturity, Growth]

1 Sam. 6:6; Prov. 28:14; Matt. 13:15

SOME people go to the podiatrist because they need him to cut off a callous where their skin has gotten really hard. It's not that they don't still have soft skin; it's just that it's been covered over for so long, they can't feel it anymore.

When you and I have gone an extended time away from God, a callous can grow, so that you don't feel the desire to be close to God. It's not that the desire isn't there. A new nature exists for Christians and the new nature always is feeling God. The reason a person might not feel the desire is because they are calloused. Their heart has become hard, many times due to ungratefulness and discontent.[446]

[Ungratefulness]
Isa. 29:13; Mark 7:6

HEAVEN, ENTRANCE INTO

WHEN citizens travel overseas, they need a passport to enter into another country. The passport must be stamped, giving the person access to enter the country. No passport, no entrance.

In order to enter heaven, a person must have a passport stamped with the blood of Christ. No passport, no entrance.[447]

[Grace; Heaven, Entrance into;
Salvation, Means of]
Rom. 4:1–8; Eph. 2:8–9

HEAVENLY MIND-SET

THE ACTOR James Dutton was the main character on the TV show *Rock*. Before Mr. Dutton became a famous actor, he was a prisoner. One day, he was being interviewed by a reporter who asked him why he never became a repeat offender. The reporter asked Dut-

ton why he didn't commit another crime like so many other men who have ended up back in prison. His answer was very informative. He said, "Unlike other prisoners, I never decorated my cell." In other words, I never made my prison cell home.

Many of us are not only in prison, we've decorated the site because it's home. We've decided since there's no way to get out of here, I might as well learn to live with it. I might as well make myself at home. I might as well get comfortable here because I'm never going to get out of this mess. I've been here too long. I've gone too deep. I will never find freedom. Let me resign to living a defeated Christian life.[448]

[Worldliness, Distraction of]
Gal. 5:1

HELL

JUST outside of San Francisco is a rock. This is where the Alcatraz prison is located. Alcatraz is in the San Francisco Bay. It is not an operating prison now, but when it held prisoners, it was considered a place of exile. In and of itself, it's a pretty tough place to get out of. But Alcatraz is also surrounded by the shark-infested waters of the San Francisco Bay. This body of water kept the prisoners from enjoying the life of San Francisco, which is not that far away.

The Bible says that hell will be placed in a lake of fire not so far from heaven that people sentenced to eternal damnation won't be able to know about the enjoyment of the folks in heaven. The lake of fire will not allow the people in this eternal prison to go anywhere.

This spiritual Alcatraz will house different folks at different levels of security, just like the Alcatraz near San Francisco. Some are under maximum security, some are under medium security, and some are under minimal security based on how bad they were. Hell will be the same way. The Bible declares that all people are not equal. The very worst of sinners go to maximum security hell. The mediocre sinners go the medium security hell. The nice people, so to speak, who just did mental sins and never did anything really bad—well, they will go to minimum security hell, but they are all on the same rock.

Why can't they go anywhere? Because the rock is in a lake. When the rich man opened his eyes in hell, the Bible says he saw Lazarus afar off. You see, from Alcatraz you can see San Francisco. From Alcatraz you can see the tall buildings and the high rises. You can see pulsating life in the big city. All a prisoner can do is to look at where they could have been and where they will never be. The worst part of hell is being able to see heaven and not go there because it is surrounded by a lake of fire and brimstone. It's a lake smoldering with fire. No one can swim across it. It is like having sharks in the water. You cannot escape this place. Even if you are a nice person and you are in minimum security, you are still on the rock. It is a place of the second death where the stench of death never leaves and the worm never dies. It is like living in a graveyard.[449]

[Eternity; Sin, Consequences of]
Luke 16:19–31; John 3:36

HELP

ONE TIME I was trapped on an elevator. The immediate reaction of all of the people was panic. We were trapped, stuck, and couldn't get out. Some people were crying, "Help! Help! Help!" Were we sincerely crying out? Yes! Were we begging for help? Yes! But it wasn't working.

Other folks were banging on the door. Bam, bam, bam! No one was hearing all that noise, but those folks didn't care. They kept right on banging. Desperate people do desperate things. They were crying out.

There was one calm man on the elevator. I simply walked to the other side, pulled out a latch, picked up the telephone, and waited.

A voice said, "Is there a problem?" I said, "We're trapped on the elevator between this floor and this floor. Can we get some help?" They responded, "We'll be right there."

See, everybody forgot about the phone. We were so into being trapped that we forgot there was a phone link to the security department. Merely by picking up the phone, we were released from our hostage situation. All the human effort we put forth, banging and yelling, wouldn't work, but picking up the phone and asking for help did. We had to seek help using the connection.[450]

[Prayer; Prayer, Deliverance through]
Phil. 4:6; James 5:13

HIGH PRIEST, SYMPATHY OF

THERE are plenty of women who have gone through the labor of childbirth. Many women have had a male doctor to deliver their baby. A male doctor can understand everything that his patient is going through. He can know what is supposed to happen during childbirth and what he needs to do to take care of the mom and facilitate the birth of the baby. In other words, he has the power to deliver the baby. But he doesn't have the ability to feel the pain.

He can see a mother struggling with the pain, but he can't experience it. He can hear the groans and functionally and informationally come to the aid of a laboring mom, but he can't say to the mother that he knows how she feels.

Now, some women have their babies delivered by a female doctor who is also a mother. She can do what the male doctor did informationally. She can do what the male doctor did medically. She can do what the male doctor did in terms of proficiency of labor and delivery. But she can also do something else. She can empathize with her patient and let the laboring mom know that she has been there too and can feel her pain.

The female doctor can do what the male doctor can do plus something more. She can sympathize and understand what it is to cry when there is no epidural. She can sympathize and understand what it is to be frustrated when the baby is taking awhile to make its way down the birth canal. She can sympathize and understand what it is to be angry with a husband in the midst of the pain. She can sympathize because she's been there.

In the same way, because of Jesus Christ, we have a Great High Priest who not only is a doctor and can deliver, but who has been where we are and can understand what we are go-

ing through.[451]

[Jesus; Circumstances, Understanding]
1 Tim. 2:5; Heb. 4:15

HOLINESS, IMPORTANCE OF

IN A hospital, cleanliness is very important. In fact, the closer you get to the operating room, the more important it is. Doctors in an operating room are very concerned that the scalpel not only is not muddy, but that it's not even dusty because the smallest amount of impurity contaminates the procedure. Great effort is made to sterilize the equipment so that all impurity is removed and no infection sets in.

If human doctors go through great detail in an operating room to make sure that the environment is totally free from contamination, then ought it shock us that God Himself must function in an atmosphere of perfection? If human doctors recognize you can't do surgery with contaminated devices, then it ought not make us too upset that God can't do the surgery on our lives that He wants to do without sterilizing our lives first.[452]

[God's Holiness; Justification; Sanctification]
Lev. 11:45; 2 Cor. 7:1

HOLY SPIRIT, FILLING OF

WHEN you leave church on Sundays, you go to your car and make your way home or out to dinner. You will deplete the reserve of gas in the tank. You don't have to be a bad person for your car to go from full to empty. You just have to use the car. If you drive, I can guarantee you, you will deplete gasoline.

Many times, when people leave

church, they are spiritually full because of the time they spent singing praises to God and hearing His Word. However, within two hours of being filled, their spiritual tank will begin to dissipate. All a person has to do to lose their "filling" is to live life. Life has its way of draining out the reality of the Holy Spirit in you.

Just like a person who drives a car has to continue to make trips to the gas station to fill up and make the car run smoothly, Christians must continue to be filled with the Holy Spirit.[453]

[Church, Attendance; Church, Role of; Power, Accessing]
Eph. 5:15–19; Heb. 10:25

HOLY SPIRIT, GRIEVING

TO GRIEVE the Holy Spirit is like letting corrosion build up on a battery so that the power of the battery cannot be accessed. In the life of a Christian, when the Holy Spirit is grieved, the charge and power available declines or is lost.[454]

[Christian Living; Sin, in the Believer]
Isa. 63:10; Eph. 4:30

HOLY SPIRIT, GUIDANCE

WHEN the Bible says, "He will guide you into all truth . . ." that's a way of saying that the Holy Spirit will be the steering wheel of your life.

There are two ways to get to a destination. One way is to look at the map and figure it out yourself as you drive. Another way is to have someone drive you who already knows where they are going.[455]

[Christian Living, New Life; Decisions; Life, Management of]

John 14:15–21; 16:7

HOLY SPIRIT, ILLUMINATION OF

MOST of us in our homes have dimmer switches. Dimmer switches are designed to progressively turn up the lights.

The Holy Spirit is your dimmer. What He does is turn up the light so that you can see things you couldn't see before. We have to be in tune with Him though. His illumination won't necessarily come on with one flip of the switch. If you are open and listening, the dimmer does work. Illumination sets in because, over time, the light gradually comes on as we study the Word.[456]

[Bible, Guidance of; Light]
John 14:26; Acts 1:8

HOLY SPIRIT, IMPORTANCE OF

DEEP sea divers enter the water with tanks on their backs. These tanks contain oxygen. The purpose of these tanks strapped to their backs is so that they can make it in a foreign world. Water is not their natural habitat; it's not the normal place for them to live, so in order for them to survive in this foreign world of water, they need to be connected to a life source from their real world. In order for them to make it in that world, they need air from this world. In other words, if they get disconnected from the air from this world, they won't last long in that world. Their connectedness is the key to their survival because they weren't meant to live in water. So they borrow from this world in order to live in that world.

That life source in the life of a

Christian is the Holy Spirit. God has given the Christian a life source because this world to the Christian is foreign territory. In order to live here and make it, you need to be connected to a life source from your real world. If you get disconnected from the life source from your real world, you won't make it in this world as a Christ follower. You'll be gagging for air that this world doesn't offer because it's foreign territory. This life source comes through the indwelling of the Holy Spirit.[457]

[Holy Spirit, Role of; World, Living in]

Col. 1:13

HOLY SPIRIT, POWER OF

THERE was a famous commercial a few years back: "Plop, plop, fizz, fizz, oh-what-a-relief-it-is!" The commercial advertised Alka-Seltzer—a medicine designed to aid an upset stomach. Alka-Seltzer would be activated by the act of dropping two tablets into water. The ensuing reaction is quite volcanic.

When people accept Christ as Savior, God drops the Holy Spirit into our new nature. The Spirit's presence is designed to bring about a change for upset lives, upset minds, and upset circumstances. God did this so that His people would discover "oh-what-a-relief-He-is."[458]

[New Life in Christ; Salvation, Benefits of]

Acts 2:1–4; 2 Cor. 5:17

A MAN had the duty of buying his grandson a birthday present. He detested the idea of going into the toy store because he thought that, with the number of toys available, he'd have trouble making a decision. When he arrived, he hunted down a salesperson and asked for help. He gave the young lady helping him the age of his grandson and asked her to lead him to toys that would be suitable. She brought the man to an aisle full of trucks. Some were nice and big; some were small and designed for collection. The man chose a big truck, thinking that it would be sturdy enough to outlast a preschooler.

The man then realized that this truck would probably require batteries. The salesperson pressed the button on top of the toy truck. The truck began to make a heap of noise. The young lady looked at the man, smiled, and said, "Sir, the batteries are included!"

This is what God says about the Holy Spirit after our salvation—batteries included. The job of the Holy Spirit is to empower the new nature to satisfy the law of God or the demands of God.[459]

[Holy Spirit, Role of; New Life in Christ]

John 16:12–15; 1 Thess. 1:5

A MINISTER was looking for some notes that he desperately needed for a presentation. He looked everywhere, multiple times, in an effort to recover the lost material. He asked around in his office, checked in his car, and retraced his steps. He gradually progressed from a random search, looking any and everywhere to an organized search, taking each room, one at a time, area by area. Exhausted, he grabbed his keys, headed to his car, and made his way to the event at which he was expected.

When it was time for him to speak, he ushered up a quick prayer

breath, expecting to hear that in order to fix their heating system, they would have to pay a pretty penny. But the pro had surprising news. The problem was minor, only a few bucks to fix. The igniter was out. The furnace was self-igniting—designed to ignite automatically. A tiny thing like an igniter was causing such a big problem. It worked but was not making the connection necessary to kick the heater into gear. The igniter was there but wasn't doing what it was designed to do because of a bad connection.

The couple didn't need a new heater. They had all the power they needed. They just needed to change out a small part that would enable them to access the power resident in their heater to heat their home.

Many new Christians wonder how they can have all the power available to them and have such cold, and sometimes miserable, lives. Their igniter is not working. When it's not operative, the available power does no good.

When we come to faith in Jesus Christ, we have all the power we need. "Old things are passed away and all things become new." We have all we need. God gives us a new heart, a new consciousness, forgiveness of sin, and empowerment. God has an igniter called the Holy Spirit. If the igniter is not working, it's because we are not allowing Him to by responding to His prompting.[465]

[God, Power of; Power, Accessing; Spirit, Power of]
Acts 1:8; 2 Cor. 5:17; 1 Thess. 1:5

HOLY SPIRIT, SENSITIVITY OF

TRAFALGAR Square in England is known for the collection of pigeons that come there. Thousands of pigeons show up to feed on the bread crumbs that people bring. Doves are not seen at Trafalgar Square. A dove is one of the most sensitive birds ever created. If a dove sniffs anything that could irritate it, it will fly away.

The Bible portrays the Holy Spirit as a dove—very sensitive. When the Holy Spirit senses anything that is contrary to the King and His kingdom, He doesn't want to hang around.[466]

[Sin, Contamination by; Sin, Stain of]
1 Cor. 3:16

WHEN TRAVELERS go through the airport and put their bags on the conveyor belt, the bags go through an X-ray machine and someone sits there and looks at it. That person sits there looking for something in the bags that don't belong. If they see a metal object in a bag or something that is questionable, they pull the bag owner off to the side and then go all through their belongings. They will get out of the bags anything that does not belong so that the traveler is free to make their trip.

The Holy Spirit does the same thing. He goes through our things. Sometimes we wonder why it is taking so long for God to make a breakthrough. It is because the Holy Ghost is going through our stuff and He may have picked up on something that's in our bag that doesn't belong there. He is not about to take off with someone who's got questionable baggage.[467]

[Holy Spirit; Sin, Contamination by; Sin, Stain of]
1 Cor. 3:16

HOPE

MANY Christians believe that hope is wishing for something you are never going to get.[468]

[Faith; Waiting]
Rom. 8:24

A BOY was at the supermarket with his mother, and he asked his mother for some chocolate chip cookies. "Mommy, get me some chocolate chip cookies."

Mother said, "No, we are in a hurry. I don't have any extra money. No chocolate chip cookies today."

As they continued shopping, the little boy said, "But, Mama, I want some chocolate chip cookies."

"No, no chocolate chip cookies today."

"Mama, please, why won't you get me chocolate chip cookies?"

She said, "Boy, you are getting on my nerves. I told you we are not getting chocolate chip cookies today." She continued to shop.

"Mama, I am begging you for chocolate chip cookies."

"You are about to get in trouble, son! I told you you're not getting chocolate chip cookies today. If you ask me again, I'm going to have to punish you."

She got in the checkout line. While waiting, the little boy stood up in the cart, clasped his hands, looked up to heaven, and said, "Jesus, my mama won't give me any chocolate chip cookies, but You told me to pray to You about anything. I am asking You to make a way for me to get some chocolate chip cookies, because my mama is not giving me any chocolate chip cookies."

People in the line started saying, "Why won't she give that boy some chocolate chip cookies?"

The little boy kept on praying, "Oh, please, Jesus, give me some chocolate chip cookies." His mother got so embarrassed, she went and got two packs of chocolate chip cookies. She came back, put them in the cart, and he said, "Thank You, Jesus."

Many Christians today are in the checkout line. They are ready to check out on God, check out on the church, or check out on their faith. We must not forget to stop, look up, and call on Jesus.

We must tell Him that we are depending on Him and relying on Him to come through. Don't check out just yet. Wait to see what God does for you in the checkout line.[469]

[Prayer; Prayer, Access in;
Provision, God's]
Luke 11:9–10; James 5:13

MY WIFE is the leftover queen. Especially, when the kids were young, she fixed these humongous Sunday meals— big roast, potatoes accompanied with sweet potatoes, green beans, macaroni and cheese, and of course some freshly baked hot bread. We'd come home after church and eat these humongous meals. After dinner, she'd take the leftovers, put them in Tupperware, and then put them in the refrigerator.

On Monday, the leftovers would come back out. I'd see her in the kitchen doing some dicing and chopping, and then some sprinkling of some cheese. I'd say, "What are we having for dinner?" She'd give me some French name and I'd think we were eating something new. You know what we were eating? Leftovers in the hands of a master.

When God gives you what seems like leftovers, He's giving you something good. He knows how to take a difficult situation and work something together in such a way that we are left in amazement at the outcome.[470]

[Second Chances]

John 6:13; 1 Peter 2:9

THERE'S a very beautiful story about a beautiful lady. Her name is Cinderella. But Cinderella was made to feel ugly. She lived with a wicked stepmother and two equally wicked sisters. We all are influenced by a wicked stepmother, the Devil, who's got two wicked daughters: the world and the flesh. Cinderella was made to live as a slave. Now, she was beautiful, but she didn't feel beautiful. She didn't think about herself as beautiful, because she was being influenced by a wicked environment that put her down, messed over her, and reduced her to nothing. The problem with Cinderella was that she was stuck there. She was locked in the situation, and for a long time, she could not get out of it.

But lo and behold, one night there was a ball. And through a series of miraculous interventions, she was transported to the ball in a chariot. There she met a prince. The prince saw Cinderella, and loved her. But the problem in the story, as you know, is that the clock struck midnight. When the clock hit midnight, she reverted back to her old ways. She became a slave again to an evil stepmother, and an evil stepsister.

But the good news of the story is the prince never forgot Cinderella. Oh, there were a whole lot of folk at the ball,

but there was something about Cinderella that made her different from the crowd. Everybody wanted the prince, but the prince wanted Cinderella. He spared no effort to find Cinderella. All he had to work with was a walking problem. There was a shoe left behind. He needed to find the foot that fit this shoe. When he found the foot that fit this shoe, he would have found Cinderella.

The prince went from house to house, trying the shoe on different women, because he wanted to get to the person on whom the shoe fit. He finally came to Cinderella's house, put the shoe on her foot, and he had found her. He gave her a kiss, and you know how the story ends. It says . . . and they lived happily ever after.

A lot of us are living like Cinderella. We're living as slaves, under the world, the flesh, and the Devil. Satan is holding us hostage. Maybe a few years ago you met the Prince of Peace, and He saved you, but you have gone back to living at the midnight hour, with that devil and his two daughters. They have you trapped in slavery. But, Jesus knows where you are, and He knows how long you've been there. When He comes knocking on your door, with those slippers, He'll let you know He wants to get you up out of there.

He doesn't just want to bring His money to you, His castle to you, or His chariot to you, He wants to take you up out of there, and let you go live with Him. He wants to remove you from those premises, and give you a brand-new place to live. He wants to show you your new position, your new glory, and your new hope. He wants to get you out of that slavery. He just doesn't want to buy you a new dress, buy you a new coat, or buy you a new car; He wants to give you a new life.

Suppose Cinderella had said, "Look, Prince. I like you, Prince. I want your money. I want your chariot. I want your castle. I want your title. But I don't want to commit myself to you." I am sure the prince would have found somebody else, because he wanted to find somebody whom he could love, not just somebody whom he could be used by. A lot of us haven't had our blessing to come through because we want to use God; we don't want God. God wants us to want Him, so that He can make us whole, so that when we connect He can say, happily ever after, because He has made us whole.[471]

[Flesh; Jesus, Relationship with; New Life in Christ; Worldliness, Distraction of]

Acts 3:19; Gal. 5:1

HUMANITY

WE ARE surrounded by radio waves. But without a radio, those waves won't do us a whole lot of good. The waves that transport the sound need a vehicle through which to express themselves. It needs something that can contain what is invisibly being distributed all around and make it make sense in terms that our five senses can understand. Our five senses can't understand radio waves. We don't pick up that signal. The radio, however, has been duly constructed to be able to catch, interpret, and dispense talk shows, music, and news and all manner of information. The radio serves as the vehicle to communicate the invisible.

So it is with our bodies. Our bodies are designed by God to be the vehicle through which God expresses His program and plan for us and for His own sake. To put it another way, our humanity is God's conduit. Our humanity is God's conduit for the purposes of achieving God's goal.[472]

[Body of Christ; Church, Role of; Christian Living, Purpose]

1 Cor. 6:19; 12:27

HUMILITY

IN FOOTBALL, they tell the offensive line, no matter how big you are, stay low. So that you can have leverage, stay low. No matter how big you get in life, stay low. No matter what title you have in front of your name, how much money you have in the bank, or how many people know who you are, stay low. The moment you use your knowledge, prestige, power, or resources to attempt to be like God, it will be made very clear, very soon, there is only one God. Humble yourself beneath His mighty hand.[473]

[Humility, Need for; Poor in Spirit; Pride, Problem of]

Matt. 18:4; James 4:10

MAN was made from the ground. He's an earthling, and on his best day he's just dignified dirt. In fact, every living person is only worth about $3.57. When a person dies, all of their components return to dirt and the value is only about $3.57.

That's why you can't think too highly of yourself. You are just not worth that much. So when you get in your Benz, it's only $3.57 driving a Benz. It's $3.57 living in the suburbs. It's $3.57 wearing designer clothes. It's $3.57 with more money in the bank than you're actually worth.[474]

[Humility, Need for]
Ps. 144:3–4; Rom. 12:3

WHEN my first grandson was being born, he had a little difficulty coming into the world. The doctor remarked that the head was in the wrong position. The easiest way for a baby to be born is for him to be facing down. Because my grandson wasn't facing down, his delivery process was an extended one. Even his mother experienced extended pain because of this. It's better if the head is turned down when delivery takes place. If the head is turned up, you get extended pain.

A lot of us have extended pain because our heads are turned up. It's in the wrong position. We haven't turned our head down and humbled ourselves beneath the mighty hand of God so that He may exalt us.[475]

[Humility, Need for; Pride]
Matt. 18:4; James 4:10

WHEN weightlifters want to strengthen their legs, there is no exercise that competes with the squat. You put the weights on your shoulders and you go down, up and down, up and down, in order to build strength in your legs. In order to build your hamstrings, in order to build your legs, you've got to squat. Most of us don't get low enough. We're not growing stronger because we're not willing to bend.[476]

[Poor in Spirit; Spiritual Maturity, Growth]
Matt. 23:12; James 1:10

FOR MOST men, getting behind the wheel in the car with their wife as the passenger can be a lesson in humility.

You are driving down the highway.

Your wife says, "Honey, do you know where you are going?"

"Yeah, I know exactly where we are." Sweat is popping up on your forehead, because you don't want to admit that you are lost.

"Well, honey, why don't you pull over, and ask somebody?"

You don't understand, ladies. To ask us to pull over and ask somebody is an attack on our manhood. What you are telling us in a nice way is, you don't know what you are doing.

The farther you drive, the harder it is to admit you're lost. So now you have to compensate for your losses. "We are almost there. Just two more lights and we should be there." All the while you are hoping, sweating, and praying that you luck your way onto the right road. Prayer meetings are going on in the car now as you silently think, "Father, show me which way to go."

All of this energy is expended to avoid having to ask for help. A lack of humility can really get in the way of reaching one's destination.[477]

[Help; Pride, Problem of]
Ps. 29: 23; Prov. 11:2

ONE time, I was driving, and the car was on empty. It's not just on "E," its passed "E." The car is going along, starting to hiccup and cough the way it does when you are about to run out completely.

My wife said, "Tony, you've got to pull over. We're going to be stuck out here on the highway, you know."

Okay, now we have two problems. One, she's telling me what to do.

Problem number two, she's telling me how to do it. I mean, I'm the man; I *need* to be in control!

"No, we're going to be fine." Now, I am sweating bullets, because I know this car could stop at any moment.

"Well, I don't know, Tony. I think we are going to run out before we get to a station."

"Oh no, we're not. We are going to be all right." In my spirit, I am begging for the next exit to come up quick. The only reason I skipped the last exit was because I wanted to be in charge. All of a sudden the car starts to jerk.

"See, this is what I am talking about."

I'm still sweating bullets. An exit is coming up, but that doesn't solve my problem. I don't just need an exit; I need a station. At that moment, I needed God to show me His creative power!

I make it to the exit and start to veer to the right. There is a station! The exit was on a decline. Just as I take the exit, the car runs out of gas, but now I'm rolling down the hill. I'm trying my best to be cool, praying that we are going to make it. At the bottom of the hill is an Exxon station. The car rolls all the way down the hill, I steer it into the station, and the car comes to a halt right at the pump.

I look at my wife and say, "See, if I tell you we don't have to stop, you don't have to question me!"

The truth is that a little dose of humility might have saved us both a lot of anxiety![478]

[Help; Men, and Their Wives; Pride, Problem of]
Ps. 29:23; Prov. 11:2

HUMILITY, NEED FOR

A BOY Scout was on a plane with a pilot, a minister, and a computer whiz. There was trouble on the plane. The plane was beginning to dive. They realized that they had to put on parachutes and jump. The only problem was there were only three parachutes and there were four people. The pilot came and said, "Well, look, I've got a wife and four kids, I need a parachute." So, he took the parachute and he jumped.

The computer whiz said, "Well, I've got all of this knowledge that the world desperately needs for the twenty-first century, and I can't have it die with me, so I need a parachute." So, the computer whiz took a parachute and he jumped.

The minister looked at the little boy and said, "Well, look, I've lived a long, full life and you're just a young man. You take the last parachute, and I'll go down with the plane."

The little boy looked at the minister and said, "Mr. Minister, don't worry about it. The brilliant computer whiz just took my knapsack and jumped out of the plane."

A lot of us are too smart for our britches. We think more of ourselves than we ought to. We think we're a life whiz and every time we jump out to do right, we fall flat on our face. God has what we need in order to jump and land on our feet. All we have to do is humble ourselves and submit to Him.[479]

[Humility; Pride, Problem of]
Prov. 16:18; Luke 22:26

HUNGER

APPETITE is one of the great indicators to a doctor of your health. Consistent loss of appetite is an indication of a much deeper problem.[480]

[Christian Living, Spiritual Growth; Sin, in the Believer]

Matt. 5:6; Luke 6:21

FROM TIME TO time in church, I'll look out in the audience as we are conducting our services and notice a mother who has a baby in her arms. Many times she's sitting toward the back of the sanctuary so that she can get to one of the cry rooms if the need arises. When the baby starts whimpering a little bit, I've noticed that the mother will try first to pull out a pacifier and give it to the baby. That's fake food. It's a piece of rubber designed to trick the kid. It's designed to make the kid feel like he's getting something and subsequently quiet down. So the kid will start sucking and gradually begin to suck harder because he realizes that nothing is happening

Now, I know this kid's a baby and hasn't lived long, but he's not crazy. That baby quickly comes to realize that the pacifier is not food and that his mother is trying to temporarily distract him from his real craving. That baby really wants milk—the real deal. The mother normally realizes that she has two options at this point. She can reach into her bag and pull out a bottle or she can go somewhere private and pull out something else. She can try to hold the baby off as long as possible, but eventually the baby will start whimpering, and then start crying, and then start screaming because he's hungry and tired of fake food. He's tired of being pacified. He's hungry for the real thing, not for a substitute.

Many people come to church on Sunday and they're satisfied with a pacifier sermon and a pacifier song because it makes them feel good, only to discover later that they're still hungry. The soul demands righteousness or else the soul goes hungry.[481]

[Christian Living, Authenticity; Materialism, Deception of; Spiritual Food]

Heb. 5:12

MANY of us have passed by beggars on the street and seen their signs, which read "Hungry," or "Help, need food." We've all, at one point or another, passed these people by. There's really one major way you can tell if they are hungry, and that is offer to take them and buy them food. Not just give them money. It is possible that they could be hungry for something else, like Jack Daniels or one of his cousins or even drugs. A lot of people are hungry for the wrong thing and are distracted from righteousness, although it is the only thing that can truly satisfy the soul.[482]

[Spiritual Food; Worldliness, Distraction of]

Luke 21:34; Rom. 12:2; James 4:4

WHEN you go to a restaurant, they give you a menu. The menu says what a particular restaurant at a particular location offers to eat. Now, you can read a menu and get real hungry. Even though your original hunger may have led you to the restaurant, a menu can make you feel like salivating. You hear lots of people say as they review their choices, "Mmmm, that looks good."

Then you have somebody who comes and proclaims the menu to you. A waiter then exegetes the menu.

They expound on the menu. They take you through the menu. They describe the menu. Then they have a Q and A session by asking if they can answer any questions about the menu. So a restaurant patron can read the menu and hear about the menu, but they don't then say amen and go home. They don't leave the restaurant talking about how great the menu was or how great the waiter did explaining it. That is not the reason why you came. You didn't come to read about it nor did you come to just hear somebody describe it. You came to experience it. So until you've eaten, you're not through.

Many people are satisfied to come to church to read from the menu, to have somebody describe the menu, and then go home not having partaken of the meal and still being hungry.[483]

> [Bible, Use of; Christian Living, Spiritual Growth; Spiritual Maturity, Growth]
> Heb. 5:12

IF THE physical man needs to eat numerous times a day for the body to function as it was designed, then how much more does the spiritual man need to eat regularly because the soul is starving to death? And how do you know the soul is starving to death? Because you're living a dissatisfied life.[484]

> [Life, Satisfaction with]
> Matt. 5:6; Luke 6:21

I

IDOLATRY

IDOLATRY is the track on which the train of demons rides.[485]

> [Demons; Ten Commandments]
> Ex. 20:3–5; Deut. 11:6

IN SOME business or media transactions, there are exclusivity clauses. These exclusivity clauses simply mean that in light of the agreement there can be no competing relationships, no competing loyalties, or no competing contractual obligations. What God calls for in the first commandment is exclusivity as to who is going to be God in our lives. He doesn't welcome competition.[486]

> [God's Standard; Ten Commandments]
> Ex. 20:3–5; Deut. 6:4

TEENAGERS have an uncanny knack for caring more about the opinion of their peers than that of their parents. They are infamous for referring to what Bob, Butch, or Betty said at one time or another as though their view is relevant. There are a couple of problems with this mentality. Those peers don't provide a roof, clothes, or food. Their thoughts should not carry the same weight as the thoughts and opinions of parents who provide for the needs of that teen. No parent wants their child being so influenced by a peer that parental authority is overruled. God shares in this sentiment. He doesn't want His children bringing the thoughts of other gods into the relationship.[487]

> [Ten Commandments]

Ex. 20:3–5; 34:14; Deut. 6:4

IDOLS

THE COMPANY that makes Arm & Hammer baking soda pretty much has a monopoly on the product. Most people associate baking soda with the Arm & Hammer brand because they sort of have the market cornered. There's just not a lot of competition. In the same way, God wants to corner the market in terms of the amount of our affection and praise. He wants to have a monopoly. Even though there are a lot of idols out there that could compete with God for a share of the market, God does not want to share us with the competition. Every time something shows up in the culture that distracts people from the true God, it encroaches on His 100 percent market share and God wants a monopoly.[488]

[Ten Commandments; Worldliness, Distraction of]
Ex. 34:14; Heb. 13:5; James 4:4

IN THE movie *Lily of the Fields*, starring Sidney Portier, there was a businessman in town who was an atheist. He didn't believe in God. However, one day, when the town was coming together to build a new chapel for the nuns, he got involved, working on the chapel. Sidney Portier asked the guy, "I thought you were an atheist."

The businessman replied, "Yes. I am."

"But I don't understand. You're up here building a house for God."

"Yes. I am."

"Why would you do that if you are an atheist?"

"Just in case."

That's what we do. We keep other gods in our back pocket just in case God doesn't work out; we keep idols tucked away. We hang on to certain people, places, or things, just to cover our backs in the event that God doesn't work out.

In the Bible, God was never satisfied with partial commitment. When His people sought to follow Him and hold on to the gods of their culture, He insisted on complete commitment and dependence on Him as the one and only true God.[489]

[God's Standard; Ten Commandments]
Ex. 34:14; 1 Sam. 7:4

ILLUMINATION

THROUGHOUT our church service, we have somebody upstairs in the control booth and he works the lights. When we're in our praise service and come to a little quieter song, the lights dim, and when we come to other features in the service, the lights brighten. That's called illumination. Illumination is when you turn up the dimmer switch and now what was dark is now clear.[490]

[Holy Spirit, Illumination of]
Luke 11:36

IMMORALITY

A WOMAN who is pregnant and takes drugs makes her baby an involuntary participant in her drug habit. A woman who is pregnant and drinks alcohol makes her baby an involuntary participant in her alcoholic habit. In the same way, a person involved in sexual immorality makes Jesus Christ an involuntary participant.[491]

[Immorality, Effects of; Sex]
1 Cor. 6:18; 1 Thess. 4:3–8

JUST as there are guardrails on a highway, designed to keep a wreck from occurring, God has put the guardrail of marriage around sex to keep wrecks from occurring.[492]

[Boundaries; Marriage; Restrictions; Sex]
Heb. 13:4

IMMORALITY, EFFECTS OF

A GIRL had her boyfriend's name tattooed on her arm, but unexpectedly they broke up. Now that she was available to date someone else, she contemplated what to do about the tattoo. She didn't want to walk around with the mark of a former lover. So, she got the tattoo removed, at great pain, and it left a great scar that took a long time to heal. Many of us today are wearing tattoos on our souls because of this infraction.[493]

[Sin, Consequences of; Sin, Effects of]
Gen. 2:24; 1 Cor. 6:18

IMPACT, POTENTIAL OF

THEY tell me that one kernel of wheat in the ground produces a stalk bearing three heads of wheat. In each head, there are fifteen to thirty-five kernels, altogether producing somewhat close to a hundred kernels from the stalk. When planted, these kernels will produce ten thousand kernels. When those ten thousand are replanted, they produce a million kernels. It's amazing what one person can do if they just start right where they are.[494]

[Ministry, Importance of; Sowing and Reaping]
Matt. 13:8; Mark 4:8; Luke 8:8

INDEPENDENCE, CONSE-QUENCES OF

A TRUE event happened a number of years ago. An airplane took off by itself. Somehow it had been left in gear, and it just taxied down the runway and took off. It's a true story. It went ninety miles, and then crashed. It took off on its own, flew for ninety miles, and then something happened.

Without God you can take off for a while. Without God you can go high for a while. Without God you can get your own name for a while or you can build something that's great for a while. But there is coming a time when you're going to run out of fuel. When you run out of fuel, that landing is going to be hard. So before you take off, make sure God is in charge. Before you take off, make sure God is calling the shots. Before you take off, make sure you have submitted to God, so that when you take off, you keep flying, and don't crash-land.[495]

[Life, Management of; Self-Sufficiency, Danger of; Surrender, Benefits of]
Ps. 127:1; Phil. 4:13

INTEGRITY, TESTING OF

A PREACHER got on a bus one day, and he gave the bus driver the fare. The bus driver gave him too much change. The preacher went and sat down, counted the money, and noted that the bus driver gave him too much change, and so he went back to the bus driver and said, "You gave me too much change. You gave me fifty cents too much."

He said, "Pastor, I really appreciate this, because I was in your church service yesterday, and I heard your sermon on honesty. So I intentionally gave you too much change to see whether you abide by what you preach."[496]

[Faithfulness; Tests]

Prov. 10:9; 11:3

INTIMACY, BASIS OF

THERE was a fire in a building and the building was burning profusely. A little boy was too high up and would soon be engulfed. However, there was an external pipe that one of the firemen used to climb up in an attempt to rescue the boy. The pipe was blistering hot. Even though he had gloves on, his gloves were smoking. Despite the extreme heat, the fireman got to the boy and then climbed back down that same pipe. When they got to the ground, the fireman immediately removed his gloves and rinsed his hands in water to relieve the pain that he was experiencing from climbing up and down on that pole that was so hot.

The boy had been brought to safety but he sadly lost his parents in the fire. Some months later, he came up for adoption. There was a professor who came into the courtroom and said, "I can make this boy a genius. I want to adopt him."

There was an engineer who said, "I want that kid, I want to adopt him."

Then there was a third man who came in. The boy looked at him, and said, "Your honor, can he have me?"

The judged asked, "Why?"

"Because I see his hands and I know who he is."

It's nice to have an engineer, it's nice to have an educator, it's nice to have a doctor, but when somebody loves you enough to burn their hands, when they love you enough to share your pain, when they love you enough to hurt when you hurt, ache when you ache, and be there when life is falling apart, when they can show you their hands, and you know they paid the price, then they ought to have the privilege of the relationship. If you want to know who loves you, look at the hands. Jesus Christ has paid the price, and He alone deserves the relationship.[497]

[Cross; Jesus, Relationship with]

Isa. 53:5; John 20:24–28

INTIMACY, IMPORTANCE OF

WE HAVE a sprinkler system in our lawn, and there was a time a few years ago that I couldn't get it to come on. I called a serviceman over and asked him to take a look at it. He looked at my water sprinkler for about an hour or so. Then he came back and said the wire that makes the electrical contact from the timer to the system unit and tells the sprinkler to come on was not connected. My lawn was supposed to be automatically watered by the sprinkler system at set days and times. The timer didn't work so the sprinkler didn't water. If you were to drive by my house, you would discover that my green lawn was starting to turn brown. The longer the sprinkler was inoperative, the more brown the grass was getting. The problem wasn't that my sprinkler system wasn't working, nor was the problem that I didn't have water. It just wouldn't turn on because the wire from the timer had broken contact with the mechanism that lets my system know to turn this on.

Some Christians have lives that are getting brown. Some of them have lost their greenness. Some of them do not have abundant life anymore. It's not because there's a water problem. Jesus says in the Word that He will give us a well that will spring up into eternal life. It's not because there is a power problem, because Jesus says in the Word that He will give us the Holy Spirit, whose job it is to power the pump and to get the water working. The problem is that the wire that connects your will with His power has been disconnected, so there is no flow of water and your life is turning brown instead of staying green. If you're developing a brown lawn in your life, it may be because there's a connection problem.[498]

[Bible, Application of; God, Knowing; Jesus, Relationship with; Prayer]

Prov. 8:34; James 1:22

INTIMACY, POWER OF

ONE time a dog was chasing my oldest granddaughter. She was only about four or five years old. She was just terrified. Now, I don't think that dog was going to do anything to her but she didn't know that. She was crying and screaming as she made her way to me as fast as her little legs would carry her. She was yelling my name, "Poppy! Poppy! Poppy!" That little girl was in a complete state of terror. I ran to meet her and gathered her up in my arms. She was huffing, heaving, and puffing, totally out of breath.

The dog ran up to me, stopped just short, and started barking away. The advance had ended. My granddaughter looked up at me and noticed that the dog was no longer a threat. She looked down at the dog, and then she looked up at me. She looked back down at the dog, and with a new verve and vigor, she said, "Na-na-nana-na!"

Intimacy breeds confidence. When you are close to someone whom you love who has a lot more power than you do, you can piggyback.[499]

[Father God; Fear]

Ps. 27:1–3

IF YOU only have a thimble worth of capacity, and you're standing on the edge of the Pacific Ocean, you have access to a lot of water, but you won't get much of it because your capacity is so small.

If you have the capacity of a bucket, you'll get more than a thimble, but once the bucket is full, the ocean can do you no more good.

If you have a barrel, then you'll get more than a bucket, but once the barrel is full, you still will only have taken advantage of a miniscule part of the ocean.

The idea is to offer God the biggest container possible. Offer Him all of you so that He can maximize what He wants to do in your life. He can do more than we think possible but according to the power that works in us.[500]

[Surrender, Benefits of]

Eph. 3:20

THERE was a little boy one day and a bully was harassing him. Every day he went to school, and the bully would beat him up. Some of his friends were telling him what to do. They gave him a lot of different advice. They told him to try another route home, but the bully found out about that route and still beat him up. Another person suggested that the little boy carry a stick. He carried the stick. The bully caught up with him, took the stick away, and then beat him with it. Everything the boy tried to get rid of the bully did not work.

One day he was walking to school—terrified. Out jumped the bully with his fists clenched and getting ready to pounce on the boy. The youngster beckoned to the bully and said, "Come on. I'm ready."

The bully couldn't believe this young man all of a sudden got some guts. "Come on. Come on you bully. I'll take you right now."

Aggravated, the bully started toward the boy intending to pummel him. All of a sudden, out stepped the boy's father from behind the bush. He was 6'10" and 275 lbs.

The bully looked up in shock and uttered, "Oh no."

See, the closer you are to the Father, the closer you are to your Daddy, the more the bully called the Devil will have to leave you alone. If your Daddy's staying home because you don't want to be close to Him, don't be surprised if the Devil wears you out day in and day out.[501]

[Father God; Satan; Victory]
Ex. 15:2; Ps. 28:7; 1 Peter 5:8

IF A person goes on a long trip and they travel the same route there and back, most time, it seems like the trip home is shorter than the trip to the destination. In actuality, it doesn't take less time, but it just seems that way. Why is that? There is something about traveling home.

No matter how far a person has traveled away from God, if they are willing to make the return trip, God will make the time coming back a lot shorter than the time moving away from Him. The trip home always seems shorter.[502]

[Repentance; Restoration; Second Chances]
Ezek. 18:31; Joel 2:12; Acts 3:19

ON ONE family vacation, we traveled to Niagara Falls. Niagara Falls has two sides, a Canadian side and an American side. On this particular vacation, we went to the Canadian side. We got in a hotel, and it was from the hotel that I first saw the falls. I looked out, and wondered at its magnificence. I was impressed.

The next morning we got up, had breakfast, then sat down at a park near the falls. You could see the falls this time too but the view was different here than from the room. Not only could we see the falls up close and see the water going over the precipice, we could also hear the thunderous roar of the water hitting the basin. The water would fly up in the air and the breeze would come in from across the street. We actually felt the water misting on our faces.

Now, there is a third way a person can see the falls. It's called the Maid of the Mist. The Maid of the Mist is a boat that rides around in the basin of the falls. It will take you up to the falls. If a person decides to take a ride on the Maid of the Mist, the crew will give that passenger a raincoat and an umbrella. The Maid of the Mist will bring them close to the falls. They will get drenched.

How much of Jesus we experience is determined by how close we choose to get to Him. His impact in our lives is determined by the level of intimacy that we choose.[503]

[Intimacy, with God; Jesus, Relationship with]

Ps. 145:18; 2 Cor. 3:17–18;
Heb. 10:22

INTIMACY, WITH GOD

A GUY was watching football on a Saturday afternoon. He had the remote in his hand when the phone rang. He walked over to the phone with the remote in his hand. Even while on the phone, he was interested in keeping up with the game so as not to miss any big plays. He couldn't see the TV but he figured that at least he could half listen in. He pointed the remote in the direction of the TV and attempted to turn the volume up. Nothing happened because he was too far. It's not that the remote didn't work, and it's not that the TV didn't work. He was just too far. Sometimes Christians will say that God doesn't work when in reality the problem is that they are simply too far. It's not that Jesus doesn't work; it's not that the Bible doesn't work, and it's not that the Holy Spirit doesn't work. If a person is not in the vicinity, then it will certainly seem that way. Closeness and intimacy with God is what provides the full experience of walking with Him.[504]

[Intimacy, Importance of; Jesus, Relationship with; God, Knowing]
Mark 7:6; Heb. 10:22; James 4:8

THERE was a sister in the church who was battling with her weight. She had tried every diet known to man but her weight kept fluctuating up and down. A few months passed without me seeing her at church. One Sunday, I happened to see her after service and I was shocked. She had virtually lost all of the weight she had fought for so long to shed. Her solution? She met a man and fell in love!

She explained to me that she knew the man she had been dating was the man she was going to marry and she wanted to look good in her wedding dress. The solution to her problem wasn't a rule-based approach to eating less. She was able to conquer in a short amount of time what had plagued her for years because she had developed a relationship and was seeking *his* pleasure. There's power in intimacy. There's power in relationship.[505]

[God, Knowing; Intimacy, Power of; Jesus, Relationship with]
John 17:3; 2 Peter 1:3

THE STORY is told of two dogs, a German shepherd and a poodle. They were arguing about who was the greatest. The German shepherd argued that he was bigger and stronger; the poodle argued that he was cuter.

The German shepherd, game for a contest, asked the poodle if he wanted to test his greatness by seeing which dog could get inside the house of the owner first. Poodle agreed to the challenge. The German shepherd went first. With its strength, it went up on its hind legs, opened its mouth, and put it on the doorknob. He couldn't turn the knob with his mouth so he took his paws and begin twisting and tweaking. After about three minutes, he had twisted and turned and tweaked it and he got the door opened. He was worn out from his effort to get inside.

It was the poodle's turn. He went over to the other door, got up on his hind legs, and scratched. The owner came and opened the door. Religion required hard work and lots of effort. Relationship required a lot less because the poodle knew how to get the attention of the owner.[506]

[God, Knowing; Jesus, Relationship with; Legalism, Danger of]
John 15:7; Eph. 2:8–9

INNER BEAUTY

ONE of my sons told me once about a pretty girl he met on his college campus. He said this girl was so beautiful that she could "stop traffic." Well, he decided to mosey on up to her and find out who she was. He walked right up to her and said, "Hello, how are you?" and then gave her his name. The girl looked at him and said, "Whassup dog?" That threw my son for a loop. Her apparent beauty simply evaporated once she opened her mouth. God's concern is that you are as good-looking on the inside as you seek to be through all of your efforts on the outside.[507]

[Character, Importance of; Spiritual Maturity]
1 Sam. 16:7

A GEODE is a hollow rock with a beautiful crystal inside. These are formed as water, high mineral water, keeps flowing through these hollow rocks. The minerals get stuck there, and the water continues to flow over it. As more minerals gather, it produces a beautiful crystal that you can buy in a jewelry store. In fact, the more water that flows, the more beautiful the crystal becomes. Now, the external covering begins to wear and weather overtime, but inside the crystal is getting prettier and prettier. This is like the woman where God continues to flow on her inside. She may be getting older, and the wrinkles may be starting to show up. She may have even picked up a few pounds. Things may not look like they used to look on the outside, because of the flow, but on the inside, she's getting prettier all the time.[508]

[Character, Importance of; Women, Value of]
1 Sam. 16:7; Prov. 31:10–31

WOMEN take a lot of time and attention to make sure they look glorious. They are a lot like my wife. If I tell her we have to go somewhere at seven o'clock, at six o'clock she "goeth" before the mirror of her glory. She goes to work. She pulls out eye mascara, eyeliner, foundation, rollers, curlers, a hot iron, and stuff I can't even pronounce. In one hour she is transformed before my very eyes.

We go to the car; the car is in the garage, so she doesn't have to go outside first to mess up her glory. She can go straight to the car, and keep all her glory intact. The first thing she does is to pull out the visor to check the glory she just put on. When we get to the building we are traveling to, we go in and come to the elevator. Guess what? There's a mirror in the elevator, to double-check her glory. When we arrive at our floor and get off the elevator, my wife will make a beeline for the powder room. Now, there is nothing wrong with a wife who seeks to be glorious. The Bible says that a woman is the glory of the man and I don't mind my wife making me look good.

But God is looking for even more. He wants us to be glorious on the inside, not merely on the outside. Far too many women are elegant on the outside, but bargain basement on the inside, evil-spirited, evil attitude, disregarding, disrespectful.[509]

[Character, Importance of;
Women, Value of]
1 Sam. 16:7; Prov. 31:10–31;
1 Cor. 11:7

WHEN most people think of Thanksgiving, they think of a turkey. But my first love isn't the turkey. My first love is the stuffing inside the turkey. The dressing gets jam-packed inside the turkey. It is filled with its own herbs and, spices and so takes on a flavor all its own. The dressing gets stuffed inside the turkey and put inside the oven. While both the turkey and the stuffing cook, the flavor of the stuffing slowly permeates the turkey, making it more flavorful than what it would have been on its own. The turkey becomes tastier because of the effect of what is on the inside.

While most of us are interested in the turkey, God is interested in the stuffing. He is interested in making the inside tasty and letting the internal flavor affect the outside.[510]

[Character, Importance of; Spiritual Maturity]
1 Sam. 16:7

J

JESUS

WHEN a man gets in trouble with the law, he doesn't want a law book. The law book is important but what he really needs is a lawyer. The lawyer is needed to reflect the law that is written in the book because the book, without the representative, a lawyer, is just information.

When a woman is sick, she wants more than just a medical book; she wants a doctor. When a potential victim is facing a criminal, they need more than the penal code; they need an officer. The Bible is a book, but Jesus has personified the book in His person.[511]

[Bible]
John 1:14

JESUS, AUTHORITY OF

GOD'S program is the summing up of all things in Christ. God's program is quite simple. God's agenda is bringing everything, everywhere, every how, under the tutelage, the authority, and the dominion of Jesus Christ.[512]

Matt. 11:27; Phil. 2:10; Col. 2:10

BRAINS don't walk. Brains don't talk. Brains don't move. Brains are the control center of thought, the mind. The job of the body is to pull off the actions, movement, and operations that come from the brain's direction. In medical science, there is the disease called myasthenia gravis and it is a disease of the nervous system. As nerves intersect with muscles, on the end of those nerves is a motor-in plate. This motor-in plate receives the signal that has been sent by the brain to the muscle and it is relayed to the muscle via the motor-in plate. If a person thinks to himself or herself, "Move your arm," the arm would cooperate because the brain sends a message through the nerves to inform the muscle what the brain wants done. But in myasthenia gravis, there is a relay switch that's not working. Even though the brain is sending the message, the muscle doesn't get it because the relay switch, the motor-in plate, doesn't transmit it. This results in the neurological disease. Now, in order to fix that, you've got to fix the motor-in plate.

Now, here is the problem Jesus has. The church's motor-in plate isn't working. Jesus sends signals and we don't hear. It's evident the church doesn't hear because we don't move. If a person tells his or her arm to move and it doesn't, something is wrong with the brain or the arm. If the church isn't moving, something must be wrong with either the church or the head. Jesus is the perfect Head. He's thinking sound and only giving correct instructions. Nothing is wrong with the head. The problem is with God's children.[513]

[Church, Role of; God's Will; World, Impacting the]
1 Cor. 12:27; Eph. 1:10

JESUS, DEITY OF

SIGNATURE stamps today have become high tech. A signature can now be put on a document by machine and still be an exact replica of the original. No one would know that the signature has been produced by a machine. In the old days, you would know someone stamped a signature because around the signature would be a hint of ink from the stamp. Now printed signatures look just like the originals. That's exactly what Jesus Christ is. He is the signature of God. Jesus Christ is the exact image of God.[514]

John 10:25–30; Heb. 1:3

JESUS, PERFECTION OF

I AM sure that many of you had in your class growing up, like I had in my class, a nerd. This particular nerd I'm talking about always made A's. He studied all the time, was kind of himself, and just always made A's. Now, there's nothing wrong with always making A's. There is nothing wrong with studying all the time. But the problem with these nerds is that they always break the curve. A regular student like me would bank on everyone doing badly on the test so that the teacher would have to grade everyone on the curve. Everyone in the class would benefit from all of the students in the class doing poorly. So it would be OK if I failed. I'd always get a little help from the teacher.

But there was this one guy in class that had to go make an A. This, of course, messed up the curve. The teacher could now argue that all of us students could have studied and done well. So we would get mad at the one person who made an A. Why? Because his success revealed our failure.

The problem with Jesus is that whenever He showed up, He messed up the curve. As long as people could compare themselves with other people, everybody passed. When Jesus showed up, He shows up with all A's. When He came and revealed the standards of God, it made everybody else see how far they fell short of the Divine Standard.[515]

[Jesus]
Matt. 12:14; Mark 3:6

JESUS, RELATIONSHIP WITH

JESUS has an impressive resume. Being born of a virgin and living a sinless life is impressive. We've all seen impressive resumes and we try to write impressive resumes. But any employer who's ever hired anyone knows a great resume isn't good enough. The resume is a start but it doesn't tell the whole story. At a glance, the resume can show where someone went to school, how much job experience they have, and what skills they have. However, references can give another piece of the picture. They tell an employer what other people think of the applicant. An employer wants to know not only what's on the resume but also what other people have to say. They want to check and see if what is on the resume is actually true. In addition to checking references, an employer will request an interview. This gives an opportunity for the employer and applicant to meet face-to-face.

Jesus has a great resume and there are plenty of people who can even testify and give Him a reference. However, the best kind of information comes from personally having an interview and being able to say that He's everything He declares Himself to be based on experience. Having a personal relationship with Jesus is to know for oneself that He is real.[516]

[God, Knowing; Jesus]
John 1:14

I'M THE chaplain of the Dallas Mavericks. As a perk for being the chaplain, I get tickets to the games. Sometimes I have tickets left over and I invite people to go with me. Now, although the folks I invite could drive their own cars and meet me at the arena, I tell them that when they go to a Mavericks game, they should not go by themselves. They should go with me. When my guest goes with me, I'll make it a much more convenient experience because I have privileges as the chaplain.

I'll say, "Now, you don't drive. You come ride with me. I have VIP parking in Parking Lot A. Parking Lot A is located twenty-five steps from the front door. I drive in and the attendant will say, 'Hello, Dr. Evans, how are you?' They will let you in not because of who you are but because of who I am. They don't know you, but they know me, and because you're with me, they're going to let you hang with me in Parking Lot A.

"Then we're going to get out of the car and we're going to go through the front door. But we're not going to go through the regular front door. We're going to go through the VIP front door. That's the Michael Jordan front door. That's the Charles Barkley front door. That's the Tony Evans front door. Guess what? If you're with me, you get to go through that front door too. There's a policeman at that front door whose job it is to not let you in until I tell him you're with me. When he finds out we're together, he's going to give you the access that he gives me. Not because of who you are but because of who I am.

"And then there is a private elevator. The private elevator is a VIP elevator. You can't get on that elevator except if you're with me. If you're with me, they're going to give you the privilege of the elevator—not because of who you are, but because of who I am.

"When we get downstairs, if you haven't eaten, don't worry about it. They have a four-course meal available for VIPs. That four-course meal is free for me, and it's also free for you because you're with me. When you're with me, you get what I get, not because of who you are, but because of who you're with.

"When the National Anthem begins to play, we don't have to go back upstairs and go through the line with all the people. We're going to wait for the Mavericks to come out of their locker and we're going to wait for them to go through the underground tunnel. You're going to line up behind me, follow me down to the underground tunnel, and you're going to get free access down through the private entrance—not because of who you are, but because of who I am.

"If you don't like cheap seats, don't worry about them. My seats are on the floor near the owner of the team. The most expensive seats of the house come at no cost to you, not because of who you are, but because of who I am. You get the best seats in the house because you are identified with me.

"When the game is over and everybody's rushing to go home, I am not going the way everybody else is going. I'm going up that private ramp, through that private exit, to that private elevator, out that private door, to that private lot, to get in my car, and be halfway home before most people have gotten out of the parking lot. All of that will happen that day because you're with me."

Jesus Christ is saying to us, "You're with Me, and if you hang with Me, you get all the rights and the privileges that come with your identification with Me." We get the privileges of having a relationship with Jesus Christ when we are linked with Him. If we are linked with him, we will see power that we did not have, privileges that

we do not own, strength that we did not possess—all because of our relationship with Him.[517]

[Christ, Union with; Power, Accessing]
John 14:6; Rom. 5:17

JESUS CHRIST, CENTRALITY OF

I HAVE a master key to the church. My key can work in any lock. It's a master key. A staff person who works here at the church may have a key to their own office, or even to the section of the building that their office is in. But they are limited in which doors they can open. Because I have a master key, I can go anywhere in the church that I want to go.

A lot of us are not getting everywhere we need to go because we don't have a master key. We've got keys for certain rooms. We come to church, hear a sermon, and receive a truth so we have a key for a certain room in our Christian lives. We must understand, however, that the key to the Christian life for the church of Jesus Christ is, in fact, Jesus Christ. The mystery of godliness is the good news. The ability to get right with God in any category comes through Jesus Christ.[518]

John 3:16; Rom. 6:23; Titus 2:11–14

JONAH

THE BIG fish that swallows Jonah is no big deal. In 1891 off of the Falkland Islands, there were two fishing boats that were whale hunting. They came across a huge sperm whale. One fishing group shot harpoons into the whale. The other boat came around and began to do the same thing to get this whale, but the whale's tail hit the second boat and knocked it over.

There were two men on the second boat. One of the men drowned. The other man was not found. Two days later, a few other boats got this same whale and killed him. They brought the whale up to the shore, slit it open, and found the second man.

The man was unconscious but still alive, and after care, resumed his life. This "Jonah and the whale" story isn't that far-fetched. Similar things have happened before. People read the Bible and say that the story of Jonah and the big fish doesn't make sense, but it does. The miracle is not that a fish swallowed a man, because that has happened before. The miracle is that the fish paid attention to the Lord.[519]

[God, Authority of]
Jonah 1:17; Matt. 12:39–41

JOY

SOMEBODY has come up with a great concept—putting playrooms in doctors' offices. Many parents bring their kids to the doctor because they are sick and they need the doctor to see them. The playrooms are designed to distract the children from the pain of their problem until their problem gets fixed. The playroom gives them joy in a bad situation.

That's the way God works. Even though things may not be going the way we want them to be on the outside, God has designed a "playroom" in our soul. In the midst of our circumstances, His joy can distract us from our pain or discomfort, until He makes provision for our change or healing.[520]

Ps. 16:11; 1 Peter 1:8

JUDGING

ONE day, a young girl asked her mother, "Mama, why do you have so much gray hair?" Her mother looked at her daughter and sternly said, "Every gray hair is representative of a time you were disobedient to me. I have gray hairs because of your rebellion." The girl looked genuinely puzzled. "Mama, so are you the reason Grandma has so much gray hair too?"[521]

[Children, Training; Parenting]
1 Sam. 15:22; James 1:22–25

CHUCK Swindoll was speaking at a camp in California. A gentleman came to him and said, "Oh, Dr. Swindoll, I have waited so long for this week, I am going to eat up everything you have to say." Swindoll thanked him.

Sunday night, the man was sitting on the front row, and the man started nodding. Swindoll figured that he'd had a long drive and was probably tired. Tuesday night, the man started nodding. Wednesday night the man nodded again. Swindoll was now getting a little upset. Here this man sat on the front row, sleeping away. As a preacher who had prepared well for this ministry opportunity, it didn't feel good to see someone sleeping on him. He was getting frustrated with this guy.

Thursday night, the man nodded and slept again.

On Friday morning, the lady who was sitting next to him came to Swindoll and said, "I want to thank you for the ministry this week. Oh, and by the way, I am sorry about my husband sleeping on you. He has two weeks to live. He has terminal cancer and the doctors have just given him a couple of weeks to live. When we talked about what he wanted to do before he died, he said, 'I want to go hear Chuck Swindoll.' But you see, Dr. Swindoll, the doctors gave him medicine to keep away the pain, and the medicine makes him sleep. I wanted to apologize to you that he has been sleeping, but I wanted you to know you made this the best week of the last part of his life."

Swindoll later said he could have crawled under a rock, because he had made a judgment and without any investigation he reacted.[522]

[Criticizing, Danger of]
Luke 7:36–50; John 8:7; James 2:2–4

JUDGMENT

SINNERS have a jar. Once the jar is full, it's over. Every time a sinner rebels against God, they fill up the jar. When the jar is full, God judges them.[523]

[God's Discipline; Sin,
Consequences of]
1 Thess. 2:16

SEEK the Lord while He may be found and before judgment falls, when it's too late to seek Him. Don't try to get right after He's already started passing judgment. Many a child has realized too late that they were headed for a spanking and tried to avoid the punishment by promising their parents they wouldn't disobey again. That's a little bit late. We must seek the Lord and His ways before He pulls out correction to address the sin. Call upon Him while He is near, let the wicked forsake his way, the unrighteous man his thoughts.[524]

[God's Discipline; Sin, Consequences
of; Sin, in the Believer]
Isa. 55:6–7; 1 Thess. 2:16

I LOVE Judge Judy, one of the TV court judges. She is my girl. Every case starts with two people who are at odds. They can't get together. They cannot fix their problem. There are lots of different problems that make it into Judge Judy's court. Both the plaintiff and the defendant lay out their complaints and concerns. Judge Judy hears their arguments and then makes a judgment. Everyone understands that once Judge Judy rules, the participants will abide by her ruling.

Now, everybody doesn't leave Judge Judy's courtroom happy. But her responsibility is to apply the law to the case, not to make the courtroom participants feel good.

God's goal is not to make everyone happy. In fact, He gets quite a few complaints! The bottom line, however, is that God is the ultimate judge. His word is final.[525]

[God, Authority of; God's Will]
Job 21:22; Ps. 50:6; Rom. 2:16

SUPPOSE you are a teacher in a high school and your son or daughter is one of your students. Let's say that your son or daughter is misbehaving in class. They are "cutting up" and so you tell them to leave the classroom and assign them to a detention. You judge your child not as your child but as a student. When they come home that afternoon from detention, they will still be your child, but even so, that would not have taken away their responsibility to be a good student. By punishing your son or daughter, you will have judged their behavior as a student.

Let's say that you have a son in business with you and he is handling the cash register. You find out that your kid is "taking from the till" and putting money in his pocket. You discover it and fire him. Did you fire him from being your son? No. You cannot judge him as your son because he is your son by birth. However, you can fire him as your servant because he was not performing the work that he was supposed to perform in the way it is supposed to be done. So he is penalized and judged as a servant.

All Christians bear two relationships to God. They bear a family relationship and they bear a relationship of service. At the judgment seat of Christ, you are going to be there because you belong to God as a child, but He's going to judge you by how you honored Christ as a servant.[526]

[Father God; God, Authority of]
Rom. 14:10; 2 Cor. 5:10; Col. 3:25;
Heb. 9:27

ICE HOCKEY is a very interesting game. There is a lot of action all the time. They have something very interesting in hockey called a penalty box. When a player disobeys the rules on the ice, they send him to the penalty box. The player is still on the team, but not allowed to participate on ice because he's broken the rules. So the referee escorts him off the ice and he sits in this little box. From this penalty box, he can see everything happening on the ice, but he just can't participate. He just can't be involved. He can watch it. He can see it. He can be dressed like everyone else. He can be in the environment, but he can't function. Depending on what this player did wrong determines how much time he is in the box. In other words,

different players stay in the box for different amounts of time.

This is what happens to carnal Christians in the kingdom. God accesses their lives and determines how they broke the rules. A Christian will be in the penalty box and, although they are still on the team, because of living a carnal life, they will not get the full benefit of being on the team and participating on the team. Their level of carnality will determine the length of time that they experience the penalty.[527]

[Carnal Christians; Sin, in the
Believer]
1 Cor. 3:12–15; Heb. 12:11

JUDGMENT DAY

IF A person wants to be a doctor, they don't wake up one day and say, "I want to be a doctor," and then start practicing. That decision to be a doctor would have been made years in advance. That decision would have determined what college they went to and would have required years of commitment to make it through an internship and residency. In other words, a person doesn't become a doctor the day they decide that a medical career is what they want to pursue. The decision about direction requires a process.

A person doesn't just wake up one day and say, "I'm going to be a lawyer," and then start trying cases the same afternoon. A decision has to be made long in advance of taking on clients.

For any professional career, there are requirements that must be met in order to enjoy the benefits of that decision. A career requires an investment of time and energy before it becomes a reality.

Some of us have retirement accounts and IRAs because we are planning for sixty-five and beyond. You don't wake up at sixty-five and say, "Let me start a retirement plan." That decision is made in advance so that when you arrive at sixty-five, you have something laid aside. Some of us, perhaps, may be saving for our children's education. You don't wake up on the day of their high school graduation and say, "I'd better put something aside for their education." That decision has to be made in advance. The point is that the knowledge of the future controls activity in the present. When you know where you are going, you will make decisions about what you must do in the now.

There is a day of reckoning coming when all men will have to be confronted by God and where every Christian is going to have to give an account. And when that day comes, it will be too late to make any adjustments. Your decision about that meeting, that day of reckoning in which you and I are going to have to meet Jesus Christ, will have to have been made long in advance of that occasion.[528]

[Salvation, Need for; Sin, Judgment on; Spiritual Death, Concept of]
2 Cor. 5:10; Heb. 9:27; Rev. 20:11–15

IT WOULD be a miserable thing to almost win the lottery. Let's say you played the lottery and you decided to listen as the winning numbers were being announced. Your excitement would rise as you realize that you've got the first number, then the second number,

then the third number, and then the fourth and the fifth numbers. You'd also be severely deflated when they call out the last number and you realize that you've missed winning by one digit. You'd probably be pouting, crying, screaming, and agonizing over this close call. For a long time, every time you pay a bill, you would remember, "I could have been a millionaire."

What God is going to do on judgment day is to show you what you could have had, what you could have been, and what He could have done with you in that kingdom that is to come. Then you will watch Him "scratch" your name off of those possibilities and give it to the man beside you.[529]

[Heaven, Entrance into]
Matt. 25:29; Luke 16:19–31

ON MY desk, I have some evaluation forms because I have to evaluate the staff. These forms give me the option of giving my staff one of two ratings: Satisfactory or Unsatisfactory.

If they get an unsatisfactory, that will have profound ramifications because unsatisfactory means a lower raise due to the fact that we give merit raises. Unsatisfactory means that staff member will not get the raise they hoped for and it will be too late to change that rating when we sit in the office to discuss their performance.

On the other hand, if a staff member gets a satisfactory rating, that means they've done a great job, and we give them a year-end expression of appreciation to say, "We recognize that you've gone above and beyond the call of duty."

Just like there are evaluations on

earth, there's coming a day when God is going to take every Christian and He's going to evaluate them or rate them.[530]

[Sin, Judgment on]
Rom. 14:10; 2 Cor. 5:10

IN 1988, an awesome event happened. Ben Johnson of Canada broke out of the starting gates like no other man in history. I remember sitting and listening to the commentator say, "Did you see that start? Ladies and gentlemen, it's Ben Johnson! It's Ben Johnson! It's Ben Johnson!"

As we watched, the time lines on the TV said that the man had broken the Olympic record. Ben Johnson had turned that sprint for the fastest human alive upside down as it had never been demonstrated before! The crowd went wild! The other runners congratulated him. What a run by Ben Johnson! Until it all hit the fan. When it went before the judges, they tested his blood and found steroids. When they found steroids, they sent word back for Ben Johnson to give up his gold medal and they awarded it to another.

The gold medal that Ben Johnson had won was snatched and turned over to another. He went back to Canada a disgrace. The crowd didn't know it when he was running it. The crowd didn't know it when he was sprinting. When he was darting out of the blocks, the people went wild. When he did his victory lap, he looked like he was a winner. He felt like he was a winner. The only problem was the judges went inside of his body and extracted what was on the inside and brought it to the light.

On that day, many of us who think we have won will find out that we have to turn in our medal because we didn't run according to the rules. The question is. will He call your name or will He strip you of your crown? Carnality will receive its just reward.[531]

[Carnal Christians; Sin, in the Believer; Sin, Judgment on]
Matt. 7:21–23

MY SON Jonathan has a highlight tape. Professional football teams have reviewed these tapes. It shows his greatest blocks, his greatest catches, and his greatest runs. It's a twenty-four-minute highlight tape showing Jonathan at his best. Now, this tape is made from extracted plays taken from all the tapes of his games.

One year, when playing against Texas Tech, he was handed the ball, got hit, and he fumbled. That's not on the highlight tape. During another game, he was on the punt team. He was one of the first ones down to the other end of the field to get the receiver, but the receiver did one of those quick moves and danced around him. That is not on the highlight tape either. The only things on the highlight tape are the highlights— the things he's proud of and the things he's excited about. He doesn't show everything.

He did get calls from a few pro football teams who have watched his highlight tape and liked what they saw. Because of the tape, they planned to watch him during his senior season. They saw enough on the highlight tape to let them know that even if Jonathan was lacking some skills in an area, he was more than talented and skilled enough to make up for those things. They knew this because of the tape. There were enough highlights to overrule whatever flaws may have been there.

One day we will all go before God and He's going to show our whole tape. However, He will also extract some highlights. The highlights will be the times where we showed love. Where we have shown love during our lives, those moments will make it onto the highlight tapes.

The question is, will there be enough highlights on your love highlight tape to cancel out all the fumbles, missed blocks, flaws, sins, failures, compromises, evil thoughts, and evil deeds you've had in your life? God wants us to know that if we have a highlight tape, a tape full of love, we can have confidence in the day of judgment.[532]

[Reward; Sin, Judgment on]
Matt. 25:21–23; Luke 19:17;
1 Cor. 3:12–15

MY MESSAGES from the ministry at Oak Cliff Bible Fellowship are played regularly over the air. They're played all over the country through The Urban Alternative. People who hear the messages over the air don't hear everything from the sermon that members of Oak Cliff hear on Sunday mornings. The messages from Sunday mornings get edited and things that are inappropriate for radio or specific to the church congregation are cut out. A forty-five- to fifty-minute message is cut down.

One day we're going to sit before the judge and He's going to roll the tape. Anything that we have done that is not for His glory gets edited out. Some of us just aren't going to have much on the reel! Acts of mercy will be left in. Acts of kindness will be left in. Serving others will be left in. However, unkind words will be edited out. Taking advantage of others will be edited out. Grumbling and complaining will be edited out. Only the things that are honoring to God will be left on your recording.

You cannot fix yesterday, but you can start today making sure you have ample material for the recording that will play on judgment day. If you're losing in a race, don't stop running. Speed up! Make up ground that you lost so that you still cross the tape a winner for Jesus Christ.[533]

[Reward; Sin, Judgment on]
Matt. 25:21–23; Luke 19:17; 1 Cor. 3:12–15

JUSTIFICATION

HAVE you ever gotten a letter in the mail from a credit card company telling you that you've been prequalified? These letters will usually tell you that you can spend five thousand dollars because they've already checked you out and decided you would be a good customer.

Now, this is just a ploy, a joke, and a gyp. They are just trying to get you to spend money so that they can charge you interest. It's a trick.

God has also prequalified us for righteousness. Unlike the trickery involved with the credit card companies, He has prequalified us by already applying the righteousness of Christ to our accounts. Our balances have already been paid.[534]

[Christ, Sufficiency of; Spiritual Identity, in Christ]
Rom. 8:31–39; Eph. 1:4–8

K

KINGDOM OF GOD

IF A man drinks Jack Daniels and comes to my house, Jack has to stay outside. In my kingdom, where I am king, Jack is not welcome. In fact, if you smoke, I don't have ashtrays available for you because you can't smoke in my kingdom. If you cuss, in my kingdom you are going to have to control your tongue 'cause I don't allow profanity in my house.

If you don't like my rules, well, there's a simple solution to that. You just don't come to my house. I pay the note, I pay the utilities, and I bought the furniture. People may think that's cold. No, I'm just head of my own kingdom. If you're under my rule, you've got to respect my guidelines.

In the same way, God is the head of His kingdom. If we want to live in, be a part of, and benefit from His kingdom, we must operate by His rules.[535]

[Boundaries; God's Will; Law, Purpose of; Restrictions; Sin, Avoidance of]

Ex. 20:1–17; Matt. 5:17; Rom. 7:21–25

IN AMERICA, ultimately, the Supreme Court makes the final decision as it relates to laws for this country. When the Supreme Court speaks, all other courts must adjust. At this point, it becomes irrelevant what the district court says or what the state court says. Once the Supreme Court speaks, the final authority of law in the land, all other decisions are canceled, reversed, or reinforced because the final authority has ruled.

A Christian is truly a "kingdom person" when he is willing to adjust his decisions to God's decisions even if God's decision is not the one preferred.[536]

[God, Authority of; God's Will; Surrender, Concept of]

Matt. 6:10; Rom. 12:1–2; James 4:7

AT A football game in Nebraska, you will see a sea of red. When their football games sell out, which is most of the time, 77,129 are in that stadium. During the 2004 Nebraska vs. Baylor game, there again was a sea of red, nothing but red, red everywhere, except this little section, up in the corner with folks from Baylor. Now, the Baylor folks didn't have on red, because red isn't Baylor's color. It's green. So there was a huge sea of red and then a little pocket of folks with green.

When the seventy-seven thousand people cheered, the folks in green weren't cheering. When the folks in green were cheering, the folks in red weren't. Red and green, they each were pulling for their own team. The folks in green, although a smaller number, were focused on their team and busy cheering them on to victory.

Christians are unique and different and are on earth to root and cheer on the cause of God. When Redskins fans come to Dallas, they are not ashamed. When Dallas fans go to Washington, they are not ashamed. They unashamedly claim their team and set their sights on victory.[537]

[Christian, Definition of; Christian Living, Identity in Christ]

Rom. 1:16; 2 Tim. 1:8

EVERY good coach has a game plan for his team. He brings a particular philosophy of the game to his particular team and the athletes then have to learn his offensive and defensive schemes. They must learn the coach's philosophy. They must adopt it and they must acclimate to it. Sometimes it's hard to pick up a particular coach's scheme, particularly if it's more technical and more detailed. The idea is that the coach brings in the scheme, and the team is to rally around and execute the scheme for maximum productivity.

Just like in games involving sports, in Christianity we have a lot of players who have been drafted into the kingdom of God and drafted out of the pit of hell, but yet they want to tell their coach how to run his team. Many Christians spend their time trying to tell God how to run His kingdom. But God's response is that He has His own program. He has His own game plan. He has adopted us into His family to be part of His plan. We each can have a strategic part to play in the game of life for His kingdom and for His glory, but only if we are operating according to His game plan.[538]

[God's Will; Self-Sufficiency, Danger of; Surrender, Concept of]
Isa. 29:16; Matt. 6:10

IN THE Olympics, competitors work hard to win medals. They go all out. At the end of each competition, there is a gold, silver, and bronze winner. When they are presented with their medals, they take their places on the platform and music begins to play. What's the music? The national anthem of the gold medal winner.

The gold medal winner doesn't get to pick any old song they like and request that to be played at the Olympics. Even though they may have competed individually, their victory is not all about them. Their victory was part of a bigger picture and was under a bigger banner. If athletes from America win the gold in an event, our national anthem is played for everyone else to hear because in the Olympics, the athletes represent their nations.

God wants us to run for His kingdom so that when the song is played it represents His song and His glory. The lyrics will reflect the idea of "Thy kingdom come; Thy will be done. Thine is the kingdom. Thine is the power. Thine is the glory. Forever and ever, amen."

I've yet to see a gold medal winner frowning because the United States is getting all the credit. Why? Because when they come home, the United States is so proud of them that they give the athletes recognition. God will not forget those who run hard for His kingdom and let His flag wave high. He will not forget what we've done for His glory.[539]

[Ambassadors, for Christ]
Matt. 6:10; 1 Cor. 9:24

KINGDOM OF GOD, KEYS TO

THE KEY to the kingdom of heaven is not a key that opens an earthly door. If you're looking for an earthly solution to your problem, and you are trying to use the key to the kingdom of heaven, you are using the wrong key on the wrong lock.

On a trip to New York, I arrived at my hotel, checked in at the front desk, and was given a card access key to enter my room. I went to my floor, stuck in the key card, on came a green light, and I had access to my room, a part of the bigger kingdom called the hotel. I had been duly authorized to have access to my own place inside the kingdom because I was a registered guest at the hotel. The kingdom received me and gave me a key so that I could access what was mine. I now had authority to go in and out of that room at my leisure.

Now, after that trip, I had to leave New York and fly directly to Chicago before coming back to Dallas. When I got to Chicago, I went to another hotel. This hotel also authorized me to be there and gave me a key card. I put the key card in my pocket, grabbed my luggage, and took the elevator upstairs to the twentieth floor. I reached in my pocket, took out my key card and placed it in the lock. A red light came on. I tried the key again. Still, I only got a red light. Now I was evangelically ticked off. It is very irritating to go to the twentieth floor with a bunch of luggage and find out your key does not work! So I got on the elevator, went down to registration, and said, "This does not work."

The front desk person apologized. "Oh I'm sorry. Let me give you a new key card." As she took the key card and looked at it, she paused, then said, "I'm sorry, sir, but this key card doesn't go to this hotel."

I had put the New York key card in my pocket, and once I arrived in Chicago, I mistakenly took that key card out of my pocket to try to open the hotel door. I pulled out the wrong key card, trying to solve my problem in the new hotel. It wouldn't work.

A lot of us come to church to get the right key, but then we take out the wrong key when we leave church. We try to use it and we hear a "click," and all we get is a red light. It doesn't work. People then go around saying, "God doesn't work," "Jesus doesn't work," "The Bible doesn't work," or "Christianity doesn't work." However, the problem is the key they are using. But if you don't use a heavenly solution to solve your earthly problems, it won't work.[540]

[Life, Fixing; Problems, Solutions to]
Matt. 16:17–20

KINGDOM OF GOD, POWER OF

EVERYBODY has heard the story of the three little pigs. Mother pig sent them out; it was time for them to build their own houses. Pig number one built his house of straw. Pig number two built his house with sticks. Pig number three built his house out of bricks. Along came the wolf who demanded entrance into their homes. He wasn't invited or solicited. He just decided that he wanted to come into the lives of the little pigs.

Pig number one said, "Not by the hair of my chin-ee-chin-chin."

So the wolf huffed and he puffed and he blew the straw house down. Pig number one's world had fallen apart, so he hurried over to pig number two's house. The wolf followed him and knocked on the door of the stick house. He said, "Little pig, little pig, let me in."

Pig number two said, "Not by the hair of my chin-ee-chin-chin."

So the wolf huffed and puffed and blew his house down. Pig one and pig two went to pig number three's house.

Now, pig number three built his

house differently than the others. Pig number three built his house of bricks so that it would stand the test of time.

The wolf tried yet again, "Little pig, little pig, let me in."

Pig number three said, "Not by the hair of my chin-ee-chin-chin." So the wolf huffed and puffed and blew and blew. Many storybooks illustrate the wind blowing and hurling and it was cast forth out of the mouth of the wolf. You could see the strength he put into trying to blow down the house, but in the pages of the nursery rhyme, the pictures of the wolf show him tiring out and the house still standing. In fact, the wolf, after unsuccessfully trying to blow down the house, decided to change his strategy and come down the chimney. He climbed up the side of the house and attempted to sneak into the house via the chimney only to enter into a pot of hot boiling water. He shot right back up the chimney. When the story ended, the three pigs were sitting around the fireplace, with the big bad wolf on the outside looking in.

If you're attached to your straw life, when stuff starts to blow, you're going to crumble. If you're attached to your stick existence, when stuff starts to shake, you're going to fall apart. But if you're part of a brick unshakable kingdom that has been built by Almighty God, I don't care what is falling apart around you, you won't be falling apart with it. If you are falling apart with it, you have not fully attached yourself to the unshakable kingdom. It is a kingdom that cannot be shaken.[541]

[Christian Living, Power; Kingdom of God]
Ps. 16:8; Ps. 62:2; 1 Cor. 3:12–15

L

LAW

LACTOSE intolerance is an allergy to milk. The problem with this condition lies not in the milk but in the biochemical makeup of a person. The flaw lies with the person who ingests the milk. The milk only reveals that fact; it doesn't cause it. The law of God is perfect in every detail. Nothing's wrong with it, but there's something wrong with us.[542]

[Law, Nature of]
Rom. 7:7

WHILE the law is valid, the law does not solve our sin problem. The law is like a mirror. When you go into your bathroom mirror, you see the hair that needs to be combed, the face that needs to be cleaned, or the tie that needs to be straightened. The mirror reveals what is wrong that needs to be made right. The mirror does not actually comb the hair, wipe the face, or straighten the tie. It is only there to reveal, not to fix.

The mirror is like the law. It's a reflector. It shows you what's wrong. It shows you what you really are. But the law can't fix your problem. The law can only reveal your problem. It can show you sin. It can show you dirt and grime. But what the law could not do, Christ did. Christ fixed it.

Many people today think that in order to be made right with God they have to keep God's law. The problem is that, even on their best day, they cannot satisfy the demands of a perfect God.[543]

[Law, Purpose of; Self-Sufficiency, Danger of]
Rom. 7:7; James 2:10

WHEN is the last time a policeman pulled you over to congratulate you for going below the speed limit? When have they ever stopped you to congratulate you for stopping at a red light? They don't do that because the law is not in place to congratulate you for the laws you keep but to curse you for the laws you break. God's law is not there to congratulate you. It is to show you and me how unlike God we are in terms of meeting His divine standard.[544]

[Law, Purpose of; Restrictions]
Gal. 3:19–22

LAW, EFFECT OF

A HONEY-DO list can be a frustrating thing. A list of four things may be left for a husband to complete. He may get a plan together to complete those four things in time to settle in for a game. It never fails, right when he finishes his list and settles in to watch his game, he will get a phone call and the list grows. Many times, that list won't seem to have an end.

That's the problem with law. There is no way to "check off the list." There is no possible way to complete the requirements of the law. There is nothing wrong with God's standard, but there's everything wrong with our capacity to satisfy it. Our flesh is contaminated by sin and will always react to God's standard.[545]

[Law of Sin and Death; Sin, Stain of; Sin, Victory over]

Rom. 7:14–25; Heb. 10:1

A FOOTBALL team met for a morning pregame talk with their coach. The coach told the guys that, although the coverage of their upcoming game would be all over the news, he didn't want them watching any of it. His words to his team were, "Under no circumstances should you look at ESPN to hear what everybody has to say about this big game."

Now, when the team came back that afternoon, the coach said, "I really don't have to tell you anything about the big game because I know that all of you have already heard about it on ESPN." He gave them a law, knowing that all that law would do was incite them to break it.[546]

[Law of Sin and Death]
Rom. 7:7

THE STORY is told of a bear that lived in a 12 x 12 foot cage. It lived there for some twelve years and so it got to know that cage extremely intimately. The bear was so proficient at moving around his small world that it could close its eyes, walk to the end of the cage, and before it hit the end of the cage, it would stop, turn around, and go to the other end. Before it hit the other end, it would spin around and do it over and over again, never ever bumping into the cage. As it got larger, the bear's handlers decided to enlarge its world, and built the animal a 36 x 36 foot cage to give it a lot more room to experience life inside of this cage. The problem was that when they put the bear, which had lived in the 12 x 12 foot cage, into the 36 x 36 foot cage, it would still only walk twelve feet and then turn around and go the other way. The bear's problem was that even though it moved to a new cage, it brought the old cage with it. The problem with the bear was that it was still hostage to the limitations of its old life. Even though it had been promoted to a whole new environment, it had not shed the habits that had been learned in the old place.

This is like the effect of the law on the lives of Christians. Many of us have been used to living under law so long and under the limitations and restrictions of a performance-based approach to Christian living, that we don't know how to handle the new freedom called grace. We keep living, limited by law, even though we've been set free to a lot more room under grace.[547]

[Christian Living, New Life; Grace, Law and; Law of the Spirit; New Life in Christ]
Rom. 7:24–25; Eph. 5:8–10; Titus 3:3–7

LAW, NATURE OF

LAW is like a standard transmission. Most people don't even use those anymore. They were a lot of work to drive. Then they came up with the automatic transmission. With the standard transmission, the driver had to work hard to move from one gear to the next. With an automatic transmission, the car switches gears itself. Automatic transmissions work to make the changes naturally that the driver used to have to make manually.

The law of sin is like trying to live life on the standard transmission. It involves a person to make all of the changes themselves. They have to do their own adjusting, twisting, push-ing, and they have to do it all at the right time. With an automatic, we don't think twice about clutches; we don't have to think twice about gears. All of those changes are already built into the transmission. The law of sin and death confines. The law of the Spirit frees.[548]

[Law of Sin and Death; Law of the Spirit]
Rom. 8:2; Heb. 7:18–19; 10:1

LAW, PURPOSE OF

THE LAW of God is like an X-ray. It will reveal a problem but it can't fix it.[549]

[Law, Purpose of; Self-Sufficiency, Danger of]
Rom. 7:7; James 2:10

THE LAW is like a speed limit sign on the expressway. If it says sixty miles an hour, that's the law. Now, that law cannot make you drive sixty miles an hour; it just gives you the law. In fact, that law means nothing to most people! However, it validates the fact that if a policeman pulls you over when you are going seventy-five or eighty miles an hour, he has the right to do it because you have broken a revealed standard.

If he pulls you over for going sixty miles per hour and there was no speed limit sign at all, then you could argue before the court that there was no law or sign posted. How could you then be condemned for going against a speed that was never told to you? In other words, the purpose of the law is to reveal the standard by which sin is to be measured.[550]

[Law, Purpose of; Self-Sufficiency, Danger of]
Rom. 7:7; James 2:10

LAW, RESPONSE TO

THERE are two reasons that drivers will stop at a red light. The first is fear of getting hurt due to an accident. The second is fear of getting caught. The law says stop; but still, late at night, when there is not much traffic out, the propensity for running a red light is higher—there is less fear of hurt and less fear of getting caught.[551]

[Sin, Source of]
John 3:19–21; Rom. 7:7

MANY folks drive down a street and clearly see the signs that say 40 mph. The very presence of the standards stirs in them the desire to go over the limit by 5 mph.[552]

[Rebellion]
Jer. 17:9; Heb. 8:7

MANY Christians react to the law by trying to work hard to obey all of the laws and do all of the right things. They are like the circus entertainer that spins plates. They put each plate on a stick and try to keep them moving, working hard to keep all plates spinning and in balance.

Just like the entertainer, Christians run all over the place trying to do the right things and keep all of the key areas of the Christian life spinning. They spin the religion plates of going to church, reading their Bible, and giving tithes, and it wears them out.

They are reverting back to a standard that the Bible says will kill you. "The letter killeth." The law will kill because sin will go crazy when it is faced with the divine standards of God.[553]

[Law of Sin and Death; Self-Sufficiency, Danger of; Surrender, Benefits of]
2 Cor. 3:6; Gal. 3:1–5; Heb. 10:1

LAW OF SIN AND DEATH

THE LAW of sin and death is like the law of gravity, which states that what goes up must come down. It is a law that is universal to our world. No matter how high you try to move up and away, gravity is going to pull you down. If you jump up, gravity says, "Come back here." It's going to pull you down every time.

Isn't that what we do in our Christian life? We get all excited on Sunday and try to jump. We say we are going to live for God, and before Monday comes, gravity pulls us down. We make New Year's resolutions, trying to jump even higher. Gravity won't let us. We make promises to ourselves and gravity yanks us back. That's the law of sin and death. It always pulls us down no matter how high we try and jump.[554]

[Failure; Sin Nature, Residue of]
Rom. 5:8; 9:16

LAW OF THE SPIRIT

THE OPPOSITE of the law of sin and death is the law of the Spirit. This law overrides sin and death. The law of gravity says what goes up must come down. However, when you get in an airplane, there is another law at work—the law of aerodynamics. This law says that if an object moves at a certain speed, and with a certain thrust, it will be able to climb out of gravity's pull. When an airplane flies, gravity hasn't stop being "gravitational"; it has simply stopped being in control. The law of aerodynamics sets you free from the law of the pull of gravity.

The law of sin and death is always at work. But when you combine the combustion of the Holy Spirit with the speed of obedience, a new law lifts you higher and into a new plane of spiritual life and victory. We ought to be rising higher, saints! You ought not to be living under the circumstances. You ought to be flying above the circumstances because you have an aerodynamic Holy Spirit. You have a law that transcends sin and death.

When Christians learn to operate by the law of the Spirit, the reality of the law of sin and death doesn't disappear. The pull of sin and death is still operational but is no longer in control.[555]

[Grace; Power of; Justification; Law of Sin and Death]
Rom. 8:2; Heb. 7:18–19

HAVE you ever seen a sidewalk turned inside out all because a little acorn fell in between a crack? As an acorn sprouts, it sends its roots deep down into the ground and over time that tiny acorn becomes a little oak tree. Now, a little acorn can't move sidewalks, but if it is set free to be what it was created to be, you no longer have a little acorn, you've got an oak on your hands. When that oak begins to grow between the crevices of the sidewalk, it moves concrete because the law of the oak transcends the law of the concrete. The concrete must now move over to give room for the law of the growth of the oak represented in the acorn.

When you accepted Jesus Christ, you received the acorn of the Spirit who wants to become the oak of your life, so that He can move aside the concrete of the problems that you face and the circumstances that you are involved in.[556]

[Holy Spirit, Power of; New Life in Christ]
Rom. 7:24–25; Titus 3:3–7; Heb. 7:28

THERE'S a law that we have in our legal world. It's called the law of double jeopardy. The law of double jeopardy simply says that you can't be tried twice for the same crime. Jesus has already been tried for your crimes, so you are under no obligation to the flesh because God has already pronounced the sentence on it. It's already been judged. Don't enter into the law of double jeopardy. Don't let the flesh try you again when it's already been pronounced guilty! You have no obligation to it.[557]

[Christ, Freedom in; Justification; Sin, Victory over]
Rom. 5:1; 8:13; 2 Cor. 5:15; 1 Peter 2:24

IF I AM holding a pen and let the pen have its way, the law of gravity will take over. If my pen could speak, it might have said, "Leave me alone. Let me have my own way." The reality is that if the pen in my hand has its own way and is independent of me, it won't be independent of gravity. It will fall.

The law of the flesh says, "Yes. You can please yourself." But the law of the flesh will also then determine the direction you are headed.

When I reach down and pick up that pen, there is another law at work. I will not have canceled the law of gravity. It will still be in effect, but I will be overriding it with the power that I have to pick it up off the floor. Gravity will still be in effect but it just won't be ruling. Why? Because it does not have life. I do. The life of the Spirit, which gives life, can overrule the law of the flesh, which pulls you down.[558]

> [Grace; Power of; Justification; Law of Sin and Death]
> Rom. 8:2; Heb. 7:18–19

LEGALISM, DANGER OF

MY GRANDDAUGHTER Kariss decided one afternoon to sit in my den and eat potato chips. I told her no eating potato chips in the den. She quickly went to the kitchen.

A few minutes later, I walked through the den for something and saw her eating cookies in the den. I said, "I thought I said don't eat in the den?"

She said, "No, Poppy. That's not what you said. You said, 'Don't eat *potato chips* in the den.'" She held up the cookie. "This . . . is not a potato chip."

The lists in legalism are always too short or too long. The lists in legalism also don't deal with the attitude behind the action. A person could do everything on a list and still have a wrong spirit.[559]

> Mark 7:9–13; Col. 2:20–23

LEGALISM, DELIVERANCE FROM

THE STORY is told of a lady who married a man named Jeff. Jeff was a very strong, rules-oriented man. He had a list for his wife every single day. She was frustrated living with Jeff, even though Jeff was a good man. It wasn't that Jeff asked her to do wrong things, it was just she was tense because she had to always wonder if she was living up to the standard that Jeff had established in the relationship. One day, Jeff died. But she had become so used to living under the tutelage of Jeff, she didn't know how to cut him loose. So she had Jeff embalmed and brought to her home. Because she had lived so long with Jeff, she didn't know how to live without him. The dead Jeff sat in a chair in the living room, and the lady would ask the dead Jeff throughout the day whether it was OK or not, do this or that or go here or there.

One day this lady went on vacation in Europe and met Bill. Bill loved her. Bill drew out of her emotions that had long since died with Jeff. Bill inspired her. Bill brought joy to her. She noticed that she did all the same stuff for Bill that she had done for Jeff, but without any of the demands. The relationship was so strong, she did things for Bill because she wanted to, not because there was a list saying she had to. They decided to get married.

They decided they would live in the U.S., not in Europe. So she brought Bill to her house. When Bill walked into the door, his mouth dropped as she introduced Bill to Jeff. She brought her new love into her old house and said, "Now Bill, I love you, but you must understand I've lived with Jeff so long I've got to keep him nearby." Bill let her know in no uncertain terms that she couldn't have a dead man named Jeff and a living lover named Bill. He told his new bride that she either had to give up her living lover and stay with her dead old love, or bury her old love so that she could can be free with her new love. She couldn't have a dead love and a living love in the same house.

Many of us have been married to

Jeff. We've been living based on a rule-based approach to the Christian life and then we met Jesus Christ and somebody told us we were free. But we're bringing Jesus Christ to live in our lives without dealing with burying old Jeff. Jesus will not live in a house with a dead man still calling the shots. It's not that the law is bad. Legalism doesn't seek to do away with the rules; however, legalism refers to a wrong viewpoint about rules. It expects a list to do what a list can never do.[560]

[Grace, Law and; Law, Effect of; New Life in Christ]

Rom. 7:11–13; Titus 3:3–7

LIFE, BREVITY OF

THE BIBLE says that a general life expectancy is three score and ten, which is seventy years. It also says, if by reason of strength, four score, which is eighty years. That's right in the range of the average life expectancy today. Men are expected to live for seventy-three years and women for seventy-nine.

Here's a little project to do. If you're a man, take your age and deduct it from seventy-three. If you're a woman, take whatever age you are and deduct it from seventy-nine. That will leave you X number of years that you have left. Multiply the number of years times 365 because that tells you how many days you have left on average. Then take some 8 ½ x 11 sheets of paper and cut them into squares. Number these squares and let them represent your days, which are numbered.

Every day, take a slip, ball it up, and toss it in the trash can. That little exercise will remind you that your stack is getting shorter. Time is running out. Whatever you plan on doing for the glory of God and the kingdom of God, you need to get around to it. Only one life will soon be passed; only what's done for Christ will last.[561]

[Death, Inevitability of; Eternal Perspective; Life, Perspective on]

Ps. 39:5; 90:12; Eccl. 8:8

THERE are many people today who consider themselves young. If I take a group of twenty-somethings and ask them if they are young, most, if not all, would raise their hands. There is only one problem. You cannot measure your age by your birthday. You can only measure your age by your death date.

See, if you are thirty-five and you're only going to live to be forty, then you're an old man. If you are forty-five and going to live to be ninety, then you're still pretty young. You can only measure how old you are by the time you have left before you die. Now, who knows when they are going to die? Nobody. So no one really knows who's old and who's not.[562]

[Death, Unexpected; Life, Perspective on]

Ps. 39:5; Luke 12:13–21; James 4:14

A DOCTOR was giving a prognosis to one of his patients. He said, "Sir, I have some bad news for you and some really bad news for you."

The patient looked shocked. He said, "OK, what's the bad news?"

The doctor said, "The bad news is that you have twenty-four hours to live."

The patient swallowed, paused a second, and then said, "Well, it can't get any worst than that. What's the really bad news?"

"The really bad news is that I should have called you yesterday."

Some of us have discovered that being a Christian cannot only be bad; it can be really bad.[563]

[Christian Living, Burden of; Death, Inevitability of; Death, Unexpected]
Ps. 39:5; James 4:14

LIFE, EMPTINESS OF

THE *PELICAN* is the world's most unwanted ship. The *Pelican* has been sailing since 1986 with no place to dock. Everywhere the Pelican goes, it is rejected; it is unwanted; and it is denied. Why does the *Pelican* wander aimlessly? In 1986, there was a political convention held in the city of Philadelphia, but during the week of the convention, the sanitation department went on strike. The sanitation workers used the political convention to make their statement. They went on strike and there was nobody to pick up the garbage. The problem got so bad that eventually the trash of Philadelphia was collected by other city workers and put on the bow of the *Pelican* just to get it out of the way. It's a huge boat; it's a 466-foot freighter. All of that garbage, unaddressed for a period of time, became toxic. The toxicity of the garbage on the *Pelican* made it an unwanted vessel. So now, wherever the *Pelican* goes, it cannot remain there because nobody wants a boatful of trash.

Life has a way of unloading its garbage on us, so that over time we become filled with trash and no one wants us around.[564]

[Pain; Problems; Trials]
Eccl. 1:2; 7:15

LIFE, FIXING

MOST of us in our cars have lights on our dashboards. One of those lights indicates when it's time to service the engine or change the oil. Now the first time the light comes on, you wonder what's wrong. Some of you may look under the hood to give the impression that you know what you're doing. Sometimes people lift up the hood and start jiggling wires trying to look like they know what in the world they are doing. After all of this, the light still won't go off.

That light that comes on in your dashboard is designed to let you know you have a deeper problem. When the light comes on, the light is not the problem. The light is an indicator that something deeper is wrong. Now unless you are a mechanic, you can't know all that the light is trying to tell you because underneath that hood are intricacies that are beyond your abilities or knowledge. So when the indicator light comes on in my car, I take it to my dealer who represents my maker, because the maker has a dealer who sold me the car. They understand the make, model, and serial number of my car. They have all the parts for my car. By delivering it to my maker, I give my maker the responsibility of servicing it.

If you've got an indicator light in your life, and it's saying things are dark, and you've done everything you know to fix that indicator light but it won't go off . . . If it just keeps shining red, letting you know that something needs to be done, that is an invitation to bring it to the Maker, and to let the Maker do under the hood what you can't do. He knows how to get down to the intricacies, fix what's wrong, and bring light to a dark situation. God wants you to bring your life to Him and let Him service you.

Oh, by the way, when I take my car in, I have an extended warranty. My extended warranty basically says, whatever is wrong, it will be fixed at no cost to me. When most people get a car, it comes with a warranty. That warranty says that whatever is wrong, broken, or out of line, it will be fixed if the owner brings it in.

On the cross, when Jesus died in your place for your sin, your salvation came with a warranty. When you accepted Jesus Christ, eternity in heaven was purchased for you. You will forever live with God when you die, because the gift of salvation is the gift of eternal life if you are trusting Jesus Christ as your sin bearer for the forgiveness of your sins. You have been forgiven and given the gift of eternal life, but God has given you a temporary warranty.

Now, you have still got to purchase the long-term warranty. It's not that you can lose your salvation. The warranty is not related to your salvation, it's related to your service. See, the warranty has to do with servicing you . . . until it's time to trade it in. One day you're going to trade in this body for a new one. One day you're going to trade in time for eternity. One day you're going to trade in this life for the life to come.[565]

[Eternal Perspective; Forgiveness, of Sin; Problems, Solutions to; Sin, Dealing with]
2 Cor. 5:15; James 5:13–16;
1 Peter 2:24

IF YOUR car fails, you go to a mechanic. If your house breaks down, you call a handyman. If your body breaks down, you go to a doctor. If your clothes are torn, you go to a tailor. If your grades aren't working, you go to a tutor. What do you do if your life breaks down? When it's a spiritual issue, only God can fix it. Anything you use to fix a problem in your life cannot compete with the presence of God. When you need to fix your life, there's no better solution than divine intervention.[566]

[Life, Management of; Problems, Solutions to; Sin, Dealing with]
Phil. 4:6; James 5:13–16

LIFE, MANAGEMENT OF

IN MY home, I have an integrated stereo system. The TV is connected to the satellite dish, which is connected to the CD player, which is connected to the cassette recorder, which is connected to the DVD player, which is connected to the tuner, which is connected to this, that, and the other. If you look behind the wall unit, there are a million different wires going everywhere. One day the DVD player wasn't working. I couldn't fix it because there were too many wires and there were too many holes. I didn't know which wire went into which hole.

So I called the people who installed it, and told them my DVD player wasn't working. I told them that I'd tried everything I knew to try and I couldn't get it going. I asked them to help me. They agreed to have a technician out to me shortly.

The technician came, took a look at my system, went to his truck to grab a couple of parts, and voila! my DVD player was working again! I have no idea how he fixed my problem, but his company manufactured the unit, so he knew what he was doing and knew exactly how to fix the problem.

Your life's got too many wires and this world offers too many holes. Instead of just trying wires, how about calling the manufacturer and letting Him send a technician who knows what He's doing?[567]

[Life, Fixing; Problems, Solutions to; Sin, Dealing with]

2 Cor. 5:15; James 5:13–16; 1 Peter 2:24

LIFE, MEANING OF

A MAN one time was with his friend. His friend was a drunkard. He just drank and drank, so his friend worried about him. He wanted to tell him, if you keep drinking this way, it's going to destroy you. The man decided to show his drunken friend an object lesson. He got a worm and filled a glassful of water and put the worm in the water. He had his friend watch the worm scurry around the water for about a minute and then he took the worm out of the water. Then he took the worm and put it in a glassful of booze in front of his friend. After about thirty seconds the worm died. He looked at his friend and he said, "Do you get the point?"

His friend said, "I get the point absolutely! If you drink a lot of booze, you won't have to worry about worms."

He missed the point. I don't want you to miss the point. I don't want you to miss the point that death is inevitable. I don't want you to not think about your afterlife and miss the point of living this life.[568]

[Death, Inevitability of; Eternal Perspective; Hell]

2 Sam. 14:14; Rom. 6:23; Heb. 9:27

AS A minister, I oversee many funerals. As a part of this duty, I've been at funeral homes many times and even a couple of times have been to the back and seen the undertakers working on the cadavers.

One time, an undertaker said to me, "You know, these cadavers are really interesting. Even after they're dead, they show semblances of life. Their fingernails still grow. So does their hair. I've even been working on a body in the middle of the night and have seen one blink. Sometimes there are muscular retractions and the body will quiver. One had such a violent muscular reaction that it threw itself right onto the floor."

By now, the undertaker was having a good time, at my expense, telling me all of these "interesting facts" about cadavers.

I said, "Now, you know I couldn't do this job. If I did, there would be two cadavers on the floor. This job doesn't bother you even the smallest bit?"

He said, "Uh-uh."

I said, "Why not?"

The undertaker smiled and said, "Because dead is dead. Even though these bodies exhibit semblances of life, I know better."

A lot of people exhibit semblances of life, but we know better. We know that what we are doing right now is not true living; it is merely a quivering of life. We do not truly live until we are living the life Christ lives in us.[569]

[Death; Salvation, Need for; Spiritual Life, Manifestation of]
Eccl. 9:4; Rom. 6:11

LIFE, PERSPECTIVE ON

A YOUNG man one day was on his way to visit a friend named John who lived on a farm. He entered the farm and began to meander up the road that led to his friend's home. He had to pass by a barn and as he got near to it, he stopped, perplexed. He saw something that both mesmerized and stupefied him. On the barn were twenty targets. In the middle of each target was a bull's-eye, and in the middle of each bull's-eye was a hole. Someone had used the barn as target practice and whoever it was, was a crack shot. There were no other holes on the barn except the holes in the bull's-eyes, centered in the targets. He couldn't believe it. He started back up the road to the house.

When he met up with John at the house, he said, "Before we begin our day together, I've just got to ask you, who in the world did the shooting on the barn?"

John said, "Well, I did."

The man looked surprised and said, "Wait a minute! I can't believe anybody can shoot that good. There are twenty targets, with twenty bulls-eyes, with twenty holes in each bulls-eye. You mean to tell me you did that?"

John said, "Yup, I made every shot."

"Where in the world . . . how in the world did you learn to shoot like that?"

John said, "It's simple. I shot first, then I drew a picture of the target around the hole."

A lot of us are like John. We just look like we're on-target. We have learned the verbiage. We have learned to carry the right Bible under our arms. We have gone through the right motions, and have learned to don evangelical smiles. It looks like we've hit a bull's-eye. It's not so much that we've hit a bull's-eye; we've just learned how to paint well. It is possible to go through the motions and not live a life on-target.[570]

[Christian Living, Authenticity]
Matt. 15:8; 23:27

LIFE, SATISFACTION WITH

I REMEMBER distinctly one Christmas all my children being gathered around in great anticipation of opening the gifts. The gifts had been voluptuously wrapped with ribbons, and my kids were excited. Paper began to fly everywhere as they hurriedly unwrapped all of their gifts. The gifts had cost a lot and they had been well packaged. With great vim and vitality, the children began the process of unwrapping them. However, I remember the statement that was made by one of them after all of the gifts had been unwrapped. The question was, "Is this all there is?" Evidently, some of you have experienced that. Many of us have unwrapped life and we want to know if this is all there is.[571]

[Life, Emptiness of]
Eccl. 1:2; 2:17; 12:8

IT IS impossible for a fish to be happy on land. A fish on land is struggling trying to make it. A fish on land is going to be squirming and flipping and twisting and jerking and jumping. It won't be able to relax because it is not where it was made to live.[572]

> [Heavenly Mind-set; World,
> Living in]
> 1 Peter 2:11; 1 John 2:15–17

EAGLES are most at home when they're soaring in the air. You know why? Because that's what they were made for. You can never be fulfilled when you're attached to earth.[573]

> [Heavenly Mind-set; World,
> Living in]
> 1 Peter 2:11; 1 John 2:15–17

AT DISNEY World there is a ride that I took my children on. If you've ever been to Disney World, you've probably taken your children on it too. It's called "It's a Small World After All." I remember well when I took my children on this ride because we rode around and around and around. On this ride you go through different cultures and see different children, dressed in different ways, singing the same song: "It's a small world after all, it's a small world after all, it's a small, small world."

The first time around it was okay; the second time around it was tolerable. The third time around it got on my nerves. The fourth time around I wanted to jump in the water and swim back, because that small world being sung by those small people was really getting on my nerves.

Life can be that way sometimes. It can seem like a real small world. Sometimes it can feel like you can't break out and see some things happen and unfold like you think things ought to.

Many of us are living lives of want—lives of dissatisfaction. We want more and the world's too small.

Every time we think we've found the thing we want, up pops a temporary sign to let us know it won't be around that long. There is one expectation after another, one disappointment after another, one strain and struggle after another, and we are just not satisfied. We soon discover when we've lived long enough, that there is no friendship, championship, scholarship, relationship, ownership, or fellowship that can fully satisfy our wants.[574]

> [Life, Emptiness of]
> Eccl. 1:2; 2:17; 12:8

THE MYTHICAL story is told of Tantalus, a king who had been found guilty of giving the secrets of the Greek gods to mortal men. His punishment was to be placed in the river called Hades. The water came up to his chin. Hanging and dangling over his head were branches of voluptuous fruits. The punishment, however, was this. Every time Tantalus got thirsty and lowered his chin to drink water, the water would recede. Every time Tantalus reached out to grab a piece of fruit, the branch would rise. So the refreshment for his thirst was right there at chin level. Food for his stomach was right above his head. But the harder he tried, the less he got. The punishment for his crime was to be in the vicinity of a blessing and not be able to get it.

The point is simply if you reach out for fulfillment in the things of this life, you'll discover that it's just out of your reach. For nothing in life was designed to give you fulfillment except God. Everything else is but a cheap imitation. The things in life that many of us cling to most for meaning, zip, and purpose must continually be hoarded because they so quickly elude us. The only lasting satisfaction in this life can be found in our relationship with God.[575]

[Abundant Life; Christ, Sufficiency of]
Matt. 16:26; Luke 9:25; James 1:17

LIGHT

ONE morning, I got up at 3:30 a.m. and decided not to turn on the light. Now, there is a light right next to me on my nightstand, but I decided not to turn on the light. I figured that I knew my bedroom and knew where things were so I didn't need the light. I figured I could make my own way in darkness, so I didn't turn on the light. However, in the middle of the floor were some shoes I'd left out from the night before.

I don't know how many times I've been told not to leave my shoes in the floor and to put them up. So there they were in the middle of the floor and I had no light so I didn't see them sitting there. As far as I was concerned, there were no shoes in the middle of the floor and I was all right. I knew how many steps it would take before I had to turn right. I knew my room. I'd been living there for a lot of years.

A few minutes later, as I tried to pick myself off of the floor after stumbling, tripping, and doing James Brown all over the carpet, because I tripped over my shoes, I was reminded that when things are dark you don't see things as they really are. You may think you're okay when you're not okay. You may think you're fine when you're not fine. You may think you know what you're doing when you don't know what you are doing—all because you are trying to do your

thing in the dark.

If I would have just turned the light on, I wouldn't have had to go through all of those issues. I wouldn't have had to face all those problems because the light would have revealed something was wrong in the middle of the floor.[576]

[Holy Spirit, Illumination of; Illumination]
Isa. 50:10; John 12:35

STARS show up at night. They burn bright all of the time; however, we can only see them at night when darkness is all around.

Christians are to be unhindered light in a generation of people that prefer darkness. In order to get us to shine, God many times allows situations in which, by reflecting His will, His perspective, and His viewpoint, we provide light to a "crooked and perverse" generation.[577]

[Witnessing]
Deut. 32:4–5; Matt. 5:16; 2 Cor. 4:6

LOFTY THING

WHAT is a partition? In a number of classrooms, there is a wall that can be brought down the middle so that one room can be made into two. It is a lofty thing. It is a high separation that can block one room from another or divide one room into two.

The reason for a partition is simple. It is there to decrease the possibility of noise on one side from passing to the other. If a group is meeting in one room and another group is in the other room, a partition will ensure that they do not disturb each other. The partition is designed to decrease disturbance. It is supposed to minimize the leaking of information from one space into another.

The way Satan creates a fortress, stronghold, or addiction is by creating in the mind a lofty thing, or a partition. This partition is designed to block the flow of the knowledge of God from entering into the thinking of the saint who is living in the fortress. It blocks out the free flow of spiritual truth and keeps it from crossing over into the thinking of the person in the fortress.[578]

[Addiction; Stronghold;
Temptation, Nature of]
2 Cor. 10:5; James 1:13–14

A LOFTY thing creates two views on the same subject. It is like the Berlin Wall. When the Berlin Wall in Germany was up, the East couldn't go West. The West couldn't go East. The two could never work together, because there was a lofty thing, a wall, or a partition that divided the same group of people, the Germans, East from West. There could never be unification and flow. The people in the East were trapped. They couldn't go West. People in the West were trapped. They couldn't get to their families back in the East—all because of a lofty thing, a wall, which had been erected.[579]

Isa. 59:2; Ezek. 14:7

LOVE

MOST people have birthmarks that are specific to them, whether moles or other kinds of unique identification marks. Designers are known by their trademarks. They have logos of various kinds that even if you don't read the name, it becomes clear who made it. God likewise has established a mark, a very clear mark, by which His children who have been birthed by the Spirit ought to be known. Love is the birthmark of the Christian. Without the birthmark of love, other people really don't know who you are.[580]

[Christian, Definition of;
Christian Living]
John 13:34–35; Rom. 13:8;
1 John 3:11

WHEN a woman is pregnant, over time, it's going to show. Early on, it may not be clear to others. There will be things happening inside of her—changes hormonally, changes with regard to taste, and changes with regard to various habits. But if the changes are happening inside, they're going to show up after awhile outside of her too. Many of God's so-called children aren't pregnant with His love, because the changes aren't showing.[581]

[Christian Living, New Life; Love,
Lack of; New Life in Christ]
Matt. 7:15–23; John 13:34–35

ONE of the things the IRS does is allow deductions for charitable giving. Uncle Sam gives folks a break on what they owe him when they show that they have supported a 501(c)(3) organization. People get credit for supporting an organization that is set up to serve other people. The IRS gives credit to people based on what they have done to help someone else.

What the government will do with your charity, God will do at the judgment seat of Christ. You and I owe God a whole bunch. We owe God not only for our salvation, but we owe Him for mercy, forgiveness, and love. There will be a payday, but on that day, God will allow for charitable deductions.

Our love for others serves as a deduction on the bill that we owe God. No matter how much we owe, when He looks at the charitable contributions in our lives, the things we have given because of His love in time, talent, and resources, He gives us credit.[582]

[Judgment Day; Service,
Motivation for]

DESIGNER clothes are known by their trademarks or designs. You can know if it's a Tommy Hilfiger or a Ralph Lauren. They have trademarks that make them very visible and very identifiable.

Those who hold an office of a unique kind can be identified by their attire. You can know a doctor by his attire or a policeman by his attire or a judge by his attire.

God has sent forth something as irrefutable evidence that we are close to God—an irrefutable test by which you can measure your own spiritual growth. In fact, so awesome is this trademark of God that He said it would be the major declaration of your faith. Jesus put it this way. He said, "By this shall all men know that you are my disciples, that you love one another."[583]

[Christian, Definition of;
Christian Living]
John 13:34–35; Rom. 13:8;
1 John 3:11

OUR fellowship with God is validated or invalidated by the love of others. When I was a boy, I went to an elementary school three blocks from my home in Baltimore. It was during the days of the old radiators that would heat the buildings. The classrooms had radiators in them and the radiators had hot water in them and they produced steam and that's how you warmed up your room. In the good old days, you would turn the knob to get more steam or turn it down to get less steam.

Well, I got to know a janitor there—we just kind of became friends—and he invited me one time to the boiler room. The boiler room was where all the mechanics were to produce all the hot water for all the rooms and the radiators in the rooms. I'll never forget the sight of this gargantuan tank in the middle of the room. When I asked about the huge cylinder, the janitor told me that the water for heating the classrooms got boiled in there.

I happened to notice that on the side of this humongous tank a little tiny cylinder hung in place. There was a little line on it with water going up to the line. The janitor explained to me that it was an indicator that showed how much water was in the tank. Because the tank itself was too hot to inspect firsthand, the indictor was in place to show what was going on inside the tank and whether or not the water was at the appropriate heat to warm the building.

Many people come to church looking to feel God in their bones, and feel Him in their feet, and feel Him all over, but that feeling is not the true indicator that God looks at to measure how full of Him we are. His indicator is our love for one another. Love for other brothers and sisters is proof positive or proof negative of our love or lack thereof for God.[584]

1 Cor 13:1–3; 1 John 4:20

FRANCIS Schaeffer, the great Christian apologist, said that love is the final apologetic. It is the defense for which there is no defense.[585]

[Love, Power of]
John 13:34–35

I HAVE seen the movie *Beauty and the Beast* three times. My wife took me to see it one time. I took my granddaughter to see it one time. We saw it yet again after that. It is the story about one ugly dude. This beast has a terrible voice and a terrible personality. He's a nothing. He's a nobody. But then there is a beauty, and you probably know the story. All the beast needed was somebody to love him. And as the story would have it, as soon as someone loved him, he wasn't a beast anymore.

There are a lot of people who look like or act like beasts. They have ugly personalities, or ugly attitudes. Even after church on any given Sunday, many people will show how ugly they are as soon as they hit the parking lot. But it is possible for other folks out there to be like Beauty. These folks find it possible to run into beasts and change them for the better through their love.[586]

[Love, Power of; Witnessing]
1 John 3:16

LOVE, LACK OF
A MAN and his friend were playing golf one day, and one of the guys was getting ready to make his chip shot. As he prepared to stroke the ball on the green, he saw a long funeral procession on the road next to the golf course. The man took off his golf cap, got on his knees, and bowed his head to pray.

His friend said, "Wow! That is the most thoughtful and touching thing I have ever seen. I can't believe how great it was for you to stop your golf swing because of a funeral procession passing by. What thoughtfulness!"

The man replied, "Yeah, well, we were married for thirty-five years. I figured that was the least I could do." That's what a lot of us do, give a nod to God, as we continue on with business as usual. First love is more than functional love. It's fiery love.[587]

[Men, and Their Wives; Passion]
Prov. 18:22; Eph. 5:25–33; Rev. 2:4

LOVE, POWER OF
A HUSBAND and wife one day were fussing. They were really going at it. So the wife suggested they write down their complaints on a piece of paper and then show the other person exactly how they felt. She thought it might cut down on the bickering. The husband agreed and got the paper. She got out the pencils. They both started writing.

They both wrote furiously for a while. The husband would pause, look at his wife, and write some more. The wife would pause, look up at her husband, and write some more. The husband paused again, looked at his wife with an even angrier look on his face, and then he would write some more. The wife did the same and then put her pencil down. Her husband was still writing. He looked up at her in fury and continued writing. He kept writing. Then he wrote some more. Then he wrote even more. The wife was getting furious because she had covered one side of the page and her husband was finishing the backside of his paper. He kept looking up at her and coming up with more to write. Every time he looked up, something new would come and he'd write some more.

The wife was in pain and agony. She was clenching her fists and tears of anger were welling up in her eyes. Finally, her husband said that he was finished. They exchanged sheets of paper and looked at each other's sheet. As soon as she gave him her sheet and looked at his, she felt terrible. She wanted to take her sheet back. For when she looked at her husband's sheet of paper, in spite of his anger and in spite of his pain, he had written on every line, "I love you, I love you, I love you. I'm ticked off, but I love you, I'm angry, but I love you. I don't want to be here right now, but I love you." When she saw that much love, it covered the multitude of sins that had brought up the argument in the first place.

When you and I love one another like that, that kind of love can cover up a multitude of sins.[588]

[Love; Men, and Their Wives; Women, and Their Husbands]
1 Peter 4:8

LOVE, RESPONSE TO

THERE is a story of a woman who had a husband who kept a list. This list contained twenty-five things he wanted her to do in order to be a good wife for him. Every day he took out the list and he checked off the things that she completed. Cooking—check! Cleaning—check! Care of the kids—check! At the end of the day, he would let her know how she scored—twenty-three out of twenty-five. Twenty-one out of twenty-five, etc. This woman was miserable. She was miserable because she didn't marry to be tied to a checklist. Not that the things she did as a wife weren't important. They were important and they were necessary. But she had higher hopes for her marriage relationship.

After a number of years, the husband died. The woman felt a weight lifted from her shoulders because she had been performing for years. She had been doing her duty and hating every minute, even though the duties themselves weren't innately bad.

Two years later, this same woman fell in love with a new guy—a guy who had no lists. He told this woman that all he wanted to do was to love her. He wanted her to wake up in the morning knowing that he loved her. In the middle of the day, he wanted to be able to call and remind her that he loved her. At night, before they retired, he wanted to reassure her that he loved her. He wanted his love for her to be her every waking thought of her day. He wanted her to know his love, not his lists.

One day she was cleaning the house. She opened up a drawer and saw a piece of paper. It was the list from the first husband. She began to giggle when she realized that everything written down, all twenty-five duties, were happening effortlessly in her new marriage. Everything she had hated doing out of requirement by the first husband, she was doing for the second husband—and loving it! All the second husband had was love. It brought joy to this woman, to her home, and all that she did for it. She was overpowered by love.[589]

[Grace, Law and; Law, Effect of;

New Life in Christ]
John 14:15; Rom. 7:11–13;
Titus 3:3–7

M

LYING

THE STORY is told of the man who didn't want the kids from the neighborhood eating his watermelons. So he put up a sign in his yard. It simply said, "One of these watermelons is poisonous." Now, none were poisonous, but he said, "One of these watermelons is poisonous." Obviously, the kids, not knowing which one was bad, would not steal his watermelons and eat them.

Now, none were poisonous. The man lied in an attempt to protect his crop from the thieves.

He came out the next day and, much to his chagrin, he saw the word *one* crossed off and the word *two* in its place. Now he'd lost his whole crop because he had no idea which watermelon the kids had messed with. Lies have a way of coming back around.[590]

[Sin, Effects of; Truth, Importance of; Truth, Speaking the]
Ex. 20:16; Prov. 12:22; Col. 3:9

MANY people admit that they lie but excuse those lies because they are only "little white ones." A little lie is like being a little pregnant, it'll all show up after awhile.[591]

[Truth, Speaking the]
Ex. 20:16; Prov. 12:22; Eph. 4:25

MARRIAGE

MOST of the grapes eaten in the United States are grown in Napa Valley, California. In order for a vine of grapes to become fruitful, the branches of the vine must be elevated. The branches are tied to a post for support. As grapes develop and grow, the vine will become too heavy and begin to droop and drag on the ground. Elevation not only keeps the fruit off of the ground but also helps them to get the full benefit of the sun. After a time the branches begin to spread along this post to which they have been tied. Having been made stable, they are then free to climb or to spread.

In the same way, stability allows a woman to feel secure and cared for. She is then free to flourish, to climb, and to be fruitful.[592]

[Men, and Their Wives]
Eph. 5:25–33; 1 Peter 3:7

A HUSBAND'S job is to set the temperature in the home. The woman is the thermometer. She is to give a temperature reading. The reading of the thermometer ought to reflect the setting of a thermostat. If a man wants a summer wife, he can't bring home winter weather.[593]

[Men, and Their Wives]
Eph. 5:25–33; 1 Peter 3:7

A MAN one day went to the Super Bowl. He was sitting in a seat with an empty seat beside him. A gentleman who sat on the other side of him said, "Is that your seat? I see no one sitting there." The man said, "Yes. My wife and I had tickets but she died, and none of my friends whom I invited could make it to the Super Bowl, so the seat is just empty."

The gentleman was puzzled. "None of your friends could make it to the Super Bowl?" he asked.

The man said, "No, they couldn't."

The gentleman was still clueless as to how this man couldn't find one friend who would love to be at the Super Bowl. "Boy, the biggest sports event in all history and they are missing it!"

The man didn't skip a beat, "Yeah, they're all at the funeral."[594]

[Men, and Their Wives]

MANY of us are disturbed in our homes. Rather than being married by the justice of the peace, it looks like we've been wedded by the secretary of war.[595]

[Family; Marriage, Unhappiness in]
Prov. 27:15

ALL OF us have either been in or been to a wedding. A wedding is a combination of discontinuity and continuity. Discontinuity speaks of a cut with the past. Continuity speaks with something that is ongoing from the past. When a couple gets married, they break a family tie that was the dominant family tie prior to their wedding. It's particularly true for the female, but normatively true for both parties as they disconnect with their mother and father as their primary point of family reference. And then they go out and begin a new household.

Yet although they disconnect with yesterday's family ties, they continue a magnificent institution called family. It's not the same as the one they are disconnecting from but it continues the same principle of family. God calls this connection a covenant. The word *covenant* can be seen all the way through the Bible as God's word to explain or describe a new relationship.[596]

[Family]
Gen. 2:24

THERE was a Catholic young lady who was thinking about marrying a non-Catholic young man. The mother said, "No way, you know that we cannot marry outside of our faith, and the only way that you can marry this guy is if you turn him into a Catholic too." The young lady went to work, very determined to change his religion. She and her mother worked hard together to turn him into a Catholic, and over time he began to break down as they sold him on the reasons why he should become a Catholic. Given his love for her, he went to catechism classes, and learned what it meant to be a Catholic. Finally, he converted to Catholicism, and in a few months they were to be married.

A week before the wedding, the young lady came to her mother, sobbing and bawling. Her mother said, "Well, what's wrong?" She said, "We can't get married." She said, "What do you mean you can't get married?" "I can't marry him," she answered. The mother said, "I don't understand why not. We sold him on our faith. We sold him, and now he is a Catholic." The young lady responded, "Yeah, we sold him all right. Now he wants to be a priest!"

When you are dating, a lot of overselling goes on. Then you get married and you find out you were sold a bill of goods.[597]

A MAN and a woman were being married by their preacher. The preacher asked if anyone had any just reason why the marriage should not occur. He told them to "speak now, or forever hold your peace." A voice rung out loud, over the whole church, crying, "I object, I object, I object!" The preacher said, "Be quiet, you are the groom, you can't object!"[598]

[Men, and Their Wives]
Prov. 18:22

SOMETIMES in baseball, a batter will have to do a sacrifice bunt. A bunt is simply taking the bat and tipping the ball so that it goes up the first or third baseline. The primary reason for bunting is to move somebody else on the offensive team farther along around the bases. A bunt is made because the team has a better chance of hitting it short and moving the person along, than swinging for the fence and perhaps striking out.

Now, when the third base coach gives the sign to bunt, it may come at a time when the batter had plans to swing for the fence. He may have planned to improve his average. He may have planned to improve his stats. He may have planned to show off his strength. He may have planned to serve notice on this pitcher that no way could he strike him out. But the third base coach tells him to give up his right to swing for the fence so that he can move his teammate along. "It is in the better interest of the team," the

coach says, "for you to sacrifice your home run swing," which usually means you are going to be thrown out, rather than to follow your own independent agenda.

God has called every man in the context of his relationship with his woman to lay down his sacrifice bunt, to not have his way simply because he is the man, and to raise the question if this decision is in the best interest of the other person.[599]

[Family; Men, and Their Wives; Submission, of Wives to Their Husbands]
Eph. 5:25–33

THERE once was a guy who was crying over a tombstone at a cemetery. He was just wailing, "Why did you have to die, why did you have to die, why did you have to die?" Another man was there visiting another lost relative. He said, "Sir, I am so sorry. Is that your wife?" The man said, "No it's my wife's first husband."[600]

[Marriage, Unhappiness in; Men, and Their Wives]
Prov. 21:9; 27:15

A MAN was looking at a couple and he said to his wife, "Look at them, they look so happy. They look like a happy couple." She said, "Don't be too sure, they're probably saying the same thing about us."[601]

[Marriage, Unhappiness in]

ON FEBRUARY 14, 2000, a very special yet unusual wedding took place. The wedding was between Benny and Brandy. You might wonder what was so special about a wedding held on Valentine's Day. Well, Benny and Brandy are two dogs. The newspaper ran a story with a picture of Brandy dressed in white and Benny with a dog tux on being brought by their owners in preparation for the unusual wedding ceremony. It turned out to be a fairly big event in Houston actually, as dog lovers from all over came to celebrate the union. That's interesting, I thought. Here we have Benny and Brandy trying to be human, and then we have married couples who act like dogs, fighting and barking at each other all the time, devouring one another. And we're supposed to be the human ones . . .[602]

[Family; Marriage, Unhappiness in]
Prov. 17:14; James 4:1

A LITTLE girl came to her grandmother and noticed that her grandmother's ring was big and gaudy and ugly looking. She said, "Grandma, those rings back there when ya'll got married were so big and heavy and gaudy looking."

Her grandmother replied, "Yeah, 'cause when I got my rings back in the day, they were made to last."[603]

[Commitment; Family]
Matt. 19:6; Mark 10:9

A GIRL ASKED her mother, "How can I keep my fiancé from spending so much money on me?"

The mother knowingly said, "Marry him. That will all stop when you marry him."[604]

[Wives, and Their Husbands]

A MAN bragged on his marriage once and said, "In our marriage, my wife and I have decided to never go to bed angry. We haven't been to sleep in three weeks!"[605]

[Anger; Marriage, Unhappiness in; Men, and Their Wives]
Eph. 4:26

MARRIAGE is like a violin. After the music stops, the strings are still attached. A husband and wife are bound together as long as they live.[606]

[Commitment; Family]
Matt. 19:6; Mark 10:9

MARRIAGE, SANCTIFICATION IN

IN OUR war against terrorism, there are Special Forces, the Army Rangers, the Green Berets, the Navy Seals, the Delta Force—these are special people who are cut out from the crowd, who are set apart from the rest of the general armed services. These are no ordinary soldiers; they are cut out from and a cut above the rest.

God is calling men to be sanctifiers, men who set themselves apart, and are set apart, for the purpose of the transformation of their mates from where they are into what they ought to be. That's sanctification, requiring a Savior first.[607]

[Discipleship; Holiness, Importance of; Sanctification; Spiritual Transformation]
Matt. 28:19–20; John 15:8

I LIKE lollipops. If I offer a wrapped lollipop to another person, they would probably take it. However, if I take the wrapper off, lick it, and then offer it to another person, they most likely wouldn't be interested anymore. Why? Because by licking it, I have made it mine. I sanctified it.

Now having licked it initially, I confirm that it is mine. As I continue to enjoy it by licking it, I actually begin assimilating what I own. If I lick it not only will I own it, but it becomes less and less its own thing and more and more a part of me. One lick won't assimilate. One lick will only give me a taste.

On a man's wedding day, he takes a lick. But in order for true assimilation to occur, he has to keep on licking until, after awhile, there is nothing left and the lollipop, his sweet thing, has become a part of him.

First a man sanctifies his wife and then he continues to sanctify her by continuously bringing her into the realm of his love and kindness and shepherding care, until they are utterly and completely one.[608]

[Marriage; Men, and Their Wives]
Gen. 2:24; Mark 10:7–9

MARRIAGE, UNHAPPINESS IN

A WOMAN once said, "My husband and I have a very happy marriage. There's nothing I wouldn't do for him, and there's nothing he wouldn't do for me. So we've gone through life doing nothing for each other."[609]

[Love, Lack of; Women, and Their Husbands]

SOME people think marriage is just three rings: the engagement ring, the wedding ring, and the suffering.[610]

[Love, Lack of; Suffering]

MATERIALISM, DECEPTION OF

THERE was a couple who had a cat. The woman loved the cat. The husband hated the cat. The cat would leave its hairs all over the place and it drove the husband insane.

One day the wife went on a va-cation and asked her husband to take care of the cat for her until she returned. Well, he didn't like the cat when the wife was home, so he certainly didn't like the cat when the wife was gone. He took the cat to the local dock and found a boat. He put the cat onto the boat so he'd never have to see the cat again. The wife came home and, of course, wondered where her cat was. Her husband told her that the cat had gone and that he didn't know where the cat was. This, of course, was the truth. He happily helped his wife look for the cat for a few weeks. She was distraught. Her husband said, "Honey, I love you so much. The cat's worth like a hundred dollars, but because I love you so much, I'm going to put an ad in the newspaper. I'll offer five thousand dollars to anybody who finds our cat."

His wife was filled with appreciation. "Oh darling, the fact that you would put up that much money for a cat because of your love for me is wonderful! Now I know how much you love and appreciate me!"

The husband put the ad in the newspaper. One of his friends saw the ad. He came to the husband and said, "I saw your ad. You're going to pay somebody five thousand dollars just to find a cat?"

The husband replied, "You have to understand. When you know what I know, no amount of investment is too much."

When you know what I know about your eternal future, when you know what I know about your welcoming committee, when you know what I know, which is that all of these earthly things will burn, it changes your perspective. Sinners don't know what I know. Sinners don't know what you know. They think that this life holds all there is. They don't know that God takes into account what you do in time for eternity. If you are a Christian, and if you know what I know, no investment for heaven should be too much. What you do in time will determine what you look like in glory.[611]

[Eternal Perspective; Money, Love of; Worldliness, Distraction of]

Matt. 16:26; Mark 8:36

MATERIALISM, NATURE OF

WE HAVE got to be the only country in the world that builds storage facilities so that people can rent space to house stuff that their house can no longer hold. We literally pay rent to keep stuff because we accumulate so much. If you want to make some money and you have some money to invest, build a storage facility because people accumulate stuff for stuff's sake. They don't take the stuff they no longer can use and share it so somebody else can use it. They accumulate it, save it, and pay rent to keep it. This is the ultimate expression of selfishness—keeping stuff for stuff's sake. We have things in our homes that we'll never use again and we just keep them. It's a shame.[612]

[Stewardship]

Amos 6:1–7; Luke 12:15; James 5:1–6

A DOCTOR, lawyer, and preacher had a mutual friend who died. They were all in the hospital room when the friend passed away. As the friend lay, taking his final breaths, he said that he had thirty thousand dollars that he wanted buried with him in his casket. He wanted to take his money with him to the grave. He gave ten thousand dollars to the doctor, ten thousand to the lawyer, and ten thousand to the preacher. He requested that at the funeral, each one of them come and place the money in the casket before it was closed.

The doctor, the lawyer, and the preacher all showed up at the funeral. They all three leaned over the casket and put something in. The casket was closed, the interment was accomplished, and they met each other afterward for a cup of coffee to discuss their friend who had died. As they talked, the guilt-ridden doctor couldn't help but confess. He said, "Well, our friend was my patient for years. I know he wanted me to put the ten thousand dollars in his casket, but I was sure that he would have wanted me to keep a little bit for myself given all the care I've provided him over the years. So, I put eight thousand in there, and I kept two thousand for unpaid bills while John was sick."

The preacher confessed. "Well, I must confess too. John always talked about our church needing a new organ. So, I only put seven thousand dollars in, and I kept three thousand toward our new organ that I know John would want us to have."

Then the shrewd lawyer spoke up. "Well let me tell you what I did. I kept my ten thousand dollars. Preacher, I went up to the casket and picked up your seven thousand, and doctor, I picked up your eight thousand, and then I wrote our friend out a check for thirty thousand dollars and put *that* in the casket!"[613]

[Money; Money, Love of]

1 Tim. 6:10; Heb. 13:5

MATERIALISM, PERSPECTIVE OF

IN ONE of his skits, the comedian Jack Benny would pretend to be robbed. A thief would approach him with a gun and say, "Sir, your money or your life?"

Jack Benny would always put his fingers up to his head and look puzzled.

The robber would repeat, "Your money or your life?"

After a brief moment of silence, the robber would ask again in frustration, "Your money or your life!?"

Jack Benny would finally answer him and say, "Hold on a minute. I'm thinking!" That's the way a lot of people are. They're so off in their perspective that they will give their life to get money—even if ultimately they only leave it to another.[614]

[Life, Management of; Materialism, Deception of; Money, Love of]
Ps. 49:10; Matt. 6:19–21

A LITTLE girl one day was given two dollars by her mother. The mother said, "Darling, one dollar is for church and one dollar is for candy after church."

The little girl started on her way to church. It was a windy day, and after a bit, she tripped and the dollars fell out of her hand. The wind took both of them, but she was able to catch one. The other one flew away. She said, "Well, God, there goes Your dollar."

Isn't it interesting that it's always God's dollar that flies away? Isn't it interesting that when you have to cut, you always cut God but not anybody else? God watches that and He weighs it.[615]

[Money; Priorities; Stewardship]

Matt. 6:24; Luke 16:13

A MAN had two prize-winning calves. These calves would win thousands of dollars. The man came to his wife and said, "Honey, this is something. The Lord done blessed us with two prize-winning calves. I'm going to honor the Lord. One calf is ours. The other calf is the Lord's. Whatever the Lord's calf brings in, we will give it to Him. Whatever our calf brings in, we are going to keep it for ourselves."

The man came home a week later, depressed and downhearted. His wife said, "Honey, what's wrong?"

He said, "Honey, the Lord's calf just died."

Have you ever noticed it's always the Lord's calf that dies? Have you noticed that when things get tight, it's always the Lord's money that gets left out?[616]

[Money; Priorities; Stewardship]
Ps. 62:10; Prov. 22:1; Matt. 6:24; Luke 16:13

MATERIALISM, REMEDY FOR

A MAN one day came to the pastor and said, "Pastor, when I was making $30,000 a year, I'd give generously to the Lord. I'm making $150,000 and I don't have anything to give to the Lord. Would you pray for me?"

The pastor said, "Let's pray. Lord, would You please take this brother back to $30,000 a year so he can start giving."[617]

[Giving; Money, Love of; Priorities; Stewardship]
Mal. 3:10; 2 Cor. 9:6–8

MEEKNESS

I LOVE the football commercials where these big, strong NFL players are shown to block and knock people off their feet and perform feats of strength. Then in the very same commercial, they are told to sit down and shut up and eat their soup by their mother. These big, strapping strong guys who are the epitome of strength on the field become humble as lambs when their mama shows up. When their mother tells them to eat their soup, it's not that the football player has lost any of his strength, his power, or his speed. None of that has changed. But now, his power is in submission to a higher authority.[618]

[Submission; Surrender, Concept of]
Matt. 5:5; James 4:10

A MEEK person bows low before God so that they can stand tall among men. It is a willingness to bow. The biggest players on a football team are the offensive linemen. They are the biggest, they are the strongest, but they're also the ones who go the lowest when it's time to run a play. The biggest and strongest get down and go the lowest because that's where they get their leverage to perform. The bigger you are, the more meek you should be, because the bigger you are or the bigger you think you are, the more out of control you might tend to be.[619]

[Submission; Surrender, Benefits of]
Matt. 5:5; Luke 6:29

THE HOOVER Dam produces enough energy for California, Nevada, and Arizona. It's concentrated power under control, producing all this energy for three states. But if you ever let that water loose, it would bring disaster to those very areas it's designed to help. When there's power with no control, and therefore no meekness, you're not blessed.[620]

[Boundaries; Self-Sufficiency, Danger of; Surrender, Benefits of]
Prov. 11:2; 1 Cor. 10:24

MEN

THERE was a special on TV about a herd of young male elephants that were running wild. They were running over trees, fighting each other, and creating havoc in their environment. They were male elephants gone wild, and experts were trying to figure out what was happening. Finally they noticed that there were no adult males in the herd. They were all teenage elephants that had lost their natural mind. The reason there were no adult male elephants is that poachers had come in and killed all of them for the ivory. So in an attempt to fix the problem, the experts flew in a group of male adult elephants, and dropped them into the herd.

When these male elephants were dropped into the midst of the chaos, they began flapping their ears, raising their trunks, and making these loud sounds. After a few days of flapping their ears, raising their trunks, and making these sounds, the teenage male elephants calmed down. As long as the teenage male elephants were calling their own shots, you had gangs of elephants that had gone crazy because of the lack of discipline. But when the adult male elephants were dropped in and they flapped their ears and raised their trunks and made the sounds, they demanded order.

We've got some teen terrorists today because there are no adult male elephants in the midst. We need a generation of adult male elephants—real men who will flap their ears and raise their trunks and sound out the truth of what a man really is in order to calm down a generation who doesn't know how to act because they've never seen male elephants in their midst.[621]

[Discipline, Love in; Fathers; Parenting; Parenting, Discipline in]
Prov. 13:24; Heb. 12:7–10

MEN can be compared to a variety of birds. First, there is the canary. The canary can usually be found singing up a storm in a cage. They just sing all day. Other folks feed them and they are pretty much powerless birds. Too many men are satisfied with the status quo. They are happy just to get their house, their beans, their potatoes, and their TV remote and they are fine.

And then you've got the buzzard. The buzzard sits on poles all day and just squawks, making this irritating sound. Far too many men want to sit on the sidelines and complain. "Well, my wife is not this, and my wife's not that; I wish she were this, I wish she were that." A buzzard is a guy who just sits around all day, complaining.

Then you've got the peacock. The peacock just wants to sit up and look good all the time. You know why? Because the peacock's interest is only itself.

Many men are eagles. Eagles just don't sit around all day. They soar. They take over. They are in complete control. Which bird are you?[622]

[Character, Importance of; Men, Weakness of]

MEN, AND THEIR WIVES

I DON'T know if you've seen one but there are square watermelons now. Of course people are trying to figure out how making a square watermelon is possible. Normally the fruit is oblong. But, somebody somewhere decided to try growing a watermelon in a square container. The idea was to control the size of a watermelon so that it can easily sit in the refrigerator. They force the watermelon to readjust from its natural tendency to become oblong, to a new shape determined by the environment.

If a man feels like he's got an oblong wife who's going in the wrong direction, maybe the environment she is growing in doesn't allow her to change her natural shape. A husband has the power to set the tone and to change the environment.[623]

[Marriage; Spiritual Transformation]
Rom. 12:2; Eph. 5:25–33

WINSTON Churchill and Lady Astor both served in the British Parliament, but they could not stand each other. Winston Churchill couldn't stand Lady Astor and Lady Astor couldn't stand Winston Churchill. One day, Lady Astor went up to Winston Churchill and said, "If I were your wife, I'd put arsenic in your tea." Winston Churchill said, "And if I were your husband, I'd drink it."

Many men feel that to go home is to go to the local graveyard, because that's where death lives.[624]

[Marriage, Unhappiness in; Women, and Their Husbands]
Prov. 21:9; 21:19; 27:15

MEN must be careful to purposefully honor their wives. If not done purposefully, time and familiarity have a way of wearing down even the nicest guys.

It's like the guy who married the lady who caught a cold every year of their marriage. The first year he said, "Sugar, darling, this cold is making you mighty uncomfortable. Why don't you let your lover boy take his baby to the doctor to get rid of this nasty cough?"

The second year of marriage he said, "Darling, that cold seems to be getting worse. Why don't you go call Dr. Miller?"

The third year of marriage he said, "You better lie down and rest with that cold before the baby wakes up."

During the fourth year of marriage, he told her, "Be sensible now and take care of that cold before it gets any worse."

By the fifth year of marriage, he would say to her, "You'll be all right, just take some aspirin. By the way, how about ironing these pants for me to wear today."

Six years into marriage, the husband would tell his wife, "Would you do something about that cold and stop barking like a seal?"

By the seventh year of marriage he sounded something like this: "Woman, do something about that cold before you give me pneumonia."[625]

[Love, Lack of; Marriage; Women, and Their Husbands]
Prov. 18:22; Eph. 5:25–33; 1 Peter 3:7

MEN, WEAKNESS OF

A LITTLE boy watched his dad leave for a business trip and figured that he was now in charge. He had two sisters, so he announced to them after his father left that he was now the head of the family. That night at dinner, he decided to sit in his dad's chair. His mother was impressed. The little boy was really trying to take over. She gave him permission to sit in his dad's chair at the table.

Well, his sisters didn't like that one bit. They reminded the boy that he was not the father and that he really didn't know what he was doing anyway.

One of his sisters decided to corner her brother. "If you are going to take Dad's place, then we'll present you with a family problem." She manufactured a family problem and then asked him what he would do about it.

The boy thought for a minute and then said, "I'm gonna do what Dad would do. Ask your mother."

Today we're living in a world of boys, in particular, who have become feminized.[626]

[Character, Importance of; Men]
1 Cor. 11:3; 1 Peter 3:7

THERE is a certain kind of wasp that stings spiders. It'll sting a spider and its sting will paralyze the spider for a few moments. The female wasp will then lay her eggs in the abdomen of the spider. So this spider now has in its belly eggs of a wasp and the spider has no idea.

After the spider regains its ability to move, sooner or later, it will begin doing what spiders do. It will make a web. After ten days, the eggs in the abdomen of the spider will begin to secrete a substance that causes the spider to stop making the web and start making a cocoon.

Spiders don't make cocoons. That's not what spiders do. But because of this foreign element that has been introduced to it by the female wasp, it is now acting very unnaturally. It's making a cocoon. When the cocoon is near finished, it's time for life to come from the egg. That life comes from the eggs, kills the spider, and the baby wasps live in the cocoon that should've never been made in the first place—except that a female wasp got ahold of the spider.

We've got a generation of males who aren't acting naturally.[627]

[Men]

Prov. 7:6–27

MERCY

JUSTICE is getting what you deserve. Mercy is not getting what you deserve.[628]

Matt. 5:7; Titus 3:5; James 2:12–13

A MOTHER, whose son had committed a series of crimes, went to Napoleon Bonaparte and asked him to have mercy on her son and to pardon him. Napoleon said he could not overlook his crimes and that justice demanded he be punished. The mother, intent on helping her son, acknowledged that her son deserved justice but reiterated that she was inquiring about mercy. The point of her request was for Napoleon Bonaparte to give her son what he did not deserve.[629]

[Grace, Need for]

Titus 3:5; Heb. 4:16

ONE time I was in such a hurry going somewhere to serve the Lord that I got pulled over by a police officer for speeding. He said, "Now, Pastor Evans, you know you're not supposed to be going this fast."

I said, "I am so sorry. I am wrong and I deserve a ticket."

Mercy kicked in. The officer said that he wouldn't give me what I deserved but he cautioned me to be careful with my speed.

Now, I figured that since I had just left a policeman, I didn't have to worry about another one for a while. I hopped on my accelerator trying to hurry up and get to my destination. Now, I had just experienced mercy. I just had been relieved from justice. But it doesn't take long to forget mercy. I went back to almost the same speed. One and half miles later, another policeman pulls me over for speeding yet again.

I got ready to plead again like I did the last time. He comes to tell me I'm speeding and I start to appeal to him for mercy. It looked like I was going to get mercy twice in a span of a mile and a half . . . until the first policeman came by. God has a way of making justice catch up with us when we don't appreciate mercy or when mercy is taken for granted.[630]

[Grace, Appreciation of]

Matt. 18:21–35

A LITTLE boy one day came to his mother. He said, "Mama, give me a peanut butter sandwich."

Mother made him a peanut butter sandwich, but then he looked at it and smiled. He said, "Mama, I asked you for a peanut butter sandwich and you put jelly on it too!"

You know what mercy is? Mercy is when God not only gives you what you asked for, but He adds a little extra on it too. He gives you more than you deserve.[631]

[Father God]

Matt. 7:11; Luke 11:13

A GUY had his picture taken. He was very upset with the photographer and very upset with the picture. He rushed back in to the photographer and said, "Look at this picture of me! This picture does not do me justice!"

The photographer looked at him and said, "Mister, with a face like yours, you don't need justice, you need mercy!"

That's exactly the situation we are in. We don't need justice, but we need a whole lot of mercy.[632]

[Grace, Need for]
Matt. 23:23; Titus 3:5; Heb. 4:16

MIND

EVERYTHING you do in your life, you do because of your brain. Without your brain, nothing else works. It is the channel that controls your motor functions, your speech, and all the other functions. When your brain dies, nothing else can work.

What the brain is to the body, the mind is to the soul. The spiritual man has reached the point where he consistently, although not perfectly, appraises, evaluates, or examines things from God's perspective.[633]

[Spirit, Walking in;
Spiritual Maturity]
1 Cor. 2:16

MINISTRY, IMPORTANCE OF

TURKEYS are interested in one thing: eating. They can't fly. They try, but they don't go anywhere. They just take food in and waddle around. Wherever you see them, they are waddling—waddling and eating, but not flying.

There are a lot of Christian turkeys today. They waddle in on Sunday morning and sit down to be fed. Then they get up and waddle out. Then they waddle back next Sunday to be fed before waddling out again . . . and they wonder why they can't fly anywhere and why they are stuck at ground level.[634]

[Christian Living, Spiritual Growth;
Family of God; Service,
Motivation for]
Mark 10:43–45; Eph. 6:7

THERE'S a clever young guy named Somebody Else. There's nothing this guy can't do. He's busy from morning to way late at night just substituting for you. You're asked to do this or you're asked to do that and what is your ready reply? Get Somebody Else to do that job; he'll do it much better than I. So much to do in this weary old world—so much and workers are few. Somebody Else, all weary and worn, is still substituting for you.

The next time you're asked to do something worthwhile, just give this ready reply: "If Somebody Else can give time and support, my goodness, so can I." Stop giving Somebody Else your job. Become a servant and watch what God will do for you, because He can also do it through you. You will discover it really is more blessed to give than to receive. What kind of servant are you?[635]

[Sacrifice; Service, Motivation for]
Mark 10:43–45; Acts 20:35

WOODY Hayes was speaking at a commencement exercise at Ohio State University. He was speaking to the graduates, giving them a challenge for life, and he said to them, "You can never pay back what this school has done for you. Even the money you paid didn't completely pay for the quality of education you received at Ohio State University. You can't pay it back. It's an investment that will last you for the rest of your life. However, even though you can't pay it back, you can pay it forward."

That concept became a movie, *Pay It Forward*. The idea was to pass along to somebody else the blessing that had been received from the school. Alumni Associations in colleges regularly call upon the alumni to reinvest in others, because of the education that they themselves have received. It is a call to sharing.[636]

> [Gratefulness; Stewardship]
> Deut. 15:10; Matt. 10:8; Luke 12:48

MONEY

IF YOU spend all of your life working and have nothing left over, then that means somehow you have failed in your work—barring something catastrophic. If for year after year and decade after decade, you are still living from paycheck to paycheck, then you have made some decisions in your life that have been generated by Madison Avenue and not by the kingdom of God.[637]

> [Money, Use of; Stewardship]
> Matt. 25:14–30; Luke 19:11–27;
> 1 Cor. 4:2

THERE ARE the haves, the have-nots, and then there are the have-not-paid-for-what-you-haves.[638]

> [Greed; Money, Use of]
> Matt. 6:19–21; Luke 12:15

MONEY is tainted. Tain't yours and tain't mine. It's all somebody else's.[639]

> [Money]
> 1 Chron. 29:11; Ps. 50:10

MANY of you think that the church only wants your money. But stop and think about this mentality. When you go to the grocery store, do you say, this store just wants my money? When you go buy a new car, do you say, General Motors just wants my money? When you go to the mall, do you say, the mall just wants my money? You don't say that about the grocer. You don't say that about the dealership. You don't say that about the mall. Why? Because that's not the issue. The issue is that you need food and the grocery store has food. The value you place on the food you need makes it legitimate for you to pay for the food you receive. You need a car so it makes sense to buy a vehicle to get you where you need to go. You need clothes, so you go to the mall in order to find what you need. In other words, it's not that these places just want your money, but they are indeed providing something you absolutely need.

We need God. We need spiritual help. We need spiritual light. We need training for our children. We need to know God's way. If we can go to the grocery store for physical food, then we ought to be willing to come to the house of God for spiritual food without whining about it. The question is not, does the church want my money. The question is, does the church serve good food.[640]

> [Church, Role of; Giving, Motivation
> for; Stewardship]
> Deut. 25:4; 1 Tim. 5:18

THERE'S a story of a young man named Danny Simpson. At the age of twenty-four, he robbed a bank in Ottawa, Canada, at gunpoint. He robbed the bank of $6,000. Shortly after, he was captured.

The real tragedy of this true story is that the weapon he used to rob the bank with was a 1918 45-caliber semiautomatic Colt worth $100,000. Danny Simpson robbed a bank for $6,000 with a weapon worth $100,000. Danny's problem was that he didn't know what he had in his hand. If he had known, he probably wouldn't have chosen to be a thief. What he had in his possession would have given him so much more.

If Christians only knew what we have in our hand, we wouldn't have to rob God of His tithes or offerings. We'd realize that He could give us so much more. If we have God in our hands, we don't have need of being thieves.[641]

[Materialism, Deception of]
Eph. 3:20

MONEY, LOVE OF

MANY a man or woman will say, "I don't love money." Okay, say you don't love it, but you date it, fantasize about it, romance it, and lose sleep over it. I don't know, sounds a lot like love to me.[642]

1 Tim. 6:10; Heb. 13:5

MONEY, USE OF

TRANSMUTATION is changing one thing into something else. For example, when you go to the pharmacist, you transmute your funds. You exchange money for medicine. The money is turned into something that helps your body. The money itself cannot help your body. You must transmute it and turn it into something else to help you.

Money can be transmuted for something else too. It can be used now for the benefit of eternity so that when you get to heaven, you'll have

things there that money cannot buy. Spend money here on earth in ways that will matter to you in eternity.[643]

[Eternal Perspective; Money; Stewardship]
Matt. 6:19–21; Luke 6:11

MOTHER NATURE

MOTHER Nature only follows the dictates of Father God.[644]

[Father God; Nature]
Ps. 19:1; Neh. 9:6

N

NATURAL MAN

A MAN went to his friend's house to hang out and watch television. His friend had a small 13" color TV, but they both sat down and relaxed in front of what turned out to be a great movie. The young man jumped up during a commercial and proclaimed that he intended to run back to his house and continue the movie on his brand-new 19" color TV.

So the man goes home, turns on his 19" color TV set, and doesn't get the movie. He keeps turning channels but can't find the movie. Even though the picture is sharp, he can't get the movie. Even though he's got great sound, he doesn't get the movie. He had no idea that his friend, even with his little-bitty TV, was hooked into a satellite that gave him the ability to pull down that great movie. His friend had the ability to pull a picture from up above that he himself did not have access to. The man may have had a bigger and better TV set but he couldn't get reception because he didn't have cable.

If you are a Christian, you have cable. You have access to God's viewpoint. If you are a non-Christian, you may have a bigger set, but you don't have cable. You can't hook in and link into a divine frame of reference no matter how expensive your life is, no matter how much money, and no matter how much power or prestige you have. So many non-Christians have a lot to show of this world but they can't pull in a divine picture because they don't have a good cable connection. This is the state of natural man.[645]

[Christian Living, Power; Holy Spirit, Illumination of; Perspective, Power of; Power, Accessing]
1 Cor. 1:20; 2:14–15

NATURE

EVERY day that you wake up, nature is preaching a sermon.[646]

[Worship]
Ps. 19:1; Rom. 1:20

NEW LIFE IN CHRIST

WHEN you take a shower, you don't put on the same clothes that you had on before. If you did, you'd be canceling out the benefit of the shower. When you clean the inside, you want the outside to match it. Having a clean inside and a dirty outside cancels the point in being cleansed. When you came to Jesus Christ, God gave you a blood bath.

You were bathed in the blood of Jesus Christ. You were cleansed from all of your sins. But what many of us have done, which wreaks havoc in the community of faith, is having been washed by the blood of Jesus Christ we

put on old clothes. The Lord wants us to take off old clothes, as they do not fit with the new cleansing.[647]

[Christ, Union with; Christian Living, New Life; Flesh; Sin Nature, Residue of]
1 Cor. 5:7; 2 Cor. 5:17; Eph. 4:22–24

BEFORE you and I were saved, we were like radios that only had one station. Everything we heard was from the vantage point of the old us. When you come to Christ, a new station has been added to your life. But unless you tune in, you will never hear the music.

Many of us are still feeding from the old station and so we are living the old way even though God has given us a brand-new channel. Unless you tune in, however, you will never hear about the power that you have in Christ. That's why you don't hang around people who are only playing old music. If you do, you are going to be . . . guess what . . . singing the same old song! What God has done is to give us a new channel once we come to Christ. He wants us to understand that we've been united with Him.[648]

[Christ, Union with; Christian Living, New Life; Sin Nature, Residue of]
Eph. 4:22–24; Heb. 12:1

OCCULTISM

IF I WOULD ask you to give me the address and phone number of the Mafia, what would you tell me? I don't know that there's a building we could locate anywhere that would be named "Mafia headquarters" because the Mafia is an invisible system of well-camouflaged evil. Many who function in the Mafia are legitimate-looking businessmen by day and hit men by night. By day many of them sign business papers; by night many of them orchestrate drug deals. It is an invisible system designed to promote evil often under the camouflage of good. Such is occultism.[649]

[Demons]

Lev. 19:31; Zech. 10:2; 1 Tim. 4:1

ON A hot summer day, here in Dallas, Texas, what good does a flashlight do? At high noon when the sun is at its peak, it is shining bright. To turn on a flashlight when you have sunlight is to depend on the inferior rather than the superior.

To go to a palm reader when you've got access to the heavenly Father is to go to the inferior rather than the superior. To call the psychic network, or to have a tarot card reading, is to turn on a flashlight when you're under the sunlight. It is to pay money for something you can have for free.[650]

[Holy Spirit, Guidance]

Lev. 19:31; Acts 16:16–21

OFFENSE

AWHILE back, there was a big deal about people burning the U.S. flag. Now, one could say, "Well, why are people getting all upset about a piece of burning cloth?" The reason has to do with what the cloth represents. People were upset because that cloth, Old Glory, represents our country. In fact, it became a Supreme Court issue. When a person burns the flag, they are in effect defaming the nation by defaming a symbol. A burning cloth represents a burning country. It's the principle of the matter.

When you are destructive in your own sinful life and it rubs off on other people, you are causing a division in the body because you are drawing people away from Christ and toward your sin.[651]

[Carnal Christians; Rebellion; Sin, in the Believer]

Matt. 18:7; 1 Cor. 11:27

OVERCOME

IF IT is raining outside, you may want it to stop, but you can't control the rain. However, you can open an umbrella. An umbrella does not change the circumstances, but it changes you in the middle of the circumstances. The wetness is no longer controlling you.

God's grace opens up an umbrella during the rainy seasons of life so that we may overcome and have the victory even when everything around us is wet.[652]

[Grace; Grace, Provision of; Sin, Victory over; Victory]

John 3:16; Titus 3:3–7

OVERCOMERS, VICTORY OF

GOVERNOR George Wallace on June 11, 1963, defied the federal court by standing in front of the doors of the University of Alabama to keep two black students from entering in. He said, "You'll enter in over my dead body." He was maintaining a system of segregation in the University of Alabama.

The only problem was that the U.S. government sent down U.S. marshals to escort the two students. They said, "Governor Wallace, you have two choices. You can remove yourself from in front of these doors, or we can remove you. But one thing is going to be the case: you're not going to block the law of the United States, which says that you must not maintain segregation at this University. Things are going to change today. Now, you decide whether you're going to get out of the way, or whether we're going to get you out of the way, but you need to know you will be out of the way."

When God joins you in the lions' den, and Satan has taken his stand against you, and he's gotten your boss to stand against you, your friends to stand against you, your family to stand against you, and everybody is standing up against you, God wants you to know that's not the final decision. There is another court up in heaven, and when that court sends in the marshals, this court can overrule whatever system is holding you down.[653]

[God, Power of; God's Deliverance; Victory]

Deut. 20:4; Ps. 18:35; 1 Cor. 15:57

OVERCOMING, POWER OF

WHEN I was a little boy, my father bought me a punching bag. It was basically a painted balloon. I would hit the punching bag every which way, but nothing I did kept that punching bag from popping right back up. I could slam it to the ground and BOOM! it came right back up. I could kick it and BOOM! it would come right back up. The only way I could keep the punching bag from coming back up was to destroy it. The reason it would come back up is because at its base, there was

a weight, and the weight forced whatever external pressure you put on it to bring it right back up.

That's biblical happiness. No matter what your circumstance is, Bang! Bing! Back up! No matter what your situation is, Bang! Bing! Back up! Your ability to recover is because there is weightiness on the inside. Whatever external pressure you experience only brings you right back up. This is the power of the blessed life. This is the power of overcoming.[654]

[Grace, Power of; Joy; Overcomers, Victory of; Victory]

Ps. 16:11; Isa. 61:10

P

PAIN

A MAN visited the doctor one day as he was in excruciating pain. The doctor asked him where it hurt and the man told him "all over." There was not a part of the man that was not hurting. The doctor told him to touch his shoulder. The man did and immediately hollered. The doctor told him to touch his own thigh. The man screamed. The doctor told him to touch his forehead. The man did and then yelled in agony. The doctor said, "I've never seen anything like this in my life. Let's try one more thing . . . touch your toes." The patient touched his toes and grimaced. "Oh Doc, everywhere I touch I hurt." The doctor examined him and said, "No wonder, you've got a dislocated finger!"

Many of us have experienced this phenomenon where everywhere we turn in life seems to be painful but only due to one specific area of hurt that is radiating into every other area of our lives.[655]

[Suffering; Trials]

I AM most certain that if you are like me, as a child one of your favorite cartoon series was Popeye the Sailorman. As you recall, Popeye was regularly brutalized by Brutus. Brutus would often seek to wreak havoc in the life of Popeye in all kinds of ways. He would try to steal Olive Oyl. I never quite understood why, but what was part of his program. He was always beating up Popeye until Popeye just couldn't take it anymore. And after he had taken all he could stand and he couldn't stand any more, he would reach for that can of spinach. After he had done everything he could to get that can of spinach and swallow it, things changed. Brutus was now the victim and no longer the victor. Brutus was now subject to this new infusion of power that Popeye possessed, and for a while at least Popeye was on top. But you could bank on this one thing: by the time that cartoon ended and another Popeye cartoon came on, he was losing again. So he needed another can of spinach.

We can liken that children's cartoon to some aspects of our lives because many of us are regularly beaten by the Brutuses of our existence— by those circumstances or people who constantly bring us pain and anguish, who are a nemesis to our lives, and who just don't go away.[656]

[Suffering; Trials]
Ps. 9:13; 25:19; 43:1

IF YOU go to the gym and lift weights, you are experiencing a burden with purpose. If you work out with a partner or a trainer, their purpose in placing weight on you to lift is to develop you. The purpose of lifting weights is to build muscle.

Now, if someone took that same weight and threw it at you, the purpose would be to harm you. The same weight causes pain but not for the same reason. One pain is to develop you. Another pain is to harm you. God allows trials or temptations in the life of the believer to develop them. Satan brings trials or temptations into the life of the believer to destroy them. Sometimes they are the same event. When you understand what God is doing and when you understand what the Devil is doing, then you understand the prayer for protection.

If you are learning how to drive and the man next to you grabs the wheel, that's to help you stay straight. When you get in the car with someone who wants to hurt you, who jerks the wheel, that's to cause damage or danger. So when Jesus says to pray for protection, He is saying to pray that God leads you into those things that are only for your development, and never let Satan get ahold of you for those things that are for your destruction. That's the prayer. Lead me not into anything that will tear me down. Only lead me into those things that will build me up. And even if I get into something I ought not be into, get me out of it quick. Deliver me from evil. That's the essence of the prayer.[657]

[Christian Living, Burden of; Satan, Strategy of; Suffering; Trials, Purpose of]

Matt. 6:13; Rom. 5:3–5; James 1:2–4

PARENTING

IN SWIMMING there is an event called the medley relay. The medley relay involves each swimmer on the relay team taking different strokes with each person doing fifty yards of each stroke. The strokes in the relay include the backstroke, butterfly, breaststroke, and then the freestyle. In the medley relay the backstroke leads off. Each stroke has a guideline that must be met. For example, the breaststroke must touch the wall with two hands and the top of his head cannot be submerged underwater after the first stroke. He's got a guideline.

The butterfly has to hit the wall simultaneously with both hands. There has to be a proper turn off the wall if you are doing the backstroke or the freestyle. If you disregard the rule, you do not only hurt yourself, you hurt the three other swimmers who are on your team.

When parents blow it in the home, they are not only blowing it for themselves, the repercussions are felt down the line. When mother and father get divorced, it's not just that the mother and father don't like each other anymore or can't stand to live together anymore. What they've done is torn asunder brother and sister and there are repercussions down the line. For good or for bad, the actions of parents touch somebody else.[658]

[Children, Training; Divorce;
Marriage; Marriage, Unhappiness in]
Ex. 20:5; Num. 14:18; Deut. 5:9

SOME parents think that by sending a child to college they are getting rid of them. What they don't realize is that by sending them away what they are really doing is increasing their phone bill, their fuel bill, and the amount of counseling time. Parenting will always be hard work.[659]

[Children, Training; Family;
Parenting, Difficulty in]

THE MARK of an authentic parent is that they are not out to please the child. They are out to do what's best for the kid. If a parent pleases their child all the time, the child is the parent.[660]

[Boundaries; Children, Training;
Discipline, Love in; Parenting,
Discipline in]
Prov. 13:24; 22:6

PARENTS ARE a child's escort through life. We have, in our culture, approximately eighteen years to escort our children safely into their own way, like a police escort that escorts specially designated travelers through traffic. Parents are to escort their children through life, safely, during the time that we have responsibility for them.[661]

[Children, Training]
Deut. 6:6–9; Prov. 22:6

RULES without relationship will always lead to rebellion.[662]

[Boundaries; Rebellion; Restrictions]
Eph. 6:4; Col. 3:21

IT TAKES fifteen years for an olive plant to become an olive tree. In the garden of Gethsemane over in Israel, there are two-thousand-year-old olive trees that still produce olives. Their roots run deep. The Mount of Olives is a mountain covered with olive trees that have lived for centuries. When those trees were saplings, they were nurtured so that they have remained productive.

Likewise the care and nurture of a child will yield the returns of a fruitful life.[663]

[Children, Training; Family]
Deut. 6:6–9; Prov. 22:6

THERE was a man who was sitting on a bank kind of meditating, and he heard somebody screaming for help from the river. This man was an excellent swimmer. So, when he looked up and saw a man drowning, he dove in, got the man, and brought him to shore. As soon as he got to shore, he heard another cry for help. There was another man drowning. He jumped in again, swam, and brought the other man to shore. Soon after, he heard yet another cry for help. He jumped in the river a third time and saved that man from drowning. This went on for five, six, and seven more times. He was totally exhausted trying to bring folk to shore. He had no energy left, and yet there were still people out there crying for help. He just couldn't help them anymore. His get up and go had gotten up and gone. He looked up to heaven and said, "Oh, God! Please show me what's happening upstream."

Sometimes, we try to deliver people without ever finding out what's going on upstream at the place that is causing people to cry for help right now. Many adults are crying for help in their lives now because of things that started earlier, or upstream, in their lives. Much of the trouble in the life of a future adult can be addressed by parents who do their job when their children are young.

Upstream, in the beginning of a person's life, God places children into families where they are to find love, acceptance, and value. Parents are the first line of defense for the well-being of life.[664]

[Children, Training; Family]
Deut. 6:6–9; Prov. 22:6

A JOB of a parent is to be the filter on their homes. Water filters keep impurities from getting into the home. Parents are the filters for their homes so junk from the world is not inculcated in the life of their children.[665]

[Children, Training; Sin, Avoidance of]

PARENTING, DIFFICULTY IN

A MAN used to lecture on child rearing. He had been a professor for a long time and had lectured through his single years and his parenting years. His lectures evolved over the years. When he was single, he started off calling his lectures the "Ten Commandments for Parenting." After his first child, he had to change the title to the "Ten Hints for Parenting." After the second child it became the "Ten Suggestions for Parenting." When he had his third child, he stopped lecturing![666]

[Children, Training]
Deut. 6:6–9; Prov. 22:6

PARENTING, DISCIPLINE IN

A LADY was in the store and her daughter was acting up terribly. She said, "Suzanne, you stop it and I mean you stop it right now. You control yourself. Suzanne, you get yourself together. Calm down. Settle down and I mean, Suzanne, you do it right now."

The store manager heard her and was impressed to hear this mother firmly give her daughter direction. She went over to the little girl and said, "You ought to be excited to have a mother like this! So your name is Suzanne, huh?"

The mother piped in, "No! My name is Suzanne. Her name is Brenda."

Instead of controlling our kids, we are trying to control ourselves.[667]

[Children, Training; Discipline, Love in; Parenting]

Deut. 6:6–9; Prov. 22:6

PARENTS, OBEDIENCE TO

A BOY was riding his bike around the block. Round and round he went, crying as he pedaled. A policeman saw the boy riding and crying and said, "Son, where are you going?" The boy replied, "I'm running away from home!" The policeman brought to the boy's attention that he hadn't even gone to the other side of the street. The boy cocked his head to the side, furrowed his brow, and smartly countered, "Yeah, I know I haven't crossed the street. I can't. My mama told me I couldn't cross the street!"[668]

Prov. 22:6

PASSION

GOD has called us into a passionate pursuit of missions in history and that of calling men out of darkness into His marvelous light. Now, you can't not talk about something about which you are passionate. If you are passionate about sports, it's going to come up. You don't have to be asked to talk about the Cowboys; you don't have to be asked to talk about the World Series; you don't have to be asked to talk about the Mavericks' season. If you are passionate about sports, it's going to come up. If you're passionate about sports, you read the front page last. You flip open

to the sports section first 'cause you feel it. Paul says knowing the fear of God, we persuade men. He says the love of Christ controls us. This is a passionate thing. Therefore, we must only conclude that if we go day after day, week after week, month after month, year after year without representing our Candidate, we don't really believe in Him. We must conclude that we're not passionate about Him because things you are passionate about, you talk about.[669]

[Witnessing; Witnessing, Motivation for]

1 Cor. 9:16; 2 Cor. 5:14; 1 Peter 3:15

PAST

IF YOU spend all your time today thinking about your failures or successes yesterday, then you will ruin your tomorrow. When today looks too long at yesterday, we are borrowing from tomorrow's time.

Yesterday is like a rearview mirror. When you go somewhere in the car, you use a rearview mirror. A rearview mirror shows you what's behind you. You need a rearview mirror but you only need a rearview mirror to glance in, not to live in. You don't move forward by focusing on a rearview mirror; you move forward by focusing on the windshield. If you live in a rearview mirror, you will hurt somebody. But in front of the rearview mirror is a much bigger piece of glass called the windshield. The windshield shows you where you are going and that's a lot bigger than where you have been. Don't let yesterday mess up today, which will ruin tomorrow.

While you are driving forward in your Christian life, every now and then look in your rearview mirror. Take a peek in your rearview mirror to see what's behind you so that you don't make a wrong turn while you're moving forward. Just don't stare too long.[670]

[Life, Management of; Second Chances]

Phil. 3:13–14

PEACE

TWO painters were in a contest where each said they could paint a picture of peace. One painter painted this sunset with the sun going down over the calm water. It all looked very nice and the picture had a very calming effect. The other painter painted a picture of a storm. In it, the sky was dark and there was lightning, thunder, and dark clouds rolling overhead. The picture showed the waves crashing against the rocks. Things looked fairly chaotic. But in the corner of the painting, at the bottom, were two big stones with a bird in the middle of them. The bird was singing. Now that's peace. Peace is where God's calm and God's tranquility overrule your concerns.[671]

[Fear; Trust in God]

Matt. 8:23–27; Mark 4:35–41; Luke 8:22–25

PEACE is a bridge and on the two sides of the bridge are truth and righteousness. You must have truth and righteousness if you're going to have peace.[672]

[Truth]

ALFRED Nobel, a Swedish physicist, created dynamite. His intentions were awesome when he created dynamite. He wanted to create an explosive that could move rock to build roads and get things out of the way to build buildings.

He wanted to create a force that was powerful and that would make life better. The problem is that people took his creation and used it for destructive purposes—to kill people and to make war. So depressed was Mr. Nobel that his good invention was being used in a wrong, destructive way, he took nine million dollars, put it in an account, and began to award people for promoting peace. We call it the Nobel Peace Prize. What motivated him was the fact that what he intended for good was being used for wrong. He wanted to award those who were doing what his intentions were. When these people get the award, they become internationally known as Nobel Peace Prize winners. They are called by that name because they make peace instead of making war. God is looking for some Nobel Peace Prize winners—some folks He can bless and award because instead of making war, they're making peace using His method that includes the blood of Christ.[673]

Matt. 5:9; Rom. 14:19; James 3:18

PERSEVERANCE

SUPPOSE the Indianapolis Colts said, "Well, we would make a first down, but the Bears keep getting in the way. We try to make progress, but the Bears keep stopping us. Since they aren't going to let us get a first down, we are just going to stop playing."

That's crazy! We'd call them chumps or sissies or fools. We would call them weak. We would call them nuts. Why? Because they don't understand that the test of true success is having the ability to move forward when other folks are trying to stop you.[674]

[Freedom, Fighting for; Trials,
Endurance during]
Rom. 5:5–9; James 1:2–4

THERE was a TV show about a very heavy man who decided to change his life. This man was very heavy . . . around a thousand pounds. All he did was lie in bed, because that's all he could do. He just lay in bed all day long waiting to die. His doctor had to come to his house to see him.

On one visit, the doctor shrugged and told the man that there was nothing else he could do for him. He said, "Well, if you are just going to lie here and do nothing, you are going to die. I can guarantee you that. Instead of lying there and waiting for death, at least die doing something."

That struck a cord. The man decided to do something. The television show fast-forwarded to a year later and showed that same man, 250 pounds thinner and walking around. He decided that he didn't want to go out like that. He chose not to settle.

Some of us have settled although we have the power to get up and do something through the power of God at work within us.[675]

[Christian Living; Faith, Acting in;
Impact, Potential of]
1 John 4:4

A FATHER WAS trying to get his son not to quit so easily. He said, "Son. you've got to hang in there and not quit. Look at Abraham Lincoln. He did not quit. Look at Thomas Edison. He did not quit. Look at Douglas MacArthur. He did not quit."

Then he said, "Look at Elmo McCringle."

The son said, "Wait a minute, Dad. Who is Elmo McCringle?"

The father said, "See. He quit."

Don't throw in the towel when the going gets tough.[676]

[Children, Training; Trials,
Endurance during]
Rom. 5:5–9; James 1:2–4

THE AFRICAN cheetah must run down its prey to eat. It can move at speeds of up to seventy miles an hour. It has a problem, however. It has a disproportionately small heart, which causes it to tire quickly. If it doesn't catch its prey quickly, the cheetah must end the chase.

We likewise rush into God's presence with excitement, but because our hearts are small we don't have staying power.[677]

[Christian Living, Commitment;
Hard Heart]
Gal. 6:9; Heb. 10:36

PERSPECTIVE

MANY people have mini TVs in their homes. In the bathroom or the kitchen, a little TV will be available to facilitate some sort of entertainment while they are involved in another activity. In the bathroom, a lady can dress, put on her makeup, and fix her hair, all while watching the news. In the kitchen, dinner can be prepared at the same time a favorite show is on. But these little TVs are not really designed for seeing the big picture. The screens are just too small. When a person really wants to see the full picture in all of its detail, they will watch TV on the bigger TV in the living room—the fifty-four-inch . . . the big screen. In the kitchen or the bathroom, you glance, but in the living room, you really see because the screen is so much bigger.

One of the reasons why Christians do not see things as they ought to be seen is that we look at the wrong screen. We tend to gaze at the wrong screen because we are so tied up in our own agendas and activities. All we have time to do is to peek at things every now and then.

God wants to give us the big picture. He wants us to see what He sees. He is inviting us to participate in His bird's-eye view.[678]

[God's Perspective; Holy Spirit, Illumination of; Perspective, Importance of]
Ps. 33:13; Heb. 4:13; 1 Cor. 13:12

WHEN a man or woman stands on the ground in a downtown area, they can't see too far up or out because buildings that are so much bigger surround them. All a person can do is stand on the corner, look down one street or another, and have a view a few blocks in front of them.

If that same man or woman takes off in an airplane and ascends to a higher position, those tall buildings now don't look any bigger than a thumb. They've gone high enough to see the big picture.

As long as you're at ground level, everything looks so big. Money problems look big, people problems look big, and job problems look big. If we'd allow God to help us see things from His perspective, our worries would begin to look a lot smaller.[679]

[God's Perspective; Holy Spirit, Illumination of; Trials]
Ps. 33:13; Heb. 4:13; 1 Peter 5:7

ONE day a teenager lost his contact lens while playing basketball in the driveway. He started looking all over the ground trying to find it, but couldn't find it anywhere. Somewhat scared, he went and told his mom that the lens was lost. She went out to help him look and found the lens in all of two minutes. Now, contact lenses are hard to find. His mother found in two minutes what the teenager had been looking for over an hour. When he asked his mother how she found it so easily, she said, "It's simple, son. We weren't looking for the same thing. You were looking for a piece of plastic. I was looking for 150 dollars."[680]

1 Sam. 16:7

WHEN I was in high school, I was selected to be a teacher's aide. At least back then, to be a teacher's aide was also to be viewed as a teacher's pet. People would make fun of you if you were the teacher's aide. You were not viewed as being sufficiently macho if you were the teacher's aide. I thought about not being the teacher's aide because I wanted to please and be accepted by my peers. As I talked to the teacher about not taking on this role, the teacher explained something to me.

She wanted me to know that the perspective of my friends and colleagues was inferior to hers. She taught me that I had a high calling as a teacher's aide. She explained to me that everybody else was taking the test while I was helping her grade the papers. She reminded me that I worked with her in reviewing the grade book. She reviewed the benefits that I would get for fulfilling this role.

After I listened to her and then

decided to stop listening to my peers, I developed a new perspective. My peers were trying to pull me down and make me think I was less than what I really was. I had to listen to the right people in order to have the right perspective. When I viewed my position from the standpoint of the teacher, it was positive. When I viewed my position from the standpoint of the peers, it was negative.

As Christians we have to constantly make sure that we are seeing ourselves as God sees us. It's God's viewpoint that counts.[681]

[God's Perspective]

AN OLD man and a young boy were walking with a donkey. Somebody saw them making their way along the road and said, "Look at that waste. The old man and the boy are walking with the donkey and not using the donkey for what the donkey was created for."

The old man thought that the passerby had a point. So the old man got up on the donkey and rode while the young boy led the donkey.

Someone else along the way saw the threesome and said, "Look at that old man making that little boy walk while he rides!" The old man thought that the second passerby had a point too so he switched places with the young boy. The young boy got up on the donkey and the old man led.

A little bit down the road, they passed a third person. That person said, "Look at that young boy making that old man walk while he rides. He is younger and stronger."

Yet again, the old man thought that the point was valid.

The next person who saw them

looked on in disbelief as the donkey was riding on the old man's back.

When you try to please everybody, you will go stark raving mad.[682]

[Truth, Importance of]

PERSPECTIVE, IMPORTANCE OF

WHEN the quarterback goes to the sidelines during a game and you see him put headphones over his ears, guess what he's doing? He's talking to the man in the booth, the offensive or defensive coordinator. Why? Because they are always situated up high looking low. The ability of the quarterback to function on the field, call the right plays, and read the right defenses is limited because he's too low in the ground. He is dependent on the perspective of somebody who's not low like he is. He makes a connection up high with somebody who sees the big picture.

In fact, it has become so sophisticated today in football that they now have a diagram of the defenses on the computer where they can see the limitations right in front of them. There are cameras situated at the top of the stadium that are taking reads of what's happening on the field. The more the quarterback is in touch with what the coordinator knows up high, the better he can deal with the team trying to stop him down on the field.

Satan is trying to stop you down here. However, God sits high but looks low. If you don't know how to pick up the headphones and get a reading from on high, you will be tackled in the backfield of life every time.[683]

[God's Perspective; Satan; Sin,

Avoidance of]

Eph. 2:6; Heb. 4:13

THERE was a boy who was looking at the reflection of the moon glistening in a pond. A friend of his threw a stone into the pond and the water began to ripple. The boy said, "What happened to the moon?" For the stone in the pond so rippled the water that he could no longer see the reflection of the moon and it looked like the moon was gone.

His older friend said, "When you can't see the moon in the pond, stop looking at the pond and look up to the moon because the moon hasn't gone anywhere."[684]

[Worship, Benefit of]

2 Cor. 4:18; James 5:13

I LIVE down in a bit of a gully. Awhile back, I had a TV put in but couldn't seem to get a clear picture. I was fiddling with knobs and couldn't get anything to work. I called the company from whom I'd bought the TV and asked them to come out and assist me in getting it working. The repairman fiddled with knobs and couldn't get anything working either. Eventually, scratching his head, he asked if he could go on top of our roof. He went up there and tried to fool with the antenna. Still nothing. He kept on twisting, turning, and tweaking. Our view on the TV went from hazy to completely straight. When the man came down from the roof, I expected him to tell me that the problem was with the antenna. He surprised me when he told me that the problem was the location of my house! Because my house is located in the gully and high trees surround us, our location basically blocked our reception of the signal. The re-

pairman actually got a long pole from his truck, took the antenna off, put the pole directly onto the roof, then added the antenna to the pole so that the antenna would rise high enough above the trees to get a signal.

The problem was not the set. The problem was not the antenna. The problem was my location. If you've been turning knobs in your life for years and your life won't get into focus, the problem might be your location. Are you living in heavenly places?[685]

[Heavenly Mind-set; Life, Perspective on]

Eph. 1:3

A MAN was getting his windshield washed and wiped at the filling station. When the attendant finished doing his windshield, the man said, "Terrible job! Redo my windshield. That windshield's as dirty as when you started."

The filling station attendant wiped it again.

The man in the car looked it over, and then in frustration said, "My goodness! Can't you even clean a windshield? This window has not changed."

The attendant did it again.

The man's wife was sitting next to him in the car, fuming. She reached over, pulled off his glasses, wiped them, and gave them back to him. The attendant had been doing his job correctly. The man himself was the problem all along.[686]

[Perspective]

2 Cor. 4:18; 5:7

A FATHER had two twin boys. He loved his boys but they had two different orientations. One boy was very negative. He found something wrong with everything. He always perceived the glass as half empty. The other son was positive. He found something right with everything.

The father was trying to figure his two boys out. He wanted to know what made them tick. So he decided to test them a bit. He put the negative boy in a room with all the toys any boy could dream of. He set him up to have a good time. He put the other boy, the positive one, in a stinky, stenchy roomful of horse manure—truly a negative situation. Then the father stepped back to see how each of his boys would react.

He came back an hour later to check on each one of his sons. He looked in on the negative boy. The young lad was sitting over in a corner with his thumb in his mouth. "Dad, I'm bored! Some of the toys that I wanted I don't even see in here." Even in a perfect toy environment for a kid, this boy found something to be negative about. This was his mind-set.

The father went over to the other son's room—the positive one. This son had a shovel and was digging through the manure! The father looked at his son in disbelief and said, "Son, what are you doing?"

"Oh Dad, I'm digging through the horse manure."

"Why are you digging through all that stench?"

The little boy paused and said thoughtfully, "Well, I figured with all of this manure, there's got to be a pony under here somewhere."

So today, if you're in a stinky situation keep digging. There's a pur-pose down there somewhere. There's a destiny down there somewhere! There's the will of God down there somewhere. You keep digging; don't let that stinky situation throw you off. Keep digging until God reveals His destiny for your life.[687]

[Life, Perspective on]
Rom. 8:28; James 1:2–4

PERSPECTIVE, NEED FOR

A MAN rushed into the house in a panic-stricken state. His wife looked at him, and said, "What's wrong?"

He said, "We're in deep trouble."

She said, "What is it?"

"It's the car."

"What's wrong with the car?"

"Water. There's water in the car-buretor. It won't work."

"What!"

"There's water in the carburetor, and the car won't work."

His wife cocked her head to the side and narrowed her eyes a bit. "Now, you don't have a mechanical bone in your body. You know nothing about automobiles. How in the world do you know the problem with the car is water in the carburetor?"

The husband hung his head and said, "The car is in the swimming pool. There has to be water in the car-buretor."

The man's problem was a lot bigger than what he said. A lot of us are more messed up than we look. We may simply say that there's water in the carburetor, when our whole life is in the pool. But we can dress it up, fix it up, tweak it up, talk it right, and lay it out, trying to make it look like there's only a little water in the car-buretor.[688]

[Pride, Problem of; Sin,
Confession of]
Isa. 64:6; Rom. 3:10, 23

PERSPECTIVE, POSITION OF

THE TECHNOLOGY of teleconferencing is commonly used now because of the money it saves in travel and time. With teleconferencing, if your company is having a meeting in Chicago and you are located in Dallas, they can pull up a video screen to include you in the meeting. Even though you are not physically at the meeting in Chicago, you are virtually in it because the teleconferencing transports you there without moving you from where you're seated. Teleconferencing can reposition you.

The same technology allows students to attend a class without ever having to leave the comfort of their living room. A teacher can reach more students than could ever fit in a classroom by broadcasting the lesson and allowing the students to ask questions via their computers. Even churches today transport their services or Bible studies, so that many people can tune in and interact.

The Bible says that God has teleconferenced you to heaven. You are really right now just like at the board meeting, sitting next to Jesus Christ. Now, what difference does that make? Well, if you've ever been on a plane, you know the difference that looking at things from on high makes. When you're down here on earth, you see the problem, the chaos, and the confusion. When you get up there high in a plane, what seems to be confusion down here becomes ordered up there. You don't even see the problems.

The problems disappear. The problems no longer have control of you because your location has changed. When you change your position, you can always change your perspective.

God wants us to know that if we are going to find liberty, freedom, and victory, we must begin living our lives from the perspective of our new position alongside of Jesus Christ. Once you take this airplane ride and get to see life as Christ sees it from where He is, it will change your perception of what is really going on in your life. It is a positional issue.[689]

[Freedom; God's Perspective; Life, Perspective on; Victory]
Eph. 2:6; Heb. 12:2

PERSPECTIVE, POWER OF

A LITTLE boy was playing in the backyard with his bat and ball. "I'm the greatest baseball player in the world." Then he tossed the ball in the air, swung, and missed.

Undaunted, he picked up the ball, threw it into the air, and said to himself, "I'm the greatest player ever!" He swung at the ball again, and again he missed.

He paused a moment to look at the bat and ball carefully. Then once again, he threw the ball into the air and said, "I'm the greatest baseball player who ever lived." He swung the bat hard and again missed the ball. Not missing a beat, he then said, "Wow! What a pitcher!"[690]

[Life, Perspective on]

PLEASURE

SURFERS enjoy temporary pleasure. They wade out, catch a wave, stand up, and for a few seconds, ride the wave for a thrilling moment. A water skier is different. They are holding on to a boat that is pulling them. While the surfer is dependent upon his own ability to stay afloat, a water skier can ride all day if they choose because they are not dependent upon their own ability to find and stay afloat of a temporary wave. Satan wants to take us surfing. He'll give us a great wave too. Even if he can't knock you off and get you addicted to some kind of pleasure, He'd be happy just to get you sidetracked to enjoy its short-lived effect. He'd love to keep you sidetracked by having you fall into a pattern of continually searching for the next wave of pleasure.[691]

> [Satan, Strategy of; Temptation;
> Worldliness, Distraction of]
> Matt. 26:41; 1 Peter 5:8

POOR IN SPIRIT

WHEN we get sick, we usually start off with over-the-counter medications. We go to the drugstore and try finding something that we think will fix our problem and help us to feel better. But if the problem persists, at some point, we will determine that this problem is beyond us. We'll decide after awhile that the medicine is not working, the syrup's not doing the job, or the pills are not strong enough. We'll realize that the stuff we have the power to purchase over the counter isn't working.

Realizing that something deeper must be wrong, we will call the doctor. We will come to the place were we recognize that we do not have the capacity to get what we need to fix what's wrong. We will go to a professional who can both diagnose and prescribe the remedy for the deeper issue that we weren't aware of.

Sometimes, in our own humanness, we can't fix our own problems. Purchasing our own pills can't fix it. Homespun remedies can't fix it. So sometimes, there may be something deeper going on. Could it be that the reason that life is not working for many of us is that we are still locked in to our own human confidence, ability, strategies, thoughts, and mentalities? Do we keep on taking over-the-counter solutions and then wonder why inside we still feel sick? Things on the outside—nicer cars, houses, and clothes—don't give true blessing. True blessing starts with poverty of spirit.[692]

> [Life, Emptiness of; Materialism,
> Deception of; Problems]
> Matt. 5:3

HOW do you know you're not yet poor in spirit? Because you're rich in worry.[693]

> [Worry]
> Phil. 4:6; 1 Peter 5:7

IN MOST athletic contests, the high score wins. In football, the highest score wins. In the game of baseball, the highest score wins. In a tennis game, the highest score wins. Even in soccer, the highest score wins. But not in golf. In golf, the low score wins. You can't finish your golf game and brag about getting a 110 for a score. If you get a 110, that means that you can't play. In golf, it is the person with the fewest strokes who wins.

Tiger Woods rules golf. The reason why Tiger Woods rules golf is he is consistent in getting the lowest score. Because he comes in the lowest, he rules the course. Because he comes in with fewer strokes, he's got a whole kingdom called the Tiger Woods Kingdom and he's running the whole show. God says that the only way we can see His kingdom is to aim low. As long as we think that the goal is to be the high man, we will not be the winner. In God's kingdom, it's the low man that wins. We have to remember that the man who is poor in spirit is the man who is better off. Blessed are the meek.[694]

[God's Standard; Meekness]

Matt. 5:3–5

ONE of my favorite songs is "Ain't Too Proud to Beg" by the Temptations. The lead singer has these lines, "If I have to beg and plead for your sympathy, I don't mind 'cause you mean that much to me. Ain't too proud to beg." God is looking for some Christians that ain't too proud to beg.[695]

[Pride, Problem of; Self-Sufficiency, Danger of; Surrender, Benefits of]

POWER, ACCESSING

MOST people get where they want to go by car. The power, the force in the car, takes them where they want to go. All the person has to do is position themselves correctly. In other words, if the car is in the garage and if the person is in the house, they may have what they need to make the trip, but they will not be located in the right relationship to it. The problem is not the individual's inability to make the trip; the problem is that they are not in correct relationship to the thing designed to bring them to a certain location.

Many times we stay stuck in the Christian life because we are not in the right relationship to the provision,

to the force, to the engine designed to get us where God wants us to be. It's not that we don't have the power or know the guidelines. The interesting thing about grace is that God has put the motor inside you. It's called the new nature. If any man is in Christ, he's a new creation. The motor has already been planted inside of you. All we have to do is be in alignment.[696]

[Christian Living, New Life; Holy Spirit, Power of; New Life in Christ]

2 Cor. 5:17; Gal. 6:15

PRAISE

AT GRADUATION there are levels of honor bestowed on those who have done a good job. There is cum laude, magna cum laude, and summa cum laude.

In the realm of giving praise, there is high praise, higher praise, and highest praise. Your friends can get high praise, and some folk who blessed you or have been merciful may deserve a higher praise, but God is the only one who deserves the summa cum laude of the highest praise. This kind of praise should be reserved for Him.[697]

[Idolatry; Worship]

1 Chron. 16:25; Ps. 96:4; Rev. 5:12

PRAISE, POWER OF

A MAN was trying to teach his horse to obey and to stop and start on command. The man was a very religious man, so he came up with a couple of religious statements to use in training his horse. He trained the horse to go on the command words, "Praise the Lord!" He trained the horse to stop on the command word, "Hallelujah!"

One day he was riding the horse and it took off. He lost control of the horse and he forgot his words. The horse had been trained to only respond to the key words. Up ahead was a cliff, and the horse was headed there full speed. The man tried thinking of every religious word he'd ever heard of. "Amen! Jesus saves! Worthy! Holy!" Nothing worked.

Just as the horse approached the precipice, the man shouted out, "Hallelujah!" The horse stopped right there on the edge. The man wiped his head and said, "Whew, Praise the Lord!"

Praising the Lord is not some kind of casual meaningless activity. There is power in praise.[698]

[Worship, Motivation for]
Ps. 150:1–6; James 5:13

PRAYER

THERE was a lady who needed a new car. Her two favorite colors were green and blue, so she prayed and asked God to give her a green and blue car. She went car-hunting and found the car she wanted—perfect green but no blue. The lady was unsure if it was the will of God for her to buy that car, because she asked for a green and blue car. After explaining her dilemma to the salesman, he asked if he could show her the hood. He lifted up the hood and the motor had been painted blue! Some of us will never know if we've heard from God, because we pray vaguely.[699]

[God's Voice; Provision, God's]
Matt. 7:7–11; Eph. 6:18; James 5:13;
1 John 5:14–15

THE CONCEPT of prayer is closely related to a sheepdog. The sheepdog, who helps the shepherd or farmer to round up the sheep, is always trained to come to his master's feet. Sheepdogs are some of the most trained dogs in the world. They learn to round up sheep and keep them in the fold, box them in, and run and corner them too. Then the dogs come right back to the master's feet. A sheepdog would always pray; that is, he would always find himself at the master's feet ready for the next instruction. That's prayer. Prayer is that abiding relationship where believers stay at the master's feet.[700]

[Jesus, Relationship with]
John 15:7; Col. 4:2

A POWER of attorney is a legal right to sign on someone else's behalf. That's exactly what happens when you pray.

When Christians pray "Our Father . . ." the Holy Spirit delivers our prayer to the Father. But before God responds, He looks over to Jesus and asks Him if He is signing the note. Jesus is our power of attorney. He is the one who signs off on prayers.[701]

[Father God; Jesus, Relationship with; Prayer, Jesus' Name]
John 16:24

IF I put a million dollars in your physical bank account, you are a guaranteed millionaire. But if you don't know how to write a check, that which is guaranteed cannot be enjoyed. Too many of us who've got bank accounts full of God's blessing are forgetting to sign our checks. We forget to draw from that spiritual reservoir, or we don't understand how to draw from that spiritual reservoir to live the successful Christian life.[702]

[Christian Living, Power; Power, Accessing; Provision, God's]

Luke 11:1–4; James 4:2–3; 5:13

WE HAVE a system in our church whereby financial requests are made. I have a budget that I take and allocate to the various staff persons based on our programming. In order to get money for a program, the staff must fill out a voucher. That voucher is designed to create accountability for the expenditures of the church's funds. If a department head wants money, that voucher must also be signed by the pastor over that area. Do you know that this department head doesn't have to come in and fuss and cuss about that money? He doesn't have to come in mad and angry and saying, "I want my money and I want it now! How come I don't have it?"

All he has to do is ask. He simply fills out a voucher and says, "I need this. It's within the purview of my budget." By filling out that piece of paper, getting it signed, and having the pastor sign off on the voucher, a check is cut by our business office to meet the total needs of the request. He doesn't have to fight. In fact, if he comes in with a bad attitude, he may be telling us he's not the person for the job! A simple authorized request is all that is required.[703]

[Christian Living, Power; Power, Accessing; Prayer, Access in; Provision, God's]

Luke 11:1–4; James 4:2–3; 5:13

SOME time ago, my two boys were arguing and fighting over something.

Anthony said, "Jonathan keeps taking my stuff!"

Jonathan said, "Well, he won't share."

Then Jonathan gets spiritual and says, "Daddy, didn't you teach us to share?"

"But he won't ask!" Anthony cried. "I don't mind sharing it if he would just ask for it and not be presumptuous and just come take it. All he's got to do is ask."

I interjected, "Jonathan, ask him."

So Jonathan reluctantly said, "May I use it?"

Anthony replied, "Yes, all you had to do is ask."

Do you know that God wants to deal with things in your life if you just ask? You do not have because you do not ask.[704]

[Power, Accessing; Prayer, Access in]

Eph. 6:18; James 4:2–3; 5:13

ALL OF us have spare tires in our car—just in case there's a flat or a slow leak of air. Most of the time, we don't even think about it until something goes wrong. But when something goes wrong, we go back to the trunk and we get out the spare to get us out of a bad situation. For most of us, prayer is like that. It's a spare tire. It's just in case. It's easy to forget about it until you really need it to get you out of a jam; it's something you are glad to have when you're caught in a dilemma you can't fix.[705]

Isa. 29:13; Matt. 15:8; Mark 7:6

FOR MANY of us, prayer is like the National Anthem before a football game. It gets the game started, but simply has no connection with what's happening on the field. It's a courtesy.[706]

Isa. 29:13; Matt. 15:8; Mark 7:6

FOR SOME of us, prayer is like putting four quarters in a Coke machine, pushing the button, and not getting a Coke. We push the button again and again, waiting for our Coke, which never comes. Finally, kicking the machine, we just wave our hand and walk away. Many of us have given up on prayer because while it is something we know we are supposed to do, we feel it just doesn't work.[707]

[Faith]

Luke 18:1–8; James 4:3

WHEN you watch football games today, you will from time to time see the coach reach in his back pocket and throw a flag out on the field. He's contesting something that the referee has called on the field and the flag shows that he doesn't agree. The coach is demonstrating that the referee didn't see the play right or call the play right. When he throws that flag out on the field, play is going to be stopped.

The referee is then going to go and look more intently at the play to determine whether the right call was made or not. On many occasions, he will reverse, because of the coach's flag.

When Christians pray right, God, in heaven, stops to take a second look. On many occasions, things will reverse because a Christian throws up a flag. God welcomes the flag of prayer. It is His communication mechanism.[708]

[God's Ways, Unpredictability of]

Ex. 32:1–14; Amos 7:1–6

THE THINGS in your house work because of electricity. Electricity is an invisible power that gives you visible privileges. It turns the lights on, turns the TV on, turns the toaster on, and turns the oven on; all that stuff is working in your house because you've got one invisible power shooting through

there called electricity. But none of those things work even though they have access to electricity until you flip on a switch. You've got to make a connection before the stuff that's there works. Every believer in Jesus Christ has stuff that works.[709]

[Power, Accessing]

James 5:13

I REGULARLY drive on empty. I stop at the filling station as a last resort. Anytime my wife has to drive my vehicle, her question is always the same. She wants to know if there is anything in the tank. To put it another way, I ride on fumes. I do it because I've gotten away with it so often! There's a little thrill getting to the station in the nick of time.

One time, my wife was riding with me while my gauge showed "E." She made no short order of telling me that I would get caught and my car would run out of gas. I did run out of gas, but I was near an exit ramp. I took the ramp downhill and coasted into the gas station just off the service road at the bottom of the decline!

There have been other times where I wasn't so fortunate. I've put up my hood at times just to avoid embarrassment and to make everyone think it was mechanical problems instead of an empty gas tank.

I live on fumes. And to live a prayer-less life is to live your spiritual life with fumes.[710]

[Independence, Consequences of;
Self-Sufficiency, Danger of;
Spiritual Food]

James 4:2–3

FOR MANY of us, prayer is like a AAA card. It's there if you need it, but you really don't plan to use it very much—unless you're in an emergency.[711]

Isa. 29:13; Matt. 15:8; Mark 7:6

A MAN was praying one day in a church in England. His English was terrible and broken. He was doing a horrible job destroying the king's English. A lady who was hearing his prayers was just beside herself as this man spoke in this manner. After he said "amen" she said, "Young man, that was the worst grammar and articulation I have ever heard in my life. I am disgusted that you would talk like that."

He turned, looked at the woman, and said, "But lady, I wasn't talking to you."

Prayer is communication with God.[712]

[Jesus, Relationship with]
Matt. 6:5–13; Luke 11:1–4

I REMEMBER when I was a boy and my mother would fry chicken. When it was my turn to pray, I'd pray with my eyes open. I'd pray to God for that thigh that I had my eyes on. Sometime during the middle of the prayer, I'd unfold my hands and let one of them slip onto the table near the chicken so that I'd be halfway to my goal when the prayer was over. I wasn't really thinking about God. I was thinking about chicken. I just had to get rid of God to get to the chicken.

Sometimes we just use prayer as a way for us to get rid of God so that we can get to the real thing.[713]

[Faith, Distortion of]
Isa. 29:13; Matt. 15:8; Mark 7:6

A LITTLE boy knelt at his bed and said his bedtime prayers. "Lord, please bless Mommy, and Daddy, and Auntie, and Uncle. Lord, give us a good day today. And please give me a bicycle for CHRISTMAAAAAAS!"

The boy's mother heard him yelling and wondered at his behavior. She walked into the room and said, "Son, son, you don't have to scream. God can hear you."

The boy looked up with big eyes and said, "Mama, I know God can hear me, but Grandma can't hear very well and she's got the money for the bike."[714]

[Christmas, Purpose of]
Isa. 29:13; Matt. 15:8; Mark 7:6

THE STORY is told of a fisherman who was not in particularly good fellowship with the Lord. He was at sea with some godless companions, and they were in trouble in a storm. It looked like the boat very well might sink. So the non-Christians called on the Christian to pray. They said, "Would you call on God?"

But he said, "Man, I've been out of fellowship with the Lord a long time and I haven't really been praying to Him regularly. In fact, I haven't even been going to church. I don't even know if I can help. But I'll try."

He bowed his head and said, "Lord, I know I have been out of fellowship with You, and I haven't been in touch with You for fifteen years. But Lord, if You will help me this time and bring us safely to land, then I promise I won't bother You again for another fifteen years."

That's how a lot of us look at prayer. It's that thing we do when everything else has failed and that we don't pick up and do again until we are in that situation again. That is a far cry from what God had in mind when He gave us this instrument of spiritual life.[715]

[Faith, Distortion of; Jesus, Relationship with]

Ps. 145:18; Eph. 6:18; Phil. 4:6

A LADY came to the great preacher of the last century G. Campbell Morgan and she said, "I only take the big things to God. I don't take the little things to God."

G. Campbell Morgan looked at her and said, "Lady, anything you take to God is little."

That is precisely the case. You can bring everything to God because anything you bring to God is little to Him, even if it is big to you.[716]

[God's Perspective]

Eph. 6:18; James 5:13–16

THE YUPPIE PRAYER
Now I lay me down to sleep
I pray my bank account to keep.
I pray my stocks are on the rise
And that my analyst is wise.
That all the wine I sip is white
And that my hot tub is watertight.
That racquetball won't get too tough
And that all my sushi's fresh enough.
I pray my cordless phone still works
And that my career won't
interrupt my perks.
I pray my microwave won't radiate,
My condo won't depreciate.
I pray my health club doesn't close
And that my money market grows.
And if I go broke before I wake,
I pray my Mercedes they
won't take.[717]

[Materialism, Deception of; Materialism, Perspective of]

PRAYER, ACCESS IN

GOD is like 7-Eleven used to be. 7-Eleven used to be open 24/7. If you ran out of milk, you could run up to 7-Eleven. If you ran out of bread, you could go to 7-Eleven. The idea would be that when everyone else is closed, a convenience store would be open to meet your needs. When the normal suppliers had gone home to go to bed, you could always go to the convenience store. They were going to be open 24/7.

The reason why we've lost sight God as our provider is we've gotten too used to the Wal-Marts in our lives. We've gotten too used to the big chains. We've gotten too used to the big boys. But the goodness of God is that He is the convenient one. He's there when everybody else shuts down. He's open when everybody else has closed down or run out. He's got more than enough and He'll be available, whether you show up or not. He is your convenience center and He is there to meet your needs. We can go to Him in prayer at anytime.[718]

1 Chron. 16:11; Ps. 5:1–3; Matt. 7:7

PRAYER, DELIVERANCE THROUGH

A WOMAN was in labor with her first baby and was experiencing much pain and anguish. That is natural for being in labor. The problem was that the pain wasn't producing a delivery. The idea is that the more the pain comes and the closer the distance between the pain, the closer you are to the delivery. But this woman was having increased pain with no birth. She was experiencing increased pain with no deliverance taking place. The doctor came in to examine the situation and told the woman and her husband that the baby's head was in the wrong position. The baby's head was pointed up. Delivery of a baby is always easier with the head facing down. When the baby's head is in the wrong position, there is a lot of pain with no delivery.

Many Christians today are experiencing a lot of pain but no delivery. We're not seeing a birth. We're not seeing new life. We're not seeing a change but we're in a lot of pain. Perhaps our head is in the wrong position.[719]

[Humility, Need for; Surrender, Benefits of]

James 5:13

PRAYER, DOXOLOGY

THEY had a sale not too long ago of items that had belonged to "The King," Elvis Presley. One of his cars sold for $277,000. One of his outfits sold for $113,000. By the time the auction was over, five million dollars' worth of The King's goods were sold. There is only one problem. The King is dead. The King is gone.

I know a King who is still alive. I know a King who still sits on the throne and His kingdom rules forever and ever. My King's sovereignty rules.[720]

[Jesus, Authority of; Kingdom of God]

Rev. 1:12–18

YOU KNOW the Supreme Court is the highest court of appeals. They've got all kind of courts that lead up to the Supreme Court. The lower courts may make all kinds of decisions but if the Supreme Court decides to hear a case, it is irrelevant what other courts have decided. If the Supreme Court decides it will hear an issue, it doesn't matter what the lower courts have decided. Only what the Supreme Court rules sticks. All other courts, no matter how powerful, just or unjust, must pale in significance when the Supreme Court rules.

I don't know who has made a decision for your life. I don't know what court has ruled on your circumstances. It may have been the court of your employer who has ruled that you will never leave this position. It may be the court of your finances has decided you will never better your lifestyle. It may be the court of the doctor that said we can't fix this disease. But at least, appeal it to the Supreme Court. At least, place it on the docket up there so that God can decide what the final rendering is. If He takes the case, it doesn't matter what the court of your employer has said, or the court of your doctor has said, or the court of your lawyer has said, because when that court speaks all other courts become irrelevant. You can be happy today because He's sovereign and He sits on the throne.[721]

[God, Authority of; God, Power of; God's Will]

Matt. 6:10; Rom. 12:1–2; James 4:7

PRAYER, JESUS' NAME

A YOUNG man sat on a park bench, bawling. A little boy saw him and said, "Sir, what's wrong? Sir, what's wrong?"

The man told him the story about his brother who was in prison. His brother was on death row and would be executed in the next few days. The man desperately wanted to see Abraham Lincoln, the president of the

United States, and ask for a pardon, but of course regular people can't just walk into the president's office. The man was hopeless.

After hearing the man's story, the little boy said, "Sir, would you come with me?" He took the man by the hand, walked him into the presidential office through the guards, past the secretary, and nobody mumbled a word. The man couldn't believe it. He couldn't have gotten in to see the president if he had tried and this little boy was walking him straight past everyone into the president's office.

President Lincoln stood up as the young man entered with the boy. He looked at the boy and said, "How can I help you, son?" You see, the reason the man could get into Abraham Lincoln's office is because he had run into the son of Abraham Lincoln, and the son could walk past all the opposition.

You can't walk into the presence of a holy God unless you are escorted by the Son. That's why we pray in Jesus' name.[722]

[Jesus, Authority of; Prayer, Access in]
John 16:24; Heb. 4:16

THE QUESTION is, "What's in a name?" If I say Bill Gates, what are you going to think of? Computers. If I say Serena Williams, what are you going to think of? Tennis. If I say Tiger Woods, what are you going to think of? Golf. These names are tied to something. When I say Tiger Woods, it's not just any name. It a NAME! Because he represents a whole industry. He represents a hundred million dollars.

Tiger Woods's name is substantive. Now, let's say you like the name

Tiger and you like the name Woods, so you name your kid Tiger Woods. Or let's say your name is Williams and you like the name Serena, so you name your kid Serena Williams. Better yet, let's say you like Bill and you like Gates, so you name your kid Bill Gates. Well, your kid may have the nomenclature and they may have the words, but they don't have what it represents.

The problem for many Christians is that we use Jesus' name powerlessly. We tag on His name without accessing the power that comes with it.[723]

[God's Name; Jesus, Authority of]
John 16:24; Heb. 4:16

ONE Friday, I was speaking in Biloxi, Mississippi, and the host pastor asked if he could introduce me to someone. I said, "Absolutely!" He said he wanted to introduce me to a young man who loved me. I said okay because I'm always interested in meeting someone who loves me. The pastor brought a young guy over to me and said, "Tony Evans, I want to introduce you to Tony Evans!"

Now this Tony Evans, whom I did not know, loved listening to my tapes. Tony Evans listened to Tony Evans's tapes! This young guy said that two or three times a week, he listened to my tapes. Tony Evans said that he not only listened, but he memorized my tapes. Tony Evans said he not only listened to my tapes, he not only memorized my tapes, but he preached my tapes when he's called upon to preach.

This guy had my name, and my messages, but he still wasn't me! You can have a name without the correlating essence and use the name, but then that use is illegitimate. The reason why more of us are not experiencing answered prayer is because of the misuse of God's name.[724]

[God's Name]
John 16:24; Acts 4:12

WHEN you go before God, you need to show an ID. When you go to the airport, and they say, "Show me your ID," it's because they want you to verify that you are who you say you are. You need an ID in order to go through security and to go back to the gate area. The ID grants you access because it shows you are authorized to go into a secured area. The Father always authorizes the Son and the Son always authorizes the children of God who carry His ID with His name. We must pray based on the authority of the name of Jesus Christ.[725]

[Jesus, Authority of; Prayer,
Access in]
Acts 4:12; Phil. 2:9–11

IMAGINE that I went to the White House and said, "My name is Tony Evans, and this is what I want the White House staff to do." As I was being booted off of the property, it would be clear that my name is really no name at all. Why? Because, in that setting, it just doesn't carry any weight. In other words, my name has no authority at the White House.

Now, if the president comes out of the Oval Office and says, "I want this, that, or the other," staff start moving and shaking because of his name. But his name is only "his name," because of his position. In other words, he's got power in his name, because he's got power in his post. His post makes his name a name above every other name in America.

Now, if you bring Tony Evans back to Oak Cliff Bible Fellowship, I've got a name. At the White House, I may not have a name; at this house, I have a name. In this house, there is authority that goes with the post, giving the name credibility.

Just shouting out the name of Jesus doesn't give you power. If you don't have the power of the person, you might as well not use His name. Having the power of the name comes through connection and relationship with the one who has the authority behind their name.[726]

[God's Name; Jesus, Relationship
with; Power, Accessing]
John 20:31; Phil. 2:9–11

PRIDE

WHEN I think about the sin of pride, the greatest sin of all, it reminds me of the army colonel. He had just been promoted to colonel. He was sitting in his office when someone knocked at the door and said, "This is Private Johnson. May I see you sir?" He said, "Just a minute." The colonel, wanting to look impressive, picked up his telephone and he said real loud, "Yes, Mr. President. I understand, Mr. President. We will take care of it right away, Mr. President." He wasn't talking to the president, but he wanted to make it seem like he was talking to the president. He wanted to appear bigger than he really was.

The colonel said, "Mr. President, just give me one second." Then he said, "Come in, Private." The private came in and the colonel asked him to talk quickly because he had the president on the other line. "What can I do for you?" "Well," the private said, "I just came in to connect your telephone."

God has a way of making you look like a fool, because "pride cometh before the fall."[727]

[Humility, Need for; Pride, Problem of]
Prov. 11:2; 16:18

PRIDE, NATURE OF

TWO brothers went away to college. One brother became a farmer. The other became a brilliant, wealthy lawyer. The lawyer brother visited the farmer brother on the farm. He said, "I can't believe you've not made anything of your life. You're out here on a farm. Look at me. Look where I am. I'm on Wall Street. I'm an investor in the stock market. I have clients who are millionaires. Here you are, stuck out here on the farm. I wonder what the difference between us is."

The farmer brother then spoke. He pointed out to his wheat field. He said, "You'll see two types of wheat out there, brother. You'll see the wheat that's standing straight up. In the head of that wheat, there is nothing. It's empty. That's why it's standing so high. You'll also see some other wheat that is bent over. That's because the head is full. It's full of wheat."

Some of us are standing straight up. We are walking tall. However, we are only able to do so because we are empty. Some of us walk a little bent over indicating that we are full. The test isn't what you have in your pocket. It's what you have in your heart.[728]

[Humility; Life, Emptiness of]
James 1:11

PRIDE, PROBLEM OF

PRIDE is the only disease that makes everyone sick, except the one who has it.[729]

Prov. 16:18; 29:23

A LADY went to her pastor and said, "Pastor, I am terribly in need of counseling. I've got this sin. I can't seem to shake it. The sin is messing with me, but I can't seem to get rid of it."

The pastor was concerned for the apparent dilemma for this lady in his congregation. "What seems to be the problem?"

"Well, I come to church every Sunday, and I can't help thinking that I am the prettiest woman in the church. I look at all the other ladies, and they can't even hold a candle to me. What should I do, Pastor, about this sin?"

He said, "Honey, that's not a sin, that's a mistake."[730]

[Inner Beauty]
Prov. 29:23; 31:30

PRIORITIES

A FAIRLY wealthy man one day was driving his BMW and had an accident — a very bad accident. The car was totaled. A policeman came on the scene and got the man out of the car. As the man came to, he said, "My BMW, oh my BMW!" The policeman said, "Sir, I'm sorry but you don't have time to worry about your BMW. It's just a car. We've got to rush you to the hospital because your arm has been severed at the elbow." The wealthy man said, "Oh, my Rolex, oh my Rolex!" He had mixed-up priorities.[731]

[Materialism, Deception of]
Matt. 16:26; 1 Tim. 6:10

PROBLEMS

IF AN alcoholic or a drug addict has an addiction they can't shake, they have to go to drastic measures to rid themselves of the problem. They get radical. Some will lock themselves up in a room for three or four days, and submit themselves to the difficult process of withdrawal. They know it will be uncomfortable. They know it will be difficult. They know it is going to drive them crazy, but they want to get better.

In order to make their lives better, they first have to make themselves worse. They have to go through three or four days in order to get those negative influences out of their system so they can start living again. Sometimes, if you want to make things right, it gets worse first.[732]

[Help; Problems, Solutions to; Trials, Value of]

Rom. 5:3–5; James 1:2–4

WHEN you have an incurable problem, entertainment can't fix it, "edumacation" can't fix it, and economics can't fix it. You simply need to be in touch with God.[733]

[Help; Prayer, Access in]

James 5:13

PROBLEMS, SOLUTIONS TO

SOMETIMES the solutions we seek from God are quite unexpected. He may tell us to do something that doesn't make sense or that contradicts our natural reactions or responses.

We've all seen movies where people get stuck in quicksand. Quicksand is, very simply, sand and water. The problem is that the water loosens up the sand so that the sand is not compact and there is nothing to stand on. Compacted sand is a surface that can support a person and give them something to move on. Once you mix that same sand with water, all of a sudden there's no traction left.

The problem is, when a person gets stuck in quicksand, the harder they try to get out, the deeper and faster they go under. The harder they try, the worse things get because the nature of quicksand is to pull them down the more they try and move.

Now, the person who gets stuck in quicksand who knows how to handle it doesn't fight to stay up. What they do is slowly paddle underneath, moving an inch here and an inch there, until hopefully they can get to a bank. The nature of some problems is that the harder you try to get out of it, the deeper you're going to wind up in it. Sometimes the answer to a problem is not a commonly prescribed approach to it.[734]

[God's Ways, Unpredictability of]

PRODIGAL SON

A YOUNG man, a successful wrestler, challenged his father once. He was the all-state wrestling champ, in the unlimited weight category in fact. He weighed 260 pounds as a senior in high school—really big and strong. He had a period of rebellion where his father wanted him to do something and he told his father he wasn't gonna do it. His father thought he was hard of hearing. "What?" The young man then got more indignant. "I said, I isn't gonna do it." The father simply turned around and started walking upstairs, beckoning his son to come with him. When they got to the top of the stairs, he said, "I'm going to help you pack, because it's obvious you are grown and don't need me. Since you are grown and can make it on your own, I'll help you pack." The young man started packing with an attitude, huffing around the room and throwing things into a suitcase. Item after item got unpacked as his dad pulled things out as he told his son, "No, that's mine. I paid for it!"

The teenager was mad. He was determined to be autonomous and independent from his dad. He took the suitcase and walked out of the house, angry and mad, only to discover that he had no car. Even his friends' parents wouldn't let them come out to help him. It was freezing outside and snow was falling heavily. This guy discovered that while he didn't prefer home, compared to what was happening outside, home really wasn't that bad.

See, the father, the loving father, had to let the prodigal son go and discover that while he didn't like everything at home, out in the world on his own there was no protection, covering, or love. He had to let him experience the harsh reality.

Thirty minutes later, that prodigal son rang the doorbell. "I'm sorry."[735]

[Children, Training; Discipline, Love in; Life, Perspective on]

Luke 15:11–30

PROVIDENCE

PROVIDENCE is the hand of God in the glove of history. It is the work of God whereby He integrates and blends events in the universe in order to fulfill His original design for which it was created. It is God sitting behind the steering wheel of time. Providence refers to God's governance of all events so as to direct them toward an end. It is God taking what you and I would call luck, chance, mistakes, happenstance and stitching them into achieving His program.[736]

[God's Will]

Gen. 50:20; Phil. 2:13

PROVISION, GOD'S

BRUCE Wilkinson, the author of *The Prayer of Jabez*, was meeting with a leader of a growing ministry. The ministry leader hoped to talk with Bruce and glean some principles from him that would help grow his own ministry. After answering many of the leader's questions, Bruce asked if he might ask a question of his own. "How many donors do you have?" The leader grew silent as he started calculating how many donors the ministry might have. After a few seconds, Bruce said, "It sure is taking you a long time." The leader apologized and assured Bruce that he wanted to give him as accurate of a count as possible. "I'm not sure. I just need a minute to think about it." Bruce halted him in the middle of his calculations. "The mere fact it's taking you this long means that you're not approaching this right." The leader looked a bit puzzled. "What do you mean, Bruce?" "Well," Bruce continued, "you only have one donor. Now, the One may work through many, but the only donor that matters is the One. The many just give the ministry what the One has given to them. Your donors aren't your true source—God is."[737]

[Blessing, Source of]

Matt. 6:33; James 1:17

PURITY

THE IVORY soap commercial says that the product is 99.7 percent pure. It has no additives, impurities, fragrances, or colors. Other soaps may look better or smell better, but Ivory distinguishes itself by its purity.

In the same way, God wants His singles to boast about and distinguish themselves by their purity.[738]

[God's Standard; Sex]

1 Cor. 6:18; Eph. 5:3; Heb. 13:4

MANY people are only interested in organic food now. They don't eat other stuff because it's been sprayed with pesticides. Nowadays, doctors and the media alike are telling us that the traditional way our food is grown, in an attempt to grow it quickly and protect it from damage, is resulting in an accumulation of pesticides and contaminates to consumers.

There are markets now like Whole Foods where it is possible to buy food that has not been so contaminated by man—that has been not touched and contaminated by man.

Man has been spraying pesticides on vegetables and fruits for years in an attempt to fix a problem. But he has only created a new problem. The pesticides are full of chemicals that when introduced to the human body are very damaging. If man would just leave it alone and let God do His thing, all of a sudden things are healthy because man's not messing it up.

When we've allowed man to spray the pesticide of this world on our souls, then we wonder why the hearts don't work right. But if we'll go back to God and stop being double minded, we'll find out that God knows what He's doing.

How did people eat before we started spraying all of this stuff? God knew what He was doing before and He knows what He's doing now. All we have to do is allow Him to do His thing and stop trying to contaminate what He's in the business of perfecting.[739]

[Double-mindedness; Nature; Sin, Contamination by]

Rom. 12:2; Col. 3:2; James 4:4

PURPOSE, UNIQUENESS OF

EVERYBODY has in their homes manufactured products. Appliances such as a toaster, refrigerator, stove, microwave, or an electric can opener are commonly found in people's homes and each of those has a different workmanship. They are designed differently. They have different parts that make them operate. Each one has its own unique reason for being. Now, if that appliance operates outside of its reason for being there, we have a problem. If you want to cook things in the refrigerator and freeze things in the stove, you are going to have a difficult situation in the home because that's not what the workmanship is for. The workmanship is used for whatever the creator designed it to do. The toaster does not tell the creator what it's going to do today. The stove does not tell the creator what it's going to do today. It is the creator that dictates to the appliance the reason why the appliance exists. The appliance does whatever it's been designed to do.

In the same way, we are God's creation and He dictates to us why we exist and can tell us what we are designed to do. He gives us our purpose. If we operate outside of our reason for being, that's when we experience problems. Walking in the purpose God designed for us is how we fulfill our unique reason for being.[740]

[Christian Living, Purpose]

1 Peter 2:9

THERE is a guy named Billy Taylor. He is a junkyard specialist. Billy Taylor goes to junkyards to find stuff that other folk have thrown away, discarded, and considered no good or worthless. Billy Taylor brings it back to his garage and turns the junk into contemporary art pieces, which he then sells for upwards of five thousand dollars a piece. He goes and finds junk that is worthless in everybody else's eyes and then turns it into a masterpiece. When Billy Taylor looks at the junk, he sees more than meets the eye. He sees a masterpiece in the making. He takes things that are worthless and makes them into something beautiful.

Well, you may have been worthless before you met Jesus, but once you meet Him, even if you were in the junkyard, He's able to go into that yard, save you, and turn you into a valuable masterpiece. Because of His grace, you are now a divine design.[741]

[Christian, Value of; New Life in Christ; Restoration; Second Chances]

1 Sam. 16:7; John 3:16

R

RACE RELATIONS

GOD is not asking blacks to be whites or whites to be blacks. He's asking both to be biblical. If I say I am a black Christian and somebody else says that they're a white Christian, what they've done is made black or white an adjective. The job of an adjective is to modify a noun.

If the word *Christian* is in the noun position and your race in the adjectival position, since the job of the adjective is to modify and explain the nature of the noun, that means you've always got to change the noun of your faith to reflect the adjective of your culture. However, the way it's supposed to work is that your history, background, race, and culture are to be in the noun position. Your faith should always be in the adjectival position, so that you're always adjusting the noun of your culture to the adjective of your faith.

In other words, you're bringing who you are—your history, your background, and your culture—to look like the adjectival description of what you say you believe about God and Jesus Christ.[742]

Gal. 3:28; Rev. 14:6

REBELLION

MANY people have a GPS system in their car. The Global Positioning System has the ability to tell a driver where they are or give them directions to where they want to go. It has a voice so it's audible and it has a screen so it is visible. It displays a red dot on the screen to show your current location and allows the driver to watch their progress toward their intended destination. The voice comes on and gives direction, telling the driver where to turn, merge, or stop and provides clear instruction of how the driver can get to their intended destination.

I was in the car one day with a guy who had a GPS and he had punched in his intended destination. We're riding along and he was following the word. The word said turn right and he'd turn right. The word said turn left and he'd turn left. He brought his driving in line with the word and therefore was making progress to his intended destination. After awhile, he decided to try a little experiment. He decided to see what happened if he didn't pay attention and if he disregarded the instructions from his GPS. So he decided to "lean to his own understanding." He decided to try the way of man rather than the way of the system. So when the GPS system said turn right, he didn't slow down. He kept going straight and totally disregarded the word that had been spoken and the word from the visual display. After he passed the exit that the GPS told him to take, the screen popped off. There was no longer any picture and no longer any word. There was no longer any direction because he was now doing things his way. After we had driven for a while in rebellion to the system, the picture came back on with the red dot showing our errant ways and how we had wandered from the path. Then the voice came on and said, "If you would like to return to your previous location, then get off at the next exit, go under the expressway, get back up on the expressway, and I will lead you back to where you went wrong."

God wants us to know that if we realize the error of our ways and simply pay attention to His direction via the Global Positioning System already in us, He will lead us in the way that we should go. We just have to be willing to follow His directions and stop leaning to our own understanding.[743]

[Bible, Guidance of; Holy Spirit, Guidance; Self-Sufficiency, Sin of]
Prov. 3:5–6; 4:11

RECONCILIATION

EVERY Christian is a minister of reconciliation and has the responsibility of bringing harmony where there is conflict. Put another way, Christians are God's Peace Corp.[744]

[Peace]
Matt. 5:9; Rom. 14:19; James 3:18

SOME women go to the hairdresser in order to get "perms." These perms change the texture of hair from one thing to another. After applying the perm to the hair, professional hairdressers will use neutralizing shampoo to assure that the harsh chemicals don't do lasting damage.

Christians are called to be peacemakers. A person who has the ministry of reconciliation has been called by God to neutralize harsh situations so that damage caused does not continue.[745]

[Peace]
Matt. 5:9; 5:23–24

I HAVE a steel plate in my right leg. It's a large steel plate that goes from my ankle all the way up to my knee. The plate is in my leg because while I was playing football one day and intercepted a pass, I got hit with a cross body block. My cleat did not come out of the mud so my leg snapped in half and I broke my tibia and fibula.

I was taken off the football field and rushed to the hospital to find that my bone had been shattered. I had been hit and hurt badly—hurt to the point where it had broken me in two. But a doctor came along who knew how to correct the problem and went with me into the operating room. He opened up my leg and placed inside of it a steel plate with screws, and then he reconnected bones that had been shattered.

Without the doctor intervening that day, my leg would even now be crooked and I'd probably be walking with a limp because of the nature of the break. But somebody who understood the problem came in with a plate, and ever since then that plate has been holding my brokenness together.

God has given all of us the scalpel of His Word in order to identify the sin that results in broken relationships. The work of the Holy Spirit is like a steel plate that brings and holds together that which has been shattered.[746]

[Holy Spirit, Power of; Relationships]
Rom. 14:19; 2 Cor. 5:18; Eph. 4:1–3

OIL AND water don't mix. This concept is exemplified in any bottle of salad dressing where things have settled and the oil and water have separated.

In order to bring that oil and water back together, the bottle must be shaken. However, the togetherness won't last forever. As soon as the bottle sits for a while, the ingredients will segregate again. They go back to their own department. They go back to separate bedrooms. They go back to separate seating places. They go back to separate communities. They go back because it is intrinsic to their nature that they will not mix.

Mayonnaise does not have to be shaken even though it is also comprised mostly of oil and water. This is because mayonnaise also contains an emulsifier—egg. An emulsifier is that which brings things together that otherwise could never come together. In mayonnaise, the egg brings together two entities that would not normally mix with one another. The egg infiltrates both so that they are able to come together and be a solid substance. The cross of Jesus Christ acts as an emulsifier to bring people together—even those who would not normally come together.[747]

[Cross; Race Relations]
2 Cor. 5:18

MANY of us have children who have braces on their teeth. Braces are designed to straighten crooked teeth or bring teeth together that are separated by too large of a space.

However, braces are also uncomfortable and can get in the way. They make eating difficult because foods get stuck easily. They can even cause pain, as every so often they must be tightened up.

God has called every Christian to be His braces—to bring together things that are separated or people who don't look like they can get along.[748]

[Cross; Race Relations]
2 Cor. 5:18

SALLY and Jack went to their grandpa's house to visit. While they were there, Grandpa took them out to teach Jack how to use a slingshot. Jack was really good at it. After a little while, Grandpa went off, and by accident, Jack threw a rock with the slingshot, hit one of Grandpa's ducks in the head, and killed it.

Sally said, "Ooh, I am going to tell."

Terrified, Jack cried, "Please don't tell."

Sally agreed and they went back to the house.

When the kids arrived, Grandma announced that she and Sally would clean up the house.

With a sly look, Sally said, "Grandma, Jack would love to do the dishes, wouldn't you, Jack? Jack doesn't mind doing the dishes. In fact, Jack, tell Grandma how much you love doing dishes."

Jack said, "Oh yeah, yeah, yeah, Grandma, I like doing dishes."

Determined to get a bunch of housework done, Grandma continued, "Well then, Sally we're going to vacuum the floor."

"Grandma," Sally replied, "let me tell you about Jack and vacuuming. That boy is a natural-born vacuum person. Come on, Jack, tell Grandma how much you like to vacuum."

Grimacing, Jack said through his teeth, "Grandma, I love being a vaccumer. Yeah, I do."

"Well, then we're going to dust the house."

"Oh, dust the house, Grandma? Jack, tell her how much you like dusting the house."

Jack was boiling now. "Yeah, I like dusting the house." He knew he was trapped, not only for now but for the rest of his life.

Later that day, well after Jack had done more than his share of the work assigned to the two grandchildren, Grandpa said, "Jack, come here. I saw that little episode earlier today. Let me tell you something, Jack. I know about the duck, but I didn't say anything, because I wanted to see how long you were going to let Sally make you her slave. All you had to do to keep her from holding you hostage was to tell me what you had done."

God knows that you've killed the duck. You don't have to hide it. Satan wants you to remember that you killed the duck and hold you hostage to your guilt. By confessing our sin to God and allowing Him to forgive us, we can release Satan's hold on us.[749]

[Satan, Strategy of; Sin, Confession of]

Ps. 32:5; Heb. 10:22; 1 John 1:9

IF YOU have a checkbook and get a bank statement whose balance doesn't agree with yours, there is a problem. There has to be reconciliation. The only way to get that reconciliation is to find out where the problem is. You have to be able to identify why those two numbers aren't the same and where the error is.

When bank balances don't match, we don't just throw up our hands and say, "It will all work out." We work to find the error and fix it!

Jesus Christ is our fix to the error of sin. He came to reconcile us to God. He lived for thirty-three years to fulfill all righteousness and to bring us into balance with God's righteousness. He did this for us because we could not do it for ourselves.[750]

[Christ, Freedom in; Salvation, Need for; Sin, Victory over]

Rom. 5:10; 2 Cor. 5:18; Col. 1:19–22

RELATIONSHIPS

A COUPLE went for marriage counseling. Both the man and the woman carried a list with them. The man had taken a sheet of paper, drawn a line down the middle, and proceeded to write all the good things about his wife down one side of the paper and all of the bad things down the other side. The woman had done the same thing. They pointed out to the counselor that they just couldn't stay married because of the lists they had compiled. Both the man and the woman had a much longer list of negatives than positives for their spouse. Having tried everything from vacations to marriage retreats, the couple had come to this counselor as the last resort before going to get a divorce.

The counselor glanced over the lists noting some serious things and some not-so-serious things. To their shock, he tore them up right in front of them, pulled over his trash can, and threw in the lists. The man exclaimed, "What are you doing? Don't you know how long it took us to make those lists?" The counselor explained that the couple's lists were useless because they examined the couple's problem from the wrong end. "You are pursuing a rule book when you should be pursuing a relationship." God meant for life to be lived by relationship, not by rules.[753]

[Legalism, Danger of; Marriage,
Unhappiness in]
Col. 2:20–23

A PREACHER owned and loved his parrot, but the parrot was evil. It had an appalling vocabulary. Every now and then it would even use profanity. Well, he figured as a preacher he couldn't keep this parrot around too long. So he decided to put the parrot to sleep. But a lady in his congregation offered to share her parrot with him. Her parrot was a female parrot and she had trained it to regularly sit on its perch and pray all the time. She thought maybe if her female parrot was in the company of his male parrot, it might have a favorable influence.

The preacher, hoping that the good parrot would rub off on the bad parrot, agreed to give it a try. So the lady brought over the female parrot and put it in the cage with the male parrot. The male parrot looked at the female parrot and said, "Hi baby, how about a kiss?"

The female parrot responded gleefully, "My prayers have been answered!"[754]

[Prayer]

REPENTANCE

REPENTANCE is when you are going south on the highway and then recognize you need to be going north. Repentance isn't just thinking about changing directions. It isn't just watching other folk go by wondering if they're going wrong too. Repentance is looking for the next exit, getting off, crossing over, and getting back on the other road on your way home. That's repentance; it's turning the other way.

If you are twenty miles out of the way and decide to change directions, you must take the exit ramp. This is the ramp of confession where you agree that you have been going the wrong way. Then you have to cross over the grace overpass where God gives you the opportunity and the privilege to turn around. Confession gets you to the place where you can make that U-turn. Grace crosses you over.

Now, there is another ramp that you have to take to get back on the highway headed in the right direction. This is the restoration on-ramp. The confession off-ramp leads to the grace overpass, which carries you over and puts you right in front of the restoration on-ramp, so that you can begin heading in the right direction.

Once the turn has been made and repentance has been accomplished, you may still be twenty miles out of the way. You might be discouraged because you've gone twenty miles wrong or maybe twenty years wrong. In fact, many folks get stuck here, thinking that since they are already twenty miles out of the way they, might as well keep on heading in that same wrong direction.

The thing to remember is that when taking a trip, the ride coming back home always seems shorter than the ride going. There's something about coming home that shortens the feeling of distance even when the actual distance to cover is the same.[755]

[Prodigal Son; Restoration; Sin, Confession of]

Joel 2:12–14; Acts 3:19; 1 John 1:9

A MAN one day was on his way to catch a train. He had to get to work because he had an important meeting. He had to catch the 8:05 train. Now, it had rained the night before and the man was rushing out the door. As he opened the back door, there was his little son playing in the mud. He was busy rubbing mud on his face, mud on his arms, and just having a good old time playing in the mud. The father, intent on catching the 8:05, jumped over his son, said good-bye, and rushed out of the house to catch the 8:05, but he slipped and fell in the mud next to his son. So now the father is in the mud and the son is in the mud. But, the father had to catch the 8:05. He had a place to go. Because of where he needed to go, he did not stay in the mud and play with his son. His son was enjoying playing in the mud and wasn't trying to go anywhere. But the father had a train to catch. He jumped up out of the mud. Best as he could, he cleaned himself off and took off running because he had a train to catch. He had to catch the 8:05 and he knew that on the 8:05 there was going to be a restroom where he could clean up the dirt that he had accumulated during the time he was in the mud.

There are two kinds of people today. There are some who are playing in the mud and are not trying to go anywhere. There are other people who are in the mud but don't want to be.

Maybe you've slipped in the mud or maybe you've walked right into the mud, but now it has dawned on you that you've got a train to catch—a place to go. You've got a God to know, a life to live, experiences to have, and you want all that God has for you. Maybe you've decided to leave the mud, to repent, to turn, and to catch the train because on this train, God has got a restroom that will clean you up. He's got the blood of Jesus Christ that will transform you and take you to the destination of God's purpose for your life.

Sin always has consequences. But the good news is that grace is greater than sin.[756]

[Restoration; Salvation; Second Chances; Sin, Confession of]

Ps. 51:1–19; Isa. 55:7; 1 John 1:9

HAVE you ever ridden a bike against the wind with the wind blowing in your face? Riding the bike in that direction is hard work because the wind is resisting you. But if you simply turn the bike around, that same wind that hindered you will now help you. It will push you.

Many of us are struggling in the hills of life because we are going against the wind. But if we simply change directions, that same wind that hinders will be the wind that helps us.[757]

[Independence, Consequences of]
Acts 3:19

REST

I HAVE Executive Platinum status with American Airlines because of the amount of miles I've flown. That means that I can upgrade my seating on a plane trip. I also have the option of upgrading a companion who is traveling with me.

One time Jonathan, my son, was traveling with me. When we got to the ticket counter, the attendant confirmed my upgrade. I then asked about my son's upgrade, as he was my traveling companion. The attendant said she didn't have a record of Jonathan's upgrade. I asked her to check because he was traveling with me and should have had the companion upgrade.

She said she would check one more time. She went through and checked again. And then she told me that she had found the problem. He wasn't ticketed with me and because his ticket was not ticketed with me, he was not viewed as a companion. Now, I knew he was a companion, but American Airlines didn't know that because we were not ticketed together. Our tickets weren't "yoked" to-

gether when they were booked.

It's not that God hasn't made provisions. It's not that God hasn't taken care of your passage to heaven. But in order for you to experience the "upgrade" of life abundantly with Him, you've got to be His.[758]

[Christ, Union with]
Matt. 11:28

WHEN an athlete talks about being in the "zone," they're talking about the fact that they are playing and functioning at a whole different level. They are flowing in their craft. I remember hearing Michael Jordan describe being in the zone. He said, "It looked like to me that the rim was this wide and I couldn't miss if I wanted to." Emmitt Smith built a whole marketing campaign around the Emmitt Zone. He described the zone as being in that place where he could smell the end zone and "neither hell nor high water" would keep him out.

God has a zone for saints. It is a realm of operating where He wants us to flow. It is operating at a new spiritual level in life. When an athlete is in the zone, that doesn't mean that there are no defenders trying to stop them or tacklers trying to corral them. It simply means that whoever and whatever is getting in the way will be overcome because the athlete is in the zone. Whatever resistance there is will not have the final word because the athlete is in the zone. So being in the zone does not mean that there are no problems in life, struggles in life, or difficulties in life. It means that challenges are no longer dictating the outcome. They are no longer calling the shots when you're in the zone.

God has a zone for His saints. It's called a place of rest. It's a realm or a sphere whereby life is to be lived.[759]

[Christian Living; Rest, Provision of]
Ex. 20:8–11; Mark 6:31; Heb. 4:9–10

THE CONCEPT of rest is a person being able to rely on what God has already done, rather what you must force yourself to do. If a quarterback receives the ball from the center, the defensive line then presses in on him, seeking to sack him behind the line of scrimmage. But the quarterback will turn if it's a running play and hand off to the halfback. The halfback takes the ball and goes in the direction of the play call. At this point, the pressure that was coming to the quarterback shifts to the halfback.

Originally, the pressure is aimed at the quarterback because he's got the ball. But when he hands it off and now everybody's going after the halfback, the quarterback has rest. He has rest because he's handed off the pressure to somebody else who's carrying the ball.

We're so determined to make things happen ourselves that we find ourselves constantly under pressure. God wants us to know that if we can learn to live by faith, we can hand Him the ball and then the enemy has to chase Him. We can rest. That doesn't mean that there's no battle on the field. It just means that we can be in a calm position, even in a tackling situation.[760]

[Christian Living; Rest, Provision of]
Ex. 20:8–11; Mark 6:31; Heb. 4:9–10

REST, IMPORTANCE OF

YOU WALK around using your cell phone all day. All day talking to this person, talking to that person, and getting stuff done. But at the end of the day, if you want to use that cell phone tomorrow, you've got to make it lie down. You've got to connect it to the charger, so that it can get new energy, new power, and new strength. If you don't make the cell phone lie down, it won't work for you tomorrow. If you don't force it to lie down, you will not be able to receive or send out a signal. It is absolutely critical that you make the cell phone lie down, if you want to restore the power of the battery. If you don't make it lie down, it won't work.

If God doesn't make us lie down, we won't work. We'll expend all of our energy, all of our strength, and will try to make it work when all of our battery will be gone. We'll still try to stay up and make it work some more. God does His best work when His children are asleep.

When we lay our cell phones down, they can't just be put anywhere. They must be connected to the power source and charged. It is only when the cell phone is in the right place, connected to the right source, that it receives new life.[761]

[Power, Accessing]
Ex. 33:14; Matt. 11:28

I REMEMBER one time that I was going through the airport. I carried two pieces of luggage that were very heavy. I had sweat coming off my head, that luggage was so heavy. Someone saw me struggling and gave me a brilliant idea. They drew my attention to the fact that my luggage had wheels. I had been carrying around what I could roll around.

Now, when I started rolling the suitcases, they still weighed the same. If they had been put on the scale, they would still register the same weight, but I could carry the weight differently by using the wheels. I could carry the suitcases with me and rest and be at ease as I walked through the airport.

Jesus says, "I am your wheels. Come unto Me, all ye that labor and are heavy laden . . . and let's roll this baby."[762]

[Jesus]
Deut. 12:10; Matt. 11:28

TWO foresters were competing against one another to see who could chop down the most trees in a day. One forester was a young guy and the other was an experienced older guy. The day of the competition, the young guy jumped up first thing and went eight hours straight chopping trees. At the end of the day, he had chopped down twenty-five trees. He knew that the older gentleman wouldn't be able to compete. The young guy knew he was young and had more strength. In addition, the young forester thought back on the day, remembering that every hour or so the older man had taken a ten-minute break. The younger guy felt more assured of his win because he hadn't taken any breaks. At the end of the day he had done his twenty-five trees only to discover the older man had done forty. In shock he asked, "How is this possible, old man? I didn't stop. You stopped every hour for ten minutes or so and yet you chopped down almost twice as many trees as I did. How is that possible?" The older man said, "Yeah, yeah,

I understand your question. You were working hard, you were sweating you were grunting, and you were groaning. But every hour I sat down for ten minutes. I did two things." He said, "First of all, I recovered. Secondly, I sharpened my axe. You were working hard but you were working with dull equipment."[763]

[Self-Sufficiency, Danger of]
Deut. 12:10; Mark 6:31; Heb. 4:9–10

REST, NATURE OF

AS I travel through various large airports across the country, I regularly see chapels. That is interesting. Why do they put chapels in airports? The airport is full of people trying to catch a plane and trying to get to their destinations. Chapels are put in airports because the airport people know that folks are bringing their pain and problems with them, even as they are rushing to go to various places. In the middle of a busy airport, there is provided a place of rest. In the midst of the hustle and bustle and hectic movement, there is a serene environment where travelers can rest spiritually between destinations.[764]

In your soul God has erected a chapel—a place of rest.

[Rest]
Ex. 20:8–11; Matt. 11:28–29

REST, PROMISE OF

IN BALLROOM dancing, the job of the man is to lead. The job of the woman, if her partner knows what he's doing, is to follow his lead. His job is to watch the floor and see where all the other dancers are. All she does is line up with his movement. She puts her hand in his hand. She puts her arm on his shoulder and he sets the pace. She yokes herself with him and as he moves, she moves. She kind of glides and doesn't worry. But he has got to keep his eyes open. He's got to watch the floor. He's got to make sure that he doesn't step on her feet. She just moves in line with him. Now, she does move but because she's yoked, she glides. He works.

Jesus wants us to know that He's willing to do the work. He's willing to take the lead. He's willing to guide and direct. He's willing to take us where we need to go, but we have to be yoked to Him. We have to be connected with Him and learn how to dance with Him. In doing so, we'll discover that He's gentle. He won't hold on too tight or choke the air out of us.[765]

[Jesus, Relationship with; Rest]

Matt. 11:28–29

REST, PROVISION OF

A FEW months ago, I had some problems with my car. I had to pull over on the side of the road because the problems were so severe. I got out of the car, opened up the hood, and pretended like I knew what I was looking for even though I didn't have the slightest idea. On top of all that, I discovered that one of my tires was flat.

Now, you can get mighty dirty and sweaty fixing a flat. I was dressed in my three-piece suit. Having to change a tire in a three-piece suit can ruin a day.

I picked up my phone and called AAA. They sent a tow truck. My car wasn't going anywhere, but that truck backed up its back to my front, and yoked my car onto the truck. I sat with the driver as he pulled my car to where it needed to go. My car wasn't cooperating. It wasn't going with the program, but AAA sent me a yoke, and the man who drove the truck took over. All I did was make the call. Because I have a relationship with AAA, when I need them, they come. They took care of everything. They got my car to where it needed to go and then made sure that all of the necessary work was done. I got to ride.

Jesus Christ is inviting us to come to Him and to take on His yoke. Being connected to Him has its benefits.[766]

[Jesus, Relationship with; Surrender, Benefits of]

Matt. 11:28–29

RESTORATION

IT WAS 1970; I was on the football field as a weak-side linebacker. A pass was thrown to the receiver cutting across the middle. I stepped in between the quarterback and the receiver and intercepted the pass. It was a pretty catch too! I tucked the ball under my arm and was ready to cut back the other way when my cleat got stuck. It didn't come up out of the mud.

As I was preparing to go try to turn and go the other way, I got hit with a cross body block. My cleat still did not come up. You could hear it across the field when I broke my tibia and my fibula, the two bones in the lower leg. My leg simply snapped in two. I lay on the field broken and unable to help myself. I couldn't get up, because I had broken these two bones in my right leg.

They came on the field with a stretcher, put me on it, and took me to the emergency room. In the hospital there were two interns who tried to help me and fix my leg. They were obviously still learning. I screamed as they attempted to reconnect and reposition my bones. Those two interns were hurting me. They were hurting me, thinking they were helping me, because they had a title in front of their name. Titles don't mean anything when you're in pain. When you are suffering, you want someone who knows what they are doing.

The interns finally called the orthopedic specialist. This doctor came in, examined the situation, and then said, "Because of the nature of the break, we just can't reset this in the normal way. Your bones shattered when they broke. We're going to have to do surgery to correct the problem and then we will have to place a steel plate in your leg to hold your bones together." In other words, to help me, he had to hurt me.

This year, I have that same steel plate in my leg, my right leg. If I were to hit my right shin, you'd hear rattling. I got steel in my right shin that was placed there in 1970 by somebody who knew what he was doing. And because he knew what he was doing, even though he had to hurt me in order to help me, nobody in this building would know that I had a steel plate in my leg unless I told you. I don't walk like there are steel plates in my leg. I don't limp when I walk. In other words, because the specialist took over, the only people who know that one day I was broken are the folk who were there when I got my leg broken. The specialist fixed my leg in such a way that it looks like there was never any pain.

When you are restored by a person who knows what he is doing, you will be restored in such a way that no one knows that you ever were broken.[767]

[Brokenness, Process of; New Life in Christ]
Ezek. 11:19; 2 Cor. 5:17

ONE day my brother did something he shouldn't have and I seized the opportunity to get him in trouble. "Ooooooh, I'm going to t-e-l-l!" When my father came home, I was the first one at the door. "Guess what he did?" and I proceeded to relate all the details. My father disciplined my brother, and I enjoyed knowing that my brother was suffering.

Soon after my father dealt with my brother, he called me to come to him. He proceeded to discipline me! I quickly questioned him and pleaded with him, "But I didn't do anything!"

My father disagreed, "Oh yes, you did. What you told me could have been corrected, before I showed up. But because you wanted to hurt your brother and wanted to see him in pain . . . because you didn't help him and want to see him delivered from pain, I am going to make sure that you know what it feels like to hurt too." I never forgot that lesson. It has since reminded me of the importance of being a restorer. [768]

[Mercy]
Matt. 5:23–24; James 2:13

WHEN people need to be cut out of cars after a bad car accident, there is often a tool used called the "Jaws of Life." These big cutters can cut away doors to give access to people who are trapped.

Even when drivers have had wrecks through no one's fault but their own, rescue crews still employ the "jaws of life" to get them out of trouble. Whether a driver was not paying attention as they talked on their cell phone or listened to the radio, when they end up in a situation where they are trapped and need help, the "jaws of life" can still be used to get them out of a jam.

Christians are supposed to be the "Jaws of Life" to one another. When a person is trapped, whether through their own fault or through the fault of another, we should be ready to rescue one another. We should be willing to offer a lifeline to our brothers and sisters when they are stuck.[769]

[Confrontation; Help]
James 5:19–20

AWHILE ago, I was sitting in my living room watching TV when my set popped and then blinked off. I got up and fiddled around with it a bit, and it popped on and off a few more times before I realized that the set was really messed up and I was probably going to need a new TV. My TV is about fifteen years old and has served me well. I figured that I'd start thinking about this as an opportunity to get myself that sixty-inch plasma flat screen, HD television. I figured that even if I was going to give away my old TV first, I'd want to get rid of it working a little bit better, so I called the repair guy who specializes in my kind of TV. He was a specialist for the brand of TV I owned.

When he arrived, I explained to him that my TV kept popping on and off and that I couldn't keep a picture. He got to work. He unscrewed the paneling and pulled out the circuitry. As he looked at the wiring, he said, "Oh, this is no big deal. You just have a little separation of the wire here. Let me put it back together again

and you'll have a picture in no time."

I see my dream dying but I figured that I'd stick with my original plan of getting the TV fixed up and still give it away. I mentioned to the repair guy that I was thinking about getting rid of this TV and getting a plasma so I could get a sharper picture. He surprised me when he said, "Well, you may want to wait. I fixed your circuitry problem but I'm not finished yet. I know this brand of TV backward and forward and most people don't know all that the set can do. Let me work on it a little bit and then tell me what you think."

He dismantled the thing, taking the screen off as well as the reflective mirror in the back. Then he sprayed this special spray on it that cleaned it up. He did some other things with the circuitry and then he put it back together again. Voila! I had an amazing picture. I virtually had a brand-new TV. I thought the TV was gone. I thought it was useless. But when I had the master come and touch it up a little bit, I didn't have to trade it in.

Some of us want to trade in our lives and throw in the towel. I know that for some of us stuff in our lives always seems to be popping on and off. Before you do anything drastic, just let the Master work with on your life just a little. He'll show you He can turn, tweak, wipe, fix, and give you a life that looks brand-new, though it may appear to be past its prime. You are a masterpiece created in Christ Jesus for good works. All you've got to do is walk in them.[770]

[Christian Living, New Life; New Life in Christ]
Eph. 2:10

RESTORATION, POWER FOR

ONE of my favorite all-time movies is *Rocky V*. In the movie, Rocky Balboa is now too old to fight. He received an eye injury in *Rocky IV* and retired. Up comes a young man named Tommy Gunn. Tommy Gunn is an up-and-coming heavyweight and has always idolized Rocky Balboa. He asks Rocky to train him and make him the kind of champ Rocky was before. Rocky agrees, thinking that this was a good way for him to stay in the game of boxing.

Rocky becomes the trainer for this young man. The young man rises and becomes contender for the heavyweight championship of the world through the training and discipleship of Rocky Balboa. The problem comes because this young man gets too big for his britches. He thinks he's something now. He's got the ladies, he's got the money, and he's got the prestige. So he figures, I don't need the old man anymore. Now, in *Rocky V*, the whole movie comes down to the last fifteen minutes because Tommy Gunn comes into Rocky's home and threatens Rocky, his wife, and his son. Rocky is furious and Tommy Gunn challenges Rocky to a fight, saying, "I will whip you right now in front of your family. I will destroy, you old man."

Rocky is angry. He tears off his shirt. The rumble in the neighborhood starts and goes out into the street. People begin showing up to watch the scene. Somebody calls the news and the news show up. Cameras are everywhere watching this brawl in the streets between Rocky Balboa and his young protégé Tommy Gunn who's gone crazy. The problem is, Tommy Gunn is too young, too strong, and too fast. Rocky can't keep up with the young man. Try as he might, he just can't keep up. At one point, Tommy Gunn reaches back and gives Rocky a right cross across his jaw that sends Rocky Balboa falling into the gutter. He is there in the gutter with his wife crying, and with his son sitting over him. The old man has been beaten, broken, and bruised. He has been defeated and destroyed. While lying in the gutter, he remembers his past. The movie screen flashes his thoughts. Pictures are shown of Rocky in his younger days when the Italian Stallion first went into the ring. His opponent said, "You're going down," and Rocky said, "Oh no, I'm not." Rocky won that fight. He fought to a draw.

After this flashback, Rocky tries to get up out of the gutter, but he can't. Then his thoughts flash to a scene from *Rocky I*. He remembers another fight where he came back to win. He remembered that he has the power to come back. Motivated again, Rocky tries to get up but can't. Then Rocky remembers Mr. T from *Rocky III*. In this movie, Rocky had been beaten and bruised and broken and defeated, but he again fought back and won the championship. When he remembers this win and tries to get up out the gutter, he still can't.

Rocky has another flashback where he remembers Ivan Glasgow in *Rocky IV*, the Russian machine, who no man could whip. He remembers how he went over to Moscow and defeated the Russian. He remembers how the Russian crowds began to chant "Rocky,

Rocky, Rocky" as he held the American flag. He remembers his victory and tries to get up, but he can't.

But then Rocky remembers one other picture. He sees his old coach Mickey. He remembers the day when he was in a fight and had been knocked to the canvas. He remembers Mickey sitting over him, saying, "Get up, get up, you bum, 'cause Mickey loves you."

Now, that's when the Rocky theme songs starts playing! All of a sudden Rocky shakes his head and pushes himself up from the gutter. Tommy Gunn is walking away, thinking he has won. Rocky says, "Yo, Tommy, come on back. We are going to go for one more round." He finds power he did not have, and he finds ability he does not have because he remembers somebody who had died and then who had "come back to life" to let him know he was loved.

No matter your status and how many times the Devil has knocked you down, two thousand years ago somebody loved you, died for you, and rose up from the dead. He says to us today, "Get up, get up, you bum, because Jesus loves you!"[771]

[Christ, Freedom in; Love, Power of; Jesus]

Rom. 8:37; Eph. 5:1–2

RESTORATION, PROVISION FOR

DEREK Redmond was a runner on the British sprint team. He was running the four-by-four hundred relay with his teammates. At the onset of the race, his team was moving nicely along the track. Then came the baton handoff to Derek. His job was to bring it home. His last leg of the race should have brought his team and good ol' England a gold medal. But as he turned the corner, he pulled an Achilles tendon and fell flat on his face. He lay there on the ground, in desperate pain. He didn't want to be there, but he was in too much pain to get up.

He began to crawl along the track. You could hear a pin drop, as all eyes focused on him trying to scratch his way forward. It was in the midst of this unfolding drama that a man came down from the stands, went over to the track, and picked up Derek Redmond.

One of the judges said, "I am sorry, sir, you must leave the track."

The older gentleman waved his hand and said, "Leave me alone, this is my boy."

Derek Redmond's father left the stands from on high and came down where Derek Redmond had fallen down to the dust, the dirt of defeat. He picked him up and put him on over his shoulder. He put his arms around his son's waist and helped him cross the finish line. The crowd stood up in applause. Derek Redmond and his father got more applause than the runners who didn't fall at all. The people who never fell didn't need help from their daddy. The people who never fell never needed help. They were sufficient to make it on their own.

Today, there is someone in the stands who sits up high, who is willing to come down, pick you up, and let you put your arm around His shoulder. He'll put His arm around your waist, and He'll drag you across the finish line. You can still come across the line, a winner, for the glory of God, by relying on Him to carry you through.[772]

[God's Deliverance; God's Presence; Help; Jesus, Relationship with]
Ps. 46:1; Isa. 40:31

RESTRICTIONS

A KID wanted ten things for Christmas. His parents bought nine things but all the kid could talk about on Christmas day was the one thing he didn't get. Because he thought his parents were going to get that one gift for him, he figured that they were just mean and didn't love him. He focused on what he couldn't have and forgot about the nine other gifts under the tree that reflected the goodness of his mom and dad.

Is there some restriction in your life that is all you can think about? Is there a restriction that you can't get off your mind? You may know that God has said to you about a certain thing, "You can't have that." Don't focus on the one restriction. Focus on all the good things God has already provided.[773]

[Blessing; Boundaries; Perspective, Need for]
Matt. 6:33

REVELATION

REVELATION is where God discloses Himself. It's like going to a play, sitting there with the curtain closed, waiting for the performance, then watching the curtain open to reveal what is behind the scene. If you go to New York and you go to a play, they've got the show bill there where you can read about that play, but you're waiting for the curtain to open because you want to see it on display. God's reasons and His rationale are called His ways. It is not good enough for you to read the bill and not see the ways. It's not good enough for you to be able to recite what's written but still not know His ways—that is, to know, based on what is written, what He is doing in your world.[774]

[God, Knowing]

REWARD

EVERY year in Dallas, the Texas State Fair comes to visit. This is fair heaven. There is more food than you could ever eat out there. Usually, I can go to the fair for free because a member of the church will give me tickets. Like salvation, my entrance into this heavenly place is free. I receive a free gift that gains me entrance.

Now, inside the fairgrounds, there is so much to do. There are animals, games, an aquarium, shows—it goes on and on. Every time we go out there, we spend six to seven hours because there is so much to see. The best part is the Midway. This is where all the fun rides and roller coasters are. It's also where most of the games are. When you play games at the fair, it ends up costing you more to play the game than to buy whatever it is that you are attempting to win. It's all part of the fun though.

All of these various activities and events are available to me simply because I have entered the fair. Entrance to the fair gives me access to a lot of things.

The free ticket gains me entrance but it does not automatically make me a full participant. All of the extra things available to me at the fair are like rewards. I can only enjoy them as much as I can afford them. I will have had to put in some work somewhere on somebody's job in order to be able to afford the additional fun that the fair offers.

Salvation is the free ticket available to those who accept Jesus Christ as their Savior. It guarantees free entrance into heaven. However, the amount we are able to enjoy heavenly rewards is tied to the amount of effort we've made on earth. Our heavenly rewards are tied to our earthly effort.

There will be many Christians who enter the kingdom. They will be at the fair. It is true that it is better to be at the fair than not be at the fair, but it's a terrible thing to be at the fair and not be able to ride. It's a terrible thing to have all the access but not be a full participant.[775]

[Heaven, Entrance into]

Col. 3:24

MY OLDEST son is the dominant person in my will. That is, most of the things that I have will go to him because of the biblical law of the first son. So I state in my will that my house goes to my first son. So as my first son, he gets the inheritance. He's not my oldest child, but if my daughter is to marry, some other man is supposed to be giving her a house. Now, my son can be disinherited, he cannot be "desoned." He will always be my son. But our will says, "If any of our children adopt a godless lifestyle, a carnal lifestyle, from which they do not repent, then the blessings are to be passed over to the other children." My eldest son is my son by birth but he is an inheritor by works. The reward

of inheritance from sonship has to be earned. It requires action.[776]

Rom. 8:17

RISK

A YOUNG preacher was preaching on a street corner in Atlanta. There was quite a bit of activity in the same area among Muslim people. While the young preacher delivered his message, a young guy of the Nation of Islam became very upset. He threatened the young preacher and told him that if he didn't stop sharing his message, that he would regret it, and he reached in his pocket.

This presented a crisis moment for the young preacher because he had to make a decision. Was he going to stop preaching at the possibility of losing his life or was he going to take the risk? He spoke to the Lord, quietly within his soul, and said, "Lord, if this is it, then I entrust my eternal destiny to You." Then the preacher kept on preaching.

There are times in our lives where we should take risks for God. When is the last time you've taken a risk for God?[777]

[Death, Fear of]

Matt. 5:10–12; 2 Tim. 1:12

S

SACRIFICE

A MAN was out with his wife and they got caught in a terrible hailstorm. This was a massive hailstorm. The hail was as large as baseballs. Under the deluge coming against them, the man realized that if he didn't do something, his wife would be severely hurt. He quickly draped himself over his wife, covering her with his own body so that instead of the storm hitting his wife, it hit him.

The hailstones seemed to get bigger as the man bent over his wife, protecting her. The large balls came down harder onto the man. They hurt him badly. After a couple of minutes, his ears started bleeding along with some spots on his head. The man tried to lead his wife to safety, but the stones were coming out faster and harder. The pounding stones took their toll. Weakened by the onslaught, the man finally collapsed over his wife, only able to shield her from the danger.

After the storm was over, the man was left with scars from where the balls had battered away at him. The remnants of sores, cuts, and abrasions would forever be reminders to him of the day he saved his wife.

This is a true story. On the local newscast, the man's wife was asked how she felt about their experience. She said, "Every time I look at that scar, on his head, on his neck, and on his ear, I love him more. Every time I see the scar, I love him more, because he sacrificed himself, for me."

When you and I get to heaven, Jesus will be the only person in eternity with scars. He will have holes in His hands, holes in His feet, and a hole in His side. He will be your eternal reminder that the only reason you are there is because He stood in between the wrath of God and judgment headed your way. He covered you with His love and allowed none of the hail to damage you. He was disfigured for you. This is the love of Christ.[778]

[Cross; Jesus; Love, Power of]
John 20:24–29; 1 Peter 2:24

A BEE one day flew into a car with a little boy riding with his father. The boy began to scream. His father reached out and grabbed the bee and squeezed it in his hand. He then opened up his hand. The bee flew back out and began to buzz around and the boy continued to scream. The father looked back and said, "Son, you don't have to scream." He held out his hand, and there inside the palm of his hand was the stinger of the bee. He said, "Son, all the bee can do now is make noise because I got the stinger in my hand."

On the cross of Calvary, Jesus Christ took the stinger. All death can do now is make noise. It has lost its sting.[779]

[Cross; Death; Jesus; Sin, Victory over]
Hos. 13:14; 1 Cor. 15:55; 1 Peter 2:24

SALVATION

IT IS impossible to lose your salvation in the same way it's impossible to stop being your parents' child. You are children by birth. Once you are born, you are born. Even if you are not acting like a well-behaved child, you are still a child because you are a child by birth.

Similarly, you don't hold on to God, God holds on to you. If a parent is holding a kid's hand, even when that kid lets go, he is still connected to their parent because the parent is still holding on.[780]

[Eternal Security, Assurance of; Fa-

ther God; Salvation, Assurance of]
John 5:24; Rom. 8:38–39

A FATHER and son were riding in a wagon, trying to outrace a prairie fire, and the prairie fire was catching up with them. They were soon going to be caught because the fire was moving so rapidly. The father and son got out of the wagon. As the fire raced to them, the father dug a little ditch and set fire in a circle around him, his son, and the wagon. He burned a big space. As the fire came upon them, the fire raged.

"Dad, we've got to get out of here."

"No, son, stand."

"But Dad, the fire."

"Son, trust me. Stand."

"Yeah, but we've got to run."

"No, we don't, son. All you've got to do is trust your father and stand."

"How can I stand when I'm surrounded by fire?"

"Because, son, this place where we are standing has already been burned once. I just set it afire. There is nothing left. All the fire can do is come up around us. It can't touch us. Once the ground has been burned, it can't be burned again."

Jesus was burned once. If you stand on Christ and His accomplishment on the cross, you can't be burned again. But we want to try to outrun the fire. We want to try to beat the Evil One. We want to try and work to avoid the fire, when all we have to do is stand on the atoning work of Jesus Christ.[781]

[Christ, Sufficiency of; Cross; Death, Fear of; Self-Sufficiency, Danger of]
2 Cor. 5:15; 1 John 2:2

SALVATION, ASSURANCE OF

ONE DAY, a lady got on a train. Now, there were a lot of trains at the station, but she had asked someone about which train was the correct train for her to get where she wanted to go. They told her which train and she followed their direction. She got on the train but she was nervous. She still wasn't completely sure that she was on the right train. She sat down with the train getting ready to pull off, wondering if she was on the right one. She didn't want to go the wrong way. Wanting to be certain that she was where she needed to be, she turned to the lady sitting next to her and said, "Excuse me, miss, is this the right train to St. Louis?"

She said, "Yep! You're on the right train."

So the lady went and sat down, but then started thinking that maybe the woman whom she had asked was on the wrong train too. She decided to check with somebody else. She turned to the man behind her. "Sir, is this the train to St. Louis?"

"Yes ma'am, this is the train to St. Louis."

She felt a little better but that man didn't look too smart. So the lady again found herself feeling uncertain, and without question, she didn't want to take a risk of being on the wrong train. At just that moment the conductor came through. The lady said, "Sir, I'm going to St. Louis; am I on the right train?"

He said, "Yes ma'am, you're on the right train to St. Louis. I will take you there as I'm running the engine." The lady lay back and went to sleep.

Hearing from the person next to her is nice, but it isn't enough.

Hearing from the nice man behind you is nice, but it's not enough. Hearing the pastor say "I think you're a Christian" is nice, but that's not enough. But when the conductor comes through, the one who is driving the train, that's enough! Sometimes you are going to check your feelings and you'll feel saved, but that's not enough. Some days you are going to be living right but when something wrong happens that's not enough. But when Jesus says, "I guarantee you eternal life because you have placed your total faith in My finished work," brothers and sisters, that's enough because He's driving the train.[782]

[Eternal Security, Assurance of; Faith, Versus Feelings]
Job 19:25–27; John 5:24; 14:1–4

THE STORY is told of a king who pardoned two criminals who were headed for death. They were on their way to be killed for their crimes but he issued a pardon. Both men could now go free. But the reactions of the two criminals were totally different. The first criminal who had been pardoned was full of joy, excitement, and exuberance. He was shouting and screaming as he looked at the pardon: "What joy to know that I was on my way to death and I have been given life, and not because of anything I have done."

The other criminal stood trembling and thinking, "Could this really be true? Was this a joke? Nobody would do anything like that for me. Look at what I have done!" He was terrified and rather than having the joy of the first criminal, he felt miserable. In fact, the second criminal tried to discourage the joy of the first criminal by telling him not to get too excited. He tried to convince him that this might not be real.

Because the first criminal believed the pardon, he had both the assurance and joy of his release. Because the second criminal questioned the pardon, he had neither the joy nor the assurance of his release. One criminal looked at the piece of paper that held his pardon and believed it. The other criminal looked inside of himself to see whether he really believed it, and because what he saw in himself was doubt, it took away the joy of his assurance.[783]

[Eternal Security, Assurance of; Joy]
John 3:16; 5:24; Rom. 10:9–10

A GREAT tragedy occurred in 1982 in Chicago, Illinois, when people went to a grocery store and bought Tylenol. Someone had laced some of the capsules in some of the bottles with cyanide. Many of the people went and picked up the Tylenol. Seven people died. They thoroughly believed they were only getting Tylenol, when the Tylenol had in fact been tampered with. They believed, but their belief was not sufficient because the contents in the bottle could not be trusted.[784]

[Trust in God]

WHEN people go shopping and pay for something, they get a receipt. That receipt validates that they made a purchase. If there is ever a question or if anything ever goes wrong, the receipt proves that the payment was made in full.

For Christians, bought by the blood of Jesus Christ, the payment for their salvation was paid in full on

Friday night when Jesus was crucified on the cross. Early on Sunday morning, the receipt was given. The resurrection of Jesus Christ is our receipt.

The resurrection of Jesus Christ is God's receipt for the payment of the death of Christ.[785]

[Eternal Security, Assurance of]
Rom. 1:1–4; 1 Peter 1:3

SALVATION, BENEFITS OF

THE LOWER that an object goes into a body of water, the more pressure there is. If a diver goes down deep enough, their jaws will even lock because of the pressure. If a boat sinks down far enough, the pressure of the water that deep will tear that boat apart, and the boat will collapse . . . unless it is pressurized.

Submarines are pressurized. They have a balance of pressure on the inside to combat the pressure from the outside.

Many people are collapsing on the outside because they don't have enough pressure on the inside, and the pressure on the inside comes from confession of Christ! The Spirit of God pressurizes Christians on the inside so that they can handle the world on the outside.[786]

[Holy Spirit, Filling of; Jesus, Relationship with]

SALVATION, COST OF

A MAN one day was low on funds and all he had was one valuable thing to his name—a family ring that had been passed down for generations. He didn't want to part with the ring that so full of memories, but he needed money to survive. He took his ring off, took it to the pawnshop, and gave it to the pawn-broker. The pawnbroker gave him a few dollars for it accompanied by a ticket. On the back of the ticket, a redemption price and date were listed.

The gentleman intended to buy his ring back but the date rolled quickly and he still did not have the money. He came and pled with the pawnbroker not to sell his ring in his shop. He begged for more time but the pawnbroker would not budge from the original agreement.

The next day was the day for the ring to be sold. The remorseful seller came by that day only to find his beautiful ring polished and sitting in the shop window. It now cost twenty-five times the price he sold it for.

Some of us today have pawned our lives for a pittance. We pawned our souls and we don't have what it takes to redeem it. But, two thousand years ago, God sent Jesus Christ to pick up the tab for the lives we pawned. The beautiful thing about the Lord Jesus Christ is that He can afford to pay the price.[787]

[Christian, Value of; Cross]
Job 19:25–27; Eph. 1:7

THE ROAD to carnality starts with a lack of appreciation. When you don't know what you have, you take it for granted. Many people feel taken for granted by their mates.

I had a lady in my office one time who said, "He doesn't know what he has and if he doesn't find out quick, I'm not going to be around much longer." She felt taken for granted. Her husband had gotten used to cooked meals, washed clothes, and ironed shirts. He'd gotten used to her.

A man once came to me and said, "I'm a hard worker, a sensitive husband, and a caring person. I feel taken for granted."

God is saying to us, "Your salvation cost Me My Son. I feel taken for granted." Now, how can you neglect that kind of salvation?[788]

[Salvation, Rejection of]
John 3:16; Acts 2:22–24; 1 Cor. 7:23

I WAS in a restaurant having lunch and it came time to pay the bill. I asked the waiter to come over and bring me the bill. He left only to come back a few minutes later and declare that I had no bill. He told me that somebody else in the restaurant had picked up the tab. Now, I would have been a fool to sit there and argue with the waiter. I would have been a fool to not accept the gift. All I could do was say thank you. I showed gratitude for a price that had already been paid.

God wants us to accept His gift. He has paid our tab. Some people are fools because they refuse to accept God's free gift. The price of salvation has already been paid and God's Son has picked up the tab.[789]

[Salvation, Rejection of]
Acts 13:46; Rom. 2:8

LIVING your Christian life is fulfilling the contract on an agreement to build a building. Let's say that you paid to get a brand-new, custom-built, top-dollar house built on your lot. The builder comes and he finishes the house with a combination of blue bricks, black bricks, white bricks, turquoise bricks, and purple bricks all mixed in together. You wouldn't appreciate that because I'm sure that's not what you would have paid for. You would probably take that contractor to court for putting in a mess when you paid a premium price. You don't pay for a top-dollar house and expect a contractor to use junk materials. You want the top-dollar material if you are building a top-dollar house.

On the cross, Jesus paid top dollar for your sins. God gave His only begotten Son that you and I might have a relationship with Himself.

The Bible tells us that God says, "I paid good money, so watch how you build. Don't use cheap material when I paid a top-dollar bill."[790]

[Life, Management of]
1 Cor. 3:10–15; 6:20

MANY students will receive a freshman orientation when they go off to college. Part of this orientation is designed to help the incoming freshmen know how to get the most out of their education at the school and how to maximize their time.

If parents find out their kids are spending too much time partying at school, they are likely to be ticked off. Why? Because the cost for college is so high. College is too expensive to waste time playing around.

Jesus Christ paid a high price for your salvation, so He doesn't want you wasting your time for development and discipleship.[791]

[Spiritual Maturity, Growth]
1 Cor. 7:23

SALVATION, GRATEFULNESS FOR

IF YOU buy an appliance, and it doesn't work after you've paid for it, that is quite irritating, isn't it? It's not a good feeling to know you've paid hundreds of dollars for an appliance that doesn't work. It drives me crazy to think that the folks at the store where I bought my appliance took my money and I received a defective product. Well, Jesus paid it all. He paid for you. He shed His blood for you so the last thing He wants to hear, having paid that expensive price for you and me, is that we're not working or that we don't feel like doing our jobs for Him today. We should be glad to serve Him out of gratitude for the gift of salvation.[792]

[Thanksgiving, Motivation for; Worship, Motivation for]

Heb. 12:2–3

SALVATION, MEANS OF

THE STORY is told of a father who had five sons. The first son was an obedient child who loved his father. The four remaining sons were to varying degrees rebellious. One of the instructions of the father was not to go near the river because it had such a traumatic torrent. It was very dangerous. But the last four sons decided not to listen to their dad. So they all went down by the river and played in the water only to be sucked up by its current and pulled downstream. No matter how hard they tried, they could not get out of the water. They were pulled downstream for miles and miles, until many miles later and almost dead, they were washed ashore a long way from home.

They had enough survival skills about them to build a fire, and around that fire they longed for home, but they didn't know how to get home and they didn't have a way back to home. They remembered their father with fondness. They remembered how joyful things were back home and lamented over how things might have gone differently for them if only they would have obeyed.

After a while one son said, "I'm going to build a hut. I'm going to make the best of things I can right here. I'm going to call this home." The second son went over to the ridge to watch the first son build his hut, and he said, "I'm going to stay here and watch what you do because I'm going to tell on you when we get back home. I'm going to tell Daddy that you forgot about him, and I'm going to tell him that you forgot your real home." The third son said, "Well, I'm going back home. I don't know my way but I'll just follow the bank and go back the way we came from."

Now, the obedient son had been sent by his father to look for his brothers. He ran into the fourth son first. He told him that their father had sent him to find his brothers and bring them home. Now that he'd located one of his brothers, he wanted to know where the other three were. Brother number four showed him where their brother number one had built his hut. They knocked on the door. The obedient brother said, "Time to go home!"

But brother number one said, "This is home now. I've been away from Daddy's house too long. I've got new friends now and a new way of life. Thanks a lot, but I'm okay where I am."

They went to the second brother who was sitting down, evaluating the first brother. The obedient brother said, "Let's go home."

Brother number two said, "I can't leave here. I'm going to keep my eye on brother number one. If I leave, then there will be nobody to watch what he is doing. There will be no one to critique or judge him."

They went to the third son, who was busy making his way upstream. The obedient brother said, "You don't have to struggle to find your way home. I've got a boat with a motor to take us upstream."

Brother number three said, "No, I've got to do this myself because then I can get home to Daddy and show him how much I love him by how hard I've worked to get back to him."

The father sent the son to bring everybody back home, but only one brother went home. Only one brother was willing to go home God's way. The first brother had gotten so comfortable where he lived that he was not willing to leave what he knew for the uncertainties of the trip back home. The second brother was so focused on somebody else that he forgot it was his sin that got him in the water in the first place. He didn't have to spend all of his time looking at his brother's sin. If he'd just look at himself, he could go home. The third brother was a "do-it-yourselfer." He felt if he tried hard enough, he could be free and climb home himself. Only the fourth brother understood that the only way to get out of the mess he had gotten himself into was to follow the son who knew how to take him back to the father so he would be home again.

So I only have one question. Which son are you? For God the Father has sent Jesus the Son to locate His brothers. If you are tired of the hut that you've made your home, if you are tired of being so focused on everybody else that you've not yet gotten around to your sin, if you are so tired of trying to work your own way back from the place you're in, God has sent the bigger brother, and Jesus is willing to take you home.[793]

[Grace, Need for; Humanity; Salvation, Need for]
Matt. 13:3–9; Luke 20:9–18; John 3:16

TWO men were climbing a mountain. They had two guides—a guide in the back and a guide in the front. They were all tied together by the same rope. As they were climbing up the mountain, the guide in the back slipped and fell. When he fell, he rolled off the edge of the mountain and yanked the two men in the middle. The guide in the front took his axe and dug it into the ice. He gripped and held on. The two men in the middle were able to climb back up on the rope because the guide in the front had dug in and not let go. Even the guide in the back was able to climb to safety because of the front guide who dug in and saved them.

In the garden of Eden, the first Adam slipped and fell, and we are hooked into him by nature. So when Adam died, we all died. When he slipped and fell, we all slipped and fell with him. We were all hanging over the edge and headed toward an eternal abyss. But there was somebody else on that rope. He was born of a virgin, a man like you and me. And

He dug in. He was born a perfect baby. He lived a perfect life. He did everything according to the will of God. He dug in, and then He died on a cross and rose from the dead. Because He dug in, all in Adam who were slipping and heading to the abyss can climb back up on this last Adam who has paid the price.[794]

[Cross; Jesus]

Rom. 5:12–19

WHAT does it mean to believe in Jesus Christ? If I'm on a luxury liner that is sinking, I should want to get off of the luxury liner and get to safety. If the crew calls out to me and says, "The liner is sinking. Get in the lifeboat so you'll be saved from drowning in the ocean," that is good news in a bad situation. The lifeboat can save me from death.

Now, I could say, "I know there's a lifeboat, but I'm going to take my chances. I'm going to stay on the big boat. I'm a little uncomfortable with the lifeboat. I heard what the crew is telling me to do, but I want to try another way." If I say this, it won't be because I don't know there is another way. I will be choosing, however, not to accept what I know.

There may be another person who says, "Well, if the captain said to get in the lifeboat, I am going to get in the lifeboat."

Believing in the Bible is not merely accepting information. It is entrusting yourself to the information that you say you accept. In other words, there is no belief until I get into the lifeboat.

Talking means nothing. I could say, "Oh, that lifeboat sure looks good. I believe that lifeboat can save somebody. I believe that lifeboat is more than able. I believe that lifeboat is the wheel in the middle of a wheel. I believe that lifeboat is so high you can't get over it, so low you can't get under it, and so wide you can't get around it. I believe that lifeboat is the Rose of Sharon, Balm of Gilead, and Bright and Morning Star." I could say all of this and still drown in the ocean if I don't get in the lifeboat.

To tell me you believe that pew you're sitting in can hold you up is meaningless until you sit down. It is the sitting down; it is the act of faith that equals real faith, not merely the discussion about faith. How do you know that you've acted in faith? Simple—you reject everything but Christ to save you. You only trust in Christ.[795]

[Faith, Acting in; Salvation, Provision of]

Gal. 5:6; James 2:14–19; Rev. 3:15–16

THE STORY is told of Farmer Dale and Farmer Pete. These were two neighbors. They really did love one another as neighbors and as fellow farmers; however, these two would always compete with one another. Every year they would enter some kind of competition where one would seek to outdo the other one. The problem was, Farmer Pete always won. Farmer Dale never won. Farmer Dale got tired of losing to Farmer Pete. He decided to come up with something he could win at. They both had horses on their farms. So Farmer Dale challenged Farmer Pete to a horse race to see which horse would win for that year's competition. What Farmer Pete didn't know was that Farmer Dale hired a professional jockey to ride his horse, figuring that would give him the edge, the little extra that he would need. The race started and the two horses shot out. Farmer Dale's horse took the lead. Farmer Dale thought that finally he was going to beat Pete at something. As they hit the stretch ready to bring it home, the horses' legs got tangled up with one another and both horses fell over. Both jockeys fell over. Both farmers were hollering, "Get up, get up!" Farmer Dale's jockey, the professional, was the first to get up. He got on the horse and started riding again, and right behind him was Farmer Pete's jockey. He got on his horse and started riding again. They crossed the finish line and Farmer Dale's jockey crossed first. He was ecstatic. He was laughing and dancing and then he looked and started crying.

Farmer Pete said, "Dale, why are you sad? You won! You've been trying to beat me all these years. You've never won, but today's your day! You shouldn't be sad!"

Farmer Dale looked at Farmer Pete and said, "My jockey got on the wrong horse." His jockey had crossed the finish line, riding the wrong horse.

Wouldn't it be tragic, after going as hard and fast as you could in this life, to cross the finish line into eternity only to discover that you were riding the wrong horse? Wouldn't it be tragic after you've done the best you could, after you had tried as hard as you know how to try, after you had sung, and gone to church, and tried to treat your neighbor right, and did the best you could, to cross the finish line laughing only to start crying? Wouldn't it be terrible to realize at the end of your life here on earth that you crossed the finish line riding the wrong horse?[796]

[Deception, Satan's; Life, Management of; Materialism, Deception of]
Matt. 7:21–23; John 14:6; 2 Cor. 4:4

SALVATION, NATURE OF

WHEN a woman is pregnant, she is carrying a seed. Her husband's sperm has fertilized her egg and now she has a unique life growing within her. The life in her is not her own. That life in her has its own DNA. The seed from her husband that fertilized her egg has produced a brand-new life. Her job is to allow the life inside of her to express itself. When that life expresses itself, she is going to get really big and that new life is going to show up.

She will have to change because of the growth within her. She'll have to get maternity clothes. She will probably have to adjust as her taste buds change. She'll have to accommodate new sleeping positions. She'll even have to adopt a new walk.

When you receive the new life of Christ, it is a different life. It's not the same life. It is a brand-new life operating in an old shell, the body. And when that new life operates in the body, it operates based on a different set of laws. The new life is righteous; the body that this new life is in is called the flesh. The body of the flesh works against the new life now within. What Satan wants to do is get the outer life to keep the inner life from expressing itself.[797]

[Christian Living, New Life; Flesh; New Life in Christ; Satan, Strategy of]
Rom. 7:23; Phil. 3:17–21;

1 John 2:15–17

BUTTERFLIES are caterpillars that have been transformed. Caterpillars are ugly, slimy, and slow. I don't find much redeeming value in caterpillars. Most of the time, I find myself stepping on them.

But once the caterpillar converts to a butterfly, all of a sudden, something new is born. Something old and ugly, something that was rejected, something that deserved to be stepped on, now begins to change. The process of change is a little uncomfortable and a little inconvenient. For a while, it looks like things are getting worse rather than better. That's because something is changing on the inside. After the cocooning process is over, and the shell flips open, all of a sudden the thing that used to be grounded can now fly. The thing that used to be a parasite now pollinates. Something beautiful has come out of something that was ugly. The seed was already there for it, but it just had to wait for development.

Now, a butterfly is not a fixed up caterpillar. A butterfly is a totally new creature that was birthed out of a caterpillar. But it's not a caterpillar. It is a brand spanking new being.[798]

[Spiritual Transformation; Transformation]
2 Cor. 5:17

SALVATION, NEED FOR

A MAN went on vacation with his family to an amusement park. Being a minister, he looked at everything theologically. So while at the amusement park, he began to do some theology on roller coasters. The entry charge per person for the amusement park was quite steep as is the norm for these fun centers, and there were six people in the minister's family. They got there at noon and left at midnight. So that's twelve hours. It dawned on the minister late in the afternoon that he was standing in line forty-five minutes to one hour to get a ninety-second ride. He began calculating. At the end of the twelve hours, he would have ridden ten rides at approximately ninety seconds a ride. That means he paid an expensive price to ride ten rides and only received fifteen minutes' worth of entertainment.

The amusement park had constructed things so that while you were in line, there were TV monitors displaying Bugs Bunny's fiftieth anniversary. They had these cartoons of Bugs Bunny playing because they wanted their visitors to forget how long they were waiting. They didn't want their guests to think about the fact that they were being robbed blind by paying such high prices for tickets worth fifteen minutes of rides.

The minister left the park with his family having had a great time but now wiser. He now knew that the people running the amusement park were aware they robbed their visitors.

That is precisely what Satan has done in our world order. He has gotten us looking at the cartoons and caused us to forget how long we are standing in line while he robs us. Yet our world does not understand and does not see its condition. People are unaware that Satan is entertaining them to hell. They are without God and are without hope. So God intervened and provided a way of salvation.[799]

[Satan, Strategy of; Worldliness, Distraction of]
2 Cor. 4:4

THE OTHER day in the mail, a credit card application arrived. The credit card application said, "You have been prequalified for a $15,000 limit." This meant that I had already been determined to be acceptable to the company. This meant that the credit card company had already given the OK. However, the invitation did not automatically grant me membership. In order to get the card, I had to fill out a form and send it in. Even though the company had already extended the credit approval, that did not mean that I would automatically get the card. I had to write back and say that I wanted it.

God has already prequalified you for heaven by paying for your sins on the cross, but He can only activate your account if you tell Him you want Him to do so. If you still believe that you must pay for it yourself, what you're saying is, "I don't need Your card. I've got my own and I'm going to satisfy You by my own human efforts." A person needs to understand that in order to receive eternal life they have to admit that they are a sinner and therefore unable to save themselves.[800]

[Salvation, Nature of]
Rom. 10:9–10; Rev. 22:17

IN OCTOBER of 1987, a little girl named Jessica McClure fell down an abandoned well shaft. The shaft was eight inches in diameter and twenty-two feet deep. She was lost to her parents with no way on her own to get out. She was trapped. In this little town of Midland, Texas, she became the focus of the whole nation. Every major news network focused in on Midland, Texas, and the girl named Jessica, who was trapped in the well.

For fifteen hours, men dug and drilled. They didn't know initially that to get to her they would have to go through some limestone. This stone cracked the bits on the drills they were using to make their way through the shaft. Getting to little Jessica took a lot longer than anyone expected. After fifteen hours or so someone was able to get down into the shaft, untangle little Jessica, and bring her up to the top. Cameras blazing upon the opening to the shaft caught the man bringing Jessica up out of the shaft and into the arms of her waiting parents. The site, filled with people hoping and praying, was filled with joy. The rescuers were crying, the parents were crying, newscasters were crying, and onlookers across the nation were crying because little Jessica, who was most certainly dead, was now alive. Little Jessica, in order to live, had to have somebody else save her.

Similarly, every member of the human race is trapped. We have fallen into an abyss out of which we can never lift ourselves. If we want to get out of this hole we're in, somebody up there has got to come down to where we've been trapped by sin. Somebody has got to drill a hole to where we are. Even though we try hard, the hole is too deep and we can't climb out.

At the heart of the gospel, that's what Jesus did. He saw you and me in a hole. We were trying to get out with good works, but we weren't getting anywhere. But God, coming as the person of Jesus Christ, entered the hole of our death, and offered deliverance from above. Not only did God offer deliverance, He also offered assurance. The same Jesus Christ not only saves, He also assures.[801]

> [Jesus; Salvation; Salvation, Means of]
> Rom. 5:8; 6:23; Eph. 2:8–9

THE RULER of the land one day passed a law that said you couldn't do certain things in the country. It was discovered that his mother had broken the new laws. The law keepers of the land brought the mother to her son, the king.

"Your mother has broken the law. You said anyone who breaks these laws would receive twenty stripes."

The ruler was caught in a catch-22. He had a standard that he could not change. It applied to everybody. He really did not want the rules or the consequences to apply to his mother. He loved his mother. How could he keep his standard of perfection and still honor and respect his mother. How could he show love to his mother without playing favorites?

The king unbuttoned his shirt, and told the law keepers to whip him. He told the man with the whip to lash him with the whip twenty times. He bent over and took the twenty lashes for his mother. He met the demands of the law, yet he showed love and mercy to his mother by taking the penalty that she deserved on himself.

Enter Jesus Christ. God says that the "soul that sinneth, it shall die." The nature of death is eternal separation from a holy God. But Jesus Christ offered Himself to be hung instead. Jesus Christ took the penalty of Calvary that you and I deserved. God obeyed the law that He Himself had set, yet provided a substitute so that you and I could be delivered. He is both just and the justifier of all those who believe in Jesus Christ. The cross shows that any man's attempt to come to God by his own works and his own power is not enough. There is no basis for self-congratulations.[802]

> [Cross; Grace, Provision of; Judgment]
> Ezek. 18:4; Rom. 3:25

LET'S SAY you crack an egg, put it in the skillet, and start to fry it only to discover it's a rotten egg. The egg is rotten. You can smell it; you can see it. It is obviously a bad egg.

Let's say that you then decide to overcome the rotten egg by frying five more good eggs with it. So you crack five eggs that are healthy and fresh and put them in the skillet, with the idea that the goodness of the five will override the badness of the one.

I've got bad news for you. It is not the righteous eggs that will overcome the diseased one; it is the diseased one that will penetrate the good ones, contaminating even the good and making you sick. The reason why being the best person you can be does not satisfy God is that the sin that is there contaminates the righteousness.[803]

> [Grace, Need for; Self-Sufficiency, Sin of; Sin, Contamination by]
> Isa. 64:6; Eph. 2:8–9

SALVATION, PROVISION OF

THERE'S a barbershop in Dallas I used to go to. I'll never forget the first time I went in. There was a sign and it said, "In God we trust, all others pay cash." In other words, this barber only accepted cash payment. You couldn't write a check; you couldn't use a credit card. Cash was the only payment the barber would accept. The death of Jesus Christ is the only payment God will accept.[804]

[Salvation, Cost of]

John 14:6

SALVATION, REJECTION OF

WHAT happens to people who die without Christ? They go to hell! There is no respectable way to say it. They go to HELL. For how long? Forever!

There is always the person who will say, "Wait a minute. I am not sure I believe in hell." This is one chance that may not be worth taking. Certain things you can afford to make a mistake on, but this isn't one of them.

If a man doesn't have food, that's bad but he can recover from that. If a man doesn't live in a good house, that's bad but he can recover from that. If a man doesn't have the best clothes, that's bad but he can recover from that. If he doesn't have the job he prefers to have, that's bad but he can recover from that. If a man has to walk because he can't afford a car, that's bad but he can recover from that. No matter how bad a person's finances are, they can recover from that. But if a man dies without a personal relationship with Jesus Christ and wakes up in hell, that's a blow that he can never recover from.[805]

[Eternity; Hell]

Matt. 25:31; John 3:36

SANCTIFICATION

MANY people buy these "strips" from the store to whiten their teeth. They use these to help restore their teeth to a better condition because after years of use, their teeth may not be as white as they used to be. Stained teeth can be covered up for a while through brushing, but eventually something stronger may be needed. Stains from coffee, dark drinks, or smoking may have set in and people buy the strips to make their teeth look better.

These strips are to be applied across the teeth. They are worn for a while and then taken off. Applied again, then taken off. Over and over, the strips are applied until over time, the strips wear down the yellow. If a person uses the strips just one time, the stains will not go away. The strips have to be applied consistently over a period of time in order for the process to work.

Many of us go for one week being diligent to live for Christ and want that effort to last all year long. We look for long-term change after short-term effort. Let me explain something: Salvation is an act; sanctification is a process.[806]

[Sin, Stain of; Spiritual Transformation]

2 Cor. 7:1; 2 Tim. 2:20–21; 1 Peter 1:2

SATAN

SNAKES don't blink, because they don't have eyelids. Snakes' eyes are open 24/7. Unlike other animals that blink, snakes don't because they have nothing to blink with. They are always looking. Their eyes go this way and that way with no end. They are in a state of constant observation. That helps us to understand the Scripture that says that Satan's on the prowl, looking for whom he may devour. His eyes are always open.[807]

1 Peter 5:8

ON A particular episode of a futuristic show called *The Outer Limits*, a man, a leader of a large armed force, was captured by creatures. They wanted information from him but he wouldn't give it up because he didn't want his army to be destroyed. The creatures then brought in a lady they said had also been captured.

Every day they came to get her, took her out, and then brought her back again to the holding room. After awhile, day after day, scales began to grow on the lady, making her look like the monsters that had captured them. The leader of the armed forces asked the lady what they were doing to her each day to make her change. She told him that each day she was exposed to certain rays that were apparently making the scales grow on her body. Each day the monsters came to get the lady and each day they asked the man for the information.

One day the monsters told the man that if he didn't tell them what they wanted to know, that they would kill the lady by continuing to expose her to the harmful rays. As soon as they left the room, the lady pleaded with the leader to tell the monsters what they wanted to know. Against his will and better judgment, he yielded because of the compassion he had for the lady whose fate was in his hands.

As soon as he gave the monsters the information, the lady then knocks on the door and calls out to the captors saying that she is ready to go. Confused, the man demanded to know what was going on. The lady turned and explained that she has always been one of the monsters. Her exposure to the rays was to rid her of her scales. Her exposure decreased a little every day to enable her to appear to be turning into a monster.

This lady was an imposter. She was made to look like the man she was trying to con. Satan does the same things with people. He can change into whatever he knows you'll respond to.[808]

[Satan, Strategy of]
2 Cor. 11:14

IN FOOTBALL, the team studies game film of the upcoming opponent in order to know their tendencies. They want to see what their rival's orientations are so that they can come up with a strategy to beat them. Well, Satan has game film on you. He has game film on me and he knows what our weak spots are. He knows where we are limited. He knows where we are prone. He knows what we would respond to. He knows what our likes are and because he is so good at what he does, he can become anything at any time, for anyone, based on what he knows your response will be. Stop looking for someone with horns, a long tail, a jumpsuit that's red, and a pitchfork.[809]

[Satan, Strategy of; Temptation, Leading to Sin]
2 Cor. 11:14

A PHENOMENAL magician presented an illusion to his audience. He had a little box and put his assistant, his wife, into the box. Then he began to fold the box in half, over and over again, until it could fit onto the top of his podium. Then, he offered to do the trick again, this time with an aid for the audience—a mirror on the other side of the box so that the audience had a full-sided view of the box. He performed the illusion again, folding it down to a small square, holding it up for the audience, and then unfolding the square to make a box again. The magician opened up the box again and his life-size wife gets out. The people watching are stupefied.

After his performance, a woman asked him to share how he does the trick. The illusionist answers, "Ma'am, it's one of the secrets of the trade. If you knew how I did it, I'd lose my edge. Because you don't know, I control the audience."

Now, if our human brains cannot figure out how an illusionist can fold human beings into a box that a baby couldn't even fit in, no matter how hard you look at it and try to figure it out, what makes you think that you can figure out a cosmic being, who not only is a spirit, but who's been doing what he does for so long that he's become an expert at it? You can't.[810]

[Deception, Satan's]
Eph. 6:12; 1 Peter 5:8

SATAN, INFLUENCE OF

ONE day a woman bought a very, very expensive dress. When she brought it home and her husband found out how much she spent on it, he said, "Why in the world would you buy that expensive of a dress? You know we can't afford it."

The woman looked at her hus-band and said, "But honey, you don't understand, the Devil made me do it! I tried it on and the Devil said to me, 'You look awesome, girlfriend, in that dress. That's you all over, you got to have that dress.'"

"Then why didn't you tell the Devil to 'get thee behind me, Satan'?"

His wife said, "I did tell the Devil to 'get thee behind me, Satan.' And he went behind me and told me I looked good there too."

You just can't get rid of Satan. He's everywhere and he's got a good argument waiting and ready for every situation you face.[811]

[Satan, Strategy of; Temptation, Leading to Sin]
Matt. 4:10; 16:23; Mark 8:33

SATAN, LIES OF

GREAT efforts have been made to seek peace in the Middle East. Every time it looks like we're taking two steps forward in our progress toward a solution to the age-old conflict there, something happens that takes us three steps back. It looks like there is an accord, and then there is an eruption, and when you didn't think things could get any worse, they do. The issue of terrorism has now changed the equation due to the phenomenon of the suicide bomber. This is a person who straps themselves with explosives, goes into a crowded area, and blows themselves up with the goal of taking as many of the perceived enemy along with them as they can.

In the news recently, we've seen a suicide bomber dressed up like an Orthodox Jew, with Jewish garb, Jewish colors, looking like he belonged to the Jewish people when he was simply an enemy in camouflage. Who would suspect that a person looking like a Jew, would, underneath the garb, be death incarnate? How do you defend your own, when the perpetrator is among you? This misleading situation is synonymous with how Satan deceives us.[812]

[Deception, Satan's; Satan, Strategy of]
1 Peter 5:8

ALL OF us know what it is to be deceived. Credit card offers arrive in the mail, luring us with the words "Congratulations!" printed on the front. We are told that because of our good credit and because we pay our monthly payments, we can have higher limits, gold membership, or preferred customer status. We can feel special because we have a different color card. We are in a higher class of people who matter. We can spend to our heart's content.

What we don't hear is that we will be paying these credit card companies for the rest of our lives. They don't tell us that they are going to own us. They don't tell us that the credit will cost us much more than what we get out of the deal. They don't tell us that they want more than payback—they want interest payments.[813]

[Deception; Materialism, Deception of]

TABLOIDS are notorious for the pictures they manufacture. They do this by creating pictures of people by matching heads with different bodies. These magazines want to paint a picture in order to sell magazines and papers. These pictures are often false creations, made up in order to achieve the goal of increasing sales. Just as a tabloid will reconfigure things to accomplish its own purposes, the Evil One is committed to changing our picture of God, in order to sell himself.[814]

[Deception, Satan's]
Gen. 3:1–4

SATAN, STRATEGY OF

WHEN the Mavericks play and the opposing team is up for a free throw, they run into opposition from the Dallas fans. The folks attending the game and sitting in the seats directly behind the basketball goals have posters put under their seats before the game. The fans hold these posters up to distract the opposing team's players from making good shots. These posters say "Brick," and they are painted to look like bricks. A "brick" in basketball is a word used to indicate a ball that is thrown so poorly that it completely misses the goal. It indicates the idea that the basketball misses just as easily as if the player would have thrown a real brick at the net. When the player gets up to shoot, the fans are ready with their posters, waving them in the air to distract him.

Now, a lot goes into getting these cardboard signs to the fans. First of all, somebody's got to cut out the cardboard. Then, the cardboard has to be painted. Then, someone has to be paid to pass out the cardboard signs before the game. All of this is done just to get the player's eyes off the goal.

But a seasoned basketball player understands one thing. No matter how many bricks are up there, he is to keep his eyes on the goal. No matter how much the fans are waving, chanting, and screaming out, he is to keep his eyes on the goal.

Satan is going through a lot of effort to put bricks up in your face to distract you from making your goals. However, God has enabled us, if we focus on Him, to be able to make the goals and for those shots to be "all net." It'll be swoosh! He makes this possible when we keep our eyes on Him. Where are your eyes? Don't be distracted.[815]

[Worldliness, Distraction of]

Ps. 141:8; 2 Cor. 4:18; Heb. 12:2

IN YELLOWSTONE National Park, there are large signs that say Don't Feed the Bears! Tourists always disobey it. They feed the bears, and every year the park rangers have to pick up dead bears. The bears get used to being fed by the tourists and they lose their ability to fend for themselves in nature. They wind up looking for a handout, and when the handout is no longer there, they die.

Satan offers us handouts—a party here, a relationship there, a thrill here, and he gets us so used to him that we forget God. When he stops handing things out, when you lose the job, when life turns upside down on you, then you don't know where to go. Satan has a strategy of tricking people into relying on cheap substitutes.[816]

[Deception, Satan's; Deception, Cost of; Temptation, Leading to Sin]

Gen. 3:1–4; Prov. 14:12; James 1:13–15

SCRIPTURE

WHEN you stand before the Bible, you are to stand before it as a mirror. This mirror will not reflect you. The wicked witch stood before the mirror and looked for the mirror to compliment her. "Mirror, mirror, on the wall, who is the fairest of them all?" She was in for a shock! A picture of Snow White appeared in the mirror. The wicked witch looked in the mirror but she saw somebody else. The purpose of the Scripture is to show you the Fair One. It is to give you a picture of Jesus Christ.[817]

[Bible; Bible, Use of]

John 1:14; Heb. 4:12

SCRIPTURE, IMPORTANCE OF

I WAS having a great deal of trouble with my cell phone. A great deal of difficulty picking things up and hearing. It kept cutting off, so I had to get another one. I walked into the store, showed them what I had, and they told me which phone model was comparable to what I was used to. I got the phone. They sent my number over to the new phone and so I was good to go. About a month after having the phone, I noticed a small but thick book in the box the phone came in. I hadn't looked at it before. I decided to thumb through it. I was just "stuptified" at all the stuff the phone could do. Its capabilities were far beyond my expectations because, fundamentally for me, a phone is to make calls and to receive calls. Upon reading the book, I discovered that it offered so much more. Without reading the book, I would have settled for basic phone use, but upon reading the book, I discovered that far and beyond the basics, there was so much more.[818]

[Bible, Use of]

Rom. 15:4; 2 Tim. 3:16

SECOND CHANCES

IN FOOTBALL, basketball, and most

sports, there is a halftime. Halftime is an extended break in the middle of a game so that the players can get themselves together. This is also a time for a coach to call in a struggling team, acknowledge the team's performance, and encourage them to do a better job in the second half.

The beauty of halftime is that there is a whole second half in which a team can turn things around. Halftime acts as a grace period. No matter how messed up the first half might have been, the second half provides an opportunity to make things right. For many Christians, they have had a bad first half of play in the Christian life. The good news is that God gives halftimes where He calls our attention to our struggles and then sends encouragement to do a good job in the second half. He gives us an opportunity to get ourselves together, to focus, and to do a better job than we did on the front end.[819]

[Grace; Life, Fixing]

SELF-SUFFICIENCY, DANGER OF

MANY of us are spiritually self-employed. We work for ourselves. There's only one negative of working for yourself. You've got to cover your own benefits. When you work for yourself you've got to pay for it. You've got to cover your own insurance. You are free to work for yourself. You are also free to bear the entire burden.[820]

[Independence, Consequences of]
Phil. 4:13

SELF-SUFFICIENCY, SIN OF

I DON'T like it when my wife asks me to go to Home Depot. I'm not a Home Depot kind of guy. Now, there are two reasons I don't like Home Depot. Number one, it's big and the aisles are packed with stuff. I also don't like fighting to get through those lines, if I happen to go during the wrong part of the day. The main reason I don't like Home Depot is because when my wife asks me to go there to purchase something, it usually means I have to fix something around the house myself.

See, Home Depot is set up for folk who want to take care of things themselves. So instead of calling a plumber, you go get the plumbing. Instead of calling an electrician, you go get the plugs and the socket so you can screw it in yourself. I don't like Home Depot because that means there is work for me to do. Home Depot has made a business of teaching people how to fix it themselves.

We've got a lot of Home Depot kind of saints today. They are used to being their own boss, captain of their own faith, and master of their own ship. They are so used to doing it themselves that, even though they will breathe a prayer every now and then, they remain fairly self-sufficient people.

These self-sufficient people are Burger King kind of people. They want to have it their way. They are sufficient within themselves and so they live their own lives.

This is what Satan wants. He wants us to operate independently of God.[821]

[Independence, Consequences of; Satan, Strategy of]
Jer. 17:5–8; Phil. 4:13

SELFISHNESS

THERE was a girl named Maria who had broken up with Jimmy. She told him she simply didn't want to be with him anymore. But after about a year of being broken up, out of the blue, she wrote Jimmy a letter. She said, "Jimmy, I miss you bad. I think of you all day and all night long. You dominate my mind and I just don't want to be apart from you anymore. Jimmy, let's reconnect. P.S. Congratulations on winning the lottery!" It's amazing how willing people are to do things when there is personal benefit involved.[822]

[Money, Love of; Relationships]
Matt. 6:24; Luke 16:13; 1 Tim. 6:10

SERVANTHOOD

DURING difficult days of war, regardless of one's particular persuasion, everyone owes a mighty debt of gratitude to the men and women of the armed forces of the United States of America who serve, and who risk their lives for freedom. Many people not long ago were touched by the story of a football player named Pat Tillman who walked away from 3.9 million dollars offered to him to play in the NFL. He walked away from a lucrative career because he felt he had an obligation to serve. That choice cost him his life. Our service to God is one that will cost much, even our lives, but we should be willing to fulfill our obligation to serve Him.[823]

[Sacrifice; Service, Motivation for]
Mark 10:45

WE HAVE a computer network in operation on our church campus. This network only functions because of its servers. Servers enable the computers to communicate with each other so that all of the campus computers can "be on the same page." Our capacity to maximize our campus productivity is enhanced because our servers are in place doing their jobs.

God wants a networked campus of hearts who love Him and who love one another because they are networked by servers—men and women who give of themselves because they have received the manifold grace of God.[824]

[Family of God; Service, Motivation for]
John 13:14; Gal. 6:2

MOST folks have a key chain and on that key chain there are a plethora of keys, each designed to open a certain lock. It is quite normal to have a number of keys. There is probably one for the house, one for the car, one for the office, and so on. Each key has been uniquely cut to fit a specific lock in order to enter or gain access to a specific location.

I have a number of keys that look alike, are the same length, and appear similar in shape, but they won't open the same door because they have each been uniquely crafted from a different master key. Each key has been uniquely crafted for a special place.

In our context, God is the master key. He opens everything, but He has uniquely crafted every believer for a specific place in which He wants you to make a difference in the lives of others as a recipient of the manifold grace of God.[825]

[Body of Christ]
Rom. 12:5; 1 Cor. 12:12–31

A WHILE back, Jackie Chan starred in a movie called *The Tuxedo*. He played a taxi cab driver. His job was to serve his customers. He wound up becoming the driver for Clark Devlin, a top secret agent.

During one scene in the movie, the car comes under attack and Clark Devlin becomes critically wounded in the attack. Mr. Devlin tells Jackie Chan to put on a tuxedo located in the car that will give him extraordinary power. The injured passenger told Chan, "When you put my coat on, then you will share in my glory." Jackie Chan put on Clark Devlin's tuxedo and he found powers to walk on walls, do all kinds of flips, and overcome the enemies who would seek to bring destruction—all because he wore the clothing of another.

When you and I put on Jesus Christ and when we wear His character and His glory, we share in His greatness. Don't think you are going to be great if you are not willing to put on His jacket, which is always the jacket of servanthood. If you really want to be somebody in time and in eternity, ask yourself if you are serving others more than they are serving you.[826]

Zech. 3:1–4; Mark 10:45; Luke 9:48

ONE of the greatest hotel chains in America is the Ritz-Carlton. It is known for one thing—its service. The company prides itself on the fact that from the time a customer drives up and gets out of their car until it is time for the customer to check out and drive away, that customer will be served like no other hotel in the country.

Most people recognize good service and they want to be the beneficiary of good service. We recognize that service is important. It makes the difference between what product or service we consider just OK, and that which we think is great.

God says that in the kingdom greatness is measured by your heart of service.[827]

[Service, Motivation for]
Mark 9:35; 10:45; John 13:35

SERVICE, APPROVAL OF

A PROFESSIONAL violinist was giving a concert. When he finished, the crowd jumped up from their seats and gave him a standing ovation. He had delivered a magnificent performance. The young violinist, with tears coming down his cheeks, walked off the stage, dejected. The stagehand saw him and said, "Why are you so sad? Those people are going crazy out there and you are crying. I don't understand."

"Do you see the one man in the center down there? He is still sitting."

The stagehand said, "Yeah, so what? There are two thousand other people who are standing."

"This is true, but you don't understand. That man down there in the middle is my dad. He's also my violin teacher. If he doesn't stand, it doesn't matter what two thousand other people do."

If God doesn't applaud when He sees how you live your life, it doesn't matter what everybody else does.[828]

[Life, Satisfaction with]
Gal. 1:10

SERVICE, MOTIVATION FOR

A FLIGHT attendant one day wanted to go on a trip and she received a seat that was available in first class. At no cost to her, she was able to fly to Europe. An emergency occurred on the airplane that made it so that they were in need of another flight attendant. She raised her hand and let them know she was a fight attendant, and even though she was on vacation taking a trip to Europe, she would be glad to serve as the additional help that was needed. She was not serving to get to Europe; that had already been taken care of. It was part of the package of being a flight attendant for the airline. But she had no problem serving on the airplane either, because she was just so grateful for the benefit to be able to ride to Europe at no cost to her. That service was a joy and not a complaint.

It is unfortunate today that many people are serving Christ in order to earn brownie points to make sure they're saved, rather than serving Christ out of the overwhelming joy of the free ride. God wants your service not as validation for your salvation. He wants your service out of your joy for the assurance of your salvation.[829]

[Salvation, Gratefulness for]
Phil. 2:1–8

SEX

ESKIMOS used to have a very intriguing way of killing the wolves that they would regularly have to fight in the cold lands. They would put a knife in the ice, blade up. They would take animal blood, put it over the knife, and freeze it. A wolf would smell the blood that was now covering the ice and begin to attempt to lick the blood off.

It tasted good to the wolf so the wolf would lick faster and faster and harder and harder, never detecting the sting on its own tongue. All the animal knew was that the blood, unknowingly his own blood, tasted good. The next day the wolf would be dead. It had eaten its own blood because it just couldn't get enough.

We are eating ourselves alive today with sex. We can't get enough. We can't get enough on the TV. We can't get enough on cable. We can't get enough on Playboy channels. We can't get enough on HBO. We can't get enough of the magazines. We can't get enough of Victoria's Secrets. We can't get enough. So, since we can't get enough, we keep licking harder and faster. What we find ourselves doing is aborting more babies, having more children out of wedlock, fighting more diseases because we can't get enough and the judgment for this sin is built in to the disobedience.[830]

[Immorality; Sin, Consequences of]
1 Cor. 6:18; 1 Thess. 4:3–7

IF YOU'RE ever stuck out on an ocean and surrounded by saltwater, don't drink it! The thirst will be real and the need for water will be real but saltwater is not the water that will help you. Saltwater contains such a large ratio of salt that it renders the kidneys unable to handle it properly. The kidneys will produce an increased sensation of thirst because they need water to solve the problem. If the only water around is saltwater and you drink more, you are in effect adding more salt to the kidneys. The excess of salt will kill you. You will end up dying of thirst in a sea of water because that water is not what you need. Indulging in more of what you desire will only lead to destruction.[831]

> [Immorality, Effects of; Sin, Consequences of; Temptation, Leading to Sin]
> 1 Cor. 6:18; James 1:13–15

SEX is the American obsession. It is in fact the drug of choice. While the Puritans may have lived as though there were no such thing as sex, Americans live as though there's nothing else but sex.[832]

> 1 Cor. 6:18; 2 Tim. 2:22

SHARING THE GOSPEL

ONE of the great tragedies in the twentieth century was the sinking of the Titanic. This large ship hit an iceberg and many people died as a result. There is another tragedy with the Titanic. Most of the lifeboats that held people saved from death were only half filled. They were unwilling to turn back and share in their salvation.[833]

> [Witnessing]
> Acts 1:8; 1 Peter 3:15

PAUL Revere is a hero. Because he feared the British, he cried, "The British are coming! The British are coming!" He sounded the alert. Paul Revere's concern was not popularity; it was sounding a warning because he took seriously the coming of the British.

God is coming. His justice is coming. His wrath is coming. Being cute ought not be your first concern.[834]

> [Judgment; Truth, Speaking the; Witnessing]
> Heb. 12:25; 1 Peter 3:15

WHEN a building is on fire and your kid is on the inside, love casts out fear.

Firemen have been known to have to hold back folks that had more love for someone in danger than fear of the danger of fire. The fire is real, but love even more so.[835]

> [Love, Power of; Witnessing, Importance of]
> 1 John 4:18

SIN

SIN is like leprosy or to put it in contemporary terms, it's like cancer. Leprosy is a modern ailment still affecting thousands of people. When you get it, it spreads. The drunk becomes a drunk because he started with his first drink. It spreads; it's like a cancer. And so, when the Bible wants to describe sin graphically, it compares sin to a leprous kind of disease.

Sickness often doesn't happen suddenly. A person may feel a little tired one day and then notice a tickle in the throat the next. Many people ignore sickness at this stage because it doesn't bother them that much or interrupt their life enough for them to take notice. They won't rush to take vitamin C or head to the pharmacy for medicine. They will go on with business as usual. But, very suddenly, something that is insignificant can become significant. Sickness can dominate, knock a person down, and then knock them out. What starts out as a tickle can become a full-blown virus.[836]

> [Temptation, Leading to Sin]
> Matt. 13:33; Luke 13:21; 1 Cor. 5:6; James 1:13–15

IF YOU go to the hospital for an operation, you want your doctor to use sterilized equipment and to be in a sterilized environment because you do not want viruses and bacteria getting in the way of your health. Sin is a spiritual virus that has no place in the sterile environment of God's holiness.[837]

[God's Holiness; Sin,
Contamination by]
2 Cor. 7:1; 1 Peter 1:16

A COLLEGE with an established football team wanted a mascot so they decided to get a goat. The question was where to keep the goat! Two of the students offered to keep the goat in their room. The head of the sports department got wind of this and approached the two students. "Well, I hear you are gonna keep the goat in your room. What about the smell?" One of the students replied, "The goat will get used to it."

Although the goat may get used to it, God doesn't. Sin is a violation, a transgression of the law of God.[838]

[God's Standard; Sin,
Contamination by]
Lev. 11:45; 2 Cor. 7:1

SIN creates an illusion. It creates an illusion that you are in control of it. When my kids were small, I would put them on my lap and drive around a parking lot, letting them hold on to the wheel. They were so excited because they were "driving." They were driving absolutely nothing! It was my foot on the brake, my foot on the accelerator, and my hand underneath the wheel. I had my hand positioned so that my kids could only go so far. They couldn't turn the whole wheel. They only had limited control of the wheel and were under an illusion. They weren't smart enough to have known any better. I'm at fault because I helped them with the illusion. I

made them feel and think that they were driving. I built them up in their excitement; but they drove absolutely nothing. I was in total control all the time. Sin creates an illusion that you are in control until it decides to bite.[839]

Prov. 16:33

SIN is like a woodpecker. It keeps pecking at your life. Now, when you look at the individual pecks, it's not all that bad. But when the job is over, you've got a hole in the tree of your life.[840]

[Sin, Consequences of]

BE UNSPOTTED. Don't be defiled by the world. If a person was to walk around with a big, red stain on his shirt, most of us would notice. We'd be thinking thoughts like, "He's got a stain on his shirt!" or "Boy, how could his wife let him come out of the house like that with a stain on his shirt?" or "Boy, he's sure unclean and unkempt." That stain would become a distraction. It would do more than damage that one spot; it would detract from the impression of the whole person.

Some Christians brag because their whole life isn't filthy. Your whole life doesn't have to be filthy. All you need is a stain.[841]

[Sin, Contamination by;
Sin Nature, Residue of]
James 1:27; 1 John 1:8

IF YOU were in an operating room and the doctor was getting ready to cut you with the scalpel, how comfortable would you feel if he said, "Don't worry. The scalpel is just a little dirty. It's not a lot dirty. I may have coughed a little bit on it but at least it wasn't rubbed in mud. Don't worry about a little dirt." You would say, "You're not the doctor and that's not the scalpel." Why? Because it doesn't take much in an operating room for bacteria to seep in and for you to become infected. You don't have to dig the scalpel in mud to believe that it's dirty. Just a little bit of lack of sterilization means you're subject to contamination.[842]

[Sin, Contamination by; Sin Nature, Residue of]
James 1:27

A LITTLE boy came to his father and said, "Dad, I'm eight feet tall." His father looked at him and said, "You can't be; you're not eight feet tall." The boy insisted, "Yes I am, Dad. I'm eight feet tall. The ruler says I'm eight feet tall." The father smiled and asked his son to show him the ruler. It was a six-inch ruler.

If you use the wrong standard, you'll come up with the wrong conclusion. You'll think you're something that you're not. The Bible says "all have sinned" and the only standard that works is the standard that Christ set by living a perfect life.[843]

[God's Standard]
Rom. 3:23; 1 John 1:8

SIN, AVOIDANCE OF

AN EVANGELIST had to travel often to preach. On one trip, he arrived at his hotel and proceeded to go to his room, which was on the fifth floor. The man got on the elevator and a lady with a lot of baggage got on too. She noticed that he had pressed the button for the fifth floor and told him that she was going to the same floor. The evangelist, being a gentleman at heart, offered to help her since they were going to the same floor anyway and because she was so

weighed down by her baggage. They arrived at their floor and the evangelist proceeded to help her carry her bags to her room. When they finally got to her door, the woman said, "Oh, sir, thank you very much, won't you come in for a while?" The minister politely declined and hurried to his room. When retelling this story to a close friend, his friend said, "So, you were obedient to the Word in fleeing immorality because of your fear of God." The evangelist replied, "No, I think I was fleeing immorality out of the fear of my wife!"[844]

[Temptation, Exit from]
Gen. 39:1–12; 1 Cor. 6:18

SIN, CONFESSION OF

I WAS attending one of my sons' football games and accidentally spilled some Coke on my shirt. It wasn't intentional, but I still did it and it still produced a stain. If I had spilled it intentionally, it would have been a stain. If I had spilled it by mistake, it would have been a stain. Either way it's a stain and it needed to be cleansed. Now, what I didn't do is take off my shirt and dip it in the Coke!

Don't let the fact that you have Tide at home cause you to dip your life in sin. Don't say that just because you've got a washing machine and a dryer at home that I should just get as dirty as I can.

God recognizes that every now and then Coke is going to spill. He recognizes that every now and then maybe you'll get sloppy and something might go wrong. He wants us to know that when sin happens, we do have a way to be cleansed. We do have a Tide. We do have a washing machine. We do have confession. But we shouldn't abuse the privilege of confession. The point is to confess our sins when we need to because life happens—not to engage in as much sin as possible because God has made it possible to confess our sins to Him.[845]

[Forgiveness, of Sin]
Rom. 6:15

SIN, CONSEQUENCES OF

THE MOMENT you pick a flower, it dies because it's been separated from its source of life although it doesn't appear dead yet. But the seeds of death are automatically built in to the breaking of fellowship. When you cut the flower off from the tree or the vine, fellowship is immediately broken between the flower and the vine. If you hand somebody that flower, you will have just handed somebody death. Now, it be may be red death, yellow death, or pink death. Just give it a little time and that death will become extraordinarily evident as the petals drop from the flower, change colors, and get old. As well intentioned as you may have been in sharing that flower, death is actually what you will have given them. Lack of fellowship of the flower with the vine results in death.[846]

[Death; Immorality, Effects of]
John 15:5; Eph. 4:17–19

YOU DON'T have to like the law of gravity, but it is in your best interest to respect it. You don't have to prefer it, but it's not going to change for you. It is a law of nature. It is a divine law, not a negotiated law.

You may say, "Gravity, you are not going to tell me what to do. It's my thing and I'm going to do what I want to do. You are not my boss, Gravity! You are not my instructor! I'm my own man and I'm going to do what I want to do!

"In fact, Gravity, just to let you know how I feel about you, I'm going to rebel. I'm going to get up on the top of this church building and I am going to despise you. I'm going to jump. What do you think about that?"

The law of gravity won't stop you. The law of gravity won't hold you back. You can jump and, for a moment, a short moment, it may appear like you have outwitted and outsmarted gravity. It may appear like you have had the last word, but a few seconds later as we sweep you up off the pavement, it will become abundantly clear that you have adjusted to gravity; gravity did not adjust to you. Sin has consequences.[847]

[Immorality, Effects of; Rebellion]
Rom. 6:23; Gal. 6:7–8

THERE was a parrot that had a foul mouth. It cursed like a sailor. A lady went into the pet store and fell in love with the parrot. It was cute to look at, even though it had a terrible mouth. The lady figured it would be OK. She would buy it and then train it to talk differently. So she took the parrot home and worked with it. She successfully turned it into a Christian talking parrot. She trained the parrot to say phrases like, "Praise the Lord!" and "Hallelujah!"

One day she forgot to feed the parrot. The parrot was ticked off and went back to his old ways. It started cussing like a sailor. The lady figured she had to teach the parrot a lesson. So she put the parrot in the freezer. After about five or ten minutes, she took the parrot out and asked it, "Have you learned your lesson?"

The parrot said, "Yeeesssss, ma'am." Everything went well for a while; he went back to praising the Lord and saying Christian things.

About four or five months later, the lady forgot to feed the parrot again. He again went back to his old ways. The lady carried him out of the cage and back to the freezer, saying, "I told you, we're not going to have this kind of language in my house!" She put the parrot in but forgot about it. It dawned on her hours later that she'd left her parrot in the freezer. She ran into the kitchen and got the parrot out. When it finally thawed out, the lady asked, "Have you learned your lesson now?"

"Oooooohhhh, yyyyyeeeeeeeesssss, maaaaa'am! But can I ask you a question?"

"Yes, what is it?"

"I thought I knew every curse word there was, but I guess that I don't. What words exactly did the turkey say?"[848]

[Immorality, Effects of; Judgment]

SIN, CONTAMINATION BY

ONE day my granddaughter decided to fix me breakfast. It really wasn't that hard for her to do because she was fixing me cold cereal. She was fixing one of her favorite cereals, Lucky Charms. When the bowl was placed in front of me, I saw that there was a problem. Lucky Charms is full of marshmallows and I don't like marshmallows. The cereal part is fine with me. It is the marshmallows that cause me great concern because I really don't like marshmallows. But, marshmallows were everywhere. They were spread throughout the cereal. So I got a paper towel, laid it beside the bowl, and began the tedious process of removing marshmallows from my cereal. One after another, I began moving marshmallows out of my cereal so I could eat. The marshmallows looked like they were multiplying. It seemed like the more I removed, the more there were to remove. It got so that after awhile, I didn't even want to eat cereal anymore. I got tired of trying to fix the good by getting rid of the bad.

Our physical frames have been absolutely and completely contaminated by sin. It is a task with no end to try to get rid of the stuff that is keeping us from being the kind of people God wants us to be.[849]

[Grace, Need for; Salvation, Need for; Sin, Dealing with; Sin Nature, Residue]

Rom. 3:23; Eph. 2:8–9; 1 John 1:8

SIN, DEALING WITH

MANY people have the habit of killing roaches, one at a time, as they appear in their homes. They will chase a roach, corner it, and stomp on it. The problem is, their success will be short-lived because they have only dealt with the roach that they see. Behind that roach, there is probably a whole family of roaches. Dealing with one roach doesn't truly address the problem. Unless the roaches hidden in the walls are dealt with, the satisfaction of getting rid of one roach is only a momentary success. In order to deal with the real problem, the Orkin man must be called.

That's the problem with sin. When a Christian is operating in the flesh, victory over sin is possible, but only for a little while. The symptoms of sin can be handled one at a time but they will keep coming back because there is always more than what we see.

When we call the Orkin man, he has never asked me to help him. He has never asked for my support. In fact, I have to leave so that he can effectively deal with my problem. When we call on Jesus Christ to come deal with our problems, He is not interested in helping me with my life. He wants to be my life.[850]

[Sin, Contamination by]
Rom. 7:24; Eph. 2:8–9

SOMETIMES, dealing with sin is not a pleasant experience. It can often be downright painful.

If you have an upset stomach, there are a few things you can do to try to feel better. Maybe you will lie down and hope that the feeling will pass. Maybe you can eat some gentle foods in hopes that will settle your stomach. Sometimes you may go to the nearest drugstore to purchase some medicine you think may help you. If that medicine doesn't help you, you may go back to the drugstore and pick up two or three more bottles of medicine that may be a bit stronger. But after all this, if your efforts don't work, if the over-the-counter solution is not working, you will make the decision to call the doctor. You decide to go to the expert because maybe something deeper is wrong.

So you go to the doctor and tell him your symptoms. The doctor may decide to put you through a battery of tests. He could take blood, or do an X-ray. In order to look into your system with specialized equipment, he may even make you drink stuff that tastes even worse than all the medicine you used before from the drugstore.

All of these tests may leave you feeling more miserable than before you came to see your doctor. With all the poking, prodding, and pressing, you may feel worse now than before. Why would the doctor make things worse? Simple: he's looking for something deeper.

When the doctor gets the tests back and tells you that you have an ulcer, you will be glad you went to see him for help. Why? Because there is no way you could have known about this problem on your own. Because of his tests, which make things worse for a while, you are able to discover the root of your problem.[851]

[Trials, Benefits of; Trials,
Endurance during]
Rom. 5:3–5; James 1:2–4

ONE of my home responsibilities is emptying the trash (yes, I still empty the trash). On Tuesdays and Fridays, my task is to make sure that the trash is in the trash can. I tend to delay emptying the trash until the trash absolutely has to be emptied. I receive help in delaying my task because I own a trash compactor. At the push of a button I can press accumulated trash down and keep from having to take it out.

What a lot of us do in our lives is accumulate trash. We just keep packing it down. We don't get rid of it. We just continue to mash it down, creating room for more of the same and allow the accumulation to control the smell of the atmosphere.[852]

[Flesh, Walking in; Sin,
Confession of]
Prov. 28:13; 1 John 1:9

WE HAVE lights in our cars today that let us know when something is not right with our engine. There are lights for checking the engine, checking the coolant system, and checking the tires.

One time, my check coolant system light was on and had been on for four months! I wished that light wouldn't come on. I didn't want that light to come on. It irritated me when it came on. But that light still kept coming on. It was trying to tell me that I had a problem and it was going to keep blinking until I took it to the manufacturer to check the car out.

Now, if I wouldn't have ever taken that car to be checked out, eventually I'd have a much bigger problem on my hands. The light was there to give me a warning that would drive me to the manufacturer.

The Bible is shining and throwing up various caution signals and lights. It shows us where we sin and where we offend God. If we don't go to the Maker and allow Him to address the issues in our life, we are going to end up with much bigger problems on our hands in years to come.[853]

[Bible, Guidance of; Conscience;
Holy Spirit, Guidance]
2 Chron. 19:10; Rom. 2:14–15

FOCUSING on your sin to get rid of your sin is like a person on a diet focusing on a Pizza Hut menu so that they can learn better what they need to avoid. It's counterproductive. If you know you need to stay away from pizza, Pizza Hut menus are not what you study. It will only make you hungrier for things you're trying to get rid of.[854]

[Temptation]
Heb. 12:2; James 1:13–15

ONE of the worst medical tests you can take is a colonoscopy. It is one of the worst tests known to man. It's not so much the test; it's the stuff you have to drink to get ready for the test. It's the nastiest stuff I've ever tasted in my life. Recently, someone thought it would be smart to give it a flavor. So, now it's flavored AND nasty.

But there is a reason they have you drink this stuff. It is designed to help the doctor keep you healthy. The nasty stuff cleans out the colon, so that the doctor can see clearly when he looks into the body for any signs of cancer or polyps. That nasty stuff helps him to do his job. When you have to undergo this procedure, you have to drink the nasty stuff so that he can do his best to make sure that you are in good health.

If we don't take the time to cleanse from sin, the risks of the polyps and cancer of sin and the consequences of sin only loom larger. When you mourn over your sin for a while, it is not a pleasant experience. Sometimes it is downright nasty. It's all good, though. God's ultimate desire is our spiritual health. We must do what is necessary, deal with our sin, so that we can stay in good spiritual health.[855]

Matt. 5:3

SIN, EFFECTS OF

OUR human understanding of God's ways is limited and hindered by our sin. When there is unaddressed sin in a Christian's life, God's way will not be revealed. When you and I have unaddressed sin in our lives, His way will not be revealed. Our sinfulness creates static on the line.

Many people have satellite systems in their home. If the weather gets rainy or stormy, the picture on the TV via the satellite may blink off and on, or even show a message that says, "Searching for a signal."

Christians today are searching for a signal. They are trying to figure out God's way and figure out what God is up to, but they can't receive the signal that God is broadcasting. This is because there is a disruption in the atmosphere called sin.[856]

[God's Voice; Immorality, Effects of]
Isa. 59:2; Luke 11:28; 2 Cor. 4:4

MANY Christians will never get clarity about their situations because there is unaddressed sin in their lives. Sin, like rotten garbage, repulses God and sends Him the other way. God will not skip sin to give blessing. He won't just ignore it and decide not to worry about it. Why? Even though He loves His children, He can't compromise His character. He can't stop being God just to make a Christian feel better.

There are people who struggle with allergies because the air has been contaminated with dust and pollen. Allergies can make life miserable. In order for the allergies to get better, the air that a person breathes in has got to get cleaner. In order for God to clarify His way, the way, the air must get holier.[857]

[God's Standard; Holiness, Importance of]
2 Chron. 7:14; Ps. 66:18; Isa. 59:2

MANY of the old football and baseball stadiums these days are being torn down and new ones are being built in their place. The older ones were okay, but they had features in them that modern technology has now improved on. One of the problems in any of the older stadiums is that much of the seating in certain areas had an obstructed view where the fans became somewhat disconnected from the activity on the field. A beam or a post would block full participation in the sporting event.

Oftentimes if you were seated in one of these seats behind a column, a fan would ask another person what happened. They'd have to get secondhand information because they couldn't see it for themselves. They could hear the noise. They could hear the shouts. They could hear the excitement, but the column kept them from being a full participant in the activities.

Many of us are in this stadium called the church and we're worshipping God with an obstructed view because of sin. We hear the noise. We hear the singing, the celebration, and the meditation, but many of us are getting it all secondhand. We're sitting in a seat, but we're sitting in a seat with an obstructed view. Sin will keep us from full participation. It will keep a Christian from experiencing the reality of God operating in their lives.[858]

[Church; Holiness, Importance of;

Immorality, Effects of]
2 Chron. 7:14; Ps. 66:18; Isa. 59:2

IF YOU listen to your favorite radio station as you head out of town, you will quickly discover that as you head down the highway, the farther you get away from the city, the weaker the signal gets. Eventually, if you keep driving away from the signal, you will not be able to get your radio station at all.

This is what sin does. It distances us from the Father. The farther we go away from Him, the less of Him we can hear.[859]

[Immorality, Effects of]
2 Chron. 7:14; Ps. 66:18; Isa. 59:2

SIN, IN THE BELIEVER

WHEN a person becomes a believer, their flesh still has a propensity toward sin. It's like having termites in the wall of a house. The structure of the house is contaminated by an invasive element that is doing damage. Now, some people's contamination is obvious. Holes in the wall and chewing on the wood are visible. It has become obvious that these folks are inhabited by something. In other people, the contamination by sin is not as visible. These people have money to hide it and to do paint jobs. Either way, the sin is there and the building is still infested.

God has condemned the flesh, the building, because it has been contaminated by sin. Your body is so condemned, God isn't even going to try to fix it. He is going to raise you up with a brand-new body because this one cannot be restored.[860]

[Carnal Christians; Flesh; Sin Nature, Residue of]
Rom. 7:14–20

SIN, JUDGMENT ON

I HAVE a basic philosophy about roaches. The only good roach is a dead roach. That's right. That's my philosophy. If I come out late at night, turn on the light, and see a roach, that roach is in big-time trouble. Why? Because I'm going to kill it dead. I'm going to kill it with passion. I won't just kill that one roach either. I'm going to kill its mother. I'm going to kill its father. I'm going to kill its children. I hope to find the roach at its family reunion so that I can wipe out the clan. I have no mercy on roaches. While one roach may be cleaner than another roach, they are all still roaches and they deserve to die.[861]

[Judgment; Sin, Dealing with]
Rom. 3:23

SIN, SOURCE OF

THE EXORCISM of Emily Rose is a very interesting movie. It is about a girl possessed by a demon and the attempt by others in the movie to get rid of it. They try everything to get rid of this demon, but the process is difficult because the girl experiences violent episodes when they are trying to exorcise it. Realizing that they need to control her episodes, they give the girl a medication called Gambutrol.

The medicine did its job and calmed her down, but it also caused a different problem. It put the girl in a state of consciousness that blocked their ability to complete the exorcism. The girl was not able to fully function and receive the benefit of the attempted exorcism. The medicine not only fixed her reaction to the demon, but it also kept her from experiencing complete deliverance.

A lot of people settle for stuff

that makes them feel better, but that also prevents them from dealing firmly with deeply rooted spiritual issues. They are content to settle for short-term solutions that provide a temporary fix, but don't get rid of the real problem.[862]

[Demons; Forgiveness, of Sin; Sin, Dealing with]

MOST of us have seen holes in apples. Most people don't eat an apple with a hole in it to the core. The reason why most people won't eat an apple with a hole in it to the core is they're afraid of what they might bite into. They wonder what exactly bore down in there and created the hole in the apple.

If you ever see an apple with a hole in it down to the core, feel free to eat. The hole to the core is a hole put there by what drilled out, not what drilled in. When the seed was growing, the larvae of the worm got on it and the apple grew up around the "problem." When the worm hatched, it bore itself out of its situation, eating its way out. The exterior of the bright, shiny apple had contamination inside.

Sin is resident on the inside. What we see on the outside of people's lives is simply the external illustration or the seed of sin inside.[863]

Matt. 15:18; 23:25–28; Luke 11:39–40

SIN, STAIN OF

IF YOU get pen marks on your clothes, they are hard to get out. Messing up clothes with pens is, in fact, a specialty of mine. I always keep my pen in either my pants or shirt pocket and sometimes I forget to put the cap on and cover the point.

I have a pair of pants that are one of my favorites. I have a big blue stain near the pocket of these pants, so every time I wear those pants, I have to wear a jacket. If I don't, people will focus on my stain, no matter how good I look in those pants. I don't want people talking about me or my stained pants so I cover it up.

Thank goodness that I now know of a great cleaners in town that specializes in getting ink stains out of clothes.

We all have stains. Some of us have really bad stains on our lives. Some of us are stained so badly that all the scrubbing we've tried to do hasn't done a thing to get the stains out. But I know a cleaners in glory that can take care of the worst possible stains that you and I have gotten on our lives. He is a specialist in stain removal and He wants to remove the stains. He wants us to be able to walk around clean so the world will have no basis of accusing us. He wants us clean so that we can stand in the day of judgment.[864]

[Forgiveness, of Sin; Grace, Need for; Salvation, Need for]

1 Cor. 7:31; 2 Peter 3:14

SIN, STANDARD OF

ONE day there was a tall man's parade in the army. In the tall man's parade, you had to be a certain height to be in the parade. In this particular bunk, there were three guys who wanted to go out and be a part of the parade. One was named Chubby. He was kind of short and plump. Another was named Jim. He was sort of midsized. The tallest of these three was named Slim, and he was fairly tall.

Well, the officer came in and he put a mark on the door. The three guys had to back themselves up against the door to determine whether they could be in the tall man's parade. Chubby looked at the mark and he didn't even bother to stand by the door. He knew it was too high and he would never qualify. Jim figured he would give it a try. He backed up against the door, but alas, he was too short. Slim began to laugh at Chubby. "You tub of short fatness! You just couldn't make it to the mark, could you? Sorry, Jim. You just didn't have enough genetic support, huh?" Slim confidently backed himself up against the mark of the door.

The officer stopped by to check Slim's height. "Sorry, Slim. You are one-eighth of an inch too short."

"But wait a minute, what do you mean? I'm taller than Chubby!"

"I know, but you're too short for the parade."

"But I'm taller than Jim!"

"You're right, but you're too short for the parade."

"But, I'm only a fraction of an inch too short!"

The officer said, "You might as well be two feet too short! We can't reduce the standard even if it's by one-eighth of an inch."

You may be taller than your neighbor, but you're too short for God. You may be taller than your co-worker, but you're too short for God. You may be only one-eighth of an inch too short, but since God's glory and His righteousness requires perfection, you might as well be a criminal on death row. When it comes to the standard of God, nothing short of

perfection is acceptable. Your best in the face of a holy God adds up to be zero.[865]

[God's Standard; Grace, Need for]
John 14:6; Rom. 3:23; Eph. 2:8–9

SIN, VICTORY OVER

MY WIFE loves to keep a clean home. But there is one thing my wife despises when it comes to cleaning: she hates cleaning tubs. She doesn't like cleaning tubs. She asked me when we first got married if I would be willing to do two housekeeping things: one was to take out the trash; the other was to clean the tubs.

I've cleaned my share of tubs and it's hard work. Number one, it's uncomfortable. You've got to get down on your knees. You've got to lean over and scrub. Then you have to rinse. If the tub is not fully clean, then you have to go through the whole process again. But as technology got better, I went to the store one day and I saw that they had come up with a cleaner that you simply poured on the tub or sprayed on the ring, and it penetrated the dirt. You would know it was working because it would bubble and foam up. It would begin to remove the dirt that had accumulated on the tub.

Many of us are getting down on our knees and trying to scrub the mess out of our lives. However, there is a shelf cleaner in the heavenly supermarket that has been designed to do the work for you. If you'll simply apply walking in the Spirit in your spiritual life, He will bubble up the mess that is in you so that all you've got to do is wipe it clean, not work it out. All you'll have to do is take advantage of what He's already done. The anointing of the Spirit means that when you think in terms of the Spirit and then you act in terms of what you think based on your new identity in Christ, He sets you free.[866]

> [Holy Spirit, Filling of; Spirit, Filled with; Spirit, Walking in]
>
> Ps. 51:7; Acts 22:16

SIN NATURE, DEATH OF

GOD wants you to know that the sin nature has died, or to put it in the words of *The Wizard of Oz*, the wicked old witch is dead. Now, when Dorothy's house fell on the wicked witch, what did they do? They partied and they celebrated because the wicked witch was dead.

Here's what we don't do. Instead of praising God that the sin factory has been shut down, we go around thinking the sin factory is still open. We are deceived by the Evil One. We ought to be praising God that the wicked witch is dead rather than thinking that the factory is still open.[867]

> [Deception, Satan's; Satan, Lies of; Sin, Victory over]

YOUR sin factory was shut down when you accepted Jesus Christ as your Savior. However, even though the factory closed down, it did not alleviate the flesh. Since the factory called sin is shut down, but the flesh has not shut down, then the sin nature and the flesh are not the same thing. What then is the flesh that's still alive and operating as opposed to the sin nature that has shut down?

Simply stated, when the sin nature shut down, what the sin nature had produced had to find someplace to lodge itself. So, the factory shut down but what it had produced had to find some place to call home, and what it found was your body. The flesh is the body that has now been inhabited by the patterns of sin established when the sin factory was alive.

The General Motors factory in Arlington, Texas, shut down. Though the factory is shut down, there are still cars riding up and down the highways that were produced at this factory. While shutting down the factory solves the problem of future production, it doesn't get rid of what has already been produced.

When you accepted Jesus Christ, God killed the old person you used to be before you met Jesus Christ. He did this without changing your essential personality or your essential soul. He shut down the factory called sin. However, that factory has been producing a lot of stuff for a lot of years, and the stuff that was produced by the factory has now lodged itself in the body. The new nature can't produce sin. It's impossible. But everything the factory of sin produced is still riding on the highway of the flesh.[868]

> [Flesh; Sin, in the Believer; Sin Nature, Residue of]
>
> Rom. 6:6; Gal. 2:20

SIN NATURE, RESIDUE OF

I KNOW that when we go to Israel and I come back from Israel, I will suffer from jet lag. I will leave the country of Israel, and return to Dallas, but when I arrive home, I'll probably be good for nothing for a few days. Why? Because

I will carry the residual effect of my trip.

When you come to Jesus Christ, He transports you to heavenly places. He seats you on the right hand of the Father. But even seated there, you carry the residual effects of the trip. When you're transported to Jesus Christ, you will still feel the residual effects of sin when you were owned by your sin nature. You're still in the body where sin has made itself at home.[869]

[Flesh; Sin, in the Believer; Sin Nature, Residue of]

Rom. 6:6; Gal. 2:20; Eph. 4:22

SINGLENESS

IF YOU are single, God says you ought to be free. Free from what? Free from concern. The desire for a marriage partner should not preoccupy you. Singles, who are concentrating on marriage, are like folks who drive and talk on their cell phones. As a matter of fact, there are laws now in various states to stop people from talking on their cell phones because they are too distracted. They are running through red lights, bumping into the cars, and causing havoc on the highway. State after state now is coming up with laws to say, "If you are going to drive, drive. If you are going to talk, talk. Don't talk and drive, because you are going to hurt somebody." People who are preoccupied with marriage put themselves in a position of being hurt or hurting others.[870]

1 Cor. 7:1–40

SINGLENESS, WAITING

I HAD to fly to Memphis once to speak briefly at a meeting and the plane was delayed. I got a little nervous because when I got to Memphis I still had to drive an hour away to Jackson, Tennessee. I wasn't dressed for the engagement. I had my clothes in a hanging bag to change into after the drive. I thought I'd have time to go to the hotel room before I spoke. An hour later, we still hadn't boarded. An hour and a half later, we still hadn't boarded. We stayed on the runway for another thirty minutes before we took off.

When we finally arrived in Memphis, a man was there to pick me up. I told him that I was worried that we wouldn't have enough time to get to the meeting. He told me not to worry. They would wait.

I told him that I was concerned that I wouldn't have time enough to change into appropriate attire. He told me not worry. He told me that he'd take me to his father's house and I could change there.

After driving for an hour, he exited the highway and took me to his father's house to change. I was rushing to change because I hate being late. My escort told me to take my time. He told me that the people would wait. I was all sweating and frustrated and irritated trying to rush and get ready. Dressed and ready to head out, I looked at the clock. We were indeed late for the engagement. The man saw me look at my watch and reminded me yet again not to worry and that the folks would wait.

A few moments later, I walked into this glorious grand ballroom filled with thousands of people. I came in and they stood up to applaud. Not only did they wait, but they celebrated my arrival.

Some single folks have been waiting at the airport a long time.

They'll wait. Some of you have been hanging on the runway a long time, but they'll wait. Yes I know, you're dressed in your old clothes and you don't look yet like you want to look and you don't yet have what you want to have or can't afford what you want to afford. They'll wait. Take your time. Those spouses you are praying for will wait. When you step into their picture, they will be ready and waiting to stand and applaud your arrival in their lives.[871]

[Marriage]

SOUL

WITHOUT the execution of the righteousness that has been planted or credited to the soul, the soul starves. The soul starves because it needs nutrition that it is not receiving. So many people, in spite of the fact they go to church, in spite of the fact they are religious, are starving spiritually because they're not hungering and thirsting after the right thing that the soul is requiring. The soul, in order to flourish, requires righteousness or at least a person seeking to align himself in accordance with the will of God.

If you fill up your car with diesel fuel, you'll be in for a rough ride. The motor of a car is not designed to receive it. Now, you may be full of diesel, but you're not going to get very far. While the gas indicator may show you that you are full, your car will be full of that which the motor cannot receive. You need unleaded fuel because that is what the car has been built to receive.

Many of us are putting stuff in our souls that the soul is not designed to receive, and we wonder why, if we're so full, we are not making strides forward. It is because we are giving our souls that which the manufacture does not require.

God requires righteousness. Seeking to align oneself with the will of God and living according to the new nature only produces righteousness. Anything else will cause problems under the hood of your life.[872]

[Christian Living; Spiritual Food; Spiritual Maturity, Lack of]

Isa. 59:2

A LADY one day was driving down the street. She noticed in her rearview mirror that a huge truck seemed to be following her a little too close. She sped up to kind of create some more distance, only to discover that the truck sped up too. The faster she went, the faster he went. She made a right turn; he made a right turn. She made a left turn; he made a left turn. She got on the expressway; he got on the expressway. She took an exit; so did he.

Terror began to sweep over her as it became clear she was being followed. It was at night and she needed to do something, so she pulled into an all-night gas station where there was light and where there were people. She rushed out of the car and ran inside; the man in the truck pulled right behind her into the gas station, rushed out of the truck, but then instead of rushing into the store where she was, he rushed to her car and pulled open the back door, reached inside, and jerked out a man who had hidden himself in the backseat.

What the lady didn't know was that the one she was running from was her savior. This would-be rapist was going to hurt her but because the man driving the truck was sitting high and looking low, he was able to see this unsuspecting character sneak into her car. The lady, however, had a distorted view. She thought she knew what was going on when in reality, she was totally unaware of what was really happening.

Many of us are living life with a distorted view; we are running in fear from the wrong thing. We spend a lot of time and energy trying to fix our souls and our personalities. We spend time making New Year's resolutions, going to self-help seminars, and promising ourselves we will do better. Our souls are not the enemy; they are not what we should try and fix.[873]

[Life, Fixing]

SOWING AND REAPING

WHEN it comes to living your life, think agriculturally, not industrially. When it comes to living your life, think like a farmer, not like a technocrat. When it comes to your life, think gardens, not microwaves.[874]

[Life, Management of]
Matt. 13:1–9; Gal. 6:7–8

WHEN a person chooses to sow into the flesh, the crop that the flesh produces is called corruption. The word *corruption* means degeneration, which is to go from better to worse. Corruption means decay.

A decaying character always results in a decaying life. You sow a thought; you reap an act. You sow an act; you reap a habit. You sow a habit; you reap a character. You sow a character; you reap a destiny.[875]

[Immorality, Effects of; Sin, Consequences of]
Gal. 6:7–8

LAST week, I went to my refrigerator to get me some milk so I could eat my Rice Krispies. Ever since my childhood, I've loved Snap, Crackle, and Pop. So on this morning, I poured the cold milk onto the cereal and prepared to enjoy it. I put the first spoonful in my mouth, and thought I was going to gag. The milk had turned on me. It had decayed. It was past the date. I spit it out. The milk had become corrupted.[876]

[Sin, Contamination by]

SPIRIT, FILLED WITH

WHEN a person is drunk, we say they are under the influence. The influence of alcohol on the brain affects their movement. A drunken person doesn't walk like they normally walk. They stagger. A person under the influence will exhibit changes in their personality. They think they can sing when they can't. Their speech and coordination are impacted. Something else has taken over the brain. The filling of alcohol leads to control by alcohol.[877]

[Holy Spirit, Filling of]
Acts 2:1–21; Eph. 5:18

MASSIVE campaigns have been launched to carry the message "Don't Drink and Drive." The idea is that if a person is going to choose to drink, they should also plan to have a friend do the driving. The person agrees to be drunk and relinquish control.

To be filled with the Spirit is to turn control over to someone else. It is to be governed and guided by the work of the Holy Spirit. It is to let the Holy Spirit do the driving.[878]

[Holy Spirit, Filling of; Surrender, Concept of]
Matt. 10:39; Rom. 12:1; Eph. 5:18

A BOY went to the country to visit his aunt and uncle. One evening, he noticed his aunt enjoying a drink.

"Hey, Auntie, what's that you are drinking?"

"Do you want to taste it?"

"Sure!"

The boy tasted it and found it to be the nastiest thing he'd ever tasted in his life. When he asked his aunt how she could bring herself to taste such terrible stuff, his aunt said, "Oh, I've acquired a taste for it."

Being filled with the Spirit may seem like quite a different experience, but if you taste it enough, you'll like the effect, and you will acquire a taste.[879]

[Holy Spirit, Filling of]
Eph. 5:18

THE MOMENT you pull away from the filling station, dissipation occurs. As you drive, you use up the gasoline. Over time you will burn gas. The length of time from full to empty depends on how far you travel, how fast you travel, and the amount of air-conditioning or heat used. The fuel indicator slowly goes from full to empty because driving the car uses the energy the fuel provides. Eventually the car will need to be filled up again with gasoline. The filling of a car is an ongoing responsibility.

In the same way, as we live life, we get drained spiritually. We go to church, have our devotions, and spend time in fellowship with other Christian believers so that we can fill our tanks. But as we live our lives, we run empty as we expend our spiritual energy doing the work God has for us. In order to continue to do the work, we have to continue to get refilled.[880]

[Spiritual Food]
Rom. 15:13

SPIRIT, POWER OF

THE ENGINE of a car lies under the hood. The engine "dwells" there. Even when the car is stopped, not moving, or sitting on the lot, dwelling underneath the hood is an invisible power source.

What is the engine there designed to do? It is designed to take the car somewhere. Only a fool would bother to push a perfectly brand-new automobile up a hill. There is no point in pushing something that has the power to carry you! Why would a person put forth effort to push a car that has the power to deliver them to their destination? Because we understand that concept, we don't push our cars; we sit inside our cars and let the cars transport us.

When the Spirit of God indwells the believer, and that believer has set his mind on Christ, he has the power to drive.[881]

[Holy Spirit, Power of]
Rom. 8:11; Eph. 3:16

SPIRIT, WALKING IN

WALKING in the Spirit involves direction, dependency, and dedication. When we walk, we do so because we are headed somewhere. That is direction. When we walk, we put one foot in front of another, leaning all of our weight on one leg for each step. That is dependency. When we walk, and are attempting to go somewhere, we take continuous steps. One step is not walking. Continuous steps are. You have to keep taking steps in order to get someplace. This is dedication. Direction, dependency, and dedication are just as necessary in our spiritual walk.[882]

[Perseverance]
Job 17:9; Gal. 6:9

YOU CAN'T put a CD in a cassette tape player. You can't do it. The CD won't fit, nor will it play because the cassette player is not constructed to take that media form. We fail to walk in the Spirit when we attempt to take spiritual information and give it to the flesh to operate. It won't work.[883]

[Flesh, Walking in]
Rom. 12:2

WALKING in the Spirit brings intimacy with God. In movie theaters, the films are shown on large screens so that the picture is visible to all. Moviegoers are usually more than a few feet away. They see the picture but from a distance. In 3-D movies, moviegoers are given special glasses. Looking at the film with these glasses creates a different viewing experience altogether. The pictures leap off the screen and seem close enough to touch.

For many Christians, God seems to be at a distance. He's way out there in the heavens. We know He created the sun, the stars, the moon, and the universe. We believe in God. We love God. But, when it comes to a 3-D experience, He doesn't seem close enough to touch.

Walking in the Spirit magnifies our experience with God and allows us to see Him with special lenses. It allows us to have a 3-D experience.[884]

[God, Knowing; Jesus, Relationship with]
Deut. 4:7; Ps. 71:12; James 4:8

MANY airports have moving sidewalks. They allow travelers to get around the airports a little faster than they would walking around on their own power. The travelers can still walk but now are able to do so with ease because of the force underneath them propelling them forward. Walking in the Spirit implies that the Christian is still on the move. They are not sitting down or being passive. They walk but with the Spirit's help guiding them, governing them, and getting them to their destination.[885]

[Holy Spirit, Guidance]
John 16:13; Gal. 5:16

LEARNING to walk in the Spirit is like a baby learning how to walk. At first, it can be awkward and a little wobbly. When a baby has been crawling for a while, it takes some time to develop the level of comfort and strength needed to walk well. Falls will happen frequently. Though the learning process is not always smooth, sooner or later the baby discovers that the ability to walk will get him a lot farther than he used to get when he crawled on his knees.[886]

[Spiritual Maturity, Growth]
1 Cor. 13:11

IF YOU have ever seen a fish out of water, you know that it just flops around, wiggling and jumping all over the place. If it's out of water, it's also out of where it's supposed to be. It's out of its intended environment. The fish is trying to move but it can't go anywhere because it's not in the environment it was made to be in. So it flops and twists and flips, absolutely going nowhere. Why? Because it's trying to be fishy in a nonwater environment and it wasn't created for that. So no matter how much flipping and flopping it does, all it's doing is running out of breath. The fish will die because it is not in its home.

A lot of Christians are flipping and flopping, trying to do better, but we are running out of breath and getting tired because we are not doing it in the right environment. The environment for living our Christian lives has to be the Spirit.[887]

[Life, Management of]
Gal. 5:16–25

SPIRITUAL AUTHORITY, CONCEPT OF

WHEN a policeman stands and directs traffic, as they put up a hand, cars will stop. But the cars do not stop because of the policeman's power. They stop because of the policeman's legal authority. That blue uniform makes him superman. He can't put out his hands and physically stop a line of cars from running over him, but when he puts out his hands, cars stop because the blue uniform, with the badge, gives him legal authority. That legal authority does what personal power can't. He doesn't have the power to stop the traffic, but he has the authority to stop the traffic. The officer is backed up by a department that backs him up.[888]

[God, Authority of; Spiritual Authority, Power of]
1 Tim. 4:12

SPIRITUAL AUTHORITY, POWER OF

DURING a Sunday afternoon football game, one of the players got upset at a referee for a call that he made. The player was twice as big as the referee and probably ten times as strong. He was angry. He did the unthinkable and the unacceptable. He bumped the referee. The rules in football are very strict. You don't put your hands or any part of your body on the referee. When a player touches a referee, that referee has legal rights, even though he's smaller than you, even though the player is bigger than the referee, even though the player has got on all of this equipment, even though the referee only has on a T-shirt and a pair of pants . . . the referee has legal rights.

The referee reached in his back pocket, pulled out a yellow flag, and flung it up in the air. He started waving his hands up and down and sent the player off the field. The referee told the player, "You are out of here."

Wait a minute! How dare a little, puny guy, who can't lift half the weight of the football player, who has no equipment to protect himself, how dare he throw a flag up in the face of a three hundred pounder? Where did he get the power? Where did he get the strength? Where did he get the confidence? It is all legal. It has nothing to do with strength or equipment or weight. It has everything to do with authority.

Satan is bigger than you. He's been lifting weights longer than you. He's got on more equipment than you. But you've got a flag in your back pocket. Based on Jesus Christ, you have legal rights. The power of the believer who uses his legal rights in heavenly places is more potent than the power of Satan. You have legal rights.[889]

[Kingdom of God, Power of; Satan]
James 4:7; 1 John 4:4

A SOLDIER one day went to the doctor. He was disturbed because he was a chain smoker and he couldn't get rid of his habit. He had tried in the past to stop smoking but he had failed each time.

He said, "Doc, these cigarettes are killing me. You know, I'm smoking two packs a day and I can't stop. Doc, do something. I need something to deliver me."

The military doctor looked at him and said, "Okay, on my lapel you see two bars. Tell me what they represent."

"They represent the fact that you are a captain."

"What are you?"

The solider said, "Well, I'm a private."

"Then, who's in charge here?"

"Well, you are, because you're the captain."

"OK, then as your captain, I command you to stop smoking permanently, beginning right now, and you must obey my orders."

This man who'd been smoking two packs of cigarettes a day for a long time stopped smoking on a dime because now he was talking to his captain. The doctor rather than going into his medicine chest reached out based on his authority. The man stopped smoking and never smoked again because his commanding officer said so. The young solider started off talking to his doctor. He wound up talking to his commanding officer. When he recognized who he was talking to and allowed the captain to be the captain over him, he was able to overcome something that he hadn't been able to overcome for a long time.[890]

[Surrender, Benefits of]
Heb. 13:17; James 4:7

I KNOW people who will say that they can't go two hours without smoking. But put them on a plane to England and they'll go eight hours without smoking. How can people who can't go two hours without smoking get on a plane for eight hours and not smoke? Because the commander of the plane tells them that they are on a nonsmoking flight. They can't smoke on the plane.

If people who smoke want to get from one point to another by plane, they have to give up something. The commander of the ship has told them that they can't take the trip if they don't abide by the rules.

As Christians, our problem is not an inability to change. Our problem is that we don't know who we are talking to. If we really knew that we were dealing with the "Commander," the all-powerful God, then we would find that power to do things we didn't think we had power for.[891]

[God, Authority of; God, Fear of]
Isa. 8:13; Matt. 10:28

SPIRITUAL BLESSING, BENEFITS OF

MANY people grew up watching *The Beverly Hillbillies*—Jed Clampett, Elly May, and Jethro. That was a fun show to watch. It really was a show about folks trying to get used to being rich. These folks didn't know how to act when they discovered how rich they were.

So here's a question. Jed Clampett one day hit black gold. He hit oil. How long had Jed Clampett been a millionaire? Did he become a millionaire on the day that he inadvertently came across the fact that there was oil, or had he been a millionaire and just was an uninformed one? There are a lot of spiritual Jed Clampetts walking around today who have untold wealth of which they are unaware.[892]

[Blessing; Christian, Value of]
Rom. 8:17; Eph. 3:6

SPIRITUAL BLESSING, CONCEPT OF

BLESSING in the Bible is not an offer of cotton candy happiness. Cotton candy is plenty sweet but it doesn't last. When you put it in your mouth, it melts soon after. Its longevity is short-lived.

The kingdoms of this world offer cotton candy. It's real sweet, but don't expect it to last long. Blessing in the Bible has to do with resources deposited on the inside that can override circumstances on the outside.[893]

[Blessing]
Phil. 4:19; Heb. 12:28

SPIRITUAL DEATH, CONCEPT OF

A LUXURY car company had a powerful commercial some time ago. There were two dummies in the car. Engineers were going to crash the car into a wall in order to show how sturdy and solid the Lexus was.

What caught my attention when I saw this commercial was what the dummies looked like. They were dressed in suits and ties. One dummy had a hat on. The other dummy had his hand on the wheel sporting an expensive watch. They were good-looking dummies headed toward a brick wall.

When we go to our cars after church with our nice dresses and our nice suits and we sit in our nice vehicles, the question is, are you a dummy behind the wheel? Those dummies in the commercial were looking good, but they were headed toward disaster. So it is possible to be a good-looking dummy. Many people are walking around today spiritually dead but don't know it.[894]

[Double-mindedness; Spiritual Life, Manifestation of]
Isa. 29:13; 1 John 3:18

SPIRITUAL DEATH, NATURE OF

ONE of my favorite shows was *Night of the Living Dead*, when all of these zombies would come out of a graveyard wrapped in grave clothes. They were dead, but they were walking, moving, and functioning.

That's what the Bible says this world is—it's a graveyard, and we are walking zombies outside of Jesus Christ. We are entombed in a casket with three locks on it. One lock is the world, another lock is the Devil, and the third is the flesh.[895]

[Flesh; Satan; Spiritual Death, Concept of]

SPIRITUAL EYESIGHT

ON TOP of my house, I have a DirecTV satellite dish. This DirecTV satellite dish links me to a satellite orbiting the Earth in outer space. That satellite in space sends a signal to my dish and to the dishes of anyone who has DirecTV. Now, you can't see the satellite, but it does send a signal to the receiver connected to my house. When my receiver, which is attached to my house, picks up the signal from the satellite that I can't see circling the Earth, I get a picture on my television.

Before I got satellite TV, I had basic television that allowed me to get about six channels. That was the extent of my reception. I had an antenna attached to my roof that helped me to get those stations. But when I got DirecTV, something graphically changed in my TV viewing. Now I could pick up stuff I never would have seen before. Now I can get stations like USA, ESPN, CNN, and TNT. I was able to get channels I never knew existed because now I was connected to something much higher. Before I was connected to a roof antenna, but now I am connected to "outer space."

When we come to Jesus Christ, God screws a satellite receiver into our souls. He quickens our spirits so that we can pick up the Trinitarian network. Because He hooks up a new receiver, we can pick up a new signal not available to us apart from Him. The Holy Spirit takes the dimmer switch and turns on the light so that we can see the spiritual nature of a thing, not merely the thing itself.[896]

[Holy Spirit, Guidance; God's Voice]
Rom. 8:9–11

MANY of us are well aware that when tornado trackers track tornadoes, they try to get close enough to them so that they can send all of these chemicals and all of these high tech pieces of equipment into the midst of the tornado in order to be able to gather information from the tornado itself. It's very dangerous to chase a tornado. If it ever turns on you, you're in trouble. It's a lot safer to track a hurricane. You wouldn't think so given the power of some hurricanes, but hurricane trackers are different from tornado trackers. Tornado trackers track from the ground. Hurricane trackers track from the air. They travel above the hurricane. They get really high. Because of their altitude, they're able to see things without being endangered by the hurricane itself even though what they're looking at is very dangerous.

Many Christians today feel as if their lives are spinning out of control, just like those hurricanes. They feel that their lives are in a state of frenzy and disaster. It's one thing to try to look at those kinds of circumstances from ground level; it's a whole different thing to look at things from a higher altitude. It's a different matter to try to see things from God's perspective.[897]

[Life, Perspective on]
Ps. 33:13; Heb. 4:13

SPIRITUAL FOOD

YOU know what food does? It satisfies hunger. There are many Christians who are hungry even though they have eaten. You see, they are filled with spiritual donuts and candy bars—stuff that tastes good but has no lasting nutritional value.[898]

[Worldliness, Distraction of]
Dan. 1:8–16; John 4:34

SPIRITUAL GIFTS, USE OF

CANCER is one of the debilitating diseases of our day. You know what cancer is? Cells that don't want to go with the program. They are deviant cells that have their own agenda. Now, this would be just fine . . . if they would leave your body. The problem with cancer is that these deviant cells still want to hang out in you. They don't want to go anywhere. They just want to be independent.

Cancer cells still want blood, they still want to eat, and they still want oxygen because they want to grow. Not only do they want to grow, they also want to spread and metastasize. So in other words, they want to siphon off the body, but they don't want to contribute to it. And ultimately, unless addressed radically, the whole body is in trouble, because what they want are the benefits.

Cancer exists in the church today too. There are cells of people that want the benefits of being in the body without the contributions. They want the sermons, they want the songs, they want the ministry to them, they want the toys for their kids, they want the foods for their pantry, and they want the counseling for their problem. They want all the things that the body is designed to give, but they don't want to be part of the body. They just want to hang out in it.[899]

[Church, Attendance]

2 Tim. 3:1–5; Rev. 3:15–16

SPIRITUAL IDENTITY, BASIS OF

WHO is Michael Jordan? Most would probably say the greatest basketball player that has ever played the game. Who is Sylvester Stallone? Most would probably say a great actor depending on the movie. Who is Diana Ross? Most would probably say one of the greatest singers of this generation. If you would say Michael Jordan is a basketball player, Sylvester Stallone is an actor, and Diana Ross a singer, you would be absolutely wrong for I would not have just described to you who they were. I would have only told you what they do. The greatest mistake in the world is to use your performance to give you your identity. The greatest mistake in the world is to define yourself by what you do. And yet it is the primary way that people define themselves.

When men get together, the first thing we want do in conversation is ask the other person what they do for a living. We then figure that if they do a big job, with a big title, for big pay, they must be somebody. However, one's self-definition, or identity, is not to be rooted in your performance because, if so, then you will always, always, always misdefine yourself.

People go to great lengths to get an identity. They'll buy identities. They go to plastic surgeons to fix their looks in order to fix their identity. They seek higher-paying jobs or nice business cards to help their identity. They pick their friends so that their friends can help elevate their identity. People go around asking for autographs so they can show other people whom they know in order to elevate their identity.

Satan knows that if he can keep you from discovering your true identity in Christ, he can keep you from discovering who you are. If in fact you are a Christian by virtue of your relationship with Christ, he can keep you hostage. He can keep you from claiming your inheritance. He can keep you from victory because you cannot be liberated if you don't know who you are.[900]

[Christian Living, Identity in Christ; Worldliness, Distraction of]
Rom. 12:2; Col. 3:2

A FEW years back, I had an intern who assisted me in the office. His name is Ikki Soma. I affectionately called him the "Ikk Man." Ikki is Japanese by birth. His mother and father, the seed that produced him, are Japanese. Now, let me tell you about Ikki. Ikki grew up black. His college roommate was black. His seminary roommate was black. He was the only Japanese on an all-black track team in college. His favorite music is hip-hop. His favorite meal is fried catfish with hot sauce, macaroni and cheese, mustard greens, corn bread, and iced tea. If you ever have a chance to hear him preach, you'll realize that he preaches black. His first girlfriend was black. He even ended up marrying a black woman. Everything about Ikki is black. But when he fills out a government form, and they ask him to check a box for his race, he doesn't put down black. While all of the external things that surround him are black, he was not born black. Therefore, when he fills out a government form, and they ask him his race, he checks Japanese. It's not his performance that defines who he is. The essence of who he is is defined by his birth. It is your birth, not your performance, that tells you who you are.[901]

[Christian Living, Identity in Christ]
John 3:5; 1 John 5:18

DURING one of the NFL drafts awhile

back, everyone was shocked when Mike Ditka gave up all of his draft choices in order to get University of Texas running back Ricky Williams. Why would Mike Ditka do that? He wanted to make him a Saint. So, he took Ricky Williams from the amateurs and made him a pro at the cost of every draft choice he had.

As an amateur Ricky Williams was a star. As an amateur he was an award-winning running back. As an amateur he was victorious. As an amateur he was a champion. As an amateur he was successful. As a Saint thus far he's been a disappointment. As a Saint, Ricky Williams didn't do so well initially, and yet Mike Ditka took all of his draft choices and made amateur Ricky Williams a Saint.

On the cross of Calvary, Jesus Christ gave everything He had so that you could be a saint. Some Christians are "fumbling the ball" saints. Some Christians are "being tackled in the backfield" saints. Some Christians are "falling on their face" saints. Some have been injured and are on the sidelines. No matter what your position, though, you are still a saint because the price has been paid to make you a saint. Now, you may have to learn to run like a saint, walk like a saint, talk like a saint, move like a saint, act like a saint, think like a saint, or dream like a saint, but a saint is who you are. You are a saint because of your identity, not how you perform.[902]

[Christian Living, Identity in Christ]

SPIRITUAL IDENTITY, IN CHRIST

I'VE GOT three envelopes: a big one,

a smaller one, and a smaller one yet. I've also got a slip of paper. The Bible says that we are in Christ and that Christ is in us. The smallest envelope has "Tony Evans" written on it. The slip of paper has "Jesus" written on it. The Bible says that when Tony Evans accepted Jesus Christ, Christ came inside of Tony Evans. Christ, the slip of paper, is inside the envelope that represents Tony Evans, but not only is Christ in Tony Evans, but Tony Evans is in Christ. The slip of paper Christ is in Tony Evans, but when Tony Evans accepted Christ, Tony Evans came inside of Christ. I put the Tony Evans envelope into the Christ envelope. Now, the Bible says that Christ is in God. So we're going to slip the Christ envelope into the God envelope. So in order to now get to Tony Evans, you've got to go through God, and then you have to go through Christ, and after you've gone through God, and gotten through Christ, then you get to Tony Evans. However, when you've gone through God, and gotten to Christ, and think you've have gotten ahold of Tony Evans, when you open up Tony Evans, he's full of Jesus Christ. So I am in Christ, Christ is in me, Christ is in God, God is in Christ, so I am well covered by Jesus Christ and His heavenly Father.[903]

[Christian Living, Identity in Christ; Father God]
John 14:20; 15:1–11; Gal. 2:20

SPIRITUAL IDENTITY, POWER OF

WHENEVER I have taken my children or grandchildren to the circus, we would normally see the elephants outside in the parking lot as they were being prepared to go in to entertain the crowd. One of the things that you will notice, if you've seen that sight, is that these huge beasts are being held hostage by a little chain around one of their ankles connected to a post that's in the ground. It is amazing to think that such a little chain, connected to such a little post, could hold such a big beast hostage. An elephant could simply swipe and either break the chain or pull up the post.

But circus elephants don't do that, because when they were baby elephants, their master, the trainer, taught them that when they felt the chain that they were supposed to submit. The baby elephants never had an opportunity to understand their identify. So circus elephants are good for entertainment only, because in the early days their identity was ripped from them.

A lot of us are being held hostage. We come to church and we hear about all of this power we have, all of this greatness we have, but just a little old chain holds us down. And we wonder what's wrong, how can we be such powerful beings and be held hostage by any little thing that shows up. It's a question of identity.[904]

[Christian Living, Power; Satan, Strategy of]
Heb. 12:1

SPIRITUAL INSIGHT

AT MANY amusement parks and museums, they have 3-D movies. When you walk into the theater, you receive a pair of glasses. If you try to watch the movie without the glasses, you see a distorted picture. No matter how hard you strain and look and twist to try to make sense of what is happening on the screen, there is still a distortion because of the dimension through which you are looking. By handing you a pair of glasses when you walk into the theater, they give you the tool you need to see the screen without distortions.

One of the problems many of us have is that we have a distorted view. We see what we see, but we don't see all that there is to be seen. If all you see is the physical, visible scenario, then you are looking at your situation without your glasses. We need to have a divine frame of reference in order to see what is really going on.[905]

[God's Perspective; Heavenly Mindset; Illumination]
Matt. 16:22–23; 1 Cor. 13:9–12; 2 Cor. 5:7; Heb. 11

SPIRITUAL INSIGHT, MEANS TO

WHEN the Word of God is linked with the Spirit of God, you have what I might call a spiritual Xerox moment. You take a piece of paper and you put it on the Xerox machine. You lay the paper on the Xerox machine because you want a copy. You push the button because you want what's on the Xerox machine to come out on another sheet of paper. Before it comes out on another sheet of paper, what happens is a light comes underneath and takes a picture of the piece of paper you laid on top. The light then transfers what it photographs onto another sheet of paper so that there is a copy, an exact copy, of what you put on top. When you come to church to hear the Word of God, it's like putting a piece of paper on top. The Word is transferred onto your life via the light and the life of the Holy Spirit. He makes sure the life of Christ, an exact copy, is transferred to you.[906]

[Bible, Application of]
John 16:12–15; 2 Tim. 3:16

SPIRITUAL LIFE, MANIFESTATION OF

WHEN a woman is pregnant, it is as a result of an intimate encounter in private. That encounter shows up in public months later. If nothing happens in public, that means that nothing happened in private.

God wants new life in Him to be manifested. He wants the life of Jesus, lived thousands of years ago, to become your experience. He wants the intimacy of your relationship with Christ to bring about the power of His presence no matter what your circumstances. He wants your joy to be full as His presence shows up in your life.

How do you know when that life is manifested? Some pregnant women I know throw up but that doesn't take away the joy of the new life. Some have trouble sleeping but that doesn't take away the joy of the new life. Some have trouble walking but that doesn't take away the joy of their new life. For when life is manifested, it overrides the inconveniences that they've had to endure.

See, a lot of Christians are looking for happiness. They want a better house, a bigger car, or nicer circumstances. There's nothing inherently wrong with that. But when they don't get those things, they don't have joy. That's because life hasn't been manifested.

Even if you have to throw up the house, if you've got life, you still have joy. Even if you have to lose the job, if you have life, you have joy. Even if you have to lose the circumstances, if you have life, you have joy. Your joy will be full because your belly is full with the manifestation of Jesus Christ.[907]

> [Christian Living, New Life]
> John 15:11

SPIRITUAL MATURITY

WHEN you travel to a country where you don't speak the language, you shouldn't be surprised when you don't understand what is being said. More than likely, you will need an interpreter so that you can communicate. There is nothing wrong with you if you don't understand. It's simply that you are new to a very different environment.

This is how things seem for an infant Christian. They are new to the Christian environment, and they may not know how to "walk the walk" and "talk the talk." They are babies born into a whole new world.[908]

> [Christian Living, Spiritual Growth; New Life in Christ]
> 1 Cor. 3:2–3; 1 Peter 2:2

IF YOU see a baby playing in the dirt, the baby may be dirty but you pretty much don't make a big deal about it because it's understood that babies play in dirt. Babies try to eat dirt. Babies scrub themselves in dirt. Dirt is a toy to a baby. But if you see a twenty-one-year-old man playing in the dirt, rubbing himself with the dirt, or trying to eat the dirt, you know you've got a crazy person on your hands! The only difference between the two is time. By twenty-one, that man ought to know that dirt is not a toy.

We have too many Christians who have been saved too long that are still playing in the dirt. They play in the dirt and they have fun in the dirt. You can't come and listen to the Word of God every week and not realize that the dirt is not where you are supposed to be.[909]

> [Spiritual Maturity, Lack of]
> 1 Cor. 3:3; 13:11

I REMEMBER a time growing up when I was sixteen and I wanted my father to let me start doing stuff. My big phrase would always be, "Well, Dad, you know I'm almost a man," or sometimes I'd say, "In two more years, Dad, I'm going to be a man and so you might as well let me start practicing some of this stuff now." My dad would always tell me, "When you start acting like a man, then you can do some of this stuff."

He basically made it his business to inform me that, although I wanted to have the responsibilities of adulthood, I was still acting like a kid. He wanted me to know that I was still riding the fence between two worlds and that I had to get straight which side of the fence I wanted to stay on.

In the same way, there are many Christians today who are not maturing. They are not producing fruit that is developing and ripening in accordance with the level of maturity they should have for the number of years they have been saved.[910]

> [Christian Living, Spiritual Growth; Spiritual Maturity, Lack of]
> Heb. 5:12

RATE multiplied by time equals distance. If I walk from our church in the southwest of Dallas to downtown Dallas, which is about eleven miles, and I start off at 11:00 in the morning, it's going to take me a long time to get there—probably about four hours or so.

If, at 11:45, you decide that you want to go downtown but you want to drive, you will get there a lot faster. Even though I started out earlier than you, you are going to get there before me because you are moving at a faster rate of speed than I am. You'll be covering more territory in a shorter amount of time than I. You'll be there and have had lunch before I even get to the Trinity River that precedes downtown. The rate of your speed will allow you to cover more distance than the slow rate that I will be traveling.

What is the relevance of that to your spiritual growth? Some folks have been coming to church for years. Some folk were almost born in church, raised in church, and they still aren't downtown yet because they are moving along at a crawl. Then there are those people who've only been saved five years, but who have reached a steady level of spiritual stability because they moved at a faster rate.

God has guaranteed maturity to every believer as a real option, but it is what each believer does with their time that will determine the rate of their speed and time to arrival at the destination of maturity.[911]

[Christian Living, Spiritual Growth; Spiritual Maturity, Growth]
Heb. 5:12; 1 Peter 2:2

SPIRITUAL MATURITY, GROWTH

AN ACORN is a small little thing—a nut to be exact. That little acorn goes and gets planted under the ground. It's hard to believe that the potential of a full-sized oak tree is in that tiny thing, but resident in that nut is growth potential that's phenomenal.[912]

Matt. 13:8; Mark 4:8; Luke 8:8

AN OAK tree is strong because of its roots. Its roots go way, way down. So whenever a storm brews, an oak tree is not intimidated. Now, your house might be intimidated but not the oak tree sitting in front of it. This tree has a solid foundation.

In the same way, the deeper your spiritual roots go, the more secure you can be when storms come your way. The spiritual maturity that occurs when you grow as a Christian keeps you rooted and able to withstand difficulties when they come your way.[913]

[Trials, Endurance during]
Matt. 7:24–25; Luke 6:48

A MAN named Frederick Handley Page, a pioneer in aviation, was flying in the Middle East one day. He had one of his best airplanes. During his journey, he was going across Arabia. Unknown to him, a huge rat had been attracted by the smell of the food that had been put in the cargo of the plane and managed to get aboard. On the next flight, Page heard the sickening sound of gnawing in his small plane. He could tell that it was a rodent. His heart began to pound when he visualized the damage that could be done to the mechanisms of the controls of the plane, and that this rodent could gnaw right through some critical lines. The question is, what could he do, because he was flying solo? Page did an amazing thing. He remembered something he learned way back in school. Rats can't survive high altitudes. When you go higher, rats can't breathe. And so he began to climb. He began to rise higher, listening intently for the gnawing sounds to cease. The sounds did stop. When he arrived at his destination, he found the rat lying dead behind the cockpit.

Many of us have the rat of sin gnawing at our lives. We have the rat of immorality nipping at us or the rat of improper language biting at us. We have the rats of marital destruction destroying us. We have the rats of secularism and worldliness devouring us, about to cause our spiritual planes to crash. But there is something you can do. You can climb higher in your spiritual life! Increasing your altitude in Christ can help ward off the schemes of the Devil![914]

[Sin, Dealing with]
Rom. 8:13; Col. 3:5; 2 Peter 3:18

GOD designed your life as a Christian to get younger on the inside as you get older on the outside.[915]

2 Cor. 4:16

SPIRITUAL MATURITY, LACK OF

MOST people have, at one time or another, been on a treadmill to work out. This equipment serves to help a person walk at faster and faster paces, creating a sweat as they attempt to burn calories. One thing is for certain, though; a treadmill has an ability to get a person moving fast without taking them anywhere.

Many Christians spiritually find themselves on a treadmill. Men and women run to and from church, to and from worship, to and from semi-nars, to and from classes, and to and from religious activities—to discover that when it's all said and done, they are still stuck in the same

place where they started.[916]
Heb. 5:12

SPIRITUAL TRANSFORMATION

POPCORN pops due to an explosion of moisture. Every kernel of popcorn has moisture in it. When you put popcorn in the microwave, the microwave heats up the moisture, creating steam. When steam rises inside the shell of the popcorn, it presses against the shell until the shell can't withstand the pressure anymore and it pops open, splitting open the shell.

What once was a small, hard little object has now increased in size and become soft and fluffy. In fact, when the popcorn pops, it's hard to even find the shell. The old outward appearance is now dominated by the inside characteristics.

God has seated deep down in your soul something that is ready to respond to the right environment. When the Holy Spirit begins to "cook" your divine nature so that the steam of your new life begins to rise and press through this outer shell called the body, you begin to "pop." You will begin to look, act, talk, and walk differently because the change occurring on the inside will show up on the outside.[917]

[Christian Living, New Life; New Life in Christ]
2 Cor. 5:17

WHEN the cordless phone has been off the hook for too long, it no longer works. The signal has lost its power and its influence. That phone must be rested back onto the base in order for it to become rejuvenated.

One of the reasons Christians are not transformed the way God wants us to be is that we've been away too long. We've been disconnected too long. Like a cell phone that cuts off because there is a bad spot on the freeway, Christians lose contact with God.[918]

[Jesus, Relationship with; Self-Sufficiency, Danger of; Sin, Consequences of]
Ps. 66:18; Isa. 59:2

THE STORY is told of a native in a foreign country who had never seen a mirror before. The missionaries brought one over. This native girl had never seen what she looked like. She walked up and for the first time in her life looked at a mirror and saw herself. The mirror had been nailed to a tree. Not liking the image before her, she took the mirror off the tree and slammed it to the ground. She did not like what the mirror had to say so she got rid of the mirror.

When we come before the mirror of God's Word, the first thing we will see is ourselves. Many of us don't want the mirror to tell us the truth because we won't like what it tells us.[919]

[Bible; Truth]
James 1:23–25

JAMES 1 says men go to the mirror, they look, and they quickly turn away "forgetting what they saw." That's not how women use mirrors. A woman will get up and go to mirror number one to check and make sure she is starting out right. Next, there is a long, full body mirror—mirror number two. Then, this woman will get in her car, pull down the visor, and check in mirror number three. Once at her place of employment, she will go to the ladies room and look at mirror number four. Now, mirror number five is in her purse. This mirror gives this lady a way to check and recheck her look in an instant.

Why do women have mirror after mirror? They never want to lose sight of what they look like.[920]

James 1:23–25

WHENEVER you see a pregnant woman, you can know for certain that she didn't get that way by reading a book about sex. Information didn't get her pregnant, intimacy did.

Transformation doesn't occur in Christians because we read about it. We are transformed because we get close.[921]

[Intimacy, Importance of; Intimacy, Power of]
James 4:8; Heb. 10:22

MANY people have experienced the frustration of putting food in the microwave to heat it up, only to find that when the timer goes off, the food is hot outside and still cold inside. There is a relatively new microwave on the market called the Inverter. It's different from every other microwave. It heats from the inside out. In this microwave, the visible effects on the outside are determined by the changes brought about internally first.

See, some Christian folks look hot on the surface. Externally, everything looks spiritual, but if we could peer into the soul, we might see that things are still cold. God is not against a hot outside. He's not against you looking blessed, or you looking on fire for Him. He's not against that.

It's a good thing to be blessed externally, but just not at the expense of the soul. God wants a smoking inside that makes its way out.[922]

[Christian Living, Authenticity; Legalism, Danger of]
Isa. 29:3; Matt. 23:27

ONE of the greatest inventions of all time is soft-serve ice cream. Where ice cream could be hard and scooped out using a lot of effort with an ice cream scooper, somebody figured out a way to make soft-serve ice cream immediately available with minimal effort.

There is a homemade way to get soft-serve ice cream too. Take the carton out of the freezer, put it on the kitchen counter, and let it set out for a while. Simply transfer the atmosphere of the ice cream and after a bit of time you will see change. Situating it in the right location, the new location will produce the transformation desired.

The reason why some Christians are so cold, callous, stingy, unloving, and evil is because they are not hanging out in the right atmosphere. God will do the work of transformation if we are in an atmosphere where He is. He is willing to do the work of change in our hearts and minds if we will allow Him.[923]

[Love, Lack of; Transformation]
Ezek. 11:19; 2 Cor. 3:18

A BUTTERFLY prances from flower to flower, pausing and moving like believers who go from service to service. They don't really DO anything. They just flitter. They are really good at looking pretty, dressed, and colorful on any given Sunday. These people go from church to church and conference to conference—fluttering.

Some Christians are like the botanist who intently studies the flower, taking copious notes, writing everything down, and observing all of the idiosyncratic details of every kind of flower there is. Although this botanist may be an academic genius, he is totally unaffected by his notes.

This person is like the Bible college student or the seminarian who can quote Greek, Hebrew, and Edgar. He can break down the syntax of a sentence and go into the grammatical construct of a verse, diagramming ALL the elements of the passage, but who walks away untransformed with all of his knowledge.

But then there's the bee. The bee is a little different; it goes into the flower and takes out the nectar; the bee does more than the butterfly, which just wants to flutter from place to place. It does more than the botanist who just wants a good grade. The bee wants to partake of the nectar of the flower. It comes in empty but leaves full. And on its way out, it deposits something somewhere so that pollination occurs and life keeps on going.

Are you a butterfly Christian? Are you a botanist Christian? or are you a bee? Are you merely fluttering from service to service to feel good about having gone to church? Are you one who writes down everything but are untransformed? Or are you one who will receive the full truth from the Word of God?[924]

[Christian Living, Purpose; Transformation]
Matt. 18:3; Rom. 12:2; 2 Cor. 3:18

WHEN a woman is pregnant, it is natural for her body to change because of the new life growing within her. The baby inside is attached to the mother, piggybacking off of her life. The baby borrows nutrition from the mother. The mother's body takes care of the growth of the baby naturally. The baby doesn't have to work to grow. It just grows and transforms because of the connection. The changes happening to the body of the pregnant woman on the inside result in changes taking place on the outside. The woman is transformed. Her shape is changed. Milk is preparing to flow. Taste buds change. All of these changes happen naturally. Nothing is coerced.

When the Spirit of God within begins to transform us, the process of spiritual transformation is natural. Changes on the inside eventually show up on the outside.[925]

[Christian Living, Spiritual Growth; Transformation]
2 Cor. 3:18; 1 Peter 1:23–25

MANY people hate dieting. In an effort to lose weight, they are miserable. They are unhappy watching other folks eat things that they wish that they could. They spend all of their energy and effort focusing on what they can't have. Many folks start diets, never to finish because they are so irritable and frustrated with the food they have to eat to lose weight. Their dieting choices for meals aren't natural. They do not have a taste for the food they need to eat in order to reach their goal.

Now, if a person develops a taste for food that is good for them, they will naturally eat the right things and get the benefit of eating healthy. Real spiritual transformation happens when we allow the Spirit to change our tastes rather than trying to force behavioral changes with human effort alone.[926]

[Holy Spirit, Filling of; Transformation]
Ps. 42:1; 63:1

MANY people regularly carry breath mints on their person. Now, breath mints can do the job of covering up a problem for a little while but they don't address the problem.

There is a new product called Breath Assure and it is different from a breath mint. It is not designed to be sucked on like most breath mints in order to change the taste in the mouth. It is designed to be swallowed so that it can enter the stomach and release oils that address the movement of the food and the effect of decay in the stomach that works its way up into the mouth.

Most times, in order for real change to occur, the heart has to be fixed first. A person can attempt to cover an issue with praise and worship or a "hallelujah" but that stuff doesn't last. It is a transformed heart that produces transformed behavior.[927]

[Hard Heart; Sin, Dealing with]
Ezek. 11:19

A MAN had a clock hanging on the wall of his office. The hands on this clock could never seem to keep the right time. Something was always off with the hands. He put a little sign under it that said, "When you look at this clock, please don't blame the hands. The problem is on the inside."

A lot of our hands are off track,

and a lot of our actions are off track, but the problem lies with a bad heart. This means that if you change the external without fixing the heart you haven't fixed the root of the problem; you've only addressed the fruit of the problem. If you address the fruit and miss the root, you will only have a temporary fix.[928]

[Hard Heart; Sin, Dealing with]
Ezek. 11:19

DISCIPLESHIP is progress over time. It doesn't happen overnight. It's like the farmer who went to the city for the first time. He saw a mall and had never seen a mall before. He was with his son and his wife. He said, "I've got to see this place. I've never seen anything like it." So, they went in and started wandering around.

Inside the mall was a bank. When they walked inside the bank, they saw the vault. They didn't quite know what it was because the farmer was used to saving his money in rudimentary ways. He would put it under his pillow or bury it in his backyard. They all stood there trying to figure out exactly what it was.

At one point a little old lady walked inside the vault. She was very old. She could barely walk and used a cane to move around. She walked shakily into the vault. About thirty seconds later, a beautiful, well-figured young lady comes out the vault. The farmer saw the old lady go in, and a gorgeous young woman come out. He leaned over to his son and said, "Hurry up, and go get your mother." He wanted an instant transformation.

The farmer's wife would not

have been immediately transformed and neither will we be in our spiritual journey. Transformation doesn't happen immediately; however, we do have control over the speed at which the process takes place.[929]

[Sanctification; Transformation]
2 Cor. 3:18; 1 Peter 2:2

STANDARD

ONE and one equals two. No matter what today is, one and one equals two. No matter what tomorrow is, one and one still equals two. But suppose tomorrow, I don't feel like it? It's still two. What if I'm not "feeling" two? It's still two. The fact of one and one doesn't adjust just because of my feelings. When it's sunny outside, one and one is still two. You know why? Because it's a standard outside of me. It is a standard regardless of how I feel about it and it still functions, whether or not I adjust.

Only God can set the standard because only He can speak absolutely without error. You cannot measure yourself by your own standards. If you are measuring yourself by the wrong ruler, you will come up with the wrong measurement.[930]

[God's Standard]
Col. 1:17; Heb. 13:8

STEWARDSHIP

WHEN I was going through seminary, money was hard to come by. I made 350 dollars a month. We weren't poor, we were "po." There is a difference. We knew that this was a temporary glitch in the progress of life but it didn't change the reality that times were difficult. One of the ways that extra money was earned during the seminary years was house-sitting. Seminary couples would be asked to come and sit at the house of a wealthy person. These would be wealthy people who were going on vacation and they did not want to leave their home unattended. So seminary couples would gladly offer to be hired out to watch over the home.

Sometimes that involved just the house. Other times it could involve the house and animals or kids. It might end up being a lot of work but seminarians jumped at this for a number of reasons. One, it paid pretty well. Also, it provided a way for seminarians to live "large" for a little while as they enjoyed the nicer accommodations of the home they watched over. It was kind of nice to have the feeling of driving up and pretending that the house was yours.

My wife wouldn't let me touch a thing! She knew that those folks were coming back home and she wanted to make sure things stayed in place. I was prone to getting a little too comfortable. Her job was to remind me that it all was not mine—that we were only visiting temporarily. She understood the mind-set of looking over the property or affairs of another. She understood stewardship.[931]

[Materialism, Deception of]
Matt. 25:14–30; Luke 19:11–27;
1 Cor. 4:2

ONE day, John Wesley's house burned down to the ground. Some people found him and said, "John, we are so sorry to tell you this, but your house just burned to the ground."

John Wesley said, "That's impossible."

"No, John! Your house burned to the ground."

"That's impossible!"

"John, we saw it with our own eyes. Your house is gone!"

"That's impossible. You see, I don't own a house. God gave me a place to live in. I only managed that house for Him. If He didn't put the fire out, then that's His problem. He'll have to put me somewhere else."

That man understood. He understood that he could have something and use something without possessing it. He didn't hold on to it so tightly that when it went down he went down too.

Some of us would lose our minds if we lost our houses or cars. We are to possess nothing.[932]

[Materialism, Deception of; Money, Use of]
Matt. 19:21–22; Mark 10:21–22;
Luke 18:22–23; 1 Peter 4:10

STRONGHOLD

I WAS supposed to be making a trip to Harrisburg, Pennsylvania. I had already checked my bags and walked to the gate when I got a phone call. As I was about to board the plane, I was told that the engagement in Harrisburg had been canceled because of a snowstorm in the area. The weather was not going to allow people to come out.

The engagement was canceled because people would be trapped inside of their homes due to the storm. That's precisely what a stronghold or a fortress is—a situation, habit, or condition that holds a person hostage. It is something that entraps you and doesn't let you out.[933]

2 Cor. 10:4; Heb. 12:1

SUBMISSION

WHEN you get on the highway, what do you do? You merge, right? You're riding on a side road called the on-ramp, coming in toward the freeway, and you are going to merge into the major traffic. Now, it would be to your betterment to slow down and look back before entering the highway because cars are coming. You are the one who is going to need to adjust. They have the right-of-way.

God has the right-of-away. He's moving alone with His plan for your life, but you have to merge. You have to blend in with what He is already doing. Your actions and plans must yield to His will for your life ahead of your own.[934]

[Surrender, Concept of]
Matt. 6:9–10; James 4:7

THERE is a campaign designed to address the epidemic of drunk driving that we have in this country. It simply says, "If you drink, don't drive." The idea is that people will choose to give their keys to someone else and let them drive when they are not sober enough to drive home. When a person is drunk, their senses have been dulled and their ability to control things has been lost. The campaign encourages a person to give their keys to someone else who is totally under control.

This world has intoxicated us, and sometimes causes us to lose our equilibrium. God is saying that we should give Him the keys to our lives, let Him steer and let Him take control so that we can safely get to where we ought to be.[935]

[Life, Management of; Surrender, Concept of; Worldliness,

Distraction of]
2 Chron. 30:8; Job 22:21; James 4:7

MANY men here have cut off the blessing of God from your family, because you are refusing to submit to the will of God related to your headship. Many women in here have cut off the blessing of God to your family because of your refusal to legitimately submit to your husbands. You can literally cut off what God has already set up.[936]

[Submission, of Wives to Their Husbands]
Eph. 5:22–23

I HAVE a will. I have four children and they are all named in my will. My oldest son came to me once to remind me that in the Bible, the oldest son got a double portion. Now, he's absolutely right. My younger son isn't too keen on that.

In the Bible, when it came to inheritance, the oldest son got a double portion because he had the responsibility of caring for the family in the absence of the father. He didn't just get a double portion so he could have twice as much. He got a double portion because he now had increased responsibility.

Now, although I have a will, and it lays out who gets what, there is a clause in my will. It states that if any of my kids adopt an ungodly, unrepentant lifestyle, they lose their inheritance. Why do I have this clause? Because I don't want them wasting what God has given. Their inheritance is connected to their submission.

Many of us have delayed our inheritance because of a refusal to submit to the legitimate authority God has ordained in our lives. Whether it's parents , or the church, or even God directly, the Bible says "to obey them that have spiritual rule over you."[937]

[Father God; God, Authority of]
Matt. 6:9–10; Heb. 13:17

SUBMISSION, OF WIVES TO THEIR HUSBANDS

ONE day, while I was out of town speaking at Promise Keepers, the National Organization for Women (NOW) was marching outside the gates of the event location. They were complaining about the word *submit*. They were saying that word makes women second-class citizens. But at the same time the president of NOW was on TV complaining about the word *submit*, I heard her call her vice president and give her instructions to fulfill a certain task. I thought to myself, *Well, if the word sub-mit is that bad, why are you, the president, calling the vice president, expecting her to do something based on your word?*

You see, it's only a bad word when it's in an arena we don't like.[938]

[Marriage; Women, and Their Husbands]
1 Cor. 11:3; Eph. 5:22–23

MANY women have a problem with submission because they think, "But I am smarter than my husband. I make more money than my husband. I am more educated than my husband. I have more common sense than my husband. I can't submit to him."

Well, let's suppose an eighteen-wheeler is trying to merge onto the freeway. Let's also assume that the Volkswagen is coming down the expressway so it has the right-of-way. The eighteen-wheeler has to yield. Now, the eighteen-wheeler may have more clout than the Volkswagen, but the Volkswagen has the right-of-way. Can the eighteen-wheeler say, "Because I have more than you have, you stop on the highway and let me on"? If there is an accident, it is the eighteen-wheeler that is going to be at fault, because even though it's got more stuff, it is operating illegitimately.

Submission has nothing to do with how much you bring to the table. Submission has nothing to do with how much education, how much clout, or how much notoriety a woman has; it has to do with God's ordained role.[939]

[Marriage; Women, and Their Husbands]
1 Cor. 11:3; Eph. 5:22–23

IF THE president of the United States were to walk into a room, everyone would stand up, even the ones who didn't vote for him. Everyone would stand, even the ones who don't agree with his philosophy or programs. Why? Because he is the president by position, regardless of your vote. In other words, enough people in this country voted for him to override your feelings and opinions about him and he is still to be respected because of his position.

Now, you can feel any kind of way you want to feel, but you must still honor his position, even if you didn't vote for the person. Ladies, God has already voted for your husband and His vote is the only one that counts. He has elevated your husband to the position of leader in the home. You must respect that position.[940]

[Marriage; Women, and Their Husbands]

1 Cor. 11:3; Eph. 5:22–23

SUFFERING

A LITTLE boy's legs were not developing as they ought. The pediatrician told his parents that their son needed to wear a leg brace, which would help to position the legs and feet to grow properly. The parents wanted to do the right thing for their son but were miserable following the doctor's orders. The bar held the little boy's feet and legs completely straight and unbendable. Each night when his parents would put the brace on and put him to bed, he would cry from discomfort and from his dislike of it. The little boy was sure to have felt hurt that his parents would treat him wrongly and possibly he even doubted their love for him. The mother was at times tempted to take off the bar but resisted because she felt in her heart that she was doing the right thing for her son.

As difficult as this time was, the doctor, the mother, and the father did what they did because of their concern and their thought for his future well-being years down the road. They were willing to sacrifice convenience now for a better life later.

God cares for His children. Right now He might use means of restraint and discomfort to achieve His desired result but He operates out of the love He has for us.[941]

[Boundaries; Pain; Restrictions; Trials, Purpose of]

Rom. 8:28; James 1:2–4

JONI Eareckson Tada hit her head when she dove into a lake and became paralyzed. Now, she has a worldwide ministry for people who are challenged physically. Today, Joni would tell you she wouldn't trade her experience for anything. She hasn't walked for a long time, but millions of people who are hurting physically are encouraged by the hope she gives, because of the suffering she's had. Her testimony is that she would have never known that God could be so real to her had she not experienced pain.[942]

[Pain; Trials, Benefits of; Trials, Purpose of]

Ps. 23:4; Rom. 8:28

THE REASON a woman can endure the pain of childbirth is because something good is coming down the pipe. She can endure because the pain will be worth it in the end as she celebrates the new birth of her child. She bears the suffering because of the joy before her. It is in weakness that God does His greatest birthing.[943]

[Trials, Benefits of]

2 Cor. 12:10

OYSTERS suffer affliction when they get a grain of sand lodged inside their shells. No matter what they do, they can't get rid of it. The sand gets lodged there and it's irritating to the oyster. It's a thorn. It drives them crazy. To bring comfort to their anguish, they begin to coat the grain of sand over and over and over again. Coating the sand doesn't get rid of it; it just comforts them.

Over time the coating of the grain of sand over and over again produces something that costs a mint. It's called a pearl. Do you know what a pearl is? A pearl is the result of an irritated oyster. Out of that came something women place great value on.

The pain resulted in beauty. Their pain resulted in elegance. The pain results in something of high value. When God allows us to suffer, He is producing something precious.[944]

[Trials, Benefits of]
Rom. 5:3–5; James 1:2–4;
1 Peter 1:6–7

SURRENDER, BENEFITS OF

WHEN a mother gives birth, her body is so constructed to make milk. The milk flows in concert with the woman's pregnancy and the birthing process. The body knows it's time for milk because a baby is here and it needs to eat. The mother doesn't have to grunt and groan to produce the milk. It's already built into the structure of her body. When life comes forth, milk flows.

The will of God flows when the life of surrender is made. It just flows.[945]

Rom. 12:1; James 4:10; 1 Peter 5:6

SURRENDER, CONCEPT OF

A FAMOUS general, Douglas MacArthur, was meeting his foe, a Japanese general. The meeting was set up for the Japanese general to officially surrender. The Japanese general stuck out his hand to shake MacArthur's hand and MacArthur said, "I cannot shake your hand, sir, until you first surrender your sword." We can't be friends as long as that sword is hanging by your side. Give me the sword and then we'll shake hands.

A lot of us want to shake God's hand while we carry our sword, the sword of our will. We must surrender our wills to God before we can be in complete fellowship with Him.[946]

[God's Will]
Matt. 6:9–10

T

TEMPTATION

A BOY climbed up in a chair and started eating cookies off of the kitchen counter. His mother had told him not to eat them earlier. Surprising him, she entered the room and asked, "What are you doing? I told you not to eat the cookies." With a full mouth, the boy replied, "You don't understand, Mama. I got up here on this chair and my teeth got caught."[947]

[Greed, Influence of]
Matt. 26:41; James 1:13–15

WHEN James uses the word "entice," it has to do with baiting or putting a worm on a hook. Why does a fisherman put a worm on a hook? To hide the real deal. It's not about the worm. The worm is the attraction. The real deal from the fisherman's standpoint is the hook, but a fish is not going to go swimming toward a hook. Fish are dumb, but they are not crazy. It won't head for a hook but it will swim toward a worm, not understanding that the worm is covering the real deal.[948]

[Deception, Satan's]
Deut. 4:19; James 1:13–16

TEMPTATION, EXIT FROM

IN OUR church sanctuary, all along

the back wall, there are exit signs. It means you can leave the sanctuary through those doors. But when you follow the exit signs and leave the sanctuary, you are still in the building. The exit sign does not take you outside of the building. There is another exit door on the other side of this exit door that takes you outside the building. So, if you're trying to leave the building, the first exit sign is not sufficient for that. It takes you outside of this part of the building, but it doesn't take you out of the whole building. There's another exit sign for that.

This is the way exits work with temptations. We are told that with our temptations, we will have a way out, an exit that will help us to endure. Most people think that an exit means they are getting out of the temptation altogether. Most people think that the exit God provides will get them out of the problem. The exits usually provided lead us to another hallway with another exit sign that leads us to a hallway to endurance. Where does the exit sign take you? It doesn't take you out, it takes you through.[949]

[Overcoming, Power of; Sin, Avoidance of]

1 Cor. 10:13; Gal. 5:22–23; James 4:7

TEMPTATION, LEADING TO SIN

A BUSINESSMAN was on a diet and experienced a craving for donuts. He drove to the donut shop and just kept circling the block. Then he prayed, "Lord, I know You don't want me to eat donuts. I know that that's not Your will, but I need You to confirm it. There are no parking spaces at this donut shop, so I'm going to drive around the block and if no parking space comes open, that will be confirmation." After going around eight more times, a spot became available. His desire gave birth to a behavior and the behavior to a sin.[950]

James 1:13–16

TEMPTATION, NATURE OF

WHAT the worm is designed to do is entice the fish so that the fish can become food for the fisherman. It is an enticement. No bear goes looking for a bear trap. No mouse goes looking for a mousetrap. What entices the mouse is cheese. But cheese is set on the trap, and because of its lust for cheese, the mouse is deceived in not recognizing the trap. Therefore, it is enticed or deceived or duped by something that is legitimate to create an opportunity for the destruction of the prey.

Most of us are in debt, because of deception. There was a desire to buy something that we either could not afford or should not have purchased, but that thing was presented in such a way so as to cause us to believe we couldn't live without it. So, we spent money we didn't have, for things we didn't need, to impress people we don't know. We were not thinking at the moment that this decision would take us the rest of our lives to pay off, at 18 percent interest.[951]

[Debt, Burden of; Deception, Satan's; Materialism, Deception of]

Deut. 4:19; James 1:13–16; 4:1–3

TEN COMMANDMENTS

ALL sporting events have boundaries. The boundaries give the lines in which the game is to be played. In football, sidelines and goal lines establish the boundaries of the game. In tennis, there are lines that establish the boundaries of the court. In baseball, there are foul lines establishing the boundary of the field of play. Those boundaries are designed to maximize the game. Remove the boundaries and you introduce chaos into the field of play. Establish the boundaries and the field of play can be maximized and thoroughly enjoyed. Picture a runner with a football, not wanting to be tackled, making his way up through the stands into the concession area, out onto the parking lot. Running to the other end, coming back up the steps, back through the concession area, down through the stands to the other end zone for a touchdown. There would be chaos. Boundaries, while establishing limitations, also establish capacity for maximizing the game. If a game is to be played, it cannot be a free-for-all where the players each do what they think they ought. Likewise, in the giving of the Ten Commandments, God established boundaries, both to establish limitations and to maximize the game of life.[952]

[Law, Purpose of; Restrictions]

Ex. 20:1–21; Deut. 5:1–22

BUILDERS use levels to measure whether something is perfectly straight or flat. In the middle of this tool, a small capsule holds a liquid with a tiny bubble that sits between two lines. A wall's construction can be determined by placing the level against the wall. If the little bubble settles between the two lines, then the builder can know the wall is flat, straight, and properly built. God's law is our level.[953]

[Law, Purpose of]

Rom. 7:7

A MAN is hanging on the edge of a cliff by holding on to a chain with ten links. Suppose only one link breaks. The nine unbroken chains don't really matter much.[954]

James 2:10–11

TESTS

WHENEVER a teacher in school gave you a test, they never had much to say during the test. Things were silent during the test. The teacher had nothing to say because the test was designed to show what you knew based on what the teacher had already taught you.

Once you get a test, you might not hear much from God. It may be silent. Knowing this, it would be wise for you to have a lot of conversations with Him before He administers the test!

Some people have problems passing their tests. In fact, they keep failing. They quit school. We have a lot of dropouts in Christianity today because people either get discouraged due to not passing the test or they decide they don't want to study.

If you are a dropout or a failing student, it is still better to graduate at twenty, having failed a few times, than to be fifty-five working on your G.E.D. It's better to keep plugging away, doing your best, even though you may have lost some time.[955]

[Trials, Patience in]

Deut. 8:2; Ps. 71:12; James 1:2–4

MANY ladies use timers when cooking so that they know when a dish is done. When the timer runs out, it says, "Bing!" Although the time indicates that the cooking time is over, a good cook will take a fork or a knife and stick it in the middle of the food to make sure that it is ready. That is a test. The timer goes off when a dish should be ready but the knife or fork makes sure that the job is done. Sometimes things can look done on the outside but still be rare on the inside.

Many Christians look done on the outside. They are all dressed up at church, carrying their Bibles, and talking using the lingo, but God doesn't just look at the outside. He has His own tests to make sure that we are done all the way through. God's got us on a timer, but when we should be done, He doesn't stop there. He tests the inside too to make sure that we are done and ready to present for His glory.[956]

[God's Standard; Spiritual Maturity]
1 Sam. 16:7; James 1:2–4

THANKSGIVING, IMPORTANCE OF

AN ATHEIST professor was walking through the woods one day, admiring the accident of evolution. He looked at the trees and the flowers; he observed the rivers and the animals, and he marveled at the magnificence of evolution. All of a sudden, he heard a rustling in the bushes, and out pounced a seven-foot grizzly bear. Immediately, the bear began chasing him. He ran feverishly to save his life, huffing, puffing, and crying, with the bear catching up with him after every step. He tripped and fell. Now the bear hovered over him, ready to pounce. That's when the atheist cried out, "O my God, help me!"

All of a sudden a light came out of heaven. The bear's paw was in the air ready to swipe at him, but the bear froze. The river stopped flowing. The wind stopped blowing. Everything was perfectly quiet and perfectly still. That's when the Voice spoke. The Voice through the light said, "Sir, do you really believe that after all these years of denying Me, after all these years of believing that this universe is merely a cosmic accident, and after all of these years of teaching your students why I do not exist that I would help you now?"

The man peering at the light said, "You know, You're right, my track record is bad, and it would be hypocritical of me to call on You now, but maybe we could approach this a different way. Even though You can't do anything for me, perhaps You could turn the bear into a Christian. If you did that, things would still turn out differently for me."

The Voice from the light said, "As you request." All of a sudden the river began to flow, the wind began to blow, and the trees began to rustle. The bear sat back, picked up its two paws, and clasped them together. It looked up, and said, "O God, thank You for this food I am about to receive."

Things can get scary sometimes. When things get bad enough, it's amazing the new direction people are willing to look.[957]

[Evolution]
Ps. 14:1; 53:1

THANKSGIVING, MOTIVATION FOR

TWO LITTLE girls one day were acting very badly. They were misbehaving. It was on Thanksgiving Day and their father told them, "Girls, go to your room. You are dismissed from Thanksgiving dinner." The girls went dejected and sad to their rooms. A few moments later, they heard their mother calling, "Girls, girls, come down to dinner, girls."

A little baffled in light of what their father had said, they sheepishly walked down to the dinner table and sat down. But they noticed something. Dad was not there. So they naturally asked, "Mother, where is Dad?"

"Dad went to his room."

"But why, Mom?"

"Because Dad loves you so much. He couldn't change his standard, but he didn't want to deny you dinner. So Dad said he would go and pay the price so that you could come and eat the meal. So, while you enjoy the meal, remember that your dad has picked up the tab and is paying the penalty."

Brothers and sisters, when you forget to say thanks for everything else, don't forget to say thanks for Jesus.[958]

[Cross, Jesus; Salvation, Gratefulness for]

John 3:16; Col. 3:16

THOUGHT LIFE

WHEN you burn a CD, you take the music or the movie and you pass it on so that on the other disc has precisely what was the original disc being burned. The copy is precisely the content of the original.

Satan does the same thing when he burns his thoughts into our thinking so that we think his thoughts after him. His goal is to get us to do this until those thoughts are burned so

deeply they become our thoughts. His thinking, which starts as a suggestion, turns into a way of thinking for us, which then turns into a way of operating. The incorrect thinking ends up creating the actions that result from the thoughts.[959]

[Satan, Strategy of; Temptation, Leading to Sin]

Gen. 3:1–6; James 1:13–15

WHEN somebody I know is on drugs, I send them to a group in New Jersey. This is a most unique place. A person addicted to drugs usually can't see themselves apart from their problem. At this place, the people there look at the individual and don't let their addiction define them.

If you are a Christian, you are not an addict. You are a blood-bought child of the Living God who already has been given victory over drugs. The staff at this drug rehab reinforces the real truth. Every time they run into a patient, that patient is supposed to identify themselves, not as a drug addict but as a blood-bought child of God who already has victory over drugs.

All of a sudden, after a week or two, the patients begin to believe what they are telling the staff about themselves. The Bible calls this "mediation."[960]

[Sin, Victory over]

TIME, PERSPECTIVE ON

HAVE you ever been to work and looked up at the clock to note the time . . . let's say that it's 9:00 a.m. Things are going slow. You may not have much to do or maybe it's just one of those slow times on the job. You glance at the clock at what seems like three hours later and it's 9:05 a.m. Time is only creeping along.

But then there are other times when you have so much to do. You start at 9:00 a.m., you work for five minutes, look up at the clock, and it's 3:00 p.m. For these times we like to say "time is flying." Guess what. Time hasn't changed.

Whether you had a lot to do or a little to do, the clock was moving the same. You know what changed when time moved fast? You. Because you had so much to do, those activities occupied your thinking. It made it appear that the clock was spinning.

There is a way we can "hurry God up" without changing His clock. God is sovereign. He controls the clock, but if you will give your undivided attention to being His advertisement, and to pleasing Him, the time that you have to wait will seem to move a lot faster.[961]

[Waiting]

Ps. 38:15; Isa. 30:18; Mic. 7:7

TONGUE

THERE was a frog that wanted to cross the lake but he did not have the wherewithal to go that distance. So he tried to figure out how to get across the water, and he came up with a brilliant idea. There were two birds nearby and he talked the two birds into each picking up a twig, a pretty solid twig, and holding it in their mouths while he grabbed and held on with his mouth in between. The plan was for the birds to fly over and of course fly him across as he held on with his mouth. The birds thought it was very brilliant for the frog to come up with a plan for overcoming an impossible situation. The frog latched his mouth on to the twig as the birds lifted off.

As they ascended, there was a man in the vicinity who saw this unusual site of two birds carrying a frog through the air. He asked out loud, "Whoa! Who came up with that brilliant idea?" The frog said, "I . . ." Opening your mouth at the wrong time in the wrong way can do great harm.[962]

James 3:1–12; 1 Peter 3:10

A LADY said to her pastor, "I struggle with my tongue. I want to put my tongue on the altar." He said, "Our altar's not that big!"[963]

A MAN went to dinner with a friend of his. He asked his friend to take him to a restaurant with the best possible meat selection. The friend took him to a restaurant that served tongue—all kinds of tongue—fried tongue, baked tongue, salad tongue, and other tongue. When he asked his friend why he brought him to a restaurant that served tongue as his choice for the best meat, his friend replied, "What other meat do you know that can bless you, encourage you, strengthen you, and affirm you?"

This same man went to dinner with this same friend and asked to be taken to a restaurant with the worst meat he could find in hopes of getting a different kind of restaurant. Again, they arrived at a place that served tongue. With a knowing look, his friend said, "Hey! What other meat do you know that can curse you, destroy you, or remove dignity from you?"[964]

James 3:9–12

THE SPACE Shuttle Challenger blew up in 1986 because some little rubber rings weren't correctly placed. They were loose. Lives were lost and destroyed because of a very little thing. Similarly, how much damage have we done or has been done to us because somebody's tongue got loose?[965]

[Sin, Effects of]
James 3:3–6

ISN'T IT amazing how, out of one mouth, both constructive and critical speech come forth?

One day a boy told his mother, "Mother, I love you."

The mother, who suffered from a self-esteem problem, said, "How can you love somebody like me who's fat and ugly?"

"Oh Mom, you're not fat and ugly. You're fat and pretty."[966]

TONGUE, POWER OF

ON October 8, 1871, Mrs. O'Leary's cow kicked over the lantern at 8:30 p.m. That led to the Great Chicago Fire. It left 100,000 people homeless, 17,500 buildings destroyed, 300 people dead, and 40 million dollars' worth of damage done—all because a cow kicked over a lantern.

One match can burn down a house. The tongue is like a match. It sets things aflame.[967]

[Sin, Effects of]
James 3:3–6

TRANSFORMATION

THE transformation you long for must come from the divine method God has prescribed. If you run out of gas in a car that requires regular unleaded and put in diesel, you are not going anywhere. At best, you are going to chug along, because that fuel has not been made for your engine. Many of us are trying to be transformed using the wrong fuel and we wonder why we are just chugging along.[968]

[Spiritual Food; Spiritual Transformation]
Isa. 59:2

WHEN a lady gets married, she often comes down the aisle with a veil obscuring her face. Her full picture is hidden. But then there comes a time when the bridegroom removes the veil. He puts the veil toward her back so that she is visibly exposed.

When you come before the Book, in order for the Spirit to do the transforming work, you must come with an unveiled face, and be willing to be exposed.[969]

[Bible, Application of; Spiritual Transformation]
2 Cor. 3:18

TRIALS

TRIALS will come. If you are spiritual, trials will come. If you are carnal, trials will come. If you are a Christian at all, trials will come. That's just how it works. Whether or not you are spiritual or carnal determines whether the trials will get you. Your spiritual maturity determines whether you experience victory or defeat when the trials come.[970]

[Pain; Spiritual Maturity; Suffering]
John 15:20; 16:33

A LITTLE boy was on a plane one day that was experiencing violent turbulence. The plane was going up and down and all over the place. The lady sitting next to the little boy was terrified. She couldn't understand why the little boy was happily playing and having fun. After a while of observing him, she just couldn't stand it any longer.

"Little boy, please stop it! Stop having so much fun! How can you have fun when the plane is going through this?"

The little boy put his hand on the lady's hand and said, "Lady, my daddy is the pilot."

When your daddy is the pilot, you can handle the turbulence because you know he's got it all under control.[971]

[Father God]
Prov. 3:5–6; John 16:33

WHEN I was growing up, there would be occasional tests of the emergency broadcast system. The national defense system would interrupt the television broadcast and the viewer would hear, "This is a test." Ordinary programming was interrupted in order to do a test. A trial is when the ordinary programming of life gets interrupted.[972]

John 16:33

JUST like a sculptor takes marble and chips away at it in order to bring out of that piece of slab an image, God chips away at the things that are not like Christ through the act of chiseling us with trouble. He calls it the testing of your faith.[973]

[Tests]
Rom. 5:3–5; James 1:2–4

WHEN you soak a sponge in water and then press down on it, what's inside comes out. A trial is the pressure on our lives that shows us what we've been soaking up. Trials show us what's really inside.[974]

[Tests; Trials, Purpose of]
1 Cor. 3:12–15

LIKE a photographer carefully develops his film in a darkroom, God allows us to go through dark times because He is trying to develop a beautiful image of Christ in us.[975]

GENERAL Motors will put two dummies in a car and ram it into a wall. There will be one dummy behind the wheel and one dummy on the passenger side. The goal for GM is not to be mean to their vehicles; they are testing them. They want to see how much their vehicles can take. They want to find out where the flaws are that need to be corrected. They want to see how much their cars can stand with the ultimate goal being to make a better car.

Some of us are just dummies! We get rammed into the wall and we think God is trying to mess us up when He is simply trying to make us better Christians. He lets us run into the wall so we can identify our flaws. He shows us things about ourselves, things we said we'd never do—Bam! language we said we'd never use— Bam! places we said we'd never go— Bam! He allows us to see our own imperfections so that we realize we are not like Him as much as we thought we were. God allows us to have encounters that show us our need for Him.[976]

[Tests; Trials, Purpose of]
James 1:2–4; 1 Peter 1:6–7

WHEN my wife is baking something in the oven, she will do what I am sure many of you ladies do: slide it out and stick it with a fork to see whether it's done or not. You do this because you want to know if the dish is ready to be eaten. You will put that cake or that pie into the oven, a fiery ordeal, and then let it sit for a while before even bothering to check it. The idea is to let the item be in the fire a sufficient amount of time to be made ready.

God may have you in the fire, but He is getting you ready for the Master. He wants to make sure you are well done for the Master. He wants to make sure that when the Master sits down, there is a well-prepared life for Him. Sometimes that means that even when you think you are ready, He puts you back in. Although you may look done on the outside, God knows that you may not been done all the way through and He wants to make sure that you are ready. God is both the cook and the Master. He makes sure that you are done and ready to present for His glory.[977]

[Tests; Trials, Purpose of]
Dan. 3:1–30; Isa. 48:10

I USED to love Pop-Tarts. You know, you put them in the toaster, and you press the toaster button down and then wait for them to pop up. Every now and then, the Pop-Tarts would pop back up before they were ready. They just were not fully toasted like I wanted them to be so I had to push the button back down again. I wanted the heat to have a chance to do its sufficient work and make those pastries satisfactory for my enjoyment.

Sometimes in trials, God pushes us down in the heat but we want to pop up and pop out. He says that if we let this difficult time have its ultimate conclusion, we'll pop up when

we're ready and then we will be blessed. So if you're going through a trial, or an adverse circumstance, don't just be concerned about popping up and popping out before God has completed His purpose. Know that He simply will push the toaster button down again to continue the process of spiritual maturity.[978]

[Tests; Trials, Purpose of]
Dan. 3:1–30; Isa. 48:10

A COMPANY asked all of its employees to give to the United Fund. They wanted to have every employee participate. There was one man who refused to give at all. He said, "I'm not going to give anything to the United Fund so don't bother to ask me." When told that the boss wanted everyone to give, the man said again, "I am not going to give any of my hard-earned money to that fund."

Word got back to the boss that this employee was not going to give. He called the employee into his office.

"Now, I know you have heard that I want 100 percent participation in the fund from my employees. So I have two choices. I can receive from you now your contribution, or I can cut you from my payroll so that I'll still have 100 percent support. Which do you choose?"

The man said, "Well, here's my money right now."

The boss said, "So, what made you change your mind?"

The employee said, "Well, nobody quite explained it to me like that before." Trials are an important and very integral part of the life of every Christian. Everyone has faced one, is facing one, or will face one. Although we might not understand them all the time, we must know that they work for our good and our ultimate goal of becoming more like Christ. This is the basic tenet of trials. This is adversity 101.[979]

[Trials, Purpose of]

TRIALS, BENEFITS OF

ONE time I was flying back from Raleigh, North Carolina. As we approached Dallas, the pilot came over the loudspeaker and said, "There are storms over the Dallas /Fort Worth Airport and the airport has shut down. We can't land. We have been rerouted to Abilene, Texas. There's too much bad weather happening over the Dallas Fort/Worth Airport and we can't get in. We can't get there from here because there is too much turbulence in the air. We will be rerouted to another location."

When we arrived in Abilene, a passenger nearby called for a flight attendant and told her that he was originally supposed to make a connection in Dallas for a flight to Abilene. Since he had already reached his destination, he wanted to know if he could just be let off the plane!

A few minutes later, I watched as a passenger with his two children get off at the back of the plane and walk to the terminal because they were home. Now, this wasn't how they planned to get home, but due to a diversion caused by turbulence in the air, they got to their intended destination quicker than expected.

God is so good that He can hit the turbulence in your life, veer off, and still take you home and make it look like that was the plan all the time.

God is able to take it, turn it, twist it, and use it and still get you home no matter where you are in your life. It's never too late. God can take a mess and make a miracle. He can hit a bull's-eye with a crooked stick.[980]

[God's Deliverance]
Rom. 8:28

TRIALS, CONFIDENCE IN

WE WERE on a ministry cruise to Alaska, spending time with some of the folks who support the Urban Alternative, when a storm broke out. It was a wicked storm. The worst storm some of the crew had ever seen. There were squalls, waves up to forty feet high. We are on a cruise liner and it was being tossed around like a tin can.

So my wife started getting a little bit evangelically ticked off. We had found out that the captain knew we were going to hit the storm, but he had to get back because he had paying customers that he had to pick up for the next cruise. So it was a business deal for him. My wife was very concerned and irritated that he would inconvenience our passengers like this. People were throwing up, the plates were falling all over the place, and everyone was a wreck. It was a wicked situation.

My wife picked up the phone and asked the operator to connect her with the captain.

"Well, I am sorry. The captain is tied up on the bridge now with this storm. He can't speak to you."

"Well, I just don't understand why he would put us through this, knowing the storm is coming."

"Well, I'll deliver the message,

but he can't talk to you."

We get a call back in a few minutes. It was the assistant captain.

He said, "I was given your message, and we will gave it to the captain. The captain has two responses. One, go to sleep. You can go to sleep because I am staying up. You can't do anything from the cabin so go to sleep and know that I am staying up. The second thing is, this ship was built with this storm in mind." He said, "I know it looks bad, but when we built this boat, we knew this day was going to come out here on this water, and we've already taken that into consideration. This storm did not catch us by surprise, and though it's inconvenient, and though it's rough, though it's difficult, you can still go to sleep because the boat can handle the storm."

I don't know what God is letting you go through, but His message to you today is go to sleep, because I am staying up. He has orchestrated your life so that you can withstand whatever trials He has allowed to come through.[981]

[Temptation]
1 Cor. 10:13

ONE of the things I love for my wife to cook over the holidays is 7-Up Cake. This cake will make a grown man cry. She gets out butter, but if I tried to eat the butter on its own, it would make me sick. It has no inherent tasty value just as butter, but she throws it into the mixer. She gets out the sugar. Now, I do like a little sugar, but if I were to take all of that sugar in, it would only make me sick. She takes the sugar and throws that into the mixer too. She gets out the flour. I would never eat the flour by itself but she throws that into the mixer. She takes a little of this, and a little of that, and throws it into the mixer. She turns the mixer on and, all of a sudden, those independent agents that were no good by themselves are intermingled with one another. They then form this gooey substance, this paste, this batter. Now, the dough is better than the independent elements. I remember growing up as a boy and licking the batter from the bowl. But even as good as the batter is, it's still not good enough. I have never eaten a whole bowl of batter!

My wife then pours that batter into a pan and sets it in a fire. All of a sudden, that batter that was in a cool environment is now set aflame by 350-degree heat, and it sits in there minute after minute. I know if that batter could talk, it would probably ask to be taken out of the fire because of the heat. However, the batter would need to know that it isn't simply being cooked; it is being created and remade into something else. My wife's goal was to take various ingredients and make something beautiful of them.

I can tell you, when the cake comes out of the oven, I could be in the back bedroom, but I will smell the cake and get levitated into the kitchen. My wife takes all things, mixes them together, and it comes out finger-licking good.

God is not just cooking us when we feel the heat. He's not just raising the temperature of our circumstances in order to make us suffer. He's up to something. He's taking the random pieces of our lives and making something out of it. We need to know that our problems will be used of God. We need to know that our disappointments are going to be used by God. We need to know that our pain is going to be used of God. We must trust that our singleness is going to be used by God. We must believe that the doctor's reports will be used by God.

We know these things, not because we can prove it but because we know Him. We must believe that He ultimately is after our good and that all of our life's circumstances will work together accordingly.[982]

[Trials, Purpose of]

Rom. 8:28; James 1:2–4;
1 Peter 1:6–7

TRIALS, ENDURANCE DURING

ONE thing I like about going weight lifting is that I don't go by myself. When I'm doing the bench press, begin to strain on number twelve or thirteen, and start making weird noises, it becomes obvious that I'm pressing more weight than what I can bear. It becomes evident that if I keep pressing the limits, I could very well drop the weights and let them fall down on me, cracking my sternum or crashing against my Adam's apple.

But just in the nick of time, the gentleman who is standing over me and there to help me, reaches over me and says, "You keep pushing, but I've got you. Keep going but I'm here too. You don't have to push up these last few on your own."

Then when I've gone up for the last one, he does a mercy thing for me. He lifts the weights totally out of my hands and puts them on the rack.

That's grace. That's what God does. When the weight of your trial is too heavy and you can't keep it up, when your arms are trembling and you're making all kinds of noises, when you're going through difficulty, God's grace steps in, carries the weight, picks it up, and puts it on the rack.[983]

[God's Deliverance; Mercy]

Joel 3:10; 1 Cor. 10:13; 2 Cor. 12:10

THERE is a story about the Lone Ranger. He and his sidekick, Tonto, are crossing the plains. All of a sudden, a group of Indians attack from the south. Tonto says, "What do we do, Kimosabi?" He says, "Well, we should go to the north." So they go north to run from the Indians but then shortly run into another group of Indians positioned on a northern ridge, prepared to attack also. Tonto says, "Kimosabi, what do we do now?" The Lone Ranger says, "Well, we should go west."

They hit the western ridge only to find a group of Indians there too. Tonto says, "Well, what do we do now, Kimosabi?" The Lone Ranger says, "Well, we can only go east. That's all that's left." The problem was that another group of Indians were positioned to attack from the east. They were surrounded! The Indians were slowly closing in on them from all sides. The Lone Ranger looked at Tonto and asked, "What do we do now, Tonto? These are your people." Tonto replied, "What do you mean *we*, Kimosabi?"

It's easy to jump ship when the going gets tough.[984]

TRIALS, PATIENCE IN

ON A Wednesday night a few years ago,

I went to the hospital, because I got a phone call that my daughter, Priscilla, was in labor. I walked inside of the room, and she said, "Dad, I've never had pain like this in my life. I thought I was going to die. I hate Eve."

On top of that she had to cooperate with the pain, because the doctors wanted her to push. There were grunts, groans, and tears. It was a painful situation. But she didn't quit. Why? Because she knew that at the end of the process, no matter how long it took, hour after hour, at the end of the process, something was going to be born. She counted it all joy, not because of the pain, but she counted it all joy because she knew what would be produced because of the pain.

If you asked her when she held that baby in her arms for the first time if it was worth it, she'd tell you yes. In fact, the reason I know she and many other ladies think that it's worth it is because they decide to do it again.

God wants us to know that when He allows or brings a trial into our lives, it is with the purpose of giving birth to something—birth to a new reality of Jesus Christ, birth to a new level of spiritual growth, and birth to new depths. In trials you don't feel happy and don't feel bad that you don't feel happy, because usually with trials there is no love and happiness. However, God wants us to know that our experiences, although painful at times, are not in vain.[985]

[Pain; Suffering; Trials, Benefits of]
Rom. 5:3–5; James 1:2–4

MY SON Anthony suffered terribly from asthma when he was a kid. I had to take him to the doctor's office quite a bit. On one trip, the doctor had to give him an epinephrine shot. Those needles hurt, but the doctor was amazing at how he handled kids and needles. He would give Anthony a lollipop and Anthony would go to licking. While he was focused on the lollipop, the doctor would hit him with the needle. Anthony was in pain and in agony. He didn't see or understand all the doctor was doing. All he knew was that the doctor who was supposed to help him was hurting him. The doctor was supposed to be relieving pressure on his lungs but was instead causing him to cry and huff and puff more. It looked like the one who was there for him was against him. However, after a few seconds, Anthony decided that since he had the lollipop in his hand he might as well enjoy it. He would go back to licking it and shortly forget about the pain.

Many of us feel that way in a trial. It seems that the God who is supposed to be for you is acting like He's against you. However, God is faithful to provide us opportunities of joy within those trials if we look for them. With tears running down your face, Jesus is your lollipop, and He is sweet, I know. Focus on the eternal perspective.[986]

[Eternal Perspective; Trials, Endurance during]
2 Cor. 4:7–18; 1 Peter 1:6–7

TRIALS, PURPOSE OF

WHEN I was dating my wife, I took her to an amusement park in Baltimore. They have this ride called the Wild Mouse. I suggested this ride very strategically. You see, it was a ride that I knew would create a little fear in her and therefore create a little situation. The ride would take us way out, dive down, and then turn back on the track, returning to the starting point. Every time we rode out and the car dipped down, my wife would scream, and she'd slide over. I created this situation because I knew if the ride got bad enough, she wouldn't stay where she was seated. She'd have to move in my direction, and of course you see where she is sitting this morning.

God creates situations, allows scenarios, and at times, causes issues. He does so because He wants to create a situation that will encourage us to slide over and to realize that we are totally and absolutely dependent on Him.[987]

[God's Discipline]
Ps. 73:28; James 4:8

A LADY saw a ranger handling a three-hundred-pound loggerhead sea turtle. These are huge turtles, these loggerheads by the sea, and this particular turtle was was just laying eggs. She became somewhat disoriented, and began walking in the wrong direction, not toward the sea but farther into the sand dunes. So the ranger came and pried her from the ground, flipping her over onto her back. The ranger put chains around the loggerhead's legs, hooked it onto his vehicle, and drug it back to the sea.

When he finally got to the edge of the water, he unhooked the animal, the loggerhead saw where it was, and it went out into the sea. I'm sure, when the loggerhead was being chained and drug, it was hard for it to understand what was happening.

Sometimes it's hard to know whether you are being killed or saved by the hand of the one turning your life upside down. When you are on your back being turned every which way but loose, you don't know whether God is doing you in or delivering you. When He puts you to lie there, you don't know which way is up, and you are lying flat on your back. Guess what, sometimes God makes us to lie down. God will take the credit for putting us on our backs to fix whatever is wrong and make us totally anemic within ourselves. He will put us in a place where there's only room for one God.[988]

[God's Discipline]
Ps. 23:2; Heb. 12:11

WHY do you iron your shirts? You iron because you want to get the wrinkles out of it. In order for the iron to get wrinkles out, it has to be hot. A "fiery trial" has to be applied to that particular piece of clothing. You want the clothes to be wrinkle-free because you are going to wear them and wearing wrinkles won't make you look good.

Jesus Christ is within you. He is inside of you and cloaked by you. But we have wrinkles on us that don't reflect well on Him, so God has to iron them out, which requires fire.

He must address the wrinkles and He does it by using trials. Now, if you insist on wearing a wrinkled life, covering Jesus Christ, thus making Him look bad, then evidently the fire is not hot enough. Since God's purpose is to conform you and me to the image of Christ, He will make that iron as hot as necessary, and keep it on the wrinkle for as long as necessary, until what we look like on the outside conforms to the life of Christ at work on the inside. Let patience have its perfect work.[989]

James 1:2–4

WHEN eagles want to get their eaglets to the next level, they stir the nest. Eagles put broken twigs in the nest, so that as the babies begin to grow, and rest on them, they become a little irritated. Then the eagles stir the nest and put grassy stuff underneath, bringing the needling to the top, so that when the eaglets try to sit down, after awhile, they can't take being stuck anymore.

When it can't take being stuck anymore, it begins to fly. The eagle knows this eaglet will never move to the next level of height, unless its surroundings are irritated. Only after being irritated does the eaglet make use of its wings. Only after being irritated does an eaglet that was stuck on the ground level begin to soar through the sky.

God wants you to soar through the sky. So sometimes, He's got to stir the nest of your comfortability.[990]

[Brokenness, Importance of; Pain]
Prov. 1:32; Rev. 3:15–16

WE HAVE all taken pictures and sent them to the developer. The pictures are originally on the negatives, which aren't really that great to look at. The pictures are small and not easy to see. So in order to get pictures that you can see, the developers have to take the negatives to the darkroom where they can be developed in secret.

When the pictures come back to you, they are larger and now in color. The final product looks nothing like the original image on the negative. In order to get to the final product, however, the negatives have to be taken to a darkroom where they are worked over by the man in the photo lab.

We can't always see what God is doing. It may look like all we are getting is one negative after another. However, there is good news. God is working on the negatives in a darkroom, in secret where we can't see. When it is the right time, He will bring them back in living color. We will see that He was up to something and working something out that we didn't know about. He has a purpose for every trial that you face. He has a reason for your development in your trial.[991]

John 16:33

MOST ladies have, at some point and time, purchased cutlery. The finest cutlery, and the most expensive, are those that have taken the most time and patience to produce. The process of producing this expensive cutlery is called tempering. It is where steel is heated to red-hot and then hammered into shape. Sparks fly everywhere when they start hammering it. Then the knives are put into water to cool it down. This process of heating and cooling is repeated over and over again. The finest cutlery is the steel that has been tempered the most.

This is what God does for us. He puts us in the furnace of a trial, hammers on you, and then He cools you off. Then just when you're getting comfortable being cooled, He lifts you out, puts you in the fire, hammers you some more, then He cools you off. That's why you'll always notice in the midst of a trial, God will periodically give you good days.

We get frustrated because the good days don't last long. We wonder why our trials can't be over. It is because we are not fully tempered. God wants us to be fine cutlery, not cheap knives. He wants us to be finely tuned.[992]

[Trials, Endurance during]
2 Cor. 4:7–18; 1 Peter 1:6–7

A DOCTOR has a knife. When a doctor makes an incision, you bleed. A mugger has a knife. If he cuts you and hurts you, you bleed. Is there a difference between the doctor's knife and the mugger's knife since both do the same thing? Both cut you. With either you are hurt and you bleed. Is a mugger and doctor the same? Of course not. Even though they do the same thing, it's not the same. The difference between a doctor's knife and a mugger's knife is intent.

The doctor's intent in cutting you is to fix something that's wrong to make you stronger. The mugger's intent in cutting you is to break something to make you weaker. They both do the same thing but their intent is different.

Satan's intent is to destroy. Satan's intent is to disable. Satan's intent is to subjugate. God's intent, even if He has to cut you and let you bleed, is always to set you free. You can thank God that when you're cut, it's designed to heal you.[993]

James 1:2–4

TENDERIZING meat can be done in a number of ways. Sometimes, you can sprinkle some tenderizing powder on it and let the meat sit and soften.

Sometimes, meat must be tenderized the hard way. It has to be hit over and over with a mallet! BAM!!!

Trials work in the same way. They are designed to soften us and make us more pliable in the hands of God. Sometimes they are long and slow and we just have to sit and wait for change to occur. Sometimes, trials are hard and tumultuous and we must respond quickly to God's prodding in our lives.[994]

TRIALS, VALUE OF

IF I take a one-hundred-dollar bill and ask a roomful of people who would like to have it, virtually every hand would go up. If I were to take that same bill and ball it up, crumpling it up badly, and then ask who would want it, most people would raise their hands yet again. If I then took that hundred-dollar bill and stepped on it, those same people would still be interested in getting it. Why? Even though that bill had been through a lot, it still would not have lost its value.

The same applies to us when we go through difficult trials. Even when you've been through a lot, stepped on, and abused, you haven't lost your value to God. Even if you've gotten dirty, when God looks at you, He does not consider you chump change. When it looks like your whole world is caving in on you and none of your prayers are being answered, there is good news: you are still worth something to God and He still wants you.[995]

[Christian, Value of]
1 Cor. 6:20; 1 John 3:1

TRINITARIANISM

ONE of the great doctrines that is unbeknownst to many but is a hot doctrine today is Trinitarianism. Muslims say that they believe in one God. Christians say that they believe in one God. Although both groups are saying the same thing, they really are not saying the same thing at all. The Christian God is not the same god as the Muslim god because the Christian God is a triune God. He is God as Father, God as Son, God as Spirit. The Muslim god is not a triune god so it is a flawed view of God. It's not Trinitarian.

If you believe that Texas has a capital and I believe that Texas has a capital, it sounds like we believe the same thing. However, if you think the capital is Fort Worth, and I think the capital is Austin, we do not believe in the same thing. Believing in one capital doesn't mean we believe in the same thing.[996]

[False Religion]

TRINITY

A PRETZEL has three holes. The first hole is not the second hole, the second hole is not the third hole, but the same dough ties all three holes together. One pretzel, three holes. There's one God made up of three distinct beings, the Father, the Son, and the Spirit, but they're all tied together by the same essence or the same divine nature. The same attributes, perfections, and descriptions of one belong to the others.[997]

[God, Knowing]
2 Cor. 13:14

TRUST IN GOD

WHEN I was boy growing up, I used to love to watch the telephone man. He was like superman to me because he could climb up on the telephone pole.

He just seemed to be good at hustling up and down that thing.

I got a chance to talk to a telephone man one day. I was trying to find out how he managed getting up and down that pole so easily. He explained that, first of all, his shoes had spikes. Secondly, he explained that, in climbing, he made it a point to rest against his belt so that he could get a firm implant with his shoes.

The telephone man admitted that as a young man he really didn't know how to do it, nor did he trust the belt. Instead of resting in the belt, he would slide down the post. As a result, he got quite a few splinters.

Many of us, because we refuse to trust God, keep getting splinters in our lives—things that keep sticking us that we can't get over, things that keep jabbing us that we can't get around. We will continue to get splinters until we learn to trust in God and to put all of our confidence in His Word.[998]

[Bible, Sufficiency of; Self-Sufficiency, Sin of]
Prov. 3:5–6; John 14:1

WHAT we need today is a generation of Christians who will have the guts to believe that following God has pleasure. It's not a boring life.

There is a story of a kite that was flying and the kite began to talk to itself. The kite said, "If only I could get rid of this string. If the string wasn't holding me back, then I could fly. I could fly above the clouds. I could fly as high as I wanted to. If I could get rid of this string, there would be nothing holding me back. I'm limited by this string."

One day the kite got its wish. The string broke and the kite came crashing down. What the kite did not realize was that the same string that kept it down kept it up. Cutting the string did not make it freer.

We will always head toward disaster when we cut the string of dependence on God in search of more pleasure. The same string that seems to hold you down also keeps you flying high. God wants us to trust him and let Him hold the string. Staying connected to Him keeps us from falling.[999]

[Independence, Consequences of; Self-Sufficiency, Danger of]
Luke 15:11–24

TRUTH

IF YOU are diagnosed with a disease, you do not want your doctor to spare your feelings and lie to you. You want your doctor to tell you the truth so that you can get your illness fixed. The saying "Take two aspirins and call me in the morning" doesn't work if you have cancer. The truth hurts, but just like a disease, you have to hear about your problem in order to address it.[1000]

Rom. 3:23; 1 John 1:8

JESUS was the only preacher who made His congregations smaller with His sermons. He would have big crowds following Him and then He would come up with a line like "Unless you deny your mother and father, yea, your own life, you cannot be My disciple." The Bible says those people left. Why? Because He never let the crowd control the truth.[1001]

[Jesus; Truth, Results of]
Luke 14:26; John 6:60–66

AN OLDER gentleman had some health problems. He went to visit his doctor and was told to change his diet. The physician lectured the man on the importance of eating well, and gave him a long list of things to eat and not eat.

The gentleman called his sons to let them know about his declining health as he knew his son would be concerned. He explained the doctor's prognosis and his prescription for restoring good health.

A couple of weeks later, one of the aged man's sons called to check on him. "OK, Dad, the doctor gave you some instructions awhile back. How is the regimen going?" The old man replied, "I've changed doctors."

Sometimes our response to the truth is not the best response.[1002]

[Truth, Results of]

A MAN came home from fishing and said, "I caught me a twenty-pound fish." His wife said, "Just a minute." She went into the pantry and brought out her scale. The man said, "Well, you know, it might not be quite twenty pounds." When there was a standard to measure the information against, the information changed.[1003]

[God's Standard; Standard]
Prov. 23:23; Eph. 4:25

A MAN asked three of his friends to tell him the meaning of truth. One of his friends was a psychologist; he said truth is what one feels it to be. Another one was an accountant; he said truth is what one needs it to be. Another one was a lawyer; he said truth is what one can make it to be.

People today talk often about the concept of "my truth" and the opinion that truth is relative and completely determined by their point of view.[1004]

[Standard]

John 14:6; 1 Cor. 8:5–6

TRUTH, IMPORTANCE OF

IT'S AMAZING. People want objective standards when it comes to everything else, but not for how to live their life. But suppose you went to the doctor and he was getting ready to perform an operation and he said, "Now, I think this is where I need to cut. Other doctors have ideas of where to cut, but this is what I think. Let's just check it out and see if I cut right." Is that the doctor whom you want?

Suppose you went to a pharmacist and he said, "Well, I think this is the medicine you should take. Now, the pharmacist down the street has another view, but this is what I think. Why don't you try it?"

Suppose you got on a plane and the pilot said, "Now, I think this is the button I'm supposed to push. Now, my engineer over here thinks I ought to push this button. My copilot over here thinks I should push that button. The flight attendant thinks I should push this other button. Well . . . let's try this button and see if it gets us off the ground."

No! At the doctor's office, you want truth. At the pharmacist's, you want truth. In the airplane, you sure enough want truth. You don't want a pilot saying, "I think," or a doctor saying, "I think," or a pharmacist saying, "I think." You're going to sue him if he thinks wrong. You want him to think right.

Well now, if you can respect the truth of a doctor and the truth of a pharmacist, and you can respect the truth of a pilot, how come God can't be trusted? He's truth—an absolute standard of reality found in the Word of God.[1005]

[Bible, Authority of; Trust in God]

John 14:6; Acts 4:12; 1 Cor. 8:5–6

TRUTH, RESULTS OF

KITTY Dukakis was interviewed on *20/20* and made public her addictions. Not only was she taking pills and drinking alcohol, but she was drinking rubbing alcohol and nail remover—anything that had a tidbit of alcohol. During the interview, she admitted that she didn't begin to come to grips with her problem until she finally faced the truth that she was, indeed, an addict. As long as she could give excuses, as long as she could blame it on the campaign, as long as she could blame it on the pressure, as long as she blamed it on something else and did not deal with the truth, she was killing herself. When Ms. Dukakis came to understand the truth, then she was able to get something done. Some of us won't get better until somebody gets the guts to tell us the truth.[1006]

[Confrontation; Truth, Speaking the]

Eph. 4:15; James 5:19–20

YEARS ago, *The Betty Ford Story* aired on television. This was a movie that told the story of her addiction and recovery. At a point during the movie, a fairly emotional scene took place. The family is all sitting around confronting Betty Ford. Her son says, "Mother, you are destroying yourself; you are destroying this family, and you are killing yourself. Mother, you are a drunk, you are an addict." The mother was infuriated. She told her son that he was being very disrespectful and questioned his right to speak to her that way. She said, "How can you say these things to me? I am your mother!" The boy said, "Mother, I can say it because it is the truth." This confrontation was the catalyst for the establishment of the Betty Ford Clinic. Now this same place helps a lot of other people overcome their addictions. Many of the people who have come to the clinic were able to face their addictions because, like Betty Ford's son, someone had the guts to tell the truth.[1007]

> [Confrontation; Truth, Speaking the]
> Eph. 4:15; James 5:19–20

IF SOME of those folks who went to Jonestown, Guyana, had asked for the truth, they'd be alive today. If somebody had asked Jim Jones about his lifestyle—his promiscuity, for instance—and asked him to validate his teachings and lifestyle with the Book of Truth, people would have seen him as a false teacher. They would have known the truth and wouldn't have willingly taken cyanide and died. No one stopped to ask, "Is this the truth?"[1008]

> [False Religion; Truth,
> Importance of]

TRUTH, SPEAKING THE

A PASTOR came to a new church. After he had been there for a few months, he got to know two of the influential men of the church who were brothers. They were multimillionaires who were not known to be very godly men, but he was determined to have an authentic ministry and preach the Word. As time went on, one of the

brothers died. The other brother who was still alive went to the pastor and said, "Now Pastor, I know that you are going to be doing the funeral in a couple of days, and I also know that you want to build a brand-new church. So I tell you what, I will put the money in the church's account to build a brand-new church if you say at my brother's funeral that he was a saint. All you've got to do is say that he was a saint and you don't have to worry about your new church building."

The pastor felt himself on the horns of a dilemma. On the one hand, he desired to be authentic, and, on the other hand, he needed the cash for his church. The question was how to build his new church with the money sitting right in front of him, and yet be authentic when this guy was a crook.

The pastor thought for a second and then said, "Well, I will do it."

The businessman wrote out a check for hundreds of thousands of dollars and gave it to the pastor. The pastor deposited it in the bank account of the church. It came time for the funeral. He got up to do the eulogy. As he stood, he said, "Ladies and gentlemen, we are here today to eulogize a very ungodly sinner. He was a very wicked man who was unfaithful to his wife, who was hot-tempered. He abused his children, he was ruthless in business, and he was a pure hypocrite. But compared to his brother, he was a saint."[1009]

Jesus is concerned with authenticity.

> [Christian Living, Authenticity]
> Zech. 8:16; Col. 3:9

U

UNEQUALLY YOKED

A MAN went to the airport, and he ran into this pretty, pretty girl. They began talking, and they began to click with each other. Something was happening; fire was starting to ignite. He finally asked her, "Where are you flying to?"

She said, "I am flying to Canada. Where are you flying to?"

The man replied, "I am flying to Mexico." And then he came up with a bright idea: "Why don't we get on the same plane?"

What he didn't think of in his stricken state is that it is impossible for two people to travel together when one's going up and the other's going down.[1010]

[Marriage]
2 Cor. 6:14

WHEN steam rises, it goes up. When snowflakes fall, they come down. They're made of the same thing; they are both water. But they are both going in two different directions. Snow can't hang out with steam, and steam can't hang out with snow. Why? Because even though they're made of the same basic stuff, they are not headed in the same direction.[1011]

[Marriage]
2 Cor. 6:14

UNFORGIVENESS

A LADY was walking her dog, and the dog was trying to get away from the leash. But every time the dog pulled away, the lady would yank it, pulling the dog back, and the animal couldn't get free. The leash held it hostage, kept it bound, and unable to break away. He couldn't break the chain.

Many of us today find ourselves held hostage by a leash. The links on the chain are many. There is the link of anger, the link of bitterness, the link of resentment, and the link of revenge. But no matter how many links are in the chain, they all boil down to one thing, unforgiveness.[1012]

[Christ, Freedom in; Forgiveness]
Eph. 4:32; Col. 3:13

A COUPLE of years ago, I was driving and getting ready to turn onto my street when someone hit me from behind. I stopped, got out of the car, went around the back, and examined the damage. The rear of my car was dented in. It was the other driver's fault, but it was my inconvenience.

I took out my license and said, "Let's exchange insurance information."

The other driver said, "I don't have any."

We had a problem. The problem is that I had a dent in my car that was caused by somebody else. Somebody would have to pay this bill because the fact remained that my car had a dent in it. However, if I waited around for him to fix it, I'd be driving for years with a dent in the back of my car. So guess what I did. I picked up the tab. The moment I picked up the tab, I didn't have to drive around with a dent anymore. I made the payment.

Many of us are living our lives with dents on the soul. Somebody has run into us, somebody has messed over us, or somebody has insulted us, and we've been driving our lives for years, waiting for their insurance package to pick it up. But they are uninsured, and they are never going to pick up the tab. Because you refused to pick it up yourself, you are forever dented in your soul.[1013]

[Forgiveness; Hard Heart]
Matt. 5:23–24; Col. 3:13

UNGRATEFULNESS

A MOTHER was trying to teach her daughter to pray, but the little girl didn't want to. Her mother tried to motivate her to pray by putting her on a guilt trip. "You have so much to be thankful for. Think of all the children who don't have food, don't have clothes, or don't have parents like you." The girl replied, "Well, then, they are the ones who need to pray."[1014]

[Children, Training; Prayer]
Eph. 6:18; Col. 4:2

THERE are many parents who have ungrateful children. It is very frustrating. Parents spend so much time working to provide for their children and to give to them so much at no cost to those children. Free food, free housing, free clothes, free spending money, free tennis shoes, and free gas. Thinking about it will make a mom or dad mad! Parents do all this because they love them. However, most kids don't recognize orappreciate the free gifts, they only see the restrictions and want to complain.

"How come I can't go?" "How come I can't stay out later?" "How come I can't have it?"

Anyone who understands the peril of living with an ungrateful teenager understands how God feels about his own ungrateful kids. God

gives good things day after day, week after week, month after month, year after year, and His children miss His goodness and His grace.[1015]

[Blessing, Source of; Grace, Appreciation of; Gratefulness; Salvation, Gratefulness for]
Deut. 8:10; Ps. 100:4

UNITY

ONE of the great experiments when it comes to nationality is the American Experiment. The American Experiment is unique because of its intentionality to bring people from all walks of life, from every nation, under the banner of a single flag and to intentionally seek to bring across to these shores people from all kinds of other nations who would make up a union called the United States of America. This Experiment brought people together who would pledge allegiance to a single flag even though their backgrounds were different, unique, and dissimilar. We acknowledge our differences by annotating our original heritages to our current nationality with terms like Irish American, Swedish American, Polish American, African American, or Hispanic American. The introductory phrase cites the uniqueness. The last word cites the unity. Whatever I am uniquely based on regarding culture, history, background, or previous location, I am that under the American Banner. There was in this Experiment an attempt to have a United States even though the people seeking to be unified were totally different. What the American Experiment represents from a cultural, historical, and geographical perspective to this nation, the church of

Jesus Christ was meant to be for the King of Kings and Lord of Lords—people from different backgrounds, cultures, and perspectives, all pledging allegiance to the cross.[1016]

[Race Relations]

1 Cor. 12:12–31; Gal. 3:28; Rev. 7:9

IF A football team is unified, it does not mean that everyone's playing the same position. It does mean everybody's going to the same goal line. If an orchestra is harmonious, it's not because they're all playing the same instrument; it's because they're all playing the same song. If a choir is singing in great harmony, it's not because they are singing the same parts; it's because they're adding their part to the same song. It is the goal that produces the unity. Unity is not sameness. Unity has to do with same purpose.[1017]

[Body of Christ; Christian Living, Purpose]

Rom. 12:5; 1 Cor. 12:12–31

THERE is a story of a little teeny pygmy who was standing over a rhinoceros that he killed. This was an odd sight to behold, a big, violent rhinoceros under the feet of a little teeny pygmy. A guy saw this dead rhinoceros and this little pygmy over it and said, "Did you kill that?" The little pygmy said, "Yeah I killed it." Curious, the man asked, "So how did you, a little tiny pygmy, kill this rhinoceros?" He answered, "With my club. Yep! I killed this rhinoceros with my club." The man was still thoroughly confused, "Well, how big is your club?" The pygmy said, "There are about a hundred of us in my club." In other words, he was surrounded by folk who had the same belief systems and worked together so that they could handle

being attacked by a rhinoceros.[1018]

[Body of Christ]

Heb. 10:25

ONE hundred pianos, all tuned to the same tuning fork, are inherently tuned to one another. In order for there to be unity, there must be something out there that everybody is tuned to. For Christians, that tuning instrument is the Spirit. The only way to be unified is that everybody is focused on going where the Spirit is going. Everyone has to have a God perspective that governs their thinking.[1019]

[Holy Spirit, Guidance; Holy Spirit, Role of]

1 Cor. 12:13; Eph. 4:4–6

V

VICTORY

PRO WRESTLING is staged. Before the wrestlers ever go out, it has been predetermined who will win. The contenders go through the battle for entertainment purposes but the point of the battle is not to decide who will win but to give the crowd a show. The winner of the match does not battle for victory but from victory. He battles knowing that he's already won.

Those who come to Jesus Christ have already won. God allows us to go through our Christian walk, not to win the victory but to show off to the world that He that is in us is greater than He that is in the world.[1020]

[Christian Living, Power; Sin, Victory over]

John 16:33; 1 John 4:4

WAITING

A COUPLE went to the airport to catch their flight. When they arrived at the gate, they were told by an agent to wait to board. So they made their way to a spot in the waiting area and took a seat. They were put to the side but didn't know why.

People began boarding and as even more people boarded and time passed, the couple began getting frustrated. They were waiting and didn't know why. After awhile, they started to get mad. They thought the airline was treating them very poorly by making them wait with no explanation and no time frame.

Now, everyone had boarded the plane but them. They were going to be last to board the plane even though they were one of the first passengers there. All kinds of things were going through the couple's minds. "What's going on here?" "This is not right." "We were here early!"

Finally, after everybody else was on, their names were called and they were told they could board. The couple walked down the Jetway and looked at their boarding passes to find their seat assignments. Unbeknownst to them, they had been upgraded to first class! All of a sudden sorrow became laughter, sadness became joy, and they each added a pep in their step because they had been bumped up from coach to first class. They realized that, sometimes, waiting just isn't all that bad.[1021]

[Trials, Patience in]

Ps. 40:1; Eccl. 7:8; James 5:7

IT WAS not too long ago that I was on a plane, headed to a destination where I had to speak. And as we got closer and closer to the destination, I noticed that we were not headed down toward the runway, as we should have been by that time. The pilot came on and informed us that we were in a holding pattern. We were circling the area. We had not been given permission to land. We were told that we were going to have to wait until such time as the control tower gave us permission to land.

I remember that I began to get very frustrated at the fact that I was in a holding pattern over which I had absolutely no control. I don't mind holding patterns that I control—because then I can land anytime I want to. But when other folks are in the cockpit, and I am in the dark and in a holding pattern, that can be a very frustrating position. It's not a good feeling to be on hold and not know how long it will last.[1022]

[Trials, Patience in]

SOME people use "pop-up" timers when they cook their turkeys. This apparatus is designed to be stuck way down in the turkey, and as the turkey heats up, the rising temperature registers with the thermometer. When the turkey gets fully cooked, the outside of the thermometer pops up and the turkey is done.

But now, this only works if it is stuck way down into the inner core of the turkey because if the turkey is not cooked, then it is not ready to eat. When the inner core is right, the external thing pops out signaling that it's time to eat!

Many people are waiting for God to pop up and say that He will give them the desires of their heart. But what they don't realize is that God is waiting for them to be fully cooked. He's waiting on them to be "done" and they just haven't finished cooking yet.[1023]

[Christian Living, Spiritual Growth]

Ps. 27:14; James 1:4

I CONFESS I pull up to McDonald's every now and then. Over the years, I've learned something about McDonald's. They are not prepared if you order something different or abnormal. They've got a mass production system going in there and anything that you order out of the ordinary throws them off. So if you want a Number Three, you are supposed to order a Number Three and say nothing else.

Once, I decided that I wanted a little special configuration in my dining. After paying, I was promptly told to pull up and pull over. In other words, I would have to wait. I had asked for something special, and they weren't prepared and ready for that. They needed more time to prepare my special request.

So I pulled up and pulled over to the side. I had to wait a few minutes, but the wait was worth it! The fries were hot and my order was just the way I wanted it.

If you want run-of-the-mill living, then just keep on like you're going. Drive through, and get what everybody else gets. But if you want something special, something designed just for you with your name written

on it, you've got to pull over to the side and let God work on your special request. He takes time to deliver something with your name on it.[1024]

Matt. 25:34; James 5:7

WAR

IN 1945, the United Nations was established and one of its primary goals was to maintain global peace and to try to facilitate harmony between nations. Because war was so natural to the human condition, there was a feeling that we needed something that would help orchestrate peace around the world. The United Nations sends in peacekeeping forces to help mediate conflicts that occur between nations.

Peace is hard to come by. In the nearly four thousand years of recorded human history, there have been only 268 years where there was no war. So war is normal.

War is not only normal for nations, it's normal for many of us. Some of us are at war with ourselves. In fact, we have our own personal civil war going on as we are at war with three people: me, myself, and I, and none of them can get along with each other. Then there are domestic wars where mates fight each other. Rather than being married by the justice of the peace, they look like they were married by the secretary of war. Every day is a new fight. For many married people, while everything looked like it was going to be good on the wedding day, one hour after the honeymoon it became apparent that they had just walked into a war zone.

There are other kinds of relational conflicts. Parents and their children war against each other. Coworkers battle against one another. People of different racial, social, or class groups face ongoing conflict—black vs. white, rich vs. poor, etc. Everywhere you turn around, there's a war.

Some people are afraid when they experience peace because they know it won't last long. They always feel that war is waiting to happen around the corner of their lives.[1025]

[Anger; Peace]
John 14:27

WEAKNESS

IN MOST church services, people attending can hear because of the process of amplification. Amplification simply takes a weak signal and makes it powerful. It takes what would otherwise be unintelligible or soft or difficult, and now allows it to make sense. What an amplification system does for a weak signal, God does for weaknesses in your own life.[1026]

[Men, Weakness of]
2 Cor. 12:9–10; Phil. 4:13

WISDOM

WISDOM requires knowledge and understanding. Just like it takes both a man and a woman to come together and form a new baby, when knowledge gets married to understanding, it has a baby, and that baby is called wisdom. When knowledge, the true nature of a thing, meets understanding, which is the enlightened purpose of that truth, a baby is born and it is called wisdom.[1027]

Prov. 9:10; 23:23; James 1:5

WISDOM, SEARCHING FOR

WHEN speaking about wisdom, the Bible says, "Seek her as silver and search for her as for hidden treasures." Silver and hidden treasure are located underneath the ground. They require digging. The fact that the treasures are hidden implies that it is not on top of the ground, obvious to the casual eye. Why would God not make wisdom available for anyone to pick up too easily? It's too valuable. He doesn't want folks to pick it up who don't intend on using it. He has placed wisdom as a hidden treasure underneath the ground for those who really want it. Just like people who truly desire to find gold don't mind digging and working to find it, wisdom is only to be found by people who value it enough to search for it.[1028]

[Wisdom]
Prov. 2:4; 23:23

WISDOM is a prize only available to people willing to work to find it. Many kids have the memory of prizes in the cereal box. The prize would always be at the bottom. Many a child would go digging around in the box but be told by their mother to take their hands out. There was this understood rule among parents that children could not just reach in and pull out the prize but had to eat their way to the prize. The prize could not be enjoyed without eating the cereal first. The prize would only be available to the child who did the job of eating first. The prize at the bottom of that cereal box would not be easily attainable![1029]

[Wisdom]
Prov. 2:4; 23:23

IF A student is too lazy to study, they shouldn't complain when they receive an F on a test. If a Christian is too lazy to find out what God says about a subject, he shouldn't be surprised when he lacks the understanding he needs to handle situations in his life.[1030]

[Prayer, Access in]

James 1:5

WITNESSING

A MILITARY man one day was talking to a young lady whom he had fallen in love with. He was soon to be overseas on assignment and wanted her to wait for his return. He told her he would write her every day just to let her know how serious he was about pursuing her.

He wrote her every single day for a year and a half and every single day she received his letters. When he came back home a year and a half later, much to his chagrin, she had married the mailman.[1031]

WHEN a witness is summoned to court but refuses to testify, he is held in contempt by the judge. When you stand before Jesus Christ, will He hold you in contempt of court because you refused to testify?[1032]

[Evangelism, Responsibility of; Sharing the Gospel]

Rom. 10:14–15; 2 Tim. 1:8

WHEN soldiers come home from war, the folks who love them are at the airport waiting to greet them. When you go home to be with the Lord, who'll be at the gates for you because you played a part in their eternal destiny?[1033]

[Evangelism, Call of]

CHRISTIANS who refuse to witness are saying to those people they choose not to witness to, "You can go to hell."[1034]

[Hell; Evangelism, Responsibility of; Sharing the Gospel]

Isa. 43:10; Rom. 10:14–15

DURING an election, people make it clear whom they stand for. They display their preferences on bumper stickers, on placards, and on commercials. They show up at rallies and stick signs in their yards. There are also those people who either don't care or who are undecided. Many Christians fit in the latter category. The world just doesn't know where we stand.[1035]

Rom. 1:16; 2 Tim. 1:12

WITNESSING, IMPORTANCE OF

WHEN the *Titanic* went under, three messages had been sent that said to watch out for the icebergs. Because everything looked all right, the folks taking the message never passed it on. They never sent the warning out to people who needed to hear and, as a result, over fifteen hundred people lost their lives. The folks who knew kept quiet.

Another tragedy of the *Titanic* was that the lifeboats, designed to carry people away from the sinking ship, were only half full. People who had made it to safety in the lifeboats didn't want to turn around and go pick up people who were dying. They didn't want to take the risk of panicking people flipping over their boat. So the people who were saved and safe kept on going. Fifteen hundred people didn't have to die, but they did. The folks who were saved didn't want to go back because it was risky.

Sharing the gospel has risks—the risk of rejection, the risk of being made fun of, the risk of being called "holier than thou," the risk of being called "Reverend," the risk of being avoided, the risk of being asked questions you don't know the answer to. Yes, there are risks, but when someone is dying, offering them the gift of salvation is worth the risk.[1036]

[Evangelism, Need for; Risk; Sharing the Gospel; Witnessing]

Rom. 1:16; 1 Peter 3:15

WITNESSING, MOTIVATION FOR

A LITTLE girl treated her mother badly because she was ashamed of her. Her mother had a big, ugly scar on her face. She looked horrible. The little girl would never bring her friends around because of the scar on her mother's face. She would never invite her mother to school functions because of the scar on her face. Her mother finally asked her, "Honey, why don't you ever bring your friends around? Why don't you ever invite me to anything?"

She said, "Mama, it's the scar on your face. I can't bear to introduce you to others."

Her mother said, "Darling, sit down. Let me tell you something I've never told you about the scar on my face. One day, I went out to draw water when you were a little girl, and when I looked back from the well, I saw the house was on fire. I rushed back in, dropped my water, and came and grabbed you, my little baby, out of the crib. The fire was engulfing you, but I got there just in the nick of time. On my way out the house, one of the beams of the house collapsed and hit me across the face. It knocked me to the ground and seethed on my face for a period of time before I could get it off, but I was able to throw you to safety. I just wanted you to know, darling, the next time you don't want your friends to see me, that the only reason I have a scar on my face is because I was saving your life."

Jesus has some scars on His hands. He's got scars on His feet. He's got a scar on His side. Let me tell you how He got those scars. You and I were on our way to hell. We were on our way to be separated from a holy God forever. But Jesus Christ looked down, and He didn't want us to suffer the consequences of sin. He told the Father, "I'll go." He came down and stretched out on a cross. They nailed His hands in the cross, His feet on the cross, and stuck a spear in His side.

So the next time you don't want to tell anybody about Him, remember how He got His scars. The next time you don't want to be a disciple, remember how He got His scars. The next time you don't want to live for Him, remember how He got His scars. When you remember, tell Him you'll follow Him for the rest of your days.[1037]

[Evangelism, Responsibility of; Salvation, Gratefulness for; Witnessing]

John 20:24–29; Rom. 1:16

WOMEN, AND THEIR HUSBANDS

THE STORY is told of two women who escaped from prison. They were running, and of course, when the guards discovered that they had escaped, they went after them with dogs to follow their scent and to track them down. The two women heard the barking in the distance and knew the guards and dogs were closing in. Panicking and needing to do something, the first lady decided to climb a tree and hide. The second lady decided to follow her lead and she climbed a tree located about fifty feet away.

The dogs arrived and picked up the scent at the first tree. They began to jump up on the tree and bark loudly. The first lady up the tree was of course panicking because she had been located, but ingeniously, she began to make cooing sounds: "Coo, coo, coo." The prison guard jerked the dog back from the tree and said, "Come on, let's go, it's nothing but a dumb bird up there." She had deflected the dog.

When the guards and the dogs arrived at the second tree, they picked up the scent of the second woman. Now, the second woman heard what the first woman had done. So she began to think, "What sound can I make to throw off the scent of the dogs?" She thought for a minute as the dogs jumped on the tree and then it hit her. She said, "Moo, moo, moo." Cows don't live in trees.

When you're confused on your role, you wind up making the wrong noise, at the wrong time, in the wrong place. A lot of women are making a lot of noise complaining about their husbands and complaining about what's wrong with their man, when they have forsaken and neglected their biblical roles. They are mooing when they ought to be cooing.[1038]

[Marriage; Marriage, Unhappiness in; Submission, of Wives to Their Husbands]
Eph. 5:22–24; 1 Peter 3:7

SO LET'S say you've got a parked car in front of you. You are trying to go somewhere. You are at a stoplight, and the car in front of you is stuck, not going anywhere. You have somewhere to go so you are getting ticked off at this parked car. You are so irritated that you may start fussing, and cussing, and complaining, and winding your window down, and doing all this kind of stuff, because this car is parked in front of you, and it's getting on your nerves. Now, having gone through all that, you still won't be able to get that car to move. You know what that car needs? That car needs somebody to come and assist it with its movement. I think the biblical word for this is "helpmate."

Guess what the job of a helpmate is . . . to help. Far too many of our ladies today, instead of being helpmates, are hurt mates, because they do what everyone else is doing to their man, putting him down, criticizing him, complaining about him, or emasculating him. The very thing many ladies are after, they are themselves destroying.[1039]

[Criticizing, Danger of; Marriage]
Prov. 21:9; 1 Tim. 5:13

ONE day a woman was trying to get her mule to move, but the mule was stubborn. She went inside the farmhouse and got a bat. She picked up the bat, and BANG! hit the mule upside the head. The mule fell over and seeing stars he jumped back up, and started moving. The woman's daughter asked, "Mom, why did you hit the mule over the head with the bat?" Her mother said, "Because you got to do something to get his attention."

Men are often mule-headed and stubborn. But God has given every woman a baseball bat, one many women are unwilling to use, and it is called respect. R-E-S-P-E-C-T.[1040]

[Marriage; Submission, of Wives to Their Husbands]

Prov. 21:19; Rom. 13:7; 1 Peter 3:1–2

IN A courtroom, in the event you get upset at the proceedings, you could blurt out, scream, yell, or fuss in defense of yourself. Even if you are right, and the person on the other side is wrong, the judge will say, "You are out of order." In fact, if you continue ranting and raving, the judge will hold you in contempt of court, because you have dishonored the courtroom.

There are many women today living in contempt of God's court, by their refusal to surrender to God's divine order. That order is clear—for a wife to respect her husband. The issue is not whether he is right or not. It is an issue of respecting him as head.[1041]

[Marriage; Submission, of Wives to Their Husbands]

1 Cor. 11:3

WOMEN, VALUE OF

A MAN walked into a flower shop on Mother's Day. He said, "What can I get for three dollars?"

The proprietor replied, "I can give you a dozen carnations, or I can give you one rose."

He says, "You mean I can get a dozen carnations for three dollars, but only one rose? How come the roses are just so expensive?"

"Oh, real simple. The scent of a carnation doesn't last very long. It's sweet for a moment, but it has no longevity. On the other hand, a rose is known for its ongoing scent. Even when you think it's dead, it can be crushed, turned into potpourri, and the smell can still continue."

Women are roses. They are valuable. However, to reject being God's kind of woman is to cheapen your worth. An ungodly woman can be found for a dime a dozen. Ladies, you are roses, you're expensive. But to reject being God's kind of woman, you can get them a dime a dozen.[1042]

[Christian, Value of]

Prov. 18:22; 31:30

WORDS, UNWHOLESOME

AS A husband and wife drove together down a highway, they noticed a mule. The husband looked at his wife and said, "There goes one of your relatives." She replied, "Yeah, I know . . . by marriage."[1043]

James 3:1–12

WORD OF GOD

WHEN a plane takes off, it needs a control tower. The control tower can see what the pilots cannot. The pilots have a limited vantage point. They can't see underneath or above them. The pilots, even with all of their instruments, cannot see all the weather conditions that will affect their flight plan. The folks in the control tower can provide the pilots information they wouldn't have because of their limited vantage point,

The Word of God is the control tower for the Christian. Where we have only a limited vantage point, God's Word can communicate to us what is going on in the spiritual realm that we can't see.[1044]

[Bible, Guidance of]

2 Tim. 3:16; Heb. 4:12

PEOPLE listen to traffic reports before heading to work so they can find out about conditions they can't see. These traffic reports are normally provided by a person flying around in a helicopter who has a large vantage point. The proof that people listen to traffic reports and believe them is evident by their decisions on which route to take.

People don't just listen to the traffic report for their listening pleasure. They listen to get information on situations they can't see themselves.

As Christians, we need eyes that we don't have. God has a greater vantage point and provides that information to us in His Word.[1045]

[Bible, Guidance of]
2 Tim. 3:16; Heb. 4:12

IF YOU drive into the Dallas/Fort Worth Airport from the south side, you'll see a big, round thing up there. That big, round thing is the Doppler radar. It was built because pilots were not able to see wind shears. In the past, these sudden bursts of wind had been forceful enough to slow down an approaching plane, press it to the ground, and cause an accident. The Doppler radar detects wind shears so that planes, pilots, and passengers can be protected from disaster, from things they can't see.

God has given you a radar to help you because there are things you can't see. The Word of God is a radar that will save us from disaster if we would only believe it to be true and act accordingly.[1046]

[Bible, Use of]
Rom. 15:4; 2 Tim. 3:16

I WAS stranded in my car once and my AAA membership had expired. I was stranded. I was stuck. So I picked up my phone and tried to find a wrecker service. Finally after hours of searching, locating, and then waiting for one to arrive, someone comes to help me out. When I arrived home, I was tired and especially frustrated with myself for not having renewed my AAA card.

At a later date, I shared this episode with someone and they hit me with information I had never heard in all the years I'd been driving. I was told that on the back of my driver's license is a number for Texas Roadside Assistance. For years, I'd been carrying around the telephone number of a savior and I had never bothered to call the number when I'd needed help.

Sadly, the tragedy is that most people don't know that the solution for their problems is already written on the back of their driver's license. Most people have never taken the time to notice or to read so they wind up stuck again and again, unaware of the help available to them.

God's Word is like Heavenly Roadside Assistance. If we would only pick it up, read it, use it, and then obey it, we would see help come alongside to provide a way out of anything the Devil brings to take us down.[1047]

[Bible, Application of; Bible, Neglect of]
Acts 17:11; 2 Tim. 2:15; 3:16

FIRST Peter 2:2 tells us to "long for the pure milk of the Word." Pure means undiluted. A lot of us want the Word but we mix it up with other information.

At most county or state fairs, you can find candied apples—apples dipped in sugar. Now, apples by themselves are a great, healthy fruit. Once you dip them in sugar, however, you've just killed the benefit of the apple although it tastes good. A candied apple is sweet but its nutritional value is diluted because something with no value has been added to it. Many of us will read the Word, hear the Word, and then talk to people about the Word but then dip it in human viewpoint.[1048]

[Bible, Application of; Faith, Distortion of]

1 Peter 2:2; 2 Peter 2:1

THERE was an old lumberjack who went to a lumberjack company looking for a job. He sought out the foreman and said, "I want to work as a lumberjack. I want to chop down some trees."

The foreman said, "Man, I'm sorry, but you are too old to chop down trees."

The old man looked stunned and said, "No, I'm not."

The foreman, a bit irritated, said, "Look, I've worked with a lot of lumberjacks and I'm telling you, you are too old, too weak, and too feeble to chop down trees."

The old man decided to prove the foreman wrong. He took the supervisor out to a tree, grabbed an axe, and chopped down a tree in record time.

The foreman said, "Where did you learn to chop like that? You are pretty fast with that heavy axe!"

"Well, have you ever heard of the Sahara Forest?"

"Uh, the Sahara Forest? Do you mean the Sahara Desert?"

"Yea, I guess that's what they call it now."

God has been around for a while. He's been chopping down stuff and mowing down stuff with His Word.[1049]

[Bible, Authority of; God, Authority of]

Heb. 4:12

WORKMANSHIP

THE GREAT painter Michelangelo came across a block of marble. He looked at the square block and said he saw an angel inside of there waiting to get out. He began the chiseling process.

In the same way, God is at work on us. We are His workmanship.[1050]

Isa. 64:8; Eph. 2:10

WORLD, CONFORMITY TO

A STORY is told of a businessman. He was in Mexico on some business. He went to a little fishing village to kind of get away from the crowd a little bit and wind down. He made his way to the dock and noticed a fishing boat coming in with a big yellow fin tuna hanging on the hook. So he went over to the fisherman and said, "Man, you had a great catch today."

"I sure did. It was a wonderful catch and I've got enough to feed my family and sell a little bit to make a little money."

The businessman asked, "Are you going to go back out today?"

The fisherman chuckled, "No, I'm through for today."

"Well, what are you going to do with the rest of your time?"

"I'm going to go home, play with my kids, and take a siesta with my wife. Then, I'm going to go out to the town tonight and get with my amigos. We're going to fellowship tonight. I'll probably go out tomorrow for a couple of hours and get some more tuna."

"Oh," said the businessman. "Look, I think I can help you. I'm an MBA from Harvard. Just looking at what you've got here, you've got something that can grow. If you work a little bit longer and catch some more fish, then you can sell it for a higher profit. When you sell it for a higher profit, you can buy more boats. When you buy more boats, bringing in more fish, you'll be able to afford to skip the middleman and become your own cannery. When you become your own cannery, then you can expand your business so that other fishermen will have to bring their fish to you. Now, you'll probably have to move, probably to Mexico City. If things continue to expand, you'll have to then move to L.A. or maybe New York. If your cannery gets to the place where things really explode, then you can take your company public on the New York Stock Exchange. You'll be a multimillionaire."

"Sounds great, Señor, but how long will this take?"

"Oh, about twenty years."

"Señor, after I become a multimillionaire, what happens next?"

"Oh, that's the best part. Then you can retire."

"What do I do when I retire?"

"Well," the businessman said with a slow realization coming upon him, "then you can go to a small fishing village, play with your kids, take a siesta with your wife, and hang out in the evening with your amigos."

Feeling a bit foolish, he continued, "Well, it was just an idea."[1051]

[Materialism, Deception of; Materialism, Perspective of]
Ps. 39:6; Matt. 16:26; Heb. 13:5

WORLD, IMPACTING THE

ONCE, when I was traveling, I stopped in at an American Airlines Admiral's Club to wait for a flight. It was one of the bigger clubs where they have hostesses come around and ask patrons if they would like something to drink. So the hostess came around and said "Sir, may I get you something to drink?"

I said, "Yes. I want something to drink."

The hostess brought me a ginger ale. She also brought me a dish full of snacks. No, I did not order a dish full of snacks. I did not request snacks. I did not intend to pay for snacks. But this dish of snacks was free. It was part of a planned evil.

She brought me this dish of snacks because it is full of salt. The goal of her bringing me the salty snacks was to get me to order another ginger ale. The goal of the salt was to create thirst, so I'd keep ordering and keep spending money.

We are the salt of the earth. The idea is that our presence in the world will create spiritual thirst so that we can offer people the living water—Jesus, the Christ, the Son of God.[1052]

[Christian Living, Purpose; Discipleship, Impact of]
Matt. 5:13

WORLD, LIVING IN

THE FARTHER you go down in the ocean, the more pressurized the ocean becomes. The farther you go down, the more you will be squashed. If you go down deep enough, the ocean's pressure will flatten you out like a pancake. The deeper you go, the greater the pressure is.

When the divers went looking for the *Titanic*, they had to make the trip in a small, pressurized submarine. It's a little podlike thing that a diver sits in when he intends to go deep. If a diver went to investigate the *Titanic* on the bottom of the ocean without a submarine, he would be totally destroyed because the pressure in his body is less than the pressure in the water. His body would collapse because of the outside pressure in the water. Even though the water is squeezing against the submarine trying to collapse it, it cannot because the sub has been pressurized. The diver can go deeper and deeper, and still remain safe and secure because the pressure on the inside is greater than the pressure on the outside.

Most Christians leave church every Sunday only to go out into the world and be under pressure. They are under pressure at work, at home, and in their various circumstances. Satan is trying to collapse them. Some people have headaches because the pressure is too great. Some people are stressed because the pressure is too great. Some people are ill because the pressure is too great.

Here's the thing—we cannot tell the ocean to stop pressurizing us. That's the nature of going deep in this world. The deeper you go, the more pressure you are going to get. The world can't help but pressure you. But greater is the pressure inside of you than the pressure outside of you. If you go deep on the inside, then when you're pressured on the outside, you won't cave in.[1053]

[Holy Spirit, Power of]
John 16:33; 1 John 4:4

WORLDLINESS, CONCEPT OF

THE WORLD is like an in-law you can't get rid of.[1054]

John 16:33

WORLDLINESS, DISTRACTION OF

SOME time ago, I was on Fifth Avenue walking and paused to look at a lifelike mannequin in a store window. I quickly realized that she wasn't a mannequin because she blinked. She almost fooled me though because everything else about her was stationary. Other people began gathering in front of the window and they attempted to get her to break her concentration. People were making faces, making fun of her, knocking on the window, and just doing everything they could to get her to move. But she held her ground. There was something more important than pleasing folk on the other side of the glass. What was more important was pleasing her employer, who was paying her to stand at that window.

For you to live a focused life, a life untouched by worldliness, you are going to have to ignore the folks on the other side of the glass.[1055]

[Focus; Focus, on the Race]
Prov. 4:25; 2 Cor. 4:18; Heb. 12:2

WORRY

A MAN was in a hurry to catch an airplane. He ran, huffing and puffing, down toward his gate. He passed a guy who was dressed in a pilot's uniform. The guy said to the breathless man,

"Where are you in a hurry to?"

"Oh," the man said, "I am late for my plane. I don't want to miss my plane." He proceeded to tell the guy what flight he was hurrying to.

The uniformed man said, "Don't be in a hurry, I am piloting that plane."

If the pilot is chilling, you chill too. Don't stress yourself out about things unnecessarily. Wait on God and trust that if He's taking His time, you can too.[1056]

[Waiting]
Ps. 127:2; Matt. 6:25–34

A MAN one day worried whether he would die of cancer, because cancer was so prevalent in the society. He worried about it for thirty years and then died of a heart attack as a result. Should you be concerned about your health? Absolutely. Should you do the best you can to stay healthy? Absolutely, but after you've done all that you can do, don't worry. That's what God says. So to worry is to insult Him.[1057]

Matt. 6:27; Luke 12:25

A MAN one day said to a friend of his, "Mister, you sure look worried." The man responded. "Man, I've got so many troubles! If something else goes wrong with me today, I'll have to wait two weeks to get around to worrying about it."[1058]

Matt. 6:25–34; Phil. 4:6–7

WORSHIP

THERE is the type of guy who says he worships God on Sunday morning on the golf course. Well, he is actually worshipping golf on God's course because he has switched the object of worship.[1059]

[Worship, Nature of]
Heb. 10:25

HOME court advantage occurs when the energy of the group magnifies what is happening on the court. With home court advantage, a basketball team struggling to put points on the board hears the energy around them and all of a sudden something feels something sparked within. All of a sudden, that energy enables the team to do better than before and push past the enemy's oppositions. The fans in the stands are not physically going through the same thing the team is, but they are joining them in spirit and in a way that gives the team a sense of power they didn't have before. Strength appears out of nowhere because of this mysterious home court advantage.

Many people ask why they need to come to church. Worshipping with other believers allows people pushing toward the same goal to gather together in spirit. Worshipping together sparks a view of God bigger than whatever situation folks may be going through.[1060]

[Worship, Benefit of]
Ps. 34:5; Heb. 10:25

WORSHIP, BENEFIT OF

HAVE you ever gone to a restaurant and the waiter had a bad attitude? The waiter didn't speak to you correctly, wasn't attentive, or kind of tossed dishes onto the table. Every now and then a waiter can act as if he or she doesn't recognize who you are.

You see, number one, your coming creates the opportunity for a job. No coming equals no customers, and no customers equals no income. The waiter is there to serve you. This is their purpose. A correct attitude will be reflected in statements like . . .

"Yes, sir."

"So glad to have you here today."

"Ah, just a moment, we'll seat you shortly."

"I'm sorry it's taking so long."

"We finally have a table for you, why don't you follow me."

"Can I get you something to drink?"

"Can I get you some appetizers?"

"This item is particularly good. I had that yesterday and I'd love to recommend it to you."

"Is there anything on the menu I can explain further to you? I'd be happy to do it."

When you get that kind of waiter, the kind who is concerned with your well-being, who doesn't think you came to the restaurant for them, who acts as if they exist at the restaurant to service you, who behaves like you are the only reason they're there, it is a wonderful experience.

All of a sudden when you get the check and you measure the tip, even folks who hate tipping, even cheap tippers, have to reconsider the agenda. Why? Because of how they've served you. Because of their consciousness to please you. Because of their desire to make you feel good about that experience at that restaurant.

God didn't create you and save you so that He could serve you. He created you and saved you so that you could serve Him. He wants you to service Him.

"God, what can I do for You today?"

"How can I please You today?"

"God, this is the best seat in the house. You can have it today."

"God, You really need to know, I know it's not about me, it's about You."

"God, I'm getting ready to go to bed but I want to let You know that between now and when I wake up in the morning, the first thought I'm going to have is of how I can serve You again tomorrow. That's why I'm here."

When you decide that He is the reason why you are here, when you look at your check, there's going to be a whopping tip because God loves to share with those who are there for Him. You're here for Him.[1061]

[Christian Living, Purpose; Service, Motivation for]

1 Sam. 12:24; Ps. 150:1–6

WORSHIP is a spark that is the result of people falling in love with their Creator, their Savior. Most folks have had the experience of dragging their foot or shoe across the carpet and then reaching out and touching someone, only to see a spark from that friction transfer through their body as they touch another person.

That's how worship is. You rub up against God long enough and something is going to shoot somewhere. Worship is our rubbing up against God, and seeing the result of that connection produce a spark or a "shock." Being close to God produces a spiritual, electric infusion of life and vitality.[1062]

[God, Knowing; Jesus, Relationship with]

Ps. 73:28; James 4:8

WORSHIP, CORPORATE

IT IS impossible to worship God privately and not want to worship Him corporately. It's one thing to sit at home and watch a football game by yourself. It's another thing to watch that same game with a roomful of people where everybody is shouting and getting excited together. The energy brought together by being with mutual fans is many times that of what it is when a person is alone at home, watching the same by themselves.

While you can listen to the Cowboys game in your car and enter into the experience of the game behind the wheel, there's nothing like the feeling of being with a group of people who are worshipping simultaneously. Anybody who's worshipping God privately will worship Him publicly.[1063]

[Church, Attendance]
Heb. 10:25

WORSHIP, MOTIVATION FOR

WHEN the American hostages came home from Iran on January 20, 1981, the first thing they did when they got off the plane was kiss the ground. No matter what star or achievement they had earned in the armed services, when they hit the ground from Iran, they bowed down. Home sweet home. Putting their clean lips on that dirty tarp, they kissed it. They went down. Because they knew where they had been and they knew where they were now. You know why folks stop bowing? Because they forget where they've come from. They forget that they have been hostages in Satan's territory, and now they have been made free.[1064]

[Salvation, Gratefulness for]
Ex. 20:2; 1 Sam. 12:24

EVERYBODY knows what groupies are. Groupies are people who follow celebrities around, like movie stars, singers, or athletes. They gather together to be near the celebrity. They follow the rich and the famous for a couple of reasons. One, they just want to be in their presence. They just want to see them. They just want to touch them. They follow because they want to be near the one whom they adore.

There is a second reason they follow them. Sometimes they want to get something from them such as an autograph. Maybe they want a hug or a kiss or some kind of attention. They are groupies because they want to be near them and they want to receive from them.

Did you know being a groupie is a form of worship? It is following the one you idolize so you can be near them and so you can get something from them.

I remember when I was doing a chapel for the Dallas Mavericks when Michael Jordan was with the Bulls and there would be groupies outside waiting for Michael to come from the hotel to the arena. They would gather around in groups with slips of paper in hand because they idolized Mike. They wanted to be in his presence and they wanted something from him.

Now, there is a legitimate side to that and there is an illegitimate side. But here is my point. God is looking for some groupies. That is my point. God wants some groupies—people who want to be in His presence and who come to Him to meet their needs.[1065]

[Jesus, Relationship with]

Ps. 16:11; 51:11; James 4:8

THERE is a story of a dog that loved its master. The master was just a little teenage boy, but this dog was full of joy and his tail wagging all the time. When the boy went to bed, the dog jumped up on the bed and lay right beside him. When the boy got up in the middle of the night to go to the bathroom, the dog would jump out of the bed, walk to the door, and sit at the bathroom door until the boy got out and then jump back up in bed. When it was time for breakfast, the boy would get up to get ready to go to school, the dog would jump up, follow the boy to the table, and then sit at the boy's feet until the boy finished eating and was on his way to school. He would walk outside with the boy until the boy went to the bus stop. Then the dog would sit down and wait for the bus with the boy. When the bus came, the boy would get on the bus. The bus would drive off. The dog would run behind as far as it could before the bus outpaced it. When the boy came home from school, the dog would be sitting right there at the bus stop, waiting for the boy to come home. The boy would then go to his home. The dog would walk with him, and sit at his feet while he ate dinner. He would then follow him around until it was time to turn in for the night. At this point, he would jump back up on the bed and go through the whole process the next day and the next, day in and day out, always wagging its tail.

How can a dog do that day in and day out for his little teenage master? Because when the boy found the dog, it was wandering the street. It was a mangy, unkempt mutt. It was headed for sure disaster by the dogcatcher. If that dog had ever been caught, it surely would not have been adopted but instead eradicated. However, this boy found that wandering, mangy dog, took it home, washed it, bathed it, resuscitated it, fed it, and best of all loved it. It became apparent from the dog's tail that the dog never forgot it. Wherever that boy was, that dog was going to be because it was evident that dog never forgot where it had been when that boy found him.

Some of us were wandering on a street called sin. We were just mangy sinners. Some of us sinned and didn't think about it. Some sinned and didn't care. Others of us were secret sinners. We didn't sin so folk could see, but if that closet ever got revealed, it would be clear that we were just as mangy as the folks who were public. Others of us were white-collar, sophisticated sinners who never did anything outright but just kept it all in our minds.

No matter what kind of sinner you were, He found you. The grace of God discovered you where you were. You heard the gospel of Jesus Christ and He saved you. And my only question is this: where would you be if He hadn't found you? Is your gratefulness evident in the way you respond to the Master?[1066]

[Salvation, Gratefulness for; Thanksgiving, Motivation for]
Deut. 8:10; 1 Sam. 12:24; Col. 1:12

WORSHIP, NATURE OF

SOME people may say that praising God is too emotional. We must understand the difference between emotion and emotionalism. Emotion is when there's a big play on the field, and everybody gets up in excitement about what the players did. Emotionalism is when you get excited and jump up and there's nothing happening on the field. We have a lot of emotionalism today where folks are getting excited about nothing. What we need, though, is legitimate emotion or praise, because God is something to get excited about.[1067]

[Praise]
1 Cor. 14:1–19

SUBJECT Index

SCRIPTURE Index

Please note that numbers refer to particular illustrations rather than page numbers.